THE ROUTLEDGE EDUCATION STUDIES TEXTBOOK

The Routledge Education Studies Textbook is an academically wide-ranging and appropriately challenging resource for students beyond the introductory stages of a degree programme in Education Studies. Written in a clear and engaging style, chapters are divided into three sections that examine fundamental ideas and issues, explore educational contexts, and offer study and research guidance respectively.

To support the development of critical thinking, debates between contributors are interspersed within sections and address the following questions:

- Do private schools legitimise privilege?
- Should the liberal state support religious schooling?
- Are developments in post-14 education reducing the divide between the academic and the vocational?
- Do schools contribute to social and community cohesion?
- Do traditional and progressive teaching methods exist or are there only effective and ineffective methods?
- Educational Research: a foundation for teacher professionalism?

Each chapter opens with an overview of the rationale behind it and closes with a summary of the main points. At the end of every chapter key questions are posed, encouraging the student to critically reflect on the content, and suggestions for further reading are made.

The Routledge Education Studies Textbook is essential reading for students of Education Studies, especially during years 2 and 3 of the undergraduate degree. It will be of interest to trainee teachers, including those working towards M level.

A companion volume, *The Routledge Education Studies Reader* by the same editors contains key classic and contemporary academic articles, and has been designed to be used alongside this *Textbook*.

James Arthur is Professor of Education and Civic Engagement at the University of Birmingham, UK.

Ian Davies is Professor in Educational Studies at the University of York, UK.

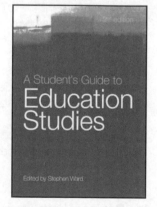

THE ROUTLEDGE EDUCATION STUDIES TEXTBOOK

Edited by

James Arthur and Ian Davies

Routledge
Taylor & Francis Group
LONDON AND NEW YORK

First published 2010
by Routledge
2 Park Square, Milton Park, Abingdon, Oxon OX14 4RN

Simultaneously published in the USA and Canada
by Routledge
270 Madison Ave, New York, NY 10016

Routledge is an imprint of the Taylor & Francis Group, an informa business

Typeset in Times New Roman by Swales & Willis Ltd, Exeter, Devon
Printed and bound in Great Britain by the MPG Books Group

British Library Cataloguing in Publication Data
A catalogue record for this book is available from the British Library

Library of Congress Cataloging-in-Publication Data
The Routledge education studies textbook/edited by James Arthur and Ian Davies.
p. cm.
Includes bibliographical references and index.
1. Education—Textbooks. 2. Education—Study and teaching (Higher)—Textbooks.
I. Arthur, James, 1957– II. Davies, Ian, 1957–
LB17.R675 2009
370.71'1—dc22 2009021906

ISBN–10: 0–415–56136–1 (hbk)
ISBN–10: 0–415–47955–X (pbk)

ISBN–13: 978–0–415–56136–5 (hbk)
ISBN–13: 978–0–415–47955–4 (pbk) ✓V AS

CONTENTS

ILLUSTRATIONS

BOX

FIGURES

TABLES

CONTRIBUTORS

Bela Arora is Academic Coordinator, Centre for Sociology, Anthropology and Politics (CSAP), University of Birmingham.

James Arthur is Professor of Education and Civic Engagement at the University of Birmingham.

Ergin Bulut is a PhD Student in Educational Policy Studies at the University of Illinois, Urbana-Champaign.

David Carr is Professor of Philosophy of Education at the University of Edinburgh.

Namita Chakrabarty is Senior Lecturer at the Cass School of Education, University of East London.

Anne Cockburn is Reader in Education at the University of East Anglia.

James C. Conroy is Professor of Religious and Philosophical Education and Dean of Education at the University of Glasgow.

Caroline Daly is Senior Lecturer at the Institute of Education, University of London.

Ian Davies is Professor of Education at the University of York.

Jon Davison is Professor of Teacher Education at Canterbury Christ Church University.

John Fox is an Advanced Skills Teacher working in association with the Department of Educational Studies, University of Oxford.

Márta Fülöp is Professor at the Institute of Psychology of the Hungarian Academy of Sciences.

Tony Gallagher is Professor of Education and Head of the School of Education of Queens University, Belfast.

Liam Gearon is Professor of Education at the University of Plymouth.

Stephen Gorard is Professor of Education Research at the University of Birmingham.

János Gordon-Győri is an Associate Professor at Eötvös Loránd University, Budapest.

Des Hewitt is Assistant Head of Teacher Education at the University of Derby.

Ralph Leighton is Principal Lecturer in Education at Canterbury Christ Church University.

Chris Kyriacou is Reader in Educational Psychology at the University of York.

CONTRIBUTORS

Lee Jerome is Principal Lecturer in Education at London Metropolitan University.

Bob Moon is Professor of Education Teaching Studies at the Open University.

Mark Newman is Reader in Evidence-informed Policy and Practice in Education and Social Policy, Institute of Education, University of London.

Norbert Pachler is Co-director of the Centre for Excellence in Work-based Learning for Education Professionals (WLE Centre) at the Institute of Education, University of London.

Michael A. Peters is Professor of Educational Policy Studies at the University of Illinois, Urbana-Champaign.

Andrew Pollard is Professor of Education at the Institute of Education, University of London.

John Preston is Professor of Education at the University of East London.

Richard Pring is Emeritus Professor of Education at the University of Oxford.

Alan Reid is Professor of Education at the University of South Australia.

Alan Sears is Professor of Social Studies Education at the University of New Brunswick.

Emma Smith is Reader in Education at the University of Birmingham.

Vanita Sundaram is Lecturer in the Department of Educational Studies, University of York.

Rupert Tillyard is Assistant Head at St Aidan's Church of England High School, Harrogate.

Bernard Trafford is Head of the Royal Grammar School, Newcastle upon Tyne.

Paul Wakeling is Lecturer in the Department of Educational Studies, University of York.

ACKNOWLEDGEMENTS

We would like to thank Primrose Paskins for all her hard work in helping to put this text together on time and with such efficiency.

We are grateful to Anna Clarkson who supported the project throughout. We are particularly indebted to Emma Joyes who collaborated with us very positively and made very many essential contributions.

The extract on pp. 158–60 is taken from Jack Demaine (ed.), *Education Policy and Contemporary Politics*, 2002, Palgrave Macmillan, reproduced with permission of Palgrave Macmillan.

ABBREVIATIONS

AfL	Assessment from Learning
ARG	Assessment Reform Group
BERA	British Educational Research Association
BME	Black and Minority Ethnic
BoE	Board of Education
CARN	Collaborative Action Research Network
DCSF	Department for Children, Schools and Families
DECS	(South Australian) Department of Education and Children's Services
DES	Department of Education and Science
DfES	Department for Education and Skills
EPPI	Evidence for Policy and Practice Information Centre
GTC	The General Teaching Council for England
GTTR	Graduate Teacher Training Registry
HEFCE	Higher Education Funding Council for England
HEI	Higher Education Institution
HMCI	Her Majesty's Chief Inspector for Schools
HMI	Her Majesty's Inspector of Schools
LEA	Local Education Authority
OFSTED	Office for Standards in Education
PGCE	Postgraduate Certificate in Education
PGDE	Professional Graduate Diploma of Education (Scotland)
QCA	Qualifications and Curriculum Authority
QTS	Qualified Teacher Status
OECD	Organisation of Economic Cooperation and Development
SATS	Standard Assessment Tests
SES	Socio-economic Status
TDA	Teacher Training and Development Agency
TTA	Teacher Training Agency
UCET	The Universities Council for the Education of Teachers
UNESCO	United Nations Organisation for Education, Science, Culture and Communications

INTRODUCTION

James Arthur and Ian Davies

The writing of this book emerged from a belief that there is a need for a textbook in more advanced Educational Studies that provides an up-to-date and informed academic coverage of key topics. This textbook is principally aimed at those students in years 2 and 3 of undergraduate degree programmes in educational studies and related areas. It is not intended to be an introductory text. There are already many good texts on the market for that audience. This textbook is designed to be appropriate for students beyond the first year of a degree programme and we are delighted to say that the high-profile and widely respected academics and practitioners who have authored the material that follows are able to provide this level of insight and challenge.

In this introduction we explain why educational studies are important, how the key issues about education are represented in the book and what students can gain from reading the chapters that have been written by our invited experts.

WHY IS EDUCATION IMPORTANT AS A FIELD OF STUDY?

Education is hugely significant and must be studied. We refer very briefly in this section to just some of the ways in which education is important.

Politicians want the best for the people that they govern but they are not being starry-eyed idealists when they claim that their priorities centre on education. Education is believed to make a difference to individuals, the economy and society more generally. An educated workforce is seen to be successful at generating wealth and, at a time when knowledge has become one of the key determinants of economic success, there is a passionate commitment to the nature and type of education that is being offered.

Of course, education – most obviously in the form of schooling – is also vitally significant as a form of consumption. Schools, colleges and universities and other educational institutions are perhaps themselves businesses or at least places that provide employment opportunities and create surpluses if not profits. They have paying 'customers' or 'clients' who, following the establishment of a contract, are required to act in certain ways in order to enjoy a service and achieve specific outcomes. Education as an economic good is an area that ought to be investigated.

We also need to consider the nature of a decent society and the relationship between that and education. If decency is achieved or demonstrated when there is individual and group fulfillment then education is obviously important. At times that achievement will be evidenced in the acquisition of what is occasionally referred to as the 'basic skills' of literacy and numeracy. But, more generally, school (or other forms of educational network) may be the places where individuals learn to do what could not be done previously. A foreign language is learned; a musical instrument may be played with increased skill; a scientific problem may be solved. There may be less tangible but still obviously important matters that are explored. Learners may become involved in the creation and celebration of cultural achievement. In this way a society presents itself through the education it offers its people. Education is not just a site of consumption; it is a means of representing what is valuable. Throughout all the differences of opinion about the nature and purpose of education one can see a tangled web of conflicting priorities and aspirations. All these matters signal the vital significance of education and raise significant questions inviting students to question what education is: what kind of schools we should have; what we should teach in them; what an educated person would look like; what it means to be educated; who has the right to an education; what the purpose of education is; how pupils are motivated to learn and so on. Education is clearly a very broad concept and refers to all the experiences in which pupils and students learn; it is also becoming increasingly internationalised.

We wish to highlight that education in its capacity to enhance the knowledge and skills of an individual and to contribute to the development of particular forms of society allows for a fascinating tapestry of aims and motivations that are worthy of study.

WHAT ARE 'EDUCATION STUDIES'?

Education Studies is a relatively new but already well-established field of study. The UK government's Quality Assurance Agency has sanctioned a benchmark statement for education studies (see http://www.qaa.ac.uk/academicinfrastructure/benchmark/honours/Education07.asp, accessed 10 July 2009). This statement is a vital point of reference for staff and students at many universities and other higher education institutions in the UK. At the time of writing approximately 50 institutions in the UK offer programmes that in whole or part contribute to the award of an undergraduate degree in educational studies. Of course there are very many more undergraduate and graduate programmes in the UK that relate directly or indirectly to education. Those who study psychology, child care, childhood studies and many other areas need to know a great deal about the ideas, issues and events that relate to education. We may look even more expansively at educational studies if we were to include those students following courses in economics, sociology, politics, history, literature. This very strong interest in developing a clearer understanding of education is not confined to the UK. There are programmes in the United States, Canada, Australia and in many other countries where an understanding of education is essential for successful graduation.

This very broad field of study is supported by an increasingly rich context. There have been for many years academic and professional bodies that focus on educational studies. Some restrict themselves to an exploration of theory and practice *about* education. For example, there are many journals – e.g. the *Oxford Review of Education* or the *British Educational Research Journal* that publish scholarly work about such matters as achievement. But there are also bodies that focus directly on the nature of education. In other words there is a great deal of work that is making a more direct contribution to the development of the field of educational studies. The Society for Educational Studies and its journal the *British Journal of Educational Studies* is perhaps the leading body in this regard although there are others, including the journal *Educational Studies*. Recently another association has been established to support research into educational studies. The British Education Studies Association has a mission to:

- support the community of students, teachers and researchers in Education Studies;
- develop a rationale and theoretical grounding for the subject; and
- promote the profile of the subject within higher education institutions.

It too has a journal – **Educationalfutures** – which can be accessed at http://www.education-studies.org.uk/journal/. These developments suggest that educational studies is becoming increasingly established and it is possible that in the near future it will acquire even more of the apparatus of a discipline in its own right.

WHAT IS CONTAINED IN THIS BOOK?

This textbook contains three main sections: 'foundations of education' (ideas and issues from the philosophy, history, sociology, and psychology of education); 'contexts: making education work' (this describes and discusses the context in which education occurs, and raises questions about the processes that are employed within those contexts); and 'doing education studies' (a guide to some of the issues involved in the writing of a dissertation to be completed by final-year undergraduates). Each chapter contains a discussion of key content and perspectives (an outline of what has been said and the different ways of looking at the key issues that are highlighted) and concludes with a summary; a list of key questions; a list of further reading that will help students explore and understand even more about education; and a link to readings in the Routledge Education Studies Reader that connect with the ideas raised in that chapter.

We have also included a series of key debates that fit between chapters. Each debate makes use of ideas and issues from the history, psychology, sociology and philosophy of education and is conducted by two protagonists. Each debater makes an initial statement in answer to a question; each gives a reply to the initial statement; and a conclusion is provided by both, as well as a suggested list of further reading. Debaters have not been restricted to simple for/against positions but have instead provided lively and stimulating intellectual explorations of subtly different standpoints.

Section 1 is principally concerned with a description and discussion of the philosophy, history, sociology and psychology of education. These are the underlying disciplines of education and will provide a foundation for further reflections as the reader progresses through the book. There are two chapters within the first part of Section 1 which deal, in turn, with the goals of education and education and culture. This will allow the reader to have a clear and in-depth understanding of the fundamental nature of education and provide a backdrop to a chapter which, by considering the history of UK state education from the beginning of the nineteenth century to the present time, shows how ideas about education have both changed and remained the same. These historical considerations provide the platform for considering contemporary education through reflections in separate chapters on gender, social class and ethnicity. These discussions that relate directly to societal matters provide in turn a way of beginning to understand the nature of learning that is undertaken by individuals. Chapters that discuss views of intelligence and how people learn make use of psychological research and scholarship. Thus, by the close of Section 1, students have been thoroughly introduced to key ideas that are associated with the foundational disciplines of education.

In Section 2 a series of chapters include descriptions and discussions of the context in which education occurs and raise questions about the processes that are employed within those contexts. This means that recent initiatives such as Every Child Matters and No Child Left Behind are subjected to focused scrutiny while broader matters about how to effect change and the relationship between politics and education can also be examined. Thus, by the end of Section 2, students should be familiar with both the general issues affecting the development and implementation of new initiatives and have some understanding about what has happened in particular cases. Section 2 also includes the consideration of matters that are more immediately connected with working with learners. Curriculum pedagogy and assessment are highlighted with reflections on curriculum by asking what should be taught, and pedagogical and assessment matters by discussing how we should teach and assess. However, we have also included chapters that highlight the issues associated with professional learning, and authors raise questions about the nature of what is provided in schools by reflecting on older and more recently established approaches to innovation. By exploring the so-called 'radical' agenda of the past (deschooling, freeschooling and reschooling) and discussing the nature of contemporary reform through e-learning we encourage students to consider alternatives to and within education.

The final part of the book, Section 3, encourages readers to reflect on the nature of the issues and data that they come into contact with as they learn about education. Readers are asked to think about how to access and understand research on education. If students are to be able to interpret research results and to consider what sort of research needs to take place in the future they need to know what research results are available (UK and internationally) and how research is done. Understanding of such matters will allow for a more sophisticated ability to assess the claims of policy makers and others as new initiatives are called for and evaluated. But this is also vitally relevant for the students who belong to our principal target audience as they will be preparing to collect and analyse data in the development of a dissertation. Issues are explored about the ways in which small-scale empirical projects may be conducted and there are references to key contemporary debates about the most appropriate ways to conduct research.

At appropriate points in the book we have inserted debates about key issues. As students read these debates they will see the intensely conducted controversies and the subtle nuances that characterise the differences between people who care deeply about education. There are debates covering a range of issues including differences of opinion about independent and state schools; faith-based and secular schools; vocational and academic education; the role of schools in promoting social and community cohesion; and 'traditional' and 'progressive' teaching methods and the future of research.

HOW SHOULD STUDENTS INTERACT WITH THE MATERIAL IN THIS BOOK?

The educational aims commonly associated with undergraduate degree programmes are shown explicitly in the benchmark statement that has been referred to above. It is important to do more than merely replicate the admonitions that have been sanctioned by a government agency. Undergraduates reading educational studies are not being trained for a profession (and, of course, beginning professionals are not to be treated as if they must acquire a set of competences mechanistically). Fortunately, the benchmark statement does not expect compliance to a narrowly framed agenda but instead highlights ideas and issues that need to be explored. We see this statement as providing a useful and provisionally framed context for the study of education. Part of the purpose of degree programmes in education will be to encourage students to learn within an agreed framework *and* contribute to the further development of education studies. It would not be reasonable or realistic to expect undergraduates to transform the area of study they are engaged with but it is important for them to consider the nature of their study and to make contributions to its further development. For some education studies will always be an area of study that uses the foundational disciplines of psychology, history, sociology and philosophy to explore contexts and issues. In some ways we are very attracted to this way of seeing education. It is a professionally related matter and people involved with it have a responsibility to make a positive contribution to the enhancement of people's lives. Expanding intellectual horizons and developing personal skills with reference to societal priorities in contemporary settings is much more than a purely academic enterprise. But of course the nature of the academic underpinning for these reflections and actions needs to be very substantial. For some, there is the perception of education studies as a discipline in its own right. The tensions and extremely varied perspectives within and perceptions of longer-established academic disciplines suggest that it is not unreasonable to regard education studies as at least potentially as much a discipline as any other. In short students who use this book should learn about education about policies and practices, ideas and ideologies; they should develop the skills of critical reflection with dispositions that allow them to consider what should be put in place to help individuals and groups; and they should ask questions and come to tentative conclusions about the nature of education studies. They should learn about education and learn about what it means to 'do' education.

The chapters and debates help realise these goals if they are read in particular ways. We do not wish students to read, remember and accept. We want them to read, criticise and reflect. We are not promoting disagreement for its own sake but we are hoping for lively engagement and reflection in the form of reaction. The debates have been included to heighten this possibility of critical engagement. The topics are obviously important and relevant; we are expecting readers to use the material in the book about fundamental principles and ideas as well as contexts as they decide which of the positions outlined in the debates are more persuasive. The debaters have chosen to work together and show in their carefully considered contributions how it is possible to disagree about both means and ends while still being committed to the achievement of high-quality education. We accept that this subtle approach risks what Freud referred to as 'the narcissism of small differences' but it avoids the sterile and falsely gladiatorial staged confrontations so beloved by the media. Real debates about education are not about who is entirely right or wrong; it is about being able to identify why people are putting forward a particular position and to weigh the likely consequences of the proposal.

No textbook can cover everything and this publication will be complemented by an additional resource. *The Routledge Education Studies Reader* contains key academic articles to support students engaging critically with educational issues. Even this extensive material will not provide the reader with all they need to know about education. What could possibly do that? It is hoped, however, that this book and its related Reader will encourage students and others to continue to engage with the most important pursuit of achieving a better society through education.

SECTION 1

FOUNDATIONS OF EDUCATION

■ **philosophy** ■ **history** ■ **sociology** ■ **psychology**

CHAPTER 1

THE GOALS OF EDUCATION

David Carr

The rationale for this chapter is:

- to provide a brief general account of past and more recent philosophical analyses of the meaning and aims of education;
- to provide an account of recent 'postmodern' scepticism regarding such analyses;
- to identify some of the conceptual confusions in such skeptical responses to philosophical analysis.

INTRODUCTION: THE NORMATIVE CHARACTER OF EDUCATION

One might naively (or pre-theoretically) suppose that the goals of education could simply be identified by drawing up a list of the sorts of things that are taught in schools as institutions generally charged with the social provision of education. The trouble with any such strategy, however, is that what is taught in schools is and has ever been subject to wide variation and there is also equally wide disagreement about whether much of this could or should be regarded as educational. At one extreme, recent history has seen Nazi schools in pre-war Germany, as well as schools in various contexts of 'white supremacism' (in apartheid South Africa or the southern USA), that have preached the racial inferiority of Jews or 'people of colour' in ways that may seem 'indoctrinatory' rather than educational. At another extreme, schools and other contexts of formation have often been sites of teaching and instruction that – however socially or humanly valuable – might still be regarded as falling short of *education*. Thus, whatever the social utility of nineteenth-century Victorian instruction of children of paupers in the skills of chimney sweeping, or even the specialist training of gifted youngsters in gymnastics skills as part of some national programme of 'cultural development', we might well have reservations about regarding such training – at any rate if focus on such skills excluded any and all other forms of learning – as 'real' education.

In short, knowledge or appreciation of the goals of education is not simply to be had by sociological or other social scientific study or survey but is unavoidably implicated in reflections or deliberations of a normative or evaluative kind that take us beyond mere data-gathering. Indeed, to recognise the evaluative character of the concept (or of concepts) of education – over which there is liable to be some human disagreement or controversy – is to regard theorising about education as implicated first and foremost in the kinds of enquiries into value in which philosophers have traditionally engaged – perhaps particularly to that branch of values enquiry usually known as ethics or moral philosophy. From this viewpoint, depending on what view one takes of the grounds or provenance of human moral claims, it would be one task of educational theory to try to identify or construct arguments designed to justify one conception of education over any rival or competing ones. But how might one begin to do this? According to one time-honoured approach to philosophy – developed and refined in modern times mainly by philosophers in Britain, Germany and the USA, but with roots going back to classical antiquity – the fundamental task of philosophy (and therefore one that must inevitably precede the construction of normative arguments) is that of determining, by so-called conceptual (or linguistic) analysis, the conditions under which we can meaningfully or coherently use such philosophically problematic terms as 'truth', 'knowledge' or 'education'. It was just this task that was first given clear and systematic direction by the founding father of Western (or at any rate 'analytical') philosophy, Socrates, who sought to discover the meaning of such philosophically vexed terms as 'justice', 'virtue' and 'knowledge' via the production of something like formal definitions.

Despite the undeniable interest in education and its social and political significance and implications on the part of many major past philosophers – not least Socrates' own distinguished pupil Plato – it is arguable that serious philosophical analysis of the concept of education (as well as of other educationally related concepts such as teaching and learning) had to await relatively recent modern attention. To be sure, this may also have had much to do with some insulation (in Britain and most other countries) of educational policy making and professional teacher training from the academic contexts in which certain key modern developments in analytical philosophy occurred: indeed, it was not only that serious philosophising about education – beyond the most superficial acquaintance with the past speculations of Plato, Rousseau or Dewey – did not generally have much place in the non-university training of teachers, but that up until the post-World War II settlement academic philosophers had not generally been greatly interested in applying their analytical methods to the discourse of education. It was precisely this perceived shortfall that such academically trained philosophers as R. S. Peters (1966) in Britain and Israel Scheffler (1960) in the USA sought to address by exploiting recently developed modern philosophical approaches and techniques (to which we shall shortly return) for the clarification of the political and professional educational discourses that they regarded as all too often unclear or confused.

THE CONCEPT OF EDUCATION IN POST-WAR PHILOSOPHICAL ANALYSIS

R. S. Peters's own main concern lay with the question of the *meaning* of education – precisely with a view to clarifying the goals or purposes of education. More precisely, Peters' approach to this question took the form of a query about the 'aims' of education (Peters 1973). In this regard, Peters asks, when people invite us to specify the aims of education what should we reply? His answer to this question is also both simple and disarming: we should properly say that it has *no* aims. Peters's point is that whereas it is proper to enquire about the aims or purposes of a wide range of human activities, education is not an activity or enterprise of this kind. From this viewpoint, Peters maintained, it is particularly important not to confuse education with other processes of learning or knowledge acquisition such as *training* – with respect to which, of course, it *is* quite appropriate to ask to what particular purpose a given schedule of training is directed. People are precisely trained to be this, that or the other – to be, for example, joiners, nurses or airline pilots – but they are not, says Peters, 'educated' for any end distinct from or located beyond education itself. It therefore makes perfect sense for people to value (say) their university education, even though that education has failed to equip them for any specific or 'useful' employment. In short, education is not a means to an end, but something that has its own inherent or ' intrinsic' worth.

Be that as it may, it is surely still reasonable to ask what exactly education *is* with a view to understanding better how we might further promote it. Peters (and others) have a fair amount to say about this, but we may confine ourselves here to five key points. First, it is integral to the value of education that it leads to the human *improvement* of those who undergo it: for Peters, the concept of education is evaluative or normative in much the same way as the term 'reform' – so that we could not say that a person had been educated but not made (in some sense) better. Second, if education is to be of intrinsic value, it must involve initiation into forms of learning or *knowledge* that are also *inherently* worthwhile: unlike (at least some of) the knowledge gained in the course of training, that may have no value beyond the extrinsic purposes it serves (such as, perhaps, computer keyboard skills), educationally valuable knowledge should be pursuable for its own sake. Third, however, education is also to be distinguished from forms of training insofar as it is not restricted to the development of some particular realm of expertise. For Peters and other liberal educationalists, education is a matter of *broad initiation*: we would not describe someone as 'educated' who had simply acquired expertise in a particular form of knowledge or skill, no matter how advanced or 'sophisticated' that expertise might be. Fourth, the knowledge that is acquired in the course of education should have *depth* as well as breadth; in particular it should involve some understanding of the 'reason why' of things and not simply be aimed at the retention of information. Fifth (for now), such educational learning should be conducted in a climate of *open enquiry* that precludes the thought control or coercion that might better be described as 'indoctrination' more than education; in short, it should conduce to the development of individual or personal rational freedom or *autonomy*.

The point of such analysis, according to Peters and other modern liberal educationalists, is precisely to distinguish education as a particular mode of formation from other processes with which it might be (or has often enough been) confused. In short, irrespective of looser applications of the term 'education' to any old processes of learning, it would seem that not all such processes of learning meet the rather strict criteria of education lately specified. Hence, as seen, though various kinds of training are clearly presupposed in education – a person's education as a mathematician or musician presumably depends at least partly upon the acquisition of basic arithmetical or musical performance skills – education is not obviously reducible to such training. Indeed, though some training in vocationally useful skills may well go on in the course of schooling – which, as radical educationalists (such as Goodman 1971, Illich 1973, Reimer 1971) have been keen to remind us, is also not identical with education – we may also succeed in producing first-rate plumbers, electricians or hairdressers, who (whatever their other valuable human virtues) we would not necessarily regard as *educated* persons. Again, education in this sense is not to be confused with wider or more general socialisation: thus, in early years and beyond, children have to master a variety of simple skills – such as doing up their buttons or tying their shoelaces – or various conventions of courtesy or etiquette that would also appear to fall short of education in Peters's more refined sense. Peters was also concerned to distinguish education in this more precise sense (as he suspected that some progressive educators – such as, perhaps, A. S. Neill (1968) – had failed to separate it) from any and all processes of quasi-psychological counselling or therapy. In this connection, he observes that 'the teacher's job is to train and instruct, it is not to help and cure' (Peters 1964). It was also claimed in further defence of this 'special' conception of education, that not only was it continuous with a long liberal educational tradition going back at least to the nineteenth century (for example, to Matthew Arnold: see Gribble 1967) – if not, as Paul Hirst (1974) claimed to classical Greece – but it was also in line with much received usage. But this now raises the awkward question: *whose* usage?

OBJECTIONS TO THE POST-WAR LIBERAL ANALYSIS

Criticisms of this modern analytical conception of liberal education were soon forthcoming, not only from quarters not especially friendly to either the liberal educational tradition or to modern conceptual analysis, but also from those broadly sympathetic to both these perspectives. As might be expected, the more modest 'internal' criticisms endorsed the overall liberal focus on the promotion of rational autonomy, but rejected some of the particular details of Peters's account of liberal education as broad initiation into forms of largely academic, theoretical or (as it was sometimes put) 'propositional' knowledge. More precisely, some 'internal' critics objected to the strongly implied liberal educational denigration of practical or technical activities or pursuits (Carr 1978); some criticised what they took to be an overdrawn distinction of 'real' or liberal education from vocational education or training (Pring 1995, 2005; Winch 2000, 2002); and some were even sceptical about any strong interpretation of the liberal idea of education as broad initiation (Warnock 1973, 1977).

These objections had also somewhat variable status and force. To be sure, to the extent that Peters's own analysis does appear to conflate the distinction between education and training with a rather different distinction between theory and practice, there is probably something to the first objection: there are many practical activities and pursuits – such as dance and even moral association – that would appear to have educational consequences and implications. On the other hand, the familiar point that the liberal account distinguished too sharply between education and vocational training is more contentious and probably much confused. If the idea here is that this account precludes any place for training of a vocationally relevant kind in schools then it is certainly misdirected; such criticism almost certainly rests on a confusion between education and schooling (see Carr 1996) – including the mistaken notion that it is the exclusive role of schools to educate – of which such post-war liberal educationalists as Peters were not obviously guilty. Peters certainly did draw a sharp (and in the present view defensible) distinction between education and vocational training and would just as surely have regarded much recent fashionable talk of 'vocational education' as oxymoronic – on the grounds precisely that the narrow focus of the vocational is inherently at odds with the broad remit of (at any rate liberal) education. But it is also not obvious that he saw such broad initiation as logically or logistically precluding other kinds of schooling in vocationally (or otherwise) useful skills.

However, more radical critiques of this analytical liberal account of education seem to have drawn mainly on intellectual trends at some odds with conceptual analysis, the liberal tradition, and the empiricist epistemology upon which these movements have often drawn. Mainly, they have been inspired by various modern (continental European and other) developments of nineteenth-century (German) idealism for which human knowledge and values are essentially social creations or constructions rather than reflections of any external mind-independent reality. The influence of such idealism and constructivism – brokered especially through the ideas of perhaps its two most influential modern interpreters Marx and Nietzsche – is also now philosophically widespread (not least in present-day philosophy of education). It may also be conceded that there has been much perfectly reasonable accommodation in wider contemporary philosophy of the deep vein of truth within such idealism: that all human knowledge and understanding is bound, at least in part, to reflect local social or cultural perspectives, and that consequently such perspectives are likely to be both limited and in some potential conflict with views developed in other places. That said, the seeds of potential corruption in such constructivism lie in its flirtation with an ancient epistemic scepticism that supposes that there can therefore be no more to knowledge than the judgements of local social consensus. It was this view, held by the ancient Greek sophists, that was stoutly resisted by Plato in his pioneering analysis of knowledge (as justified true belief) in the dialogue *Theaetetus* (Plato 1961). In short, for Plato, since knowledge entails *truth* – to be understood, at the very least, in terms of some test of our knowledge claims that transcends arbitrary local consensus – knowledge is not finally or entirely reducible to (either individual or collective) judgement. This is a lesson that much modern 'non-analytical' – Marxist, 'neo-Marxist', 'post-structuralist', 'post-modernist' and even (some) pragmatist – speculation seems to have ignored at its peril.

For present purposes, we may identify two common versions of such 'constructivist' views. The first (weaker) claim is that insofar as human knowledge and the concepts in terms of which such knowledge is construed are but human constructions, they may reflect only the epistemically limited perspectives on experience of locally situated agents. In this light, human knowledge claims cannot be taken to reflect anything much worth dignifying with the status of objective, universal or absolute truth. On the contrary, knowledge claims are at best *provisional* and *fallible* – ever liable to refutation in the light of further enquiries or discoveries. However, the second (stronger) claim – perhaps most famously articulated for our times by Marx (Marx and Engels 1968) – is that insofar as knowledge is a social construction, it is also clearly designed to serve or secure explicit human purposes. From a Marxist perspective, one such key human purpose is precisely to maintain an appropriate level of social order – an order that has for most of human history been maintained by imposition of the ideas and values of dominant elites on subservient masses. On a radical interpretation of such control or dominion, moreover, the ruling ideas of the controlling elites – what such classes are disposed to promote as objective knowledge – has all too often little or no genuine objective status or value; on the contrary, it serves solely as a tool for control and dominance of 'subaltern' groups. For example, the religious (and, on this view, entirely fabricated) ideas of (other-worldly) salvation and redemption, promoted in Western Christendom from the Holy Roman Empire onwards, are and were simply the means by which an ecclesiastical hierarchy and its appointed secular vassals kept the masses in a state of (often brutally exploited) oppression. Crucially, moreover, Marx and his followers regarded the various common processes of knowledge transmission – from church sermons to state-sponsored schooling – as key mechanisms of such control and dominion.

Hence, in this more radical view, any idea that it is the goal or purpose of school-based education to promote the learner's grasp of objective knowledge and truth is illusory: on the contrary, it is the principal goal or purpose of such education to ensure (at best) that school pupils are duly conditioned or indoctrinated into the order-sustaining values, principles and practices of the status quo – irrespective of the 'truth' (a term that cannot on this view anyway be written outside of scare quotes) of what is taught – or (at worst) to maintain existing hegemonic arrangements and ensure that the dominated do not rise above their station. From an educational philosophical viewpoint, however, it at least means that we cannot take any given account of the concept of 'education' – even (or perhaps especially) if it claims to be supported by received 'usage' – to be an objective account of the meaning of education *per se*. The point is that if this or that concept of education does claim to reflect common usage it is more than likely that such usage is itself infected by ideas of the social purposes of education and schooling that are irredeemably hegemonic. In fact, this is just what many latter-day radical educationalists have been inclined to say of the sort of analysis of education and the purposes of schooling defended by such post-war liberal educationalists as Peters and Scheffler; educational sociologists of knowledge, radical educationalists of 'de-schooling' and post-structuralists (all invariably influenced by Marx) have precisely argued that such analyses are informed by a distinctively Western liberal conception of education and schooling that is endemically colonialist (if not actually often racist) and class-based (for some influential latter-day views of this kind, see Apple 1979, 1982, 2000; Freire 1972; Giroux 1981, 1992; Young 1971). It is a conception of education that also elevates effectively useless academic learning – generally accessible only to a privileged few in possession of the required 'social capital' – over the really relevant and useful practical knowledge traditionally possessed by lower social classes. At any rate, from this viewpoint, we cannot safely assume that the analysis of education offered by the likes of Peters, Scheffler and other post-war liberal educationalists provides an objective account of the nature of education as such – that is, as it might be apart from such local hegemonic interests and influences; for, if education is a social construction like other human concepts, there simply cannot be any such 'objective' account.

THE 'CONTESTABILITY' OF EDUCATION

Thus, with respect to any proposed account of education, we ought as educational philosophers always to ask – in the spirit of Alasdair MacIntyre's (1987a) recent enquiries into notions of rationality and justice – *whose* education? To be sure, in terminology that MacIntyre (1973–74) has himself contributed significantly to popularising, 'education' is one of those concepts that has to be considered 'essentially contested', Indeed, MacIntyre – whose impact on recent educational philosophy has been considerable – has argued in one place (MacIntyre 1987b) that the social and epistemically fragmenting conditions of much (particularly Western liberal) modernity are such as to preclude the conception of general education for which philosophers like Peters and Scheffler argued, and in another (MacIntyre 1999) that this must imply a diversity of locally adapted educational provision in (at any rate) Western culturally pluralist contexts. Be that as it may, it has now become a routine matter for educational philosophers of different – 'analytical' as well as post-analytical' – persuasions, to claim that 'education' is a *contested* concept. However, assuming that contestability does not here just mean simply (and trivially) the mere possibility of argument over the meaning of a term – in which case all concepts would be contested (so that we might as well say that none are) – we should perhaps here ask in what sense precisely education *is* supposed to be contestable.

In this respect, going back to the accounts of this notion of Gallie (1955–56), MacIntyre (1973–1974) and others, the idea of (essential) contestability would appear to be that there are concepts that are so deeply implicated in rival value perspectives that there could be no question of overarching rational agreement or consensus over their meaning. It is also certainly arguable that there are concepts that are contestable in this radical sense. Thus, suppose that Tom, asked to spell out what he regards as 'sexual fulfilment', says that it is to be found in emotionally involved sexual expression with a partner to whom one is personally committed. However, Harry contests this by saying that he can only find sexual fulfilment in free sexual encounters with many different partners from whom he is emotionally detached. This is at least arguably a case in which different agents ascribe different senses to the term 'sexual fulfilment' and have divergent – quite conflicting or incompatible – understandings of the condition indicated by this term. Indeed, for Tom, to say that 'sexual fulfilment is emotionally disengaged promiscuity' is *false* – and likewise, for Harry, it is no less false to say that 'sexual fulfilment is emotionally committed monogamous sexuality'. In short, Tom and Harry are always and forever doomed to differ on the question of sexual satisfaction. But if this is what it is for a concept to be contestable, it seems far from clear that education *is* a contestable concept in anything like this sense.

One trouble is that educational philosophers and theorists who talk freely of the contestability of education seldom specify – or provide clear examples of – what they have in mind. Still, some such fairly relativist – or at least social constructivist – interpretation of the idea of the contestability of education seems fairly conspicuous in the work of Wilfred Carr. Indeed, according to Carr's avowedly 'post-modern' perspective, there is utterly irresolvable disagreement of this essentially normative or evaluative kind as to whether the aims or goals of education are 'emancipation' or 'socialization', 'liberal' or 'vocational', or concerned with 'fulfilling individual potential' or 'meeting the needs of society' (see Carr 1997, 2006). On the face of it, however, there would seem to be nothing – post-modernly or otherwise – of a conceptually irresolvable character about such alleged antinomies. At all events, such 'disagreements' about the aims of education seem not at all like those between Tom and Harry over 'sexual fulfilment'. In that case, given that sexual fulfilment for Tom is emotional attachment to one partner, it *cannot* for him be promiscuous detachment – and the same goes *mutatis mutandis* for Harry. But it would seem that what most sane and sensible people would want from educational provision, or at least (with some tightening or clarification of what is probably here meant by 'education') *schooling*, is neither 'socialization' rather than 'emancipation', nor 'liberal' rather than 'vocational' learning – but *all* these things. In short, what most people (policy makers, professionals and the general public) require of school education is a diversity of goods and services – that, whatever the logistical problems of providing these in the space of a short school day, are not obviously at odds in any deeper conceptual sense.

To be sure, a rat might here be smelled in the talk above of the need for some 'tightening' or 'clarification' of the sense or senses of 'education' in contexts in which questions of the aims or goals or education are at issue. Indeed, in light of constructivist analyses of education of the kind favoured by Carr and others, this might simply appear to beg the question. For is not one consequence of assuming a constructivist perspective that any such 'tightening' or 'clarification' of the concept of education can only serve to endorse or confirm some particular partisan conception of education – that, in all probability, also reflects the vested interests of some dominant group? In this connection, by the way, it is important to grasp that the objections to the account of education canvassed by the likes of Peters and Scheffler by recent post-this-and-that philosophers are not objections to such accounts in particular, but objections to the whole method of conceptual analysis on which these accounts rest. Wilfred Carr seems fairly typical of a general loss of faith among recent educational philosophers in the power of modern analytical methods to assist clarification of the concept of education or any objective identification of the goals and purposes of education. However, without ignoring the limits of what may be philosophically achieved by conceptual analysis alone (notwithstanding that such analysis has clearly continued to be the dominant approach in serious mainstream philosophy for something like the last century), it is also arguable that recent critiques of the use of conceptual analyses in educational philosophy have been mainly misplaced and confused.

DIFFERENT SENSES OF 'EDUCATION'

Fairly direct insight into some of the deepest confusions here may be had by briefly examining the work on meaning of the great twentieth-century philosopher Ludwig Wittgenstein (1953). Indeed, Wittgenstein's ideas are significant in this context insofar as his work has clearly had much influence on both post-war analytical philosophers of education (Peters, for example, draws explicitly on his work) *and* on constructivist critiques of educational uses of conceptual analysis. Thus, in constructivist or relativist quarters, the contestability of such concepts as democracy, freedom and education – the idea that there are rival conceptions or traditions of thought concerning these notions – has sometimes drawn on the 'anti-essentialist' Wittgensteinian notion of 'language games'. This idea, so the story goes, clearly shows that such terms are firmly anchored in local socially constructed discourses that reflect radically different concepts of human association and practice. We also need not doubt that Wittgenstein did hold – in line with both some idealist influence on his thought and the findings of modern anthropology – that communities may differ much in their conceptions of democracy, freedom and education. Be that as it may, it is just as clear that Wittgenstein's idea of language games is not generally or primarily advanced as an argument for linguistic or social relativity, but as a rule of analytical method (influenced by his great teacher Frege – the founding father of modern analytical philosophy (see Frege 1978)) – that encourages us to seek for the sense or meaning of a term in its *context* of use. So, for example, the sense of the term 'good' may differ in 'that's a good hammer' from its meaning in 'Good morning'. However, that does not mean that the term 'good' is essentially *contested* between those who think that it means (in this context) fitness for purpose and those for whom it means (in that one) wishing prosperity – and it would clearly be absurd for people to debate about whether it must *always* mean one thing or the other.

It would be difficult to overstate the confusion that has been caused in latter-day educational philosophy and theory by failure to apply (even on the part of those who pay it regular lip service) this basic rule of analytical method. Indeed, such failure has been perhaps most conspicuous precisely in contexts of debate about that most basic of educational concepts, 'education' itself – and/or of the goals and aims of education. For, in different contexts of human discourse, the term 'education' clearly has widely different – though, one should quickly add, not necessarily *incompatible* – senses. Thus, for example, at its most fast and loose the term 'education' may be used to describe any old experience from which it might be thought we have learned. In this spirit, someone might say that: 'mucking out those cows was a real education'. From this viewpoint, one is tempted to wonder whether Carr's (1997) post-modern professor would insist that there are communities who have a completely different concept of education from ours because they frequently speak of it in relation to shovelling dung. Be that as it may, it is clearly safer to suppose that those who may speak in this way – quite in accordance with popular usage – would not also want to deny that education in schools and universities has quite another sense and purpose in such contexts (and not wish to insist, for example, that dung-shovelling should feature in the school curriculum). Indeed, it should be clear that the term 'education' is commonly applied to a wide variety of processes of acculturation or learning in a no less wide range of human contexts. While these senses of 'education' may differ from those that the term has in more formally instituted or organised contexts of knowledge acquisition, they are not obviously (conceptually) incompatible with them.

In this regard, as we have already indicated, another very common – and also very fast and loose – use of the term 'education' is to refer to the social institution of schooling in which education is widely provided. In fact, in much policy documentation, not to mention professional theorising, the terms 'schooling' and 'education' are employed more or less synonymously. Just as clearly, however, such terms are not co-extensional; we can say many things about schooling and schools (that, for example, they have headmasters or a particular spatial location) that we cannot say of education – and vice versa. It is also no contradiction to claim – as those radical educationalists known as 'deschoolers' (such as Goodman 1971, Illich 1973, Reimer 1971) have sought to show that 'schools do not educate' – or, of course, that 'education does not require schooling'. Indeed, it is clear that 'education' in the sense of schooling serves a much wider range of purposes than the more narrowly defined liberal idea of education as broad critical appreciation of knowledge for its own intrinsic worth. Schools exist in our own and other societies to provide child-care, a range of welfare (health and child-protection) services, counselling, some vocational training, careers advice, examination and certification for purposes of vocational selection, introduction to sports, games and other leisure activities (and so on) – as well as the broad educational initiation into intrinsically worthwhile knowledge and understanding beloved of liberal educationalists. But, from this viewpoint, it is more than likely that Carr's false educational oppositions between 'emancipation' or 'socialization, 'liberal' or 'vocational', 'fulfilling individual potential' or 'meeting the needs of society' follow simply from his own failure to distinguish the more refined sense of education – that liberal educationalists want to contrast with (say) socialisation or vocational training – from the common popular understanding of education as 'schooling' that would encompass *both* such broad initiation *and* vocational training.

THE IMPORTANCE OF CONCEPTUAL ANALYSIS

In short, it is something of an irony that the deep muddles to which Carr and those who share his post-modern 'anti-essentialist' perspective on the concept of education are prone, are actually the direct consequence of failure to engage precisely in that close scrutiny of the complex usage to which the term 'education' is given in received discourse – and which it is precisely the concern of properly conceived conceptual analysis to achieve. Such failure readily gives rise to the sort of false oppositions that Carr invents between rival camps of 'liberal educationalists' and 'vocationalists', 'emancipators' and 'socialisers' and so forth. In fact, on any close reading of the work of Peters and other post-war liberal educationalists, it seems fairly clear that while their distinction between 'liberal education' and 'vocational training' was drawn for serious theoretical and practical purposes – precisely in the interests of showing that we should not want to say that children who have only been taught vocational skills (say of plumbing or hairdressing) have been fully *educated*, as well as of specifying the criteria to which any such fuller education should conform – they were not generally inclined to insist that this is the *only* sense in which the term 'education' is ordinarily used, or that in its broader popular sense of 'schooling', education would have to exclude child-minding, socialisation or vocational learning. Above all, the idea that educational goals or aims are contestable between 'emancipation' or 'socialization', 'liberal' or 'vocational' learning, 'fulfilling individual potential' or 'meeting the needs of society', seems to be an untenable post-whatever sophism.

In this light, most parents would surely want education in the sense of schooling to socialise children *and* assist them to some mature independence; to help them realise their potential *and* to help them to be productive members of society; to have intrinsic appreciation of a broad range of cultural achievement *and* to have acquired vocationally useful skills. There may be considerable logistical problems in meeting such a tall order, but these aims and goals are not obviously at any serious conceptual odds – and, in fact, it is probably safe to say that all good teachers are in the normal course of their working lives simultaneously concerned to achieve many of these diverse goals. So, in contrast with what many 'post-analytical' educational philosophers have recently claimed – indeed, even in contrast to what many leading analytical educational philosophers have routinely come to assert – we are forced to conclude that it is far from obvious that 'education' *is* a contestable concept or that any of the goals that interested parties – policy makers, professionals and the wider public – have been accustomed to associate with education are 'contested' either. If we simply care to distinguish carefully between different common uses of the term 'education', we may recognise that in the looser sense of education (to mean something like school learning) it embraces a range of aims and goals, which (while no doubt diverse) are not inherently incompatible, and that in a theoretically or professionally more refined sense it identifies a notion of broad liberal initiation that is nevertheless not inherently incompatible with some parallel vocational learning. Thus, notwithstanding political or other controversies (about how best, say, to publicly provide education), and the usual philosophical difficulty of arriving at strict definitions in such matters as these, the idea that we really do not know what education actually *means* (or could not recognise an educated person if we saw one) is at least overstated and at most sophistical.

Still, it might yet be insisted that these arguments – however persuasive – perversely miss the point. For surely, it is just a fact that education is a contested concept in so far as many *do* contest it – and fairly heatedly at that. Indeed, leaving aside the intellectual or 'academic' challenges to the idea of the kind raised by Carr and others, it is clear that there are serious contemporary controversies about the content of state or public schooling and the kinds of teaching that go on in them. To take just one striking example, religious (Christian, Muslim and other) fundamentalists around the world have voiced much disquiet about the kind of open critical questioning of beliefs that seems to be encouraged by (secular) liberal education and have sometimes contested the teaching of modern scientific theories taken to be at odds with this or that religious text. They advocate a concept of education as uncritical initiation into the teachings of this or that deity or prophet. As earlier indicated, however, mere disagreement is not sufficient proof of contestability. For example, while it is clear that people can disagree about pretty well anything, disagreement about whether or not the earth is flat does not render the roundness (or otherwise) of the earth an essentially contestable issue in the special sense of Gallie and MacIntyre – precisely because flat-earthers do not have much (in the current state of human knowledge) of a rationally defensible case. But how does this example support the present case against educational contestability? Insofar as (evaluative) views on the purposes of education are clearly not at all like (factual) knowledge of the shape of the earth, is there not here still some flagrant avoidance of the key issue? Indeed, further to this, would not the fundamentalist opponents of critical education precisely have a supportable *rational* case, if – as would also be nowadays widely accepted – they have a parental *right* to some say in their children's development *and* they regard critical education as inimical to such development?

SUMMARY

In short, while we lack space to do full justice to this question, it is arguable that the fundamentalist stance on education is actually much closer to the flat earth defence than to a genuinely contestable issue – and is therefore not at all question-begging. For surely, while not denying that parents clearly have a right to some say in the educational treatment of their offspring, we should not want to uphold such rights on the basis of *any* norms or values – to whatever extent such values were consensual. From this viewpoint, it would seem not only reasonable, but morally imperative to overrule – in the interests of the flourishing of *any* child and of any community to which it might belong – a claim by parents of a Nazi community to have their children taught the racial superiority of some and the inferiority of others. To whatever extent we might disagree over definitions of rationality, given the basic concern of rationality with the discernment of truth, any and all coercion of the young into uncritical acceptance of (at best) dubious beliefs, could not be considered rationally defensible – and, indeed, would have to be considered closer to indoctrination than education. However, to regard indoctrination – even in the name of local consensus – as a rationally defensible *alternative* form of education rather than as (what it is) a rationally indefensible form of anti-education, is not to be post-modernly open-minded about the possibilities of education, it is effectively to talk nonsense. That being so, it is also in the reasonable hope that even contemporary advocates of post-this-or-that educational contestability would also wish to draw the line at such nonsense that we presently rest our case.

KEY QUESTIONS

1. What is the meaning of education?
2. What is the difference between education and training?
3. Is it possible for us to agree about what constitutes 'good' education?

FURTHER READING

Carr, D. (2003) 'Philosophy and the meaning of "education"', *Theory and Research in Education*, 2, 195–212.

Carr, W. (2006) 'Education without theory', *British Journal of Educational Studies*, 54, 2, 136–159.

Peters, R.S. (1973) 'Aims of education', in Peters, R.S. (ed), *The Philosophy of Education*, Oxford: Oxford University Press.

This chapter links with readings 1, 2 and 4 of *The Routledge Education Studies Reader.*

CHAPTER 2

EDUCATION AND CULTURE

Michael A. Peters and Ergin Bulut

The rationale for this chapter is:

- to understand the contemporary theoretical debates around the concept of 'culture';
- to review and analyse some of the main approaches in the field of education to cultural studies;
- to provide a review of British cultural studies approaches and especially the work of Paul Willis and to chart its influence on debates in education.

INTRODUCTION

In line with the main lines stated above, our chapter charts the contested concept of 'culture' and its influence on theories of education purporting to explain cultural differences in achievement and development. The concept 'culture' is a difficult one to understand because its meanings have changed over time and it has been vitiated with assumptions of Western cultural and cognitive superiority, largely as a result of its early association with theories of evolutionism and social Darwinism. One of the main arguments of this chapter is that culture in the pre-war context was strongly tied to the notion of the other – the concept applied to other cultures and employed anthropological tools and theories to understand them. The other main use of the term culture was applied to the arts and related to 'high culture' (as opposed to 'popular culture'). These two notions of culture – one external, the other internal – increasingly came in for criticism as scholars and commentators first criticised the imperial roots of anthropology and accounts of so-called 'primitive' cultures, and second, turned their attention to the class implications of high culture and began to experiment with notions of subcultures, class cultures, multiculturalism, cultural capital, consumer culture, and the growth of post-war youth cultures. In both cases we see the increasing differentiation of cultures (in the plural) and their increasing complexity, so much so that scholars are reluctant to claim any explanatory power at all for the concept today. And yet the concept plays a central role in education theory and is used to underpin ethnographic studies in education of class and reproduction as well as research in relation to multiculturalism, youth cultures, postmodernism and so on. This chapter investigates some of these developments: it begins by charting the contested history of the concept of culture; next, the chapter reviews influence of British cultural studies focusing on the work of Paul Willis in his seminal ethnography *Learning to Labour*. We conclude the chapter with some suggestions for the future of cultural studies in education.

THE CONTESTED HISTORY OF THE CONCEPT OF 'CULTURE': EVOLUTIONISM VERSUS CULTURAL RELATIVISM

The concept of 'culture' has a rich and complex history tied to European colonialism, expansionism and Victorian moral assumptions. One source of its use in the modern period begins with the formation of the discipline of anthropology in the nineteenth century, when the term was linked to the theory of social evolutionism based on an application of the work of Charles Darwin's *The Origin of the Species*, published in 1859. This early evolutionary anthropology treated 'culture' from the perspective of a standard recording all cultural variations as stages of development starting with the most 'primitive' and ending up with the most developed, which was considered to be that of Victorian England. This developmental anthropological framework gave rise to grand theories that mapped human cultures in terms of their evolutionary stages on the basis of the reports of travellers, navigators, explorers, traders and missionaries. Such theories, based on a social application of Darwin's evolutionary to human cultures, led to 'armchair' theories that hypothesised different stages of development in a linear sequence, leading from higher primates to first identifiable human cultures to the industrial culture of the Victorians as the highpoint of development and evolution. This evolutionary framework also became the basis for a series of false assertions concerning race and racial characteristics linked to statements concerning genetic endowments for whole populations. Brian Schwimmer,[1] the anthropologist, notes that the theses of early anthropology are evident in Edward Tylor's 1871 work, *Primitive Culture*, which includes the first formal definition of culture: 'Culture or Civilization, . . . is that complex whole which includes knowledge, belief, art, morals, law, custom and any other capabilities and habits acquired by man as a member of society.' As Schwimmer indicates,

> The telling point of this definition is that, although labeled a whole, culture is actually treated as a list of elements. In effect, culture traits were understood as representing one of a series of stages of mental and moral progress culminating in the rational society of industrializing England.

This evolutionary perspective easily led to the ideology of social Darwinism based on Darwin's theory of natural selection applied to human cultures which held that differences in human populations were the outcome of competition for limited resources, leading to the 'survival of the fittest'. The doctrine, which developed during the early nineteenth century, rested on a combination of ideas that predate Darwin, based on the work of Herbert Spencer (*Progress: Its Law and Cause*, 1857), Thomas Malthus (*An Essay on the Principle of Human Population*, 1789), and Francis Galton (*Inquiries into Human Faculty and its Development*, 1883), the founder of eugenics. The ideas of cultural evolution had been formulated earlier by such philosophers as Hegel and Nietzsche, and their interpretation in Ernest Haeckel's *Welträtsel* (*The Riddle of the Universe*) led to notions of racial hygiene and later, as some critics claim, also directly to the underlying racist ideologies of modern Fascism and the race doctrines driving Nazism. It is aptly claimed that many of the social Darwinist ideas also found their way into laissez-faire capitalist economics and the culture of liberalism that together emphasise competition and comparative advantage as founding principles.

Against this view Franz Boas (1920) elaborated an approach on the basis of cultural relativism that directly opposed the evolutionist perspective. As Schwimmer notes, this position rested on four postulates:

1 Cultural aspects of human behaviour are not biologically based or conditioned but are acquired solely through learning.

2 Cultural conditioning of behaviour is ultimately accomplished through habituation and thus acts through unconscious processes rather than rational deliberation, although secondary rationalisations are often offered to explain cultural values.
3 All cultures are equally developed according to their own priorities and values; none is better, more advanced, or less primitive than any other.
4 Cultural traits cannot be classified or interpreted according to universal categories appropriate to 'human nature'. They assume meaning only within the context of coherently interrelated elements internal to the particular culture under consideration.

These two opposing positions – evolutionist and cultural relativist – are still dominant in anthropology today and together define the study of culture, especially in terms of its traditional anthropological outlook toward other cultures. Evolutionary anthropology, becoming dominant, sees itself as scientific and as the discipline that applies modern evolutionary theory to the analysis of human biology, behaviour, and culture. The differences in theory and methodology could not be more marked: Should anthropology be a scientific or interpretive discipline? Can cultures be validly compared? If every culture is unique and should be analysed in its own terms what of universal values, rights and standards? What are the colonial roots of anthropology and does the discipline have the capacity to overcome its imperial beginnings? To what extent if at all can ethnography overcome the subjectivity of its methods and perspectives? Are cultures whole, separate and distinct, or are they radically intermingled and hybridised based more on models of exchange, mobility and intermarriage than 'pure' and integral to themselves? What are the cultural effects of globalisation and are there now world cultures? These are some of the theoretical questions that face the study of cultures determining approaches, methodologies and field procedures.

The famous definition Tylor gives in *Primitive Culture* provides a definition of human culture from the viewpoint of an evolutionist interested in stages of human development. It was Franz Boas who referred to cultures in the plural and successfully displaced the notion of 'race' as the major signifier of cultural difference:

> Culture may be defined as the totality of the mental and physical reactions and activities that characterize the behavior of the individuals composing a social group collectively and individually, in relation to their natural environment, to other groups, to members of the group itself and of each individual to himself.
>
> (1948: 159, cited in Sökefield, 1999: 14)

While cultural difference under Boas's definition came to be seen less as a matter of descent and evolutionary development and rather more as a matter of acquisition, Boas's new concept still retained a certain determinism and exhibited homogenising tendencies, treating individuals and groups merely as cultural exemplars. Yet, as many scholars have pointed out, the concept of culture is itself *an implicit instrument of Othering*, epistemologically constructing the anthropologist as 'subject of knowledge' and the other as its scientific object. This epistemological problem of reflexivity has led to the observation that anthropological knowledge creates or constructs difference: it is actually produced by anthropological texts as well as being an aspect of empirical reality (Clifford and Marcus, 1986). Yet at the very moment in which the concept in anthropology is dissolving itself into a series of epistemological and ethical puzzles, the concept of culture has been advanced as a *political concept* (see Sökefield, 1999).

COLONIALISM, RACE AND CULTURE

For much of the nineteenth and twentieth centuries the relation between metropolitan (colonising) and local (colonised) cultures – traditional cultures and the European culture of modernity – came to be seen officially perceived as largely a problem of *modernisation*, of making the latter more like the former. Education was often viewed as one of the principal means for bringing about this 'evolution' to liberal modern society. Modernisation was not just a form of 'assimilation' or 'integration': the logic of modernisation was taken to supersede all forms of traditionalism. Tribalism, in particularly, was perceived to be inimical to the interests of the liberal State because it promoted historic 'we–they' attitudes and thereby militated against the liberal conception of 'one language, one culture, one state'. Only recently in the Western development of political theory has it even seemed a remote possibility that the enhancement of traditional ways of life might actually contribute to, rather than hinder, the 'development' or 'progress' of a people.[2] The development question is raised again in a different context when talking of transition to the 'knowledge economy'.

There is probably no more pressing set of philosophical problems in cultural theory than those that fall under the broad issue of cultural difference. The question of cultural difference in the era of modernity is normally considered in abstract terms, in terms of the logic of alterity, of Otherness, but it cannot be thought without examining the historical context of colonisation, its consequences for imperial, white-settler and indigenous cultures, and the historic struggles against the exercise of imperial power: the myriad forms of decolonisation, cultural re-assertion and self-determination. We have a reasonably clear though contested historical picture of the consequences of the clash between traditional cultures and cultures of modernity. It is a familiar story of cultural disintegration: language death, dislocation of rural extended family structures, the decline of traditional values, urbanisation (with all that that entails), and the official relocation of male labour to work in factories. What about the philosophical reflections of these above-mentioned phenomena?

In *Phenomenology of Spirit*, Hegel (1977, orig. 1807) defines 'consciousness' in terms of 'self-consciousness' and what he calls the 'truth of self-certainty', and he develops a model of consciousness, of self and identity, which inaugurates a new way of thinking that helps to define these concepts for Leftist thinkers of modernity: not only Marx but also Kojève, Sartre, Lacan and Fanon. Broadly speaking, we can characterise Hegel's modernity in terms of the dialectic of self and other, governed by the logic of negation. This model informs versions of Marxism (particularly notions of 'alienation' and imperialism), phenomenology (Kojève's interpretation of 'unhappy consciousness'), existentialism, and psychoanalysis, and philosophies of decolonisation and cultural liberation, as they have been articulated by Fanon (the 'coloniser' and the 'colonised') and Freire (the 'oppressor' and the 'oppressed'). Hegel defines what he calls 'self-consciousness' in terms of the dependence/independence of 'lordship' and 'bondage'.

Hegel's dialectic of 'lordship' and 'bondage' – of self and other – defined through the process of negation, and his analysis of 'consciousness' has exerted a powerful sway over modern thought. In particular, his account of consciousness in terms of the 'struggle of recognition' and his picture of 'Spirit' as a progression towards freedom, exercised considerable influence over many of the precursors of poststructuralist philosophy. A certain Hegelianism also became important for the founders of the Frankfurt School – Horkheimer and Adorno – and later, for Habermas. Certainly, it is Hegel's dialectic of self and other that provides the fundamental duality informing the work of Paulo Freire. One can understand how previously colonised peoples found in Freire a logic of self-recognition that helped to define the colonial experience. Hegel's account provided the most comprehensive account of the dualistic or oppositional logic characterising modernity – not only labour/capital, capitalism/socialism, coloniser/colonised, man/woman – yet it is also a product of its age.

There are philosophical resources and an understanding of 'difference' that tend to characterise the present historical phase – what we might provocatively call 'postmodernity' or 'postcoloniality' – better than Hegel's dualistic logic of alterity. This is one of the main lessons that so-called postcolonial theorists (e.g., Said, Spivak, Bhabha) have learned from the French poststructuralists.

STRUCTURALISM, SEMIOTICS AND CULTURE

The structuralist notion of culture as a system of positive differences represented a marked shift from the organicist, humanist version embraced by Williams.[3] In the structuralist notion of culture based upon the model of semiotics, identity is relationally defined and is purely a function of *differences* within the system. The relationship of signified to signifier is entirely arbitrary. One of the distinguishing features of Saussure's linguistics and an advance over the comparative grammar of the time, is his emphasis on the autonomous form of the system as a whole which comprises and organises phonic and semantic elements not directly accessible in sensory experience. Jonathan Culler (1976: 49) explains the *structuralist* Saussurian view of language that came to define 'culture'.

> [It is] not simply that a language is a system of elements which are wholly defined by their relations to one another within the system, though it is that, but that the linguistic system consists of different levels of structure; at each level one can identify elements which contrast with one another and combine with other elements to form higher-level units, and the principles of structure at each level are fundamentally the same.

Yet it was Jakobson who first coined the term 'structuralism' in 1929 to designate a structural-functional approach to the scientific investigation of phenomena, the basic task of which was to reveal the inner laws of the system. Jakobson (1973), following the success of the First Prague International Slavistic Congress, came to frame his programmatic statement in these terms:

> Were we to comprise the leading idea of present-day science in its most various manifestations, we could hardly find a more appropriate designation than *structuralism*. Any set of phenomena examined by contemporary science is treated not as a mechanical agglomeration but as a structural whole, and the basic task is to reveal the inner, whether static or developmental, laws of this system. What appears to be the focus of scientific preoccupations is no longer the outer stimulus, but the internal premises of the development: now the mechanical conception of processes yields to the question of their functions.

The 'linguisticality' of culture came to provide a method for structural anthropology. Jakobson introduced Claude Lévi-Strauss to structural linguistics at the New School for Social Science Research in New York in the early 1940s. Lévi-Strauss published an article relating structural linguistics and ethnology for the first time in Jakobson's newly established journal *Word* in 1945. It becomes an early chapter of *Anthropologie Structurale* published in 1958, comprising a collection of papers written between the years 1944 and 1957. Lévi-Strauss (1958: 21) acknowledges his debt to Saussure and Jakobson and proceeds to describe method in anthropology focusing upon the notion of the *unconscious structure*:

> If, as we believe to be the case, the unconscious activity of the mind consists in imposing forms upon content, and if these forms are fundamentally the same for all minds – ancient and modern, primitive and civilized . . . – it is necessary and sufficient to grasp the unconscious

> structure underlying each institution and custom, in order to obtain a principle of interpretation valid for other institutions and other customs. . . .

Lévi-Strauss (1958: 33) suggests that we apprehend the unconscious structure through the employment of the *structural method* developed by structural linguistics, declaring 'Structural linguistics will certainly play the same renovating role with respect to the social sciences that nuclear physics, for example, has played for the physical sciences'. And he goes on to define the structural method in terms of the programmatic statement made by Nikolai Troubetzkoy (a member of the Prague Linguistic School) in his seminal *Principles of Phonology*:

> First, structural linguistics shifts from the study of *conscious* linguistic phenomena to the study of their *unconscious* infrastructure; second, it does not treat *terms* as independent entities, taking instead as its basis of analysis the *relations* between terms; third, it introduces the concept of *system* . . .; finally, structural linguistics aims at discovering *general laws*, either by induction [or deduction].
>
> (1958: 33)

Employing this method, Lévi-Strauss (1958: 34) suggests that social science is able to formulate necessary relationships, 'new perspectives . . . open up' where the anthropologist can study kinship systems in the way the linguist studies phonemes: 'like phonemes, kinship terms are elements of meaning; like phonemes, they acquire meaning only if they are integrated into systems' and kinship systems like phonemic systems 'are built by the mind on the level of unconscious thought'. Three years later in 1961 in his inaugural lectures at the Collège de France Lévi-Strauss publicly recognised his debt to Saussure and defined anthropology as a branch of semiology.

The notion of culture becomes central in these discussions and in the space of the nation, the adoption of an anthropological concept of culture as a set of *lived practices* and even, 'a structure of feeling', certain conceptual gains were made, including, the recognition of class cultures which permitted political analyses of 'national' culture and popular formations. Certainly, the move from the notion of culture considered in the singular and as a synonym for 'civilisation', to cultural studies provided the grounds for recognising 'culture' as a more *differentiated* concept that no longer gained its respectability from the discipline of cultural anthropology alone.

BRITISH CULTURAL STUDIES: THE ENCOUNTER OF CULTURE WITH POLITICS

What is cultural studies? In what context and which historical conditions did it emerge? This section aims to briefly answer these questions and then focus on Paul Willis's pathbreaking work *Learning to Labour* in relation to cultural studies of education. It is indeed hard to define cultural studies. Even Stuart Hall, certainly the most renowned figure within the tradition of British Cultural Studies, states that 'it was always a set of unstable formulations. It was centered only in quotation marks' (Hall 1996). Nevertheless, it is not impossible to chart the main figures and the traditions that had an impact on the emergence of British Cultural Studies.

This significant school emerged at the end of the 1950s.[4] As far as the political climate which gave birth to British Cultural Studies is concerned, we can list the following reasons: defeat, the working class's lack of interest in politics and the decreasing morale of the intellectuals, orthodoxies of the 1930s, the revisionist manner of Labour (Dworkin 1997), critique of old Marxism, and a recovery of 'values' against Stalinism (Johnson 1986–7: 38). Richard Hoggart and Raymond Williams played a central role in creating British Cultural Studies, placing literary criticism at its heart. Hoggart adopted an interdisciplinary approach in *The Uses of Literacy* and analysed popular publications. Yet, it is argued that he was still working within the framework of the cultural conservative F. R. Leavis and 'nostalgia is central to his project' (Turner 2003: 39). While Hoggart was never a Marxist (Sparks 1996), Raymond Williams was and he criticised not only the economistic type of Marxism but also the distinction between high and low culture.[5] While Williams acknowledged 'that culture was subject to bourgeois power (notably through education) he also argued that it contained contributions from other classes and challenges to the dominant ideology by those who were bourgeois themselves' (Dworkin 1997: 91). When one looks at Williams's *Long Revolution*, it becomes evident that a culturalist approach based on experience and common people is at the very centre. As Richard Johnson mentions, a similar trend was going on within the realm of history. Social historians emphasised 'popular culture, or the culture of the people especially in its political forms' (Johnson 1987: 38; Kaye 1984). Thus, this school of British Marxist historians, as Johnson further states, became a second matrix for cultural studies. Yet, this culturalist strand would be replaced by structuralism due to the encounter with Western Marxism.

The institutionalisation of British Cultural Studies was realised by the foundation of Birmingham Centre for Contemporary Cultural Studies in 1964 under the directorship of Richard Hoggart. Tom Steele (1997) reminds us that British Cultural Studies began principally as a political educational or pedagogical project in the field of adult education. He argues that:

> Adult education has, since the nineteenth century, been a critical place of dialogue and negotiation between the forced attempt to modernise the British state and the emergent social movements, especially that of labour or 'working-class' movement.

Steele suggests that 'interdisciplinary study in adult education was an important precursor of academic British cultural studies' (1997: 2) rather than an offshoot of English and he documents the involvement of Hoggart in extramural studies at Hull (founding the Birmingham Centre for Contemporary Cultural Studies in 1962), Thompson as a tutor for WEA and later in extramural studies at Leeds, and Williams as a member of the Department of Extramural Studies at Oxford.

Yet, only 'after Marx' (Sparks 1996: 79) and under the directorship of Stuart Hall (1968–1979) would the centre bear fruit and initiate 'an academic revolution from below' (Mills & Gibb 2004: 206). In relation to encounters with Marxism, Louis Althusser and Antonio Gramsci were the primary sources of inspiration. As far as the notion of culture in relation to British Cultural Studies is concerned, Richard Johnson's checklist is worth quoting as it demonstrates the impact of both Althusser and Gramsci:

> 1 Cultural processes are intimately connected with social relations, especially with class relations and class formations, with sexual relations, with the racial structuring of social relations and with age oppressions as a form of dependency.
> 2 Culture involves power and helps to produce asymmetries in the abilities of individuals and social groups to define and realize their needs.
> 3 Culture is neither an autonomous nor an extremely determined field, but a site of social differences and struggles.
>
> (Johnson 1986–7: 39)

Thus, as opposed to the Raymond Williams-ian phase of cultural studies, the Althusser effect resulted in 'the heroic age of cultural studies, during which socialist humanism was rejected, the relative autonomy of culture was stressed and a new emphasis on ideology was initiated (Sparks 1996: 84). Although this relationship with Althusserian Marxism was not unproblematic (Hall 1996), it had a considerable impact on the quality and content of the work produced by the Birmingham School. The theoretical flirting with structuralist Marxism led to the creation of works on media and subcultures (Lee 2003: 114). Even though this interest in subcultures was not new, it is undeniable that Paul Willis's seminal work – *Learning to Labour*[6] – introduced a critique (but not a total break from Althusser) of the structuralist account of education and social reproduction and foregrounded the agency of working class youth.

Published in 1977, *Learning to Labour* first of all constituted a response to another seminal work within the realm of education, *Schooling in Capitalist America* (Bowles & Gintis 1976). Secondly, it was written in a UK that was not yet de-industrialised and therefore there was a working class and its culture to be reproduced. However, what was put on the table by Willis was the manner through which the reproduction of culture and society took place. As has been argued, *Learning to Labour* is 'a key marker in the development of social scientific epistemology integrating an analysis of structure and agency that was unprecedented' (Arnot 2004). Criticising the structuralist account of education, Willis 'steered a middle course between the extremes of structuralism and humanism' (Dworkin 1997: 163). He argued that working class kids in Wolverhampton got working class jobs not just due to structural reasons, but because they chose to be like their fathers. As Lee argues, 'the failure of the lads is not due to their inability; on the contrary, the lads are genuine rebels and the school is a battleground' (Lee 2003: 117). They were rebels since they opposed the meritocratic ideology which promises success in exchange of hard work. In this respect, the 'lads' – as opposed to the ear'oles who were more 'submissive' when compared to the 'lads' – considered mental labour to be feminine and therefore preferred manual labour. These reasons pushed Willis to come up with a new class analysis in which 'structuralist interpretations needed to be supplemented by a conception of the "cultural", the semiautonomous domain through which social agents lived the meaning of structure, understood and represented it, resisted and transformed it, and frequently reproduced it' (Dworkin 1997: 163). Thus, his argument in *Learning to Labour* is such that

> the cultural forms cannot be reduced or regarded as the mere epiphenomenal expression of basic structural factors . . . Social agents are not passive bearers of ideology, but active appropriators who reproduce existing structures only through struggle, contestation and a partial penetration of those structures.
>
> (Willis 1981: 174–175)

In his conceptualisation of semi-autonomous culture, Willis came up with two different concepts with regard to the agency of the lads: penetrations and limitations. Penetration is 'meant to designate impulses within a cultural form towards the penetration of the conditions of existence of its members and their position within the social whole but in a way which is not centred, essentialist or individualist' (Willis 1981: 119). Thus, this concept refers to youth's critique of school authority and their production of style, whereas limitation means 'blocks, diversions and ideological effects which confuse and impede the full development and expression of these penetrations' (1981: 119). In this respect, these limitations caused the self-domination of the working class youth. Yet, Willis's emphasis on agency has become more dominant and the concept of cultural production, as opposed to reproduction, has become foregrounded (Willis, 1983).

What about the evaluations of *Learning to Labour*? Willis was accused of romanticising the 'resistance' of the lads (Walker 1985) and reducing patriarchal relations to class (McRobbie 1980). On the other hand, it was asserted that Willis offered pivotal insights into how masculinity/sexuality could become the key to social class resistance to unjust systems (Arnot 2004). The book has also been appreciated in terms of its emphasis on the category of class and the possibility of attaining class consciousness (McLaren & Annibale 2004). In a similar vein, other scholars also contend that Willis demonstrated both the potential and limitedness of youth agency (Nolan & Anyon 2004: 148).

In relation to this possibility of attaining class consciousness, Willis later analysed the impact of de-industrialisation and globalisation and its impact on education (Willis 2003). Questioning the feasibility of modernist education, he suggested that radical educators should see the resistant actions of youth – rather than approaching them as pathological patterns – and engage with them. However, with a growing emphasis on agency as exemplified by his concepts including grounded aesthetics and life as art (Willis 1990, 2000), Paul Willis today seems to have overplayed the agency card and bears the risk of falling into a liberal-humanist position – rather than a socialist humanist perspective – totally disregarding structure. Moreover, there is a general tendency in contemporary cultural studies to overstress the meaning-production of agents, move away from the 'transformative' project it initiated and biographise the social structure and structuralise the biography (Arnot, 2004).

SUMMARY

The collapse of the USSR, the demise of real socialism, the 'triumph' of free market capitalism,[7] and the end of ideology and metanarratives have all had their impact on social sciences. The study of political economy has been despised while identity and multiculturalist arguments have become the rising stars in social sciences. In today's so-called postmodern society, the superiority of Western cultures seems to have been eroded by the philosophical and political trends we have tried to chart above. At first sight, this is a development to be celebrated. Nevertheless, we argue that this multiculturalist atmosphere (both in politics, educational studies and social sciences) can even lead to another type of racism which still implicitly favours the supremacy of Western culture and actually tells us: 'Look, you can also be like us. You *are* like us.'[8] In other words, to what extent can we argue that this 'democratisation' of culture paves the way for a real equality among societies? How different is this project from the fetishisation of democracy and cultural differences? How possible is it to locate this shift within social sciences and cultural studies in education in the larger context of multiculturalism? Can we really expect an intellectual and political emancipation from discourse that is implicitly racist and disguises structural economic inequalities? Does the overemphasis on agency and paralysing respect towards the choice of people (Birkan, 2002) really create space for possibilities for a theoretical and practical opening? We believe that the democratisation of culture always has potential, if that potential can pave the way for more access to resources around the world. That is, rather than being a meaningless discourse of choice and a top-down process, this democratisation has to correspond to the needs of people. Especially regarding the debate around a wireless world and open access, we argue that these are meaningful and can bear a stronger potential if there is not a skill divide throughout the globe (not only in terms of North–South but also within nations). In line with this argument, we would like to once again remind readers that we have learned much from Pierre Bourdieu's concept of cultural capital and how it operates. This concept has also helped us to understand how culture in different forms might become a means of social reproduction. When we say in different forms, we aim to point to Bourdieu's understanding of cultural capital as: a) an embodied state (that is, it is related to one's body); b) an objectified state (writings, paintings, cultural artifacts); and c) an institutionalised state (academic credentials and qualifications). In other words, not only the abundance of access but one's cultural capital matters in an increasingly globalising society.

Additionally, starting as a politically transformative project and giving birth to real intellectual endeavours within the field of education, cultural studies in education particularly and cultural studies in general seems to have forgotten its wrestling with theory (as once suggested by Stuart Hall), with the objective of grasping the world in all its complexity. We would argue that the discipline today runs the risk of falling into another type of cultural relativism which falls short of suggesting pedagogy, as opposed to its initial roots within the field of adult education. Rather than diagnosing and then fetishising the infinite differences in a globalised world, contemporary cultural studies has to remember its roots, and engage in pedagogical activity in terms of establishing links between oppressed groups across the planet. Otherwise, the relation between culture and politics is doomed to be lost and culture is headed to become just another object of inquiry, rather than a means of understanding and changing the asymmetrical relations in which we are increasingly enmeshed.

KEY QUESTIONS

1. Explain Bourdieu's idea of 'cultural capital'.
2. What is the central argument in Willis's book *Learning to Labour*? Do you agree with it?
3. Do you think that the 'democratisation' of culture paves the way for a real equality among societies?

FURTHER READING

Gaztambide-Fernández, R. A., Harding, H. and Sordé-Matri, T. (eds) (2004) *Cultural Studies and Education Perspectives on Theory, Methodology, and Practice*. Cambridge, MA: Harvard University Press.

McCarthy, C., Durham, A. S., Filmer, A. A. and Giardina, M. D. (2007) *Globalizing Cultural Studies: Ethnographic Interventions in Theory, Method, and Policy (Intersections in Communication and Culture)*. New York: Peter Lang.

Weaver, J. A, Carlson, D. and Dimitriadis, G. (2006) The Cultural Studies of Education: Introduction to a Special Issue of *Journal of Curriculum Theorizing*. *Journal of Curriculum Theorizing*, 22(2): 3–6.

NOTES

1 See his webpage at http://www.umanitoba.ca/faculties/arts/anthropology/courses/122/module1/concept. html.

2 Along with that, this perspective has also its limits. A sound and legitimate critique might be that this approach can be watered down within the context of globalisation and lead to an understanding that each and every different culture is aimed to be integrated with global capitalism.

3 Hall's (1980, 1988) response to the 'crisis' in cultural studies represented by the contradictions between Williams's 'culturalist' paradigm and the structuralist paradigm was to turn to Gramsci and, in particular, his notion of 'hegemony' which analyses political domination as a contested struggle. For a detailed discussion of these moves and a strong critique of 'postmodern cultural studies' see Katz (1997).

4 This decade also witnessed the rise of the New Left. It comprised ex-communists, socialist students and Labour supporters. It originally comprised two groups and their journals: *The Reasoner* (edited by E. P. Thompson and J. Saville) and *ULR* (*Universities and Left Review*). Some articles in *ULR* hinted at the birth of the kind of academic works to be produced by British Cultural Studies (Dworkin 1997: 60).

5 However, a theme that united these two people – and a critique raised against British Cultural Studies in general – is the very Britishness and whiteness of the project (Logue & McCarthy, 2008).

6 In a nutshell, we can summarise the book as follows. Emphasising the agency of the working class kids in a working class school, the book demonstrates that they create an autonomous environment for themselves at school through which they ultimately find themselves at the lowest part of the occupational ladder. Some of the working class kids (lads) differentiate themselves from the 'hardworking' students (ear'oles) in terms of how they get dresses and how they live. They fulfil only the minimum of the required things, not more. They enjoy having a 'laff' at school and they choose how to behave. Thus, by looking at culture, the book presents a non-mechanistic perspective on reproduction.

7 This assertion of Francis Fukuyama was put forward well before the recent global financial crisis.

8 Yet, it is still us who decides and can teach you that you are like us. Furthermore, you are like us as long as you are willing to participate in the global capitalist economy.

This chapter links with readings 3 and 6 of *The Routledge Education Studies Reader.*

CHAPTER 3

EDUCATION AND THE STATE 1850 TO THE PRESENT

Paul Wakeling

The rationale for this chapter is:

- to chart the evolution of the British state's involvement in the provision of primary, secondary and higher education since 1850;
- to put these events in context by relating them to developments in three comparable countries (France, Germany and the USA);
- to identify themes cutting across time and type of education, especially as they relate to broader social, economic and political trends.

INTRODUCTION

In today's Britain, the intimate relationship between state and education system is taken for granted. Education spending eats up substantial chunks of public spending. Education policy and legislation is an important aspect of government business, featuring prominently in political debate. The state regulates education through various inspection and assessment regimes. It builds schools, employs the teachers to run them and enjoys a virtual monopoly in this universal system. Through the National Curriculum, the state stipulates what shall be taught in schools, for how long and to whom. Education and the state in Britain, at the school level at least, are mutually dependent: education is a fundamental part of the state's functions; and the education system relies on state funding.

In this respect, Britain is little different to most of the industrialised world where there is no example of a privatised school system. Alternatives exist in other countries, as in the UK – charitable foundation schools, private schools, home schooling – but everywhere the state is the monopoly provider, laying on education from late infancy to mid-adolescence, free at the point of use and funded by general taxation. Actually in many other countries, state domination over education is even greater, reaching further into nursery education and higher education, with greater public spending as a result.

France, Germany and the USA are the three countries most often cited by politicians and scholars when comparing education in Britain with that of her 'rivals'. The state's first forays into education happened considerably later in Britain than in the former two countries and with a degree more reluctance than in the USA, traditionally seen as a *laissez faire* state. In 1850, there was little in the way of state-provided education in Britain, and during the nineteenth century this situation changed slowly and unevenly. Secondary education was neither compulsory nor free in Britain until the end of World War II. The British National Curriculum, only 20 years old, is a mere youngster by international standards.

Still, the British state has, sometimes reluctantly, staged a long-term takeover of education from the voluntary sector and the Church. Despite occasional panics about contraction of the state's role in education and encroachment of the private sector, taking a long historical view suggests such matters are relatively insignificant. The history of the state's role in education from 1850 is of a long march to almost complete oversight. It is a march which has sometimes been a quickstep, often a trudge. Occasionally it threatens to turn into a retreat or it seems the columns are marching in different directions; but in the battle for the control of education since 1850, it has on balance been a march to victory.

UNDERSTANDING THE BRITISH STATE'S ROLE IN EDUCATION

In considering the history of the British state's involvement in education one must beware of three easily committed errors. The first is to suppose the state's takeover and expansion of education was inevitable. At each key historical point the state's actions were resisted and contested – sometimes bitterly – and could have turned out differently. Indeed the recent history of state education shows this clearly. Different parts of the state – central government, local government, autonomous state agencies and latterly devolved administrations – are engaged in struggles for control of education. They are joined in this struggle by the private sector and groups in civil society who seek to reclaim aspects of education (institutions, the curriculum and sometimes funding) from the state.

The second potential mistake is to assume state omnipotence. The state is but one player, albeit an important one, in its own story. To misquote Marx, states make history, but they do not do so in circumstances of their own choosing. The British state, in expanding its role in education, was frequently reacting to concerted pressure: from business, from the church, from campaigners, from the educational establishment itself and perhaps most importantly, from comparisons with rival states. It has been as often follower as leader. Moreover concerted attempts by governments to change schooling and higher education and to reduce educational inequalities have met with only limited success.

Finally, the history of the British state in education should not be conflated automatically with that of the state in *English* education. England and Wales may legitimately be considered together, but education in Scotland has remained distinct: it arose earlier, has different institutional arrangements, is covered by separate legislation and maintains a separate trajectory. Whilst England and Wales, by virtue of their far larger combined population, comprise much of what counts as the British education system, because the Scottish system has retained its difference it is problematic to talk about a unitary relationship between the state and education. At various points since 1850 the British state has shown contrasting approaches to education north and south of the border.

WHAT IS 'THE STATE'?

Although it is a term in common usage, giving a precise definition of 'the state' is tricky. It typically refers to a group of institutions which together form the legitimate authority for a particular territory. Modern states usually incorporate an executive (the government, cabinet, ministries etc.), a legislature (parliaments), a legal system (courts, police force, prisons) and some form of welfare provision (social security, education, sometimes healthcare). States are backed up by taxation systems and by control of the legal use of force to impose their will.

PRIMARY EDUCATION AND THE STATE

The British state's entry into education began with primary (or 'elementary') education. Prior to 1944, primary education was the overriding concern; afterwards focus shifted increasingly to secondary and higher education.

The 1833 Factory Act had introduced, for the first time, a requirement that all children between the ages of 9 and 13 received at least two hours of schooling per day, mainly in response to concerns about the exploitation of child labour in factories rather than through concern with the benefits of education *per se*. Before 1870, state involvement in elementary education was slight. There were no state-run schools, there was practically no bureaucracy in place to regulate educational provision, nor was there anything but the most minor expenditure of public funds: the education budget was just one-quarter of a million pounds in 1861 (Green, 1990, p. 7), a mere trifle compared to the £78 million spent on the Crimean War of 1853–1856 (Curtis and Boultwood, 1966, p. 68). Poor children in workhouses received nominal daily instruction, but quality was low. Parliament was hostile to state provision of education because it was believed educating the poor would lead them to feel discontent with their lot and hence to unrest and rebellion. Victorian governments had to resort to convening a special committee of the Privy Council established by Royal Prerogative to effectively bypass Parliament on educational matters, a constitutionally unusual practice, even for the time.

There *was* elementary schooling available to the British population; however provision was extremely patchy, in terms of quality, geographical distribution and accessibility to ordinary families. In 1851, the Census indicated that only about one in every eight children actually attended school, although the enrolment rate was three times that figure (Green, 1990, p. 53 and p. 13) Children in south-eastern England and Scotland were better provided for than Welsh children or those living elsewhere in England. In Scotland there developed, during the eighteenth century, a system of parish schools. Local landowners were legally obliged to provide a schoolhouse and appoint a teacher, but it was down to the Church to ensure the arrangements worked in practice. School was neither compulsory nor free and the state did not provide funding (Anderson, 1995). In England and Wales, there was a hotchpotch of elementary schools: some districts had charitable schools akin to the Scottish model, provided by a benevolent local landowner or notable; others were provided by charitable bodies, usually associated with the churches. Fees varied, with some being free or levying only a nominal charge. However most poor children received only a few years of schooling, if any, because their family needed the income they could earn in the field or factory. Before about 1870 then, primary education in Britain was not free, it was not compulsory and it was dominated by the Church. It was certainly not universal and state-provided.

As Andy Green (1990) notes, British schooling in the nineteenth century, even in Scotland, was a mere shadow of Prussia's[1] and somewhat behind France and the USA. Prussian schools were state-provided and compulsory, with an effective national system emerging as early as the late eighteenth century and well-established by 1840. France's development was slightly slower, with the state gradually taking over from the Roman Catholic Church as the main educational provider. An extensive system was in place in France by the 1860s and free public primary provision finally attained in 1882. Similarly, the USA had a fairly well-formed public system of primary education by the mid-nineteenth century, even though education was (and remains) largely within the remit of the individual states rather than the federal government.

Many contemporary commentators bemoaned the quality of education in England compared to that on the Continent and in North America (although few drew comparisons with Scotland). The Prussian schools in particular were commended, it being asserted – apparently with justification according to the balance of historians' opinions – that they were better organised, with higher standards of teaching and achievement than English (or indeed British) schools. Whilst periodic panic at the state of schooling in Britain prompted, in the period before 1870, the setting up of various commissions on education, the resulting reforms were piecemeal. Frustrating the ambitions of a growing body of opinion in favour of a national system of elementary education for England and Wales, the reforms did not interfere fundamentally with the voluntary nature of school provision, adding restricted state intervention through small increases in expenditure, a skeleton inspection system and some limited quality control.

The Elementary Education Act of 1870 and the Education (Scotland) Act of 1872 signalled the arrival of the British state as an education provider, although it was another two decades before universal, free primary education would be guaranteed by the state; and into the twentieth century before secondary schooling began to come under the state's remit. The key feature of both Acts was the establishment of elected local School Boards to oversee the provision and quality of primary education. In England, the Boards worked with the existing schools, 'filling the gaps' in provision (Curtis and Boultwood, 1966). This meant building and staffing new schools, financed by local taxes, in some areas, but largely it meant subsidising the voluntary schools, most of which chose to remain independent rather than come directly under the control of a Board. The 1870 Act did not compel school attendance, nor did it abolish tuition charges, although the poorest families were generally exempted. Meanwhile, the creation of the School Boards prompted the voluntary societies and the churches to build new schools themselves which only gradually came under state control, largely due to an inability to match the resources available to Board schools and their successors. Even today, approximately one-third of state-funded schools have a religious affiliation (Gardner, 2005).

In Scotland, where there was something more of a national 'system' of education, the creation of the School Boards and a Scottish Education Department as part of the Scottish Office was more of a state-sponsored consolidation, although, as in England, there was also an element of gap-filling. In addition to the parish schools in rural areas, in the large towns and cities there were 'burgh' schools and Scotland too had many voluntary schools which were incorporated into the system. Unlike in England, elementary education was made compulsory by the 1872 Act (Anderson, 1995).

In 1902, the 'Balfour' Act replaced the School Boards with Local Education Authorities (LEAs) and in doing so tied education to local government such that it became a state responsibility like other infrastructural services such as roads, sewage, police force and fire brigade. In essence, the Acts of 1870, 1872 and 1902 laid the foundation for the national system of primary education which remains in Britain today, although the nationalisation of the voluntary sector proceeded in a slow and fragmentary manner and a watered-down state–church partnership endures in England's denominational and 'voluntary-aided' schools.

After and including the 1902 Act, the state's focus in terms of debate, legislation and expenditure moved from primary to secondary education and indeed post-compulsory education. That is not to say that the state has neglected primary education since 1902; far from it. Rather the nature of its engagement has changed from questions of organisation and funding to matters of curriculum and performance. This change of attention has been manifested in a move from local to central state control over primary education and with it an increasingly regulatory role for the state. These processes have affected all stages of education, but have perhaps been felt strongest in primary schooling. The National Curriculum, introduced in the Education Act of 1988, represents a statutory code for the subjects to be taught in state schools. Appearing far later than equivalent codes in western European countries, it formalises a long-term trend for intervention in matters of curriculum, with a reduction of autonomy first on the part of individual teachers and later the local state. Of particular concern in primary education has been emphasis on the '3Rs' (reading, writing and arithmetic), seen especially in a state-supported backlash against 1960s 'progressive' teaching methods which de-emphasised formal grammar teaching. Latterly this has resulted in the introduction of literacy and numeracy strategies, complete with dedicated classroom time (the 'literacy hour', for example) and national testing regimes with associated targets and league tables of performance. In Scotland however there is no statutory curriculum.

It is worth briefly considering the state's approach to nursery or pre-school education. In some rich industrialised nations, nursery provision is largely state-provided (Netherlands and Sweden are examples) and kindergarten teachers are typically university-qualified. In Britain, nursery education is mostly run as a private, for-profit business; indeed according to the OECD, England has the highest proportion of privately provided childcare in Europe (OECD, 2006). Although it is regulated (in England and Wales by OFSTED) to ensure educational standards, attendance is voluntary and largely fee-paying. Since 2004, free part-time places have been available to all three- and four-year-olds in England under the 'SureStart' programme and some schools offer

BOX 3.1 EDUCATION AND THE BRITISH STATE FROM 1850: A TIMELINE

1851	Census records 12 percent attendance rate and roughly 40 percent enrolment rate in schooling
1856	Privy Council Education Committee renamed Education Department
1861	Newcastle Commission on the state of elementary education
1864	Clarendon Commission into conditions in the nine major public schools
1868	Taunton Commission: inquiry into secondary education
1870	Elementary Education Act: School Boards established for England
1872	Education Act (Scotland): School Boards established for Scotland
1889	Boards of Education established for Wales
1891	Primary education becomes free
1893	School leaving age raised to 11
1899	School leaving age raised to 12
1902	The 'Balfour' Act: state grammar schools created; Local Education Authorities (England and Wales) established
1918	School leaving age raised to 14
	Education (Scotland) Act creates education authorities
1919	University Grants Committee established
1944	Education Act establishes free universal secondary provision to age of 15 in England and Wales in 'tripartite' system
1951	GCE O- and A-levels introduced
1960	Anderson Report recommends mandatory funding for full-time undergraduate students
1964	Committee on Higher Education (Robbins) reports
1965	Comprehensivisation begins
1966	Polytechnics established
1972	School leaving age raised to 16
1988	National Curriculum introduced
	Polytechnics and Further Education colleges removed from local authority control and 'incorporated'
	Grant Maintained Schools
1992	Further and Higher Education Act allows polytechnics to apply for university status
1997	Committee of Inquiry into Higher Education (Dearing Report): undergraduate tuition fees of £1,000 introduced
2004	Undergraduate tuition fees raised to a maximum of £3,000. Limited maintenance grants reintroduced
2007	Plans announced to raise school leaving age to 17 by 2013 and 18 by 2015

limited part-time provision. Similar initiatives run in Scotland. However, in contrast to much of western Europe, funding comes mainly from parents rather than the state. In many respects, the British state's approach to pre-school provision mirrors that for elementary education in the nineteenth century: there is limited state support, a regulatory framework of some description but little direct state provision. If the private sector were rapidly to collapse, the state cannot simply step in to replace it.

SECONDARY EDUCATION AND THE STATE

The British state's engagement in secondary education trailed its interest at elementary level. State-funded secondary education did not begin until 1902 and in England at least it was as late as 1944 before secondary schooling would be universal and free. In the post-war period however the state has concentrated on secondary education such that, in the twenty-first century, it has become one of the state's main concerns.

If the availability of elementary education in nineteenth-century Britain was somewhat uneven, access to secondary education was even more of a lottery of birth, generally only enjoyed by the elite or the more privileged middle classes. Provision was sparse. There were the nine 'great' public secondary schools in England, most of which were long-established aristocratic boarding schools, with a few dozen other boarding schools in England, Scotland and Wales. Many towns and cities had an endowed 'grammar' school, founded originally by the Church to educate those destined for a clerical life. Most had been secularised after the sixteenth-century dissolution of the monasteries. Almost all were fee-paying and only catered for boys, mainly from the affluent middle-classes. Finally, there were a larger number of private secondary schools, whose pupils were generally the children of lower-middle-class parents.

As with primary schooling, British secondary schooling did not stand comparison with that available in France, Germany or the USA. Both France and Prussia had established a national system of elite secondary schools during the Napoleonic period (the *lycée* in France, 1802; and the *Gymnasium* in Prussia, 1812) to provide an academic education culminating in a leaving certificate which would confer university entrance. Enrolment rates were fairly low however. In the USA, high school was free and attendance slightly higher (Green, 1990). In addition to the low quantity of secondary scholars, the quality of British secondary education was also generally held to be inferior to that of the French, Prussians and Americans. Concern over standards in secondary education triggered two commissions: Lord Clarendon's in 1861 into the state of the 'great' public schools and Lord Taunton's inquiry of 1868 which covered all other secondary schools. Both found fault with the curriculum (mainly classical and 'moral' in nature) and with teachers (generally untrained and ineffective). In some of the so-called 'endowed' schools, conditions were woeful, as captured in contemporary fiction (such as Dickens' *Nicholas Nickleby* and *Hard Times*). In both cases though the state was reluctant to intervene and the resulting legislation failed to enact most of the recommendations made (Curtis and Boultwood, 1966). Arguably the real purpose of secondary schooling in the nineteenth century was preparing privileged boys for professional and governmental positions (in the Army, Church, civil service and so on); the emphasis was on the maintenance of class distinctions and was certainly not directed at the needs of commerce and industry.

Only in 1902 did the state intervene directly in secondary education. The newly created LEAs were mandated to provide grammar-school education and in many instances to provide state funding to existing independent secondary schools. Secondary education became available – in principle – to more children, but local variation in provision continued: in Scotland, universal secondary education began (nominally) in 1918; in some Welsh and English authorities, grammar school provision was generous and scholarships available. However this system was deliberately elitist, providing in England what had been created in France, through the *lycées*, exactly one century earlier. British children would have to wait until the 1944 Education Act (1945 in Scotland) for a true national system of schooling from age five to 15, finally establishing the three phases of primary, secondary and further education, with the decisive post-primary break at age 11. It also established the state's control over the training and licensing of teachers working in the state system. In a typical British compromise, elements of the previous system were allowed to continue, not least the independent and voluntary-aided schools.

Much government attention from the 1960s was concerned with reform of the 'tripartite' system, as codified in the 1944 Act. Grammar schools were open to the minority of pupils who had passed the '11 plus' examination, with others being directed to 'secondary modern' and 'technical' schools (although few of the latter ever opened). From the mid-1960s a policy of 'comprehensivisation' was pursued by the Labour education minister Anthony Crosland, acting on evidence that the grammar schools were socially and not just academically selective. His policy was continued (in deed, though not word) by the succeeding Conservative government. Comprehensive schools were intended to provide an academic education to all pupils, with no selection at age 11 (although there remained 'streaming' by ability within schools) (Jones, 2003). These reforms proceeded unevenly: Scotland was fully comprehensive by 1979, but in England there remain in 2009 15 local authorities with a selective system.

There have been a number of important developments in the British state's relationship with secondary education since 1944, with the pace of change accelerating since 1988. The introduction of the National Curriculum in 1988, discussed above in connection with primary education, also impacted on secondary education. Equally important was the creation of national examination systems. The General Certificate of Education, with 'Ordinary' and 'Advanced' levels, was introduced for pupils aged 16 and 18 respectively;[2] The 'O' level was replaced by the General Certificate of Secondary Education (GCSE) for examinations in 1988; 'A' levels continue in revised form and are typically required for entry to higher education. Other credentials, including National Vocational Qualifications and a range of awards intended to fit the middle ground between vocational and academic certificates, have also been introduced. Much popular and state attention has come to be taken up by performance in the examinations by different types of pupils and schools. Increasingly British governments are judged (and judge themselves) according to the level of attainment of school pupils in public examinations.

This state concern with school effectiveness and performance has been another important facet of secondary education over the last quarter-century, a concern which has persisted across governments of different political hue. Whilst the Conservative government of 1979–1997 sought to ensure maximum efficiency in the face of reductions in public spending and to introduce an ideologically driven market-led choice into secondary education, the Labour government of 1997 onwards has added the improvement of attainment among under-achieving groups. These policies have been implemented using 'performance management' tools such as league tables of examination results, the introduction of standardised National Curriculum tests (the 'SATS') at ages 11 and 14 and the intensification of school inspection regimes through OFSTED.

Detailed performance management is part of an increasing centralisation of education policy in England with power shifting from LEAs to the education ministry. In Scotland and Wales, education is part of the brief of the devolved governments, but although this represents a reduction in Westminster's reach, it is the devolved ministries rather than the LEAs in Scotland and Wales which preside over secondary education. In England this centralisation has been accompanied by a granting of autonomy to individual schools through quasi-independent 'grant-maintained' status (echoing the nineteenth-century state/voluntary sector compromise) and latterly the creation of 'academies', state schools outside of LEA control.

Finally, a recurring theme in the British state's interest in secondary education has been its consequences for economy and employment. As with higher education, high-quality secondary schooling has been seen as increasingly necessary in securing Britain's economic prosperity in competition with other countries for high-skill 'knowledge economy' jobs. State investment in education is viewed as 'something-for-something', with the payback of public spending on education being growth generated in the economy by skilled and productive workers.

HIGHER EDUCATION AND THE STATE

Contemporary debates about higher education in Britain often characterise the state as attempting to limit or actively reduce its commitment in favour of the private sector, be this students' financial contribution to the cost of their studies or encouraging business to have a greater input to the planning of courses. A longer historical perspective suggests a different conclusion. Prior to World War I, the financial contribution of the state to higher education was tiny. Compared to the current multi-billion pound budget the £15,000 allocated to the new university colleges in 1889 is but a drop in the ocean.

In 1850 there were only eight universities in Britain. The Church had more influence than the state in the affairs of the universities, which supported themselves through endowments and income from property (Oxbridge) and tuition fees paid by students (especially important in Scotland). That is not to say the universities and the state had no relationship. The British political class in the period 1850–1919 followed a path from the major public schools through Oxford and Cambridge to parliament and the civil service. Parliament too showed periodic concern about the quality of education at Oxbridge during the nineteenth century.

The establishment of new higher education institutions between 1850 and 1919 was mainly due to the efforts of local committees, philanthropists, reformers and industrialists. Only after World War I did governments begin to show interest in higher education. Most importantly, in 1919 the University Grants Committee (UGC) was established for the distribution of state funding to higher education. Designed as a 'buffer' body, it established a model whereby higher education was increasingly publicly funded but simultaneously insulated from direct government intervention. The development of higher education in Britain over the twentieth century needs to be understood with this quintessentially British compromise in mind. Whereas continental universities are largely public institutions directly funded by the state, the British universities are formally independent of the state and technically free to do as they please within the limits of their charter and the law. However unlike the great American private universities, they depend on the state for their income, which (inevitably) comes with a whole series of obligations.

The British state's approach to higher education was still relatively 'hands off' in the period to 1963. It provided financial support for teaching and research and, from 1960, funding for all full-time undergraduates through the LEAs. It also supported a modest expansion of the system with several new universities appearing before 1960 (Stevens, 2004).

As with secondary schooling, the 1960s saw rapid change in the higher education system as a whole and in the state's approach to it. Lord Robbins was commissioned to examine the demand for and provision of higher education in the UK. His committee's recommendations, which were accepted in full by the Conservative Government, included an expansion of places to accommodate all those qualified to benefit from higher education and the conversion of the existing 'Colleges of Advanced Technology' to university status, underwriting a process which was to some extent already in train.

The precedent of state intervention in higher education, given a substantial push by Robbins, continued in two other developments of the 1960s. One was the Open University, an institution designed to provide teaching via radio, television and correspondence and which would, through waiving entry requirements, open up higher education to those who had missed out first time around. The other was the creation of the polytechnics in 1966. Intended to provide vocational, professional and industry-focused courses, 28 were founded. The 'polytechnic experiment', seen historically, was rather short-lived, lasting only 26 years. It gave a much more interventionist role to the state, with polytechnics, like the schools, directly under LEA control and with degrees validated by a state agency. Perhaps this decidedly anomalous position contributed to the eventual unravelling of the polytechnic system as first polytechnics were granted independence from LEAs in 1988 and then allowed to apply for university status (which all did) under the 1992 Further & Higher Education Act.

The 20 years which followed were, in contrast, unremarkable. Higher education slipped off the national stage and the 1970s were a decade of consolidation, with the state preoccupied with the OPEC oil and industrial action crises. In the 1980s, consolidation gave way to contraction, as the steady growth in student numbers stalled. Cutbacks followed, pursued with an ideological zeal by the New Right Conservative government of Margaret Thatcher. Some universities saw budgets cut by 40 per cent, although others escaped relatively unscathed (Stevens, 2004). Student funding arrangements were adjusted, with loans gradually replacing grants for maintenance support.

Contemporary accounts of these changes, including the government's, situated cutbacks as part of a broader process of 'rolling back' the state and a key element of the New Right political philosophy which emphasised 'traditional' values, individual responsibility and a greater role for markets in providing public services. Taking a longer view, these claims seem largely rhetorical. Reductions in spending commitments were temporary, private higher education did not materialise and with an upturn in the economy student numbers recovered. Indeed it was the same Conservative government which responded to increasing public demand by presiding over a massive expansion in student numbers in the early 1990s. Far from withdrawing from higher education, the state increased its interactions with universities through the establishment of various quangos such as the Quality Assurance Agency for Higher Education and funding councils for each of England, Scotland and Wales. The overall trend was towards centralisation of the state's functions in higher education, not retreat.

The Dearing Report of 1997 was initiated by the Conservatives to address universities' complaints that reduction in funding per student was eroding the quality of the student experience and hence Britain's international competitiveness in higher education. Delivered to the incoming Labour administration it recommended the introduction of a flat-rate undergraduate tuition fee of £1,000, with loans and means-tested grants for maintenance. Instead, the government abolished grants in favour of loans, with tuition fees means-tested. The principle of a student contribution thus established, a substantial increase in tuition fees (£3,000) was introduced in 2004, accompanied by a complex set of maintenance support arrangements including state loans, state grants and institutional bursaries, the latter paid for by redistributed tuition fee income.

There are plenty of continuities in the state's relationship to higher education across the last two decades, regardless of the party of government. Micro-management of higher education, at least according to critics, is one aspect, as government ministers express opinions on university admission policies, relationships with various 'stakeholders' (business, parents and so on), recruitment of fee-paying overseas students and research output. Another is the use of higher education as a tool in pursuit of broader policy objectives. Two have featured prominently in the last decade: higher education's contributions to the economy; and 'social justice'. Thus the expansion of higher education has been lauded for producing highly skilled 'human capital' for the 'knowledge economy', placing Britain at a global competitive advantage with universities also producing economic benefits for their host cities and regions by transferring to enterprise the knowledge they generate through research. Education as the route to social mobility for able but disadvantaged children has also been a key theme, with a sustained emphasis on 'widening participation' to reduce the social class inequality in access to university. Significant state expenditure in this area has barely impacted on these inequalities. Critics suggest the introduction of tuition fees has been a disincentive to university entry for those from lower social class backgrounds, contradicting New Labour's espousal of social justice, but neither have fees affected participation rates. It would seem this is an area where the state's influence is limited.

A final trend in the higher education–state relationship since 1997 – and which by contrast, *does* mark a break with the past – is devolution. To some extent, these recent changes signify more general shifts in the character of the British state and are consistent with the experience of formally federal states such as the USA, Germany and Australia. However the prominence of higher education policy in the short history of the devolved Scottish Government and Welsh Assembly is remarkable. Both bodies have responsibility for education and both appear to have used student funding arrangements as a self-conscious symbol of autonomy from Westminster, eschewing the English 'top-up fee' policy. An unintended consequence has been fragmentation: there now exists a complex set of funding arrangements which vary considerably depending on a British student's 'home' nation and the location of their university.

CHANGING CONCERNS IN THE EDUCATION/STATE RELATIONSHIP

Over the course of the last 150 years, the nature of the British state's engagement with education has shifted substantially. At the beginning of the period the state's main concern with education was child protection, intending that younger children avoided working long hours in poor conditions and had some basic education. Throughout the nineteenth century the state was reluctant to become an educational provider, taking the role of regulator instead. This was something of a defensive strategy, aimed at delaying engagement for as long as possible and continuing reliance on voluntary provision.

Why was the British state so reluctant to intervene in education when other states forged ahead? Interestingly, opponents of state provision cited the detrimental effect they believed it would have on social control and public order: they argued educated workers would be unhappy with their lot and would become unruly. Conversely in Prussia (and to some extent France), desire for social control was behind early state intervention: the school curriculum was seen as a tool for instilling nationalist values and suppressing disorder! It has been argued that provision of education was important for the very formation of states themselves – Prussia, post-revolutionary France and the USA were relatively young states compared with Britain, where the *laissez faire* tradition dates at least to the seventeenth century, bringing with it a suspicion of 'etatist' top-down planning. These differences endure in the late adoption of a National Curriculum, the continued existence and disproportionate influence of private sector schooling and in the relative autonomy of British universities from the state (Green, 1990).

Economic considerations also feature prominently in the British state's involvement in education. Some have argued that relatively high literacy rates (especially in Scotland) prior to the creation of mass schooling contributed to Britain's Industrial Revolution (West, 1994). Indeed, the demand for child labour in British industry during the nineteenth century, together with families' reliance on children's wages, may have suppressed the development of mass schooling. Elsewhere state schooling preceded economic take-off (France, Germany) or happened alongside (USA). National pride, perhaps as much as a desire for economic competitiveness through education, seems to have been behind the eventual entry of the state into schooling in England and Wales; however economic concerns have become ever more important in justifying state expenditure on education.

After 1944, once universal and free state-provided primary and secondary education had been achieved a key concern has been about which parts of the state control education. Contrary to the earlier abdication of responsibility by central government first to the voluntary sector and then to local government, there has been an increasing centralisation of state control over education, with policy increasingly driven by the ministries rather than the LEAs. Alongside the NHS and the economy, education has become a key area on which British governments are judged by the electorate and this is reflected in increasing state regulation and monitoring of performance in education at all levels, even where there has been some marketisation or privatisation of finance (such as in higher education).

Finally, issues around that great British obsession – social class – have often driven state involvement in schooling, although the state's attempts at (to use the unfortunate term) 'social engineering' have altered considerably in their intent. Before 1918, government sought to preserve distinctions of social background through the types of schooling available to the population: public schools for the upper class, grammar school education for the middle classes and basic education for the working classes. These divisions were more or less consciously maintained until 1944. The partitions in the tripartite system, whilst notionally based on educational grounds, effectively replicated class-based differences; these demarcations of status can also be spotted in contemporary debates about parental choice, 'sink schools' and 'bog standard comprehensives'. However the state has latterly sought to use education as *the* engine of social mobility, introducing policies with the explicit objective of raising the educational attainment of disadvantaged groups, particularly post-16.

SUMMARY

The state has a near-monopoly of schooling, but not higher education, in Britain. The relationship between education and the state differs across England, Scotland and Wales and also at different levels of the system (primary, secondary, etc.). A state-provided national education system arrived late in Britain compared to many other countries. There is considerable continuity in the state's role in education across governments of different political parties. Recent trends have been in favour of centralisation and an increased intensity of state engagement with education.

KEY QUESTIONS

1. Choose three key dates in the development of state education and justify your choice.
2. What are the differences between the role of the state in education in Britain as compared with other nations?
3. Is state education necessary? Why?

FURTHER READING

Green, A. (1990) *Education and State Formation: The rise of education systems in England, France and the USA*. London: Macmillan.

Lawson, J. and Silver, H. (2007) *A Social History of Education in England*. London: Routledge.

Simon, B. (1994) *The State and Educational Change: Essays in the history of education and pedagogy*. London: Lawrence & Wishart.

NOTES

1 Prussia was a large state in what is now modern Germany and was one of the most powerful in nineteenth-century Europe. Its territory stretched from the Rhine to parts of modern Poland and the Baltic States.

2 In Scotland the equivalent examinations are the 'Standard' and 'Higher' grades of the Scottish Certificate of Education.

This chapter links with reading 5 of *The Routledge Education Studies Reader.*

DEBATE 1

DO PRIVATE SCHOOLS LEGITIMISE PRIVILEGE?

Bernard Trafford and Rupert Tillyard

A debate between Bernard Trafford (head of the independent Royal Grammar school, Newcastle upon Tyne and Chairman 2007–2009 of the Headmasters' and Headmistresses' Conference – HMC) and Rupert Tillyard (assistant head, St Aidan's Church of England High School, Harrogate).

Both writers have served for some years on the Council of their professional association – the Association of School and College Leaders (ASCL) – so they have considerable experience of working together on shared problems across the sectors. Despite a high degree of mutual understanding and respect, they nonetheless hold strong views on opposite sides of this debate, as the contributions that follow demonstrate.

There are difficulties inherent in debating this particular topic. Each author having worked for many years on opposite sides of the sectoral divide, their strongly contrasting views are perhaps predictable, while nonetheless authoritative. However, though they speak from considerable experience, there is little research background to support their arguments. Indeed, although the private–state debate has been argued for decades, and continues unabated, it is generally conducted on the basis of mere assertion. The Sutton Trust (see 'Further Reading') has commissioned some research in recent years into the lack of penetration by young people from poorer homes into top universities, and into the alleged domination of the traditional high-status professions by independent-school-educated men and women. These first steps into this highly charged area, little more than statistical surveys, have been criticised for bias in some quarters, not least for being quantitative rather than qualitative. Whether or not the studies are reliable, they are certainly too few to shed much real illumination on the issues. It is perhaps unsurprising, therefore, that this debate, while lively and heartfelt, is ultimately unsatisfying. The two authors, dedicated teachers, seek common ground and a way forward. The fact that, to their regret, they find little of either arguably illustrates the need for extensive and useful research in what remains almost unexplored territory.

BERNARD TRAFFORD

Private schools: Not a mechanism for perpetuating privilege

In any discussion of the way in which private schools are alleged to perpetuate or legitimise privilege, there is the underlying assumption that they are all the same; that they will admit their members to an old-school-tie network, to an exclusive club.

Even the most cursory examination of the independent school sector will demonstrate how diverse it is. There are around 3,000 independent schools in the UK, encompassing a bewildering range of institutions: boarding, day, small, large, urban, rural, highly academic, non-selective, primary, secondary, all-age, single-sex, coeducational, authoritarian, liberal – or combinations of the above. Many have particular specialisms: in sport, drama, music, dance, Special Educational Needs.

The histories of those schools vary enormously. The old 'public schools', those ancient boarding establishments, were once bastions of the ruling elite. Yet during the nineteenth century many far less grand imitators sprang up to produce the officers and administrators of the British Empire. The former grammar and direct-grant schools comprise a powerful group: the academic backbone of the tripartite maintained system from 1944 until the 1970s, these mostly ancient foundations reverted to independence when local authorities went comprehensive. Still other schools have grown up over the years to meet a unique need in their setting.

The diversity within this tiny sector – which educates just 7 per cent of the nation's children – is remarkable and defies simplistic generalisation. However, there are three things that unite them, and all have a bearing on this debate.

First, they share a passionate commitment to excellence. Second, among all their distinctive characteristics they prize most highly their independence. Third, without exception they feel wounded by accusations of exclusivity, and are deeply committed to widening access.

Excellence is perhaps an overused word: yet the independent sector has a claim to it. The most recent (2008) OECD PISA study rated UK independent schools as the best group in the world. Opponents would see this accolade as an inevitable consequence of their unfair, their privileged position. Those working in the sector would point to the ultimate accountability that they live with but also relish: parents pay significant amounts of money to have their children educated and (in contradiction of much of the rhetoric) make significant sacrifices to do so. They demand the best. If their children don't receive the best opportunities, they will remove them. Independent schools have in the main no funding apart from the fees paid for each pupil: this focuses minds. Commitment to the best is the hallmark of the sector: to allow it to slip would be suicide.

As its second common and defining feature the private sector cites its very independence. Though in general preparing children for the same qualifications and university entrance as their maintained-sector counterparts, independent schools are infinitely less regulated and enjoy the freedom to ignore much of what they would see as government interference and meddling; to experiment and to innovate; in short, to run themselves in whatever way suits them best.

Independence itself is widely recognised nowadays as the sector's greatest asset. Moreover, it is arguably essential to have an independent sector. A country that had only schools of one model and operating in ways dictated by government would be poor indeed: history shows how little innovation and enterprise come out of a totalitarian system. The existence of an independent alternative also encourages divergence and creativity in the majority sector controlled by government.

The concept of independence lies at the heart of the Academies programme. Its architect, then Schools Minister Lord Adonis, always described academies as independent state schools. He was adamant. Some observers have wondered whether the Academies are indeed as independent as is claimed, and the present Secretary of State, Ed Balls, appears to play down their independence and seek to diminish it. If he tightens his control he risks losing what for many is the jewel in the crown.

Third, the sector's alleged exclusivity is a myth that needs to be challenged. For example, when the former grammar schools reverted to independence in the 1970s they were without exception committed to remaining accessible to children from lower-income families. In the 1980s and 1990s they participated enthusiastically in the Conservative government's Assisted Places Scheme. When that ended in 1998 they reactivated their appeals and sought endowment or revenue funding for bursaries.

Independent schools seek to broaden access not as a result of political pressure, nor of wrangles over public benefit, but because they know that it is not in the best interests of any pupils to learn and develop in a narrow social grouping: that would simply not be good education. A recently formed group, the Forum for Independent Day Schools, has been challenging the major parties to fund places at their schools at maintained-sector cost. It is a sincere offer. Where, in the past, government did work with the same schools to widen access, they became involved with great enthusiasm: witness the Assisted Places Scheme.

The most famous names in private education commit enormous resources to widening access through bursaries. Some 20 per cent of Eton's pupils receive financial support to allow them to attend: the school aims to raise that figure to a third – a move, as the College says, in keeping with the intentions of its fifteenth-century royal founder. But, whatever the school, it takes enormous levels of benefaction to fund places for even a small percentage of its students.

If private schools are clear about what they are trying to achieve, what about parents, and the choices they make? Are they wrong to seek the best school for their child? Are not top-performing state schools also a problem? The top-scoring state schools are academically selective, as are many independent schools. Many Specialist Schools (popular with parents) are allowed to select according to 'aptitude', not academic ability. Is not this also to do with privilege? If so, there is little honesty in discussing the matter. In some political circles selection in education is seen as a greater problem than the independent sector: yet politicians turn a blind eye.

The affluent buy themselves into the catchment area of a desirable school: are they buying privilege? The articulate talk (or prep) their children into the school of their choice: is that fair? Can one blame them for doing all they can for their children? Or are they wrong only if they pay school fees, rather than inflated house prices or tutors' charges? When does canny parental choice become the (by implication) morally unacceptable purchase of privilege?

John Prescott complained that 7 per cent of children go to independent schools, yet some 80 per cent of the judges, barristers and politicians in this country come from independent schools. Is that the sign of a set of self-perpetuating wealthy class at work? It could be: yet the old grammar schools, so many of which are now independent, were for decades the engine of social mobility. They provided a fast track for children from poor and poorly educated homes to build careers by way of the best universities. In offering bursaries in order to widen access, independent schools are conscious of trying to play their part in increasing social mobility: in effect, they can reach only a few. Under the present government, social mobility has reached rock-bottom.

So what should be done? To agree that gaining the advantages of an excellent education is to be privileged is to accept that the provider of that education legitimises that privilege. If to be privileged in that way is somehow wrong, society has to be prepared to sacrifice excellence and the limited social mobility provided by bursary schemes on the altar of equality. To mix a metaphor, that sacrifice would involve an orgy of social engineering on a near-Soviet scale.

If, on the other hand, the discourse can grow up and move on; if the dirty word 'privilege' (a term, when used pejoratively, that is born of jealousy) is replaced by the aspirational phrase 'best life chances', perhaps it is time that this country and its government finally engaged properly with its independent sector. The sector has been urging it: it is governments that have stood back, as does the apparent government-in-waiting. Real engagement could reduce and remove the danger of the legitimising or perpetuating of privilege. The discourse could move beyond unhelpful words like privilege and elitism and talk – or better than talking, do something – about providing better opportunities for all. It could remedy a situation where, even in 2008, a lottery of birth and geography still determines whether children will find the best educational opportunities within their reach.

Society should not blame the private sector for its inequalities but should do something, and do something positive; not look for abolition of what is good but seek engagement with it; use the language not of privilege and envy but of opportunity and aspiration. Those are the terms that should be the starting point of a useful debate, a far more useful debate, and one that is long overdue.

RUPERT TILLYARD

The whole point of private schools is to gain privileges over others

To anyone unfamiliar with the facts, the costs of sending one child – let alone two or three – to private schools for up to 13 years seems unimaginable. Boarding at a famous public school costs nearly £30,000 a year. Even a day pupil at a more modest establishment will cost parents £10,000 or more. For most people these sums are beyond consideration. That fact alone means that only those who are already privileged enough to be earning a great deal more than most are in the running.

So why would parents spend so much of their hard-earned cash for this privilege? Or, rather, exactly what privilege are they after? The most commonly expressed reason, because it is the most acceptable and easily understood, is that they are buying a better education. So poor is the local comprehensive that they could not possibly subject their child to it. It would not be fair. In London, for example, infant and junior schools often have children from very varied backgrounds, but when the time comes to move to the secondary phase the local school is not regarded as an option. Of course, parents do not necessarily have to buy this escape; some – even Labour Ministers or Prime Minister – have effected the escape for their children by other means. But if parents do not have recourse to entrance exams, the right address or faith that can help them, money may be the only answer. The truth is, though, that many of those with sufficient money to afford the fees year after year could afford to domicile themselves within the catchment area of what they see as the best the state can offer. Yet they would rather pay the school fees.

Is it the case, then, that these costly schools really do provide a better education? Results alone will not support this. Many state schools clearly can rival in added value and raw results what money can buy. However, results are not all that we mean by education. The whole school experience, including the extra-curricular, adds a great deal to what we mean by a good school. Here the expensive well-endowed private schools really can offer something better. From cricket pitches to swimming pools, from libraries to stables for the child's own pony, they do offer facilities that are beyond even the imagining of most state schools. People outside the educational sphere may be unaware just how gross these inequalities are. Eton has its own Olympic standard boating lake; whole golf courses with their own green keepers are commonplace; most of the famous public schools can boast a cricket ground with a properly cared-for pitch, some the envy of county cricket clubs. Virtually all have swimming-pools, squash courts, fives courts: and one privilege found only in the paying sector is that, as in America, they have many sports played by themselves alone. The Eton wall game, Rugby fives and real tennis are just the better-known ones. Later on in life these exclusive sports will ensure that 'birds of a feather' can recognise each other. Of course, it is not just sport: fully equipped theatres, indoor and out; art galleries; orchestra pits; and so on. It is true that five-star hotels offer more than B&Bs and, the more paid for one's holiday, the better place and facilities. These superior physical resources are certainly part of what parents are paying for.

Perhaps, though, parents might feel these are just the pastimes that money can buy and not really the most essential part of what they are paying for. Are they in the end paying all that cash simply for better teaching resources? Perhaps so: they will get them. Far smaller classes would be the best-known privilege. It would go against the grain to claim the teachers are better – after all, many of them are not qualified in the sense of nationally accredited teaching certificates. Let us assume, however, that if they were really hopeless they would leave and replacements would be easily found: that is not always the case in deprived areas of the British education system. (In London itinerant Australians have frequently been used to fill the teaching gaps, staying for a year or so to finance their travels: the only people from the other side of the world to be found in the private sector are elite sportsmen and women taking a year or so to do some coaching.) Certainly many of the teachers will be well qualified in their subjects, having been to such schools themselves and gained degrees from Oxbridge, returning to the fold in order to help keep the wheel turning. Generally speaking independent schools are smaller in terms of pupil numbers, however much larger they may be in terms of lands and buildings, but still they have the funds to pay for small A-level groups.

More importantly for improving the opportunities for learning, though, will be the fact that all the children will have been selected: by money first, of course, but also (in almost all cases) by ability – simple intellectual ability. Private schools do not count how many children gain 5 A*–Cs: they all do. As one happy private school teacher said to me at a standardisation meeting: 'To paraphrase Oscar Wilde, I am happy to say I have never seen a D.'

After checking that it will not have any difficulties with pupils' intellects, the next step is for the school to ensure that they are – how do they term it? – 'suited to boarding' or 'able to benefit from the particular kind of education we offer': in other words, character and background. The wrong kind of character will not gain admittance. So once the school has a homogenous mix of wealthy, able, positive pupils, away it can go and make the claims for its superior teaching.

Interestingly, in these superior schools with their carefully selected pupils, a new curriculum is emerging. They have never had to conform to the national curriculum, KS2 and KS3 levels unless they wanted to but, up to now, they have had to do the same A-level and GCSE exams as everyone else. Not content with what they have already, however, they have recently decided that they want their own system of assessment. (Why is this? Could it be that it is becoming increasingly difficult to prove superiority when state school pupils are getting the same grades?) So now independent schools have iGCSE and Cambridge pre-U. That should ensure that it is clear where their products come from.

Parents with certain means also have other choices – privileges – not accorded to those who cannot afford it except by chance. They can choose what kind of school will suit their child: boarding or day; single-sex or co-ed. Moreover, they can have holidays outside the peak periods and get cheaper prices. (Naturally they will need to save money on the skiing when they have paid those fees.)

If this is all it was, though, perhaps one could simply accept that there is an imbalance and seek to gradually reduce the difference. But better physical resources and smaller classes are by no means the key privilege that ambitious parents are after. Perhaps the most important privilege of all will be the connections their children make, contacts that prove so useful later in life. Next comes the entrée to the famous universities, the army, the places of power: for the 'masters or mistresses' will know how their pupils should apply, whom they should talk to.

But most of all the privilege that parents seek when they pay is freedom from having to mix with hoi polloi. That is the key: in the words of a famous television comedy, 'no riffraff'. By definition, apart from the odd scholarship boy or inner city child plucked out for a reality TV show, everyone the private school pupil meets will be wealthy and most likely better connected. Their social experience will be similar. (Holidays in north Norfolk and Rock in Cornwall, skiing and flotilla sailing: 'One meets such awfully nice people.') Some parents are so keen to preserve the social difference that this, and this alone, is worth all the money. They will put up with what are clear disadvantages in some smaller schools: small choice of A-levels; or what are really non-viable teaching situations, A-level Drama groups of one pupil, for example. Even poor accommodation and dreadful food can be borne if it is with 'people like us'.

This emphasis on difference is made clear by those hugely important markers of identity – clothes. The uniform will be distinctive, really quite extreme in some cases. The expectation of just how many kinds of clothes a pupil will need to get through a school year: blazers and tweed jackets; suits and maybe boaters; a dozen or so different kinds of games (games, not sports) clothes – 'all with name tapes, please!' The other useful social marker will be the language the young people speak. There are arcane names for things – High Masters and 'beaks' – and the traditional slang of the school. Most important of all is the accent, RP (Received Pronunciation), a way of speaking invented in the public schools and carefully preserved generation by generation.

After all, there's no point in parents paying for all the privileges if no one knows their child has them! The so-called 'haves and the have-yachts' (a term coined just before the credit crunch started to bite) will never give up these privileges voluntarily. They have fought long and hard to preserve them. The truth is that they do not want to share: and the schools they use make sure they don't have to.

BERNARD TRAFFORD: RESPONSE TO RUPERT TILLYARD

Looking beyond the stereotypes

How good it would have been to be able to employ irony and comedy to open this debate! But the defence never gets the best jokes. The caricature presented of independent schools is a glorious Aunt Sally to throw things at. The toffs; the haves and the have-yachts; the arcane sports; the uniforms, funny accents and coded language. All that was needed in addition was that famous old photo of the Eton schoolboys and street urchins, with an amusing own caption: then the picture would have been complete!

But it is not a picture those working in the private sector can recognise. Simply, it does not exist. To be sure, there are some independent schools whose uniform, for reasons historical and sometimes hysterical, is eccentric, flamboyant even. But beware: smart uniforms are the hallmark of an improving school in the maintained sector nowadays. Politicians love them, and any self-respecting Academy has a smart blazer to distinguish its proud pupils from the rest.

Some privileged young people behave badly in Rock, Cornwall. Some parents may well want to keep their children away from 'riff-raff'. But there are obnoxious, intolerant people in every walk of life. They do not make all of us bad, nor our society sick. They do not define private schools any more than a few hooligans fighting on a Saturday afternoon define the majority of football fans.

It was inevitable that Eton's boating lake would be mentioned. Mainly from its own resources, with far less lottery support than rumour had it, Eton created a world-class facility where Great Britain's rowers train and where the 2012 Olympic rowing events will be held. Britain is doing rather well at rowing nowadays: it is hard to see that as problem.

My first piece described how independent schools are trying to broaden access: the more exclusive their history and/or repetition, the more they strive to render themselves more accessible, more inclusive – for reasons of good education and of doing what is right, not because of outside pressure.

At bottom lies a 'weasel' word, privilege. Parents want the best for their children: they are likely to buy it if they can. Who has any right to prevent them? John Prescott insists that they buy privilege, an entrée into a magic circle. As a serving head, I regularly stand up in assembly and say that I am privileged to run my school. I tell my students that they are lucky to have all the opportunities they get, and they have a duty – as we all do – to make the most of their gifts and good fortune for the benefit of all.

Are they lucky? Yes. Have their parents bought them some kind of unfair advantage? I do not believe so. Nor do I believe that they will emerge as the spoilt brats, ruined by privilege, portrayed above. The depiction was like a Bosch painting: an allegory; a lesson; a warning; and hilarious too. But it was not a true picture.

RUPERT TILLYARD: RESPONSE TO BERNARD TRAFFORD

Privilege still prevails

Bernard Trafford sets up a very reasonable – dare one say liberal? – defence. Of course, that is one of the tricks the system employs, calling on decent, well-intentioned, generous professionals, handy defenders of the privileged.

His defence lays claim to a diverse sector, not comprising all famous public schools. One might concede that there are a few admirable experimental schools: Summerhill, of course; and Bedales. There are certainly a few 'crammers' and 'bucket shops' that may take pupils of all abilities and difficulties. But for the vast majority, and certainly the largest and most powerful institutions, the ability to select by ability is paramount. That is why the famous city grammar schools go private when the state system went comprehensive. Seven percent of children are in private schools, according to the statistics: but the percentage privately studying A-levels is 20 per cent, an inevitable consequence of the initial selection. Those are the pupils the private schools are really interested in. How many of this very diverse group of educators have sought to join in vocational education, for example? Painfully few: the diversity is somewhat limited.

There is excellence, of course. No-one could dispute that some excellent education is on offer, but it is an excellence absolutely dependent on exclusivity. What Bernard Trafford calls the 'myth of exclusivity' is the very foundation and cornerstone of the entry policies of independent schools. The governors – often old pupils themselves – make sure of that. Parents simply have to have plenty of money to send their children to private schools. The Assisted Places Scheme – so often cited as a defence – scarcely scratched the exclusivity of wealth and, by definition, supported the exclusivity of academic ability. It seems that Tories and private schools alike think that only clever poor children deserve better.

It is, of course, not exclusively the already rich and privileged who seek to get the best for their children. The middle classes fight as hard as they can to get their children into the popular state schools, though the point about top-performing state schools being selective merely serves to illustrate what those who use private schools grade as 'success'. The 'top performing' selective state schools are only top in raw scores. In any value-added table they fall well down the scale. But then, private schools are simply not interested in most children.

Independence is indeed a valuable attribute. Freedom from government interference, which so often seems to be motivated by successive secretaries of state looking for headlines or trying to avoid them as much as any pedagogical considerations, is a virtue. This is the one aspect that inhibits the desire to do away with the sector altogether.

Any scrutiny of the actual situation as it is – any close look at those who go to the majority of these rich and powerful institutions and at where they end up – reveals the already-privileged looking after themselves. If private schools really believed in wide and fair access, if they actually believed in their charitable and often Christian foundations they would become comprehensive and seek alternative funding from the pockets of wealthy parents. But that would assume a sort of independence they have never exhibited.

CONCLUSION FROM BERNARD TRAFFORD AND RUPERT TILLYARD

Is there any common ground or scope for joint action?

In considering what has been said there clearly are some points of agreement. First it is clear that, as teachers, both writers have a broad general (liberal) agreement about what education is for and what moral values we share. They work with young people and find them rewarding and full of both energy and (most of the time) idealism. Both feel that they want the best for the most, believing – as far as it can be managed – that from those to whom much is given much is (or should be) expected. Also they value learning for its own sake and think that intrinsic rewards are the most worthwhile in the end. But not everyone acts as though this were so: it is an uneven and unfair world. So both feel the need to ask (and preferably answer) the question: do we have a duty to 'even up the playing field', at least to some extent?

Both also agree on the necessity for an independent strand to provide alternatives to the government's orthodoxy. It would be hard really to argue the case for denying people the right to spend their money on education if they want to. Where they continue to disagree, however, is that the main purpose of the purchasers of private education is to gain an advantage. Rupert Tillyard has no faith that those purchasers would ever surrender that advantage but would continually seek it out wherever it were available (much as those using the state sector seek the maintained schools they perceive to offer greatest advantage to their children).

Since both want to seek more equality – or, rather, more of a sense that 'we are all in this together' – Rupert Tillyard feels an attempt should be made to force the issue: how about thoroughly demoralising and undermining the private sector by insisting that they too follow the National Curriculum and fully implement government initiatives? Unsurprisingly that is not a course that appeals to Bernard Trafford, who observes that it would remove the freedom that makes the independent sector independent; a totalitarian move indeed.

More seriously, Rupert Tillyard argues, charitable status could be removed unless certain guidelines were met: for example, no academic selection. Or the problem could be approached from the one area of the education system that is very largely not private – the universities. Should the Russell group of 'leading' universities be forbidden from recruiting more than 25 per cent of their entrants from fee-paying schools? Again, Bernard Trafford fears social engineering and discrimination: but that is arguably a predictable, inevitable response from him.

In the end, though, Rupert Tillyard holds out virtually no hope of forcing the issue: this pleases Bernard Trafford who is simultaneously depressed that it seems so hard to find common ground, despite the close agreement between the two about the purposes of education and our mission in it as teachers and leaders of teachers.

Rupert Tillyard asks, could the problem be tackled from the other direction? Could HMC take a lead and say, 'We do not want to be elitist: we want to recruit pupils from everywhere'? Given the boarding tradition and the location of many schools it would be difficult: but perhaps a start could be made in London? Famously the state secondary sector there is regarded as something to escape from (as demonstrated by some Labour cabinet ministers). Could the famous independent schools in London and other fee-paying schools of reasonable size each go into partnership with a large comprehensive and manage and teach all the pupils between them? To be fair, there are partnership moves in the form of sponsorship of Academies. And schools such as Eton are publicly setting out to make themselves 'needs-blind' (ironically, it is the wealthiest schools that seek this path, because it requires huge levels of funding): but they will still select according to academic ability, or even more so.

Rupert Tillyard will claim they are doing this entirely on their terms. Bernard Trafford says that it is at least a start.

Neither writer wants this great divide. But both acknowledge that society is a long way, a vast distance, from bridging it. Both wish it were otherwise.

KEY QUESTIONS

1. Do private schools provide a mechanism for perpetuating privilege?
2. Does the variety of educational provision that is evidenced in the private sector provide support for the argument to retain this form of schooling?
3. Do private schools achieve higher standards than state schools?

FURTHER READING

Adonis, A. and Pollard, S. (1997) *A Class Act: Myth of Britain's Classless Society*. London, Hamish Hamilton.

Johnson, R. (2007) 'Haves and have-yachts', *The Times*, 18 February: http://www.timesonline.co.uk/tol/comment/columnists/rachel_johnson/article1400086.ece

Sutton Trust research reports (http://www.suttontrust.com/annualreports.asp) including:

http://www.suttontrust.com/reports/UniversityAdmissions.pdf

http://www.suttontrust.com/reports/Journalists-backgrounds-final-report.pdf

http://www.suttontrust.com/reports/APS_report_FINAL.pdf

Trafford, B. (ed.) (2002) *Two Sectors, One Purpose: Independent Schools in the System*. Leicester: Association of School and College Leaders (www.ascl.org.uk).

Walford, G. (ed.) (2003) *British Private Schools: Research on Policy and Practice*. London: Woburn Press.

This debate links with readings 7, 8, 9 and 18 of *The Routledge Education Studies Reader.*

CHAPTER 4

GENDER AND EDUCATION

Vanita Sundaram

The rationale for this chapter is:

- to examine competing explanations for differences between men and women;
- to explore the concept of 'gender' and its role in ordering social relations;
- to examine key issues in gender and education, including debates concerning achievement, learner identities and teaching.

INTRODUCTION

The field of gender and education is a shifting one; in a 'post-feminist' era where individual identity construction is emphasised, the role of gender in macro-analysis is subject to scrutiny. This chapter explores the significance of gender to education in the UK context. We will consider how entrenched conceptualisations of gender continue to underpin current concerns about participation and outcomes in formal schooling. Key contemporary issues that will be addressed in this chapter are gender and achievement, gendered identities and behaviour in the classroom, and the 'feminisation' of the educational sector – and the inter-linkages between the three. In doing so, this chapter will argue for the continuing relevance of gender as a structural category, but will also highlight the importance of multiple subjectivities in identity construction and therefore, the pitfalls of binary thinking about gender in relation to education and social life.

This chapter is divided into five parts. It begins with a brief outline of the nature of gender, seeking to introduce readers to predominant explanations for behavioural, and other, differences between boys and girls/men and women. Second, the chapter introduces you to a key issue within educational studies: gender and achievement. We will explore the prevalent understanding that boys' underperform relative to girls, and third, we consider reasons put forward for the lower performance of boys in compulsory schooling. These include gender differences in ability, identity and behaviour, and the feminisation of the educational sector. We also explore strategies suggested to remedy the gender gap, including the (re)masculinisation of schools. The fourth section of this chapter focuses on critiques of these explanations for gender differences in achievement, drawing heavily on the notion that gender binaries are not always helpful in explaining differences between boys and girls (or men and women). The final section subsequently explores how gender can (and should), nonetheless, still be considered a salient factor in the learning experiences of boys and girls. We will discuss the role of gender in structure, as well as everyday experience and practice, in maintaining hierarchies and specific social roles.

WHAT IS GENDER?

Men and women tend to behave in different ways across society as a whole, as well as in education in particular. Many theorists have sought to explain these patterns of behavioural difference, as well as the many instances where individual men and women behave atypically, or where groups of men and women behave similarly. Explanations for the differences observed between men and women mainly address two theoretical perspectives: the position that behavioural differences between men and women are due to inevitable biological distinctions between them, and the position that differences observed between men and women are socially constructed, or rooted in social expectations and representations of appropriate male and female behaviour.

Biological difference between men and women

Differences between men and women have been attributed to their specific and different biologies. The physiological differences between men and women have thus been used to explain intellectual, emotional, behavioural, and sexual differences. The view that men and women are 'naturally different' is held across disciplines, including within feminism. Feminist scholars have thus argued that women's biological, and thus behavioural, difference from men should be celebrated (e.g. Gilligan, 1982). Advocates of the innate differences perspective often refer to variation between men and women as 'sex' difference. Evolutionary development, hormones and brain structure are thought to underlie oppositional patterns of behaviour in men and women. Thus, the biology of men supposedly produces more aggressive behaviour, higher sexual drive, logical patterns of thinking, and linear communication. Conversely, women's biology renders them more peaceful, emotional, intuitive and nurturing. Such innate qualities are seen to present a 'natural' obstacle to full gender equality and have thus been used to justify discrimination (primarily against women) at many levels of society (e.g. Jackson & Scott, 2001).

Socially constructed difference between men and women

In contrast, some theorists view differences between men and women as socially developed, or constructed. The term 'gender' is used to describe a social (rather than natural) division between men and women that positions them in hierarchical opposition to one another. In other words, what is viewed as 'male' or masculine behaviour is defined not only as different, but as opposite, to behaviour which is regarded as 'female' or feminine. Further, qualities that are represented as 'male' (e.g. logic) are positioned as superior to those represented as 'female' (e.g. creativity). A defining feature of 'gender' is that while the division itself is fixed, modes of being 'male' or 'female' may vary (Delphy, 1993). Thus, gender identities may be diverse within the separate categories that men and women are seen to belong to. Jackson (2005) argues that gender is constituted at intersecting levels, from the level of structure to that of subjective practice and identity. While the difference between men and women is socially and structurally maintained (through marriage, for example), individual men and women can transgress behaviours that are seen as appropriate only for men, or only for women. However, the institutionalisation of gender at multiple levels of society naturalises differences between men and women, and may thus impede the disruption of gender norms.

The relevance of gender to education

Gender is an important issue to consider in relation to education in terms of access to, participation in, and outcomes of, schooling. In a global context, marked gender differences (inequalities) in access to education exist. Girls are less likely to be enrolled in primary and secondary schooling and even where official national statistics suggest that there is gender parity in enrolment, attendance and equitable participation remain significantly lower for girls than for boys. Inequality in access to and participation in education is justified by biological as well as social perspectives on differences between boys and girls (although the two often intertwine). Girls are argued to be intellectually less capable than boys, and money spent by relatively poor families on educating girl children is thus seen as wasteful. Girls and women are also viewed as being *re*productive in function, rather than productive, and education for future employment is therefore not considered necessary (UNICEF, 2007). The social roles of girls also determine their limited participation in education; in many contexts, girls marry 'out' of their parental family, so any financial gains to be made from educating them would not benefit their parents. Further, the organisation of teaching, including curricula and the attitudes of teachers, has been argued to disadvantage girls across national contexts. The gender bias in education has been acknowledged in international conventions and declarations aimed at eliminating this inequality (International Covenant on Economic, Social and Cultural Rights, 1976; Convention on the Elimination of all Forms of Discrimination Against Women, 1981; Convention on the Rights of the Child, 1990; Vienna Declaration and Programme of Action, 1993; Beijing Declaration and Platform for Action, 1995; World Summit for Social Development, 1995).

While it is important to bear in mind the global scope and pertinence of gender as an educational issue, the focus of the current chapter is the UK educational context, and core issues of concern in this setting. Selected key areas have consistently been identified as sites of gender inequality in national educational policy and practice. Research into these areas has primarily set out to document gender differences in experiences and outcomes of education, and increasingly, to explain these differences with reference to gender.

GENDER AND ACHIEVEMENT

The gender gap in achievement

An issue that has received much attention in recent years is that of gender inequality in achievement, particularly the 'underachievement' of boys. Gender gaps in educational achievement in the UK are typically ascertained on the basis of General Certificate of Secondary Education (GCSE) exam scores. Both boys' and girls' educational performance have improved during the last 25 years. However, the predominant image of gender and achievement is that the improvement in girls' exam performance has been greater and more rapid than for boys. This has resulted not only in the elimination of previously existing performance gaps in some subjects, but has led to girls overtaking boys' performance in many subjects. In 2007, there was a 9 per cent gender gap (in favour of girls) for those achieving five A*–C grades at GCSE (DCSF, 2007, quoted in Eden, 2007). Girls are now excelling at subjects once considered to be more suited to boys. Girls thus not only pass the Maths GCSE in higher numbers, but are also attaining a bigger proportion of the highest grades. In 2003/2004, 51 percent of A*–C GCSE grades in Maths went to girls (Gorard & Smith, 2004).[1]

Girls' improved performance in maths and science-related subjects, as well as their continued dominance in language-based subjects has been linked to the removal of barriers to girls' attainment, such as biological and medical theories regarding the harmful effects of overworking girls, the reservation of more grammar school places for boys and the upward adjustment of boys' scores in order to secure places in selective schools (Martin, 2004). The changing attitudes of female pupils themselves, their parents and teachers to the academic potential and ability of young girls is also thought to have influenced girls' performance. In recent media and political discourse, however, girls' improved achievement is typically presented as occurring at the expense of boys.

Multiple explanations have been put forward for boys' supposed lower performance in secondary schooling in particular. Three competing and current discourses which seek to explain (or excuse) the gender gap are the existence of innate, or genetic, differences in ability; differences in learner identities and behaviour; and the 'feminisation' of the educational sector. While these constitute three distinct explanations for the current 'disadvantage' of boys in compulsory schooling, we will explore how they overlap and draw on similar conceptualisations of gender for their reasoning.

Explaining achievement gaps

Innate differences between boys and girls

Historically, the tripartite system of schooling was actually skewed in favour of boys, as they were thought to mature less rapidly than girls, and were therefore disadvantaged in terms of taking selective tests, namely the 11-plus examinations. More places were thus reserved for boys in grammar schools and girls were required to score higher than boys in the 11-plus examination in order to obtain a grammar school place as they were considered to be biologically advantaged in terms of concentration and ability to pass exams. The representation of boys as naturally more energetic and boisterous remains salient in current academic and practitioner discourse, as does the related notion that boys' and girls' mental development occurs at different rates and along different pathways (Raphael Reed, 1999). Boys' and girls' brains are thought to be specifically structured, such that the 'male' brain struggles with emotional or intuitive tasks, while the 'female' brain operates optimally with exploratory and reflective tasks. Innate and gender-specific ways of thinking and 'knowing' can explain differential test performance and subject-choice in school (Becker, 1995). Males are thus thought to gain knowledge in a logical, rigorous and more abstract fashion, while females 'know' in a more intuitive, creative and exploratory way. Such, primarily psychological and neurological, evidence has been used to argue that current and predominant classroom practices which encourage dialogue and emotional reflection seriously disadvantage boys, and further, that boys will inevitably perform worse in subjects that primarily require creativity and exploration, e.g. language-related subjects. These representations of gender difference may also feed into a historically normalised and binary portrayal of males as logical and rational and females as emotional and irrational in their behaviour. As Raphael Reed (1999: 39) has argued, gender as a social and structural category 'is replaced by idiographic descriptions of learner orientations, with gendered preference embedded in the brain'. In fact, recent research has established that while differences in neurological processing, including visual–spatial ability and working memory, have been found to exist, language tests conducted in controlled conditions revealed no gender differences in performance (e.g. O'Hara, 2005).

Nevertheless, this representation of gender-specific learning pathways has led to a call for making learning experiences more reflective of and responsive to boys' interests and (innate) needs, including the curriculum, classroom dynamics and teaching methods and resources. It is the latter two to which we turn now.

Gender-specific identities and behaviour

Closely related to the discourse of innate differences between boys and girls as an explanation for boys' lower performance, is the notion that gender-specific identities and behaviours displayed in the classroom may influence academic performance. While not founded in psychological research, this viewpoint often draws on naturalised and essentialised representations (and expectations) of appropriate behaviour by girls and boys. The concern surrounding boys' engagement with, and behaviour in, school is not new (e.g. Willis, 1977) but was more recently fanned following an assertion by then Schools Standards Minister, Stephen Byers, regarding the 'laddish' behaviour of boys (*The Guardian*, 1998 cited in Francis, 1999). This specifically male behaviour is seen as anti-school and incompatible with educational engagement and success. While not construed as desirable in terms of educational success, boisterous and 'laddish' behaviour by boys is viewed as problematic, but 'normal'. Indeed, the disruptiveness typically associated with 'laddish' behaviour is frequently viewed as a consequence of the girl-friendly school environment which neglects to respond to boys' natural liveliness, and thus, to keep boys interested in academic success.

Older boys in particular, are thus viewed as possessing natural confidence, and an action-oriented and competitive disposition – which is neither valued nor responded to by current school structures and practices (Skelton, 2006). By many accounts then, 'laddish' behaviour is 'problematic' primarily in so far as schools are failing to respond to boys' needs appropriately. Accordingly, it has been argued that rather than attempting to uncover the genuine emotional needs underlying 'laddish' behaviour, educationalists tend always to classify boys' behaviour as a discipline problem (Pollack, 1998 cited in Skelton, 2006), thus alienating them further from a successful pupil identity and academic success.

The discourse of gender-specific identities and behaviours is a powerful one in explaining gender differences in performance, and the underachievement of boys in particular. Francis (1999: 359–360) found that young people themselves invoke discourses of natural differences between boys and girls to explain why boys display 'laddish', anti-school behaviour. The gender difference was cast in terms of boys' particular genetic makeup and girls' (natural) greater maturity. However, there was also some recognition of the social and gendered pressure to adopt particular identities in school. Numerous studies have found that boys display disruptive or aggressive behaviour in order to maintain an appropriately 'masculine' identity and thus to be accepted by peers (e.g. Salisbury & Jackson, 1996; Younger & Warrington, 1996). Particular and prevailing constructions of masculinity demand an overt display of disdain for academic success and high educational performance can often be a starting point for homophobic bullying and harassment in school (Reay, 2001; Renold, 2006).

In contrast, the qualities which are viewed as appropriate and expected for girls represent female pupils as diligent, hard-working, mild-tempered and passive. Female pupils are thus discursively positioned to perform well in school and in traditional assessments. However, this gendered expectation of appropriate female behaviour does not consistently favour girls in school settings. Reay (2001) argues that, within schools, gendered power relations are more complex than the predominant 'boys versus girls' discourse suggests. While prevalent educational discourses which draw on crude binaries of 'mature/high-achieving girls' and 'immature/low-achieving boys' could be argued to be empowering for female pupils, some constructions of femininity – even those seen as successful – may be constraining for girls. These rigid stereotypes are maintained by girls themselves, their male peers and their teachers. When girls attempt to disrupt and resist conventional expectations of feminine behaviour, this has been found to be more negatively interpreted by teachers than when boys display similarly subversive behaviour. Studies of teacher responses to rebellious behaviours in the classroom consistently find that boys who display challenging behaviours are viewed more positively than their female counterparts (Clarricoates, 1978; Connolly, 1998). Gordon *et al.* (2000) found that boys who 'talked back' to teachers were viewed as 'curious' or 'inquisitive' while girls were constructed as challenging teacher authority.

Nonetheless, the discourse of gender-specific identities and (the enactment of) gendered behaviour is widely accepted as a significant explanatory factor in the lower performance, primarily, of boys. Further, this reasoning resonates with teachers' perceptions that girls are academically successful because they work hard, while boys who do well are naturally clever (e.g. Francis, 1998); boys' underachievement is thus constructed as a consequence of their disadvantage to succeed in stifling, girl-oriented school environments. Explicit demonstrations of gender identity are also maintained by teachers themselves, particularly in terms of gender-specific banter between male teachers and pupils (e.g. Francis & Skelton, 2005). Male teachers may thus emphasise and encourage characteristics which are constructed as desirable for boys to possess, such as competitiveness, athleticism, a 'healthy interest' in females, and so on. These gender-matched relationships have been considered so important to maintaining appropriate gender identities and behaviour that the under-representation of men in the teaching force has been argued to be a major fact or in the disaffection, laddish behaviour and poor achievement of boys.

This leads us onto the next principal factor in explaining boys' lower performance relative to girls: the 'feminisation' of the educational sector. In this chapter, 'feminisation' is taken to mean the under-representation of men in the teaching profession.

'FEMINISATION' OF THE EDUCATIONAL SECTOR

There exists a widespread perception that the gender gap in achievement is rooted in an educational bias in favour of girls, including in terms of classroom dynamics and teaching methods and resources, as discussed earlier. A further aspect of the 'feminisation' of schooling is the absence of many male role models for male pupils. The targeted recruitment of men to the teaching profession has thus been viewed as an obvious and powerful solution to boys' underachievement and disaffection with school.

The over-representation of women in the teaching profession is not a recent phenomenon. Teaching has historically been associated with caring for or nurturing young children, in particular, and has thus been viewed as more appropriate work for women (especially as they began to take up employment outside the private sphere). The apparent underachievement of boys and the 'laddish', disengaged behaviour many low-performing boys display has been linked to the dearth of suitable male role models, particularly in primary education. In the UK, concern surrounding the absence of male primary teachers is so great that in 2001 the Teacher Training Agency specified a 15 per cent recruitment target for male entrants to primary initial teacher training[2] (Mills *et al*., 2004). It has been argued that pupils respond better to teachers of the same gender and that female teachers are thus less likely to provide learning experiences that reflect, and respond to, the needs and interests of boys. Further, female teachers do not constitute adult figures with whom boys can identify as they are inherently (biologically) different to them in terms of emotions, behaviours and interests. It is thus argued that boys need same-gender role models to foster and promote appropriate male values and qualities, such as 'boyish energy' and discipline, as well as to respond to the gender-specific learning styles of boys (as their brains are argued to be structured differently to those of girls). By virtue of the over-representation of women in the teaching profession, girls are thought to be advantaged in terms of appropriate adult role models, and classroom environments, teaching practices and assessment methods that are oriented towards 'female' needs and interests. The discourse of girls' performance improving at the expense of boys is thus reinforced by the 'feminised' schools stance.

There is an emerging body of evidence to show that matching teachers and pupils by gender does not significantly influence pupils' achievement or their attitudes towards school. Indeed, Carrington *et al*. (2008) found that boys' attitudes towards school may improve when they are taught by female teachers. Nevertheless, gender-matching is viewed as an essential measure in raising boys' academic performance. Male teachers are seen, and many view themselves as, better equipped (by virtue of their gender) to provide the 'father figures' that boys are seen to be lacking. The discourse of firm but indulgent (of boys' natural energy and enthusiasm) parenting permeates policies directed at recruiting male teachers. This particular 'parenting' discourse also reinforces notions about the ideal (heterosexual) nuclear family, in which male and female influences are seen as necessary to shaping balanced and successful children.

Male teachers are thus thought to be more capable of dealing effectively with boys' unruly and 'laddish' behaviour, and to provide positive, school-oriented role models for young men. Identifying pathways to engage boys with school is, of course, not in itself problematic. However, as we now go on to consider, the reasoning which positions men as definitive and essential role models for boys is based on rigid conceptualisations of gender that locate certain qualities as universal to all boys (and not to girls). Further, this view on gender precludes women from being able to respond to boys' needs (and men from being able to respond to girls' needs). So, a binary (and hierarchical) thinking about gender is reproduced, and differences within gender categories are obscured, as are distinct factors that may be more important to the achievement of boys and girls. What is known as a 'recuperative masculinity politics' (Mills *et al.*, 2004) has thus fuelled the debate on boys' apparent disadvantage in the educational system. The use of such strategies as gender-matched teaching, boy-friendly curricula, and the increased presence of male teachers to raise boys' academic engagement and achievement, have drawn on essentialised notions of masculinity. Boys are assumed to possess innate and unchangeable qualities which are oppositional to those which characterise girls (for example, boisterous and disruptive versus quiet and well-behaved). These qualities are viewed as essential to the nature of boys and, therefore, the hierarchical and constructed content of gender categories is negated. As Arnot and Miles (2005: 173) have noted, the masculinisation of schooling has 'ignored the impact of the *production* of hierarchical masculinities and laddishness' (emphasis added). Further, the focus on disadvantaged masculinities has masked barriers to engagement and success for working-class girls in schools, and the gendered power relations negotiated by girls in their performance of femininities (Reay, 2001).

In an equality-of-opportunity framework where boys are accorded a disadvantaged status, recuperative strategies thus invoke a naturalised masculinity that is to be restored (*inter alia* by male teachers) and celebrated. These policies to raise male achievement actually reproduce binary and hierarchical thinking about masculinity and femininity as gender identities. The view of 'feminised' schools as inherently 'anti-male' also reinforces the oppositional nature of gender categories. Mills *et al.* (2004) point out that despite the supposed feminised climate of schools, this has done little to favour female teachers in terms of salary or career progression. As is the case with other 'feminised' professions, overall wages are lower and men tend to occupy managerial or leadership positions.

Treating 'boys' and 'girls' as though they are static and homogenous groups is problematic – also in terms of analysing achievement. Much research has shown that the differences within gender categories may be greater than those between them. In other words, in different contexts and at various points in time, girls may share more commonalities with boys than with other girls (and vice versa). We now turn to critiques of the arguments put forward for boys' supposed underachievement relative to girls. First, we briefly examine the contentious concept of 'underachievement' before discussing in more detail the promise and limitations of gender analysis in relation to achievement.

REASSESSING ACHIEVEMENT GAPS

Interrogating 'underachievement'

Despite its pervasive use in educational policy and practice, underachievement is not a widely agreed-upon term. Gorard and Smith (2004) note that it may be used to denote low achievement in one group of pupils, or lower achievement in one group relative to another, or low achievement in one group relative to their perceived ability or expected performance. In the latter use of the term, 'underachievers' could thus belong to any group of pupils: high-achieving, middle-achieving or low-achieving. As Myhill and Jones (2006) point out, in this sense 'underachievement' can be defined more positively, as the potential to perform better, rather than in the negative sense of failure to perform. However, the concepts of 'achievement' and 'underachievement' are also highly gendered; underachievement has become so closely linked to the gender identity of boys that underachievement in girls may be rendered invisible. Thus, teachers perceive underachievement (or the potential to do better) to be epitomised by the 'clever but bored' boy. Underachievement as a masculinised phenomenon is therefore related to untapped potential and lacking intellectual stimulation among boys, rather than wanting ability. However, if underachievement is overlooked or unrecognised in girls, then their achievement centres solely on high or low performance and not their inherent ability – including their potential to do better. Jones and Myhill (2004: 531) note that it is problematic for low-achieving girls if they are cast immutably as low performers, rather than as 'could-do-betters'.

A key question to ask is thus, *who* are we comparing boys to when we claim that 'they' are underachieving? Is this a statement about the unfulfilled potential of boys; is it a claim about the absolute achievement of boys; or is it a comparison of boys with girls? In educational policy and discourse, the use of the term 'underachievement' is predominantly based on a comparison of boys' performance in relation to the achievement of girls. Of particular concern is the image that the performance of girls is improving more rapidly than boys and some of the reasons thought to underlie this 'widening gap' have been discussed in this chapter. However, the notion that boys' performance is low at all and that the gender gap in achievement is growing is increasingly being questioned. It has been pointed out that different scholars use varying uses of the term 'low' when they refer to achievement, such as failure to obtain grade C at GCSE, which actually represents the middle of the range of possible grades (A*–G). Further, in reporting on the gender gap in GCSE performance, observers tend to confuse percentages with percentage points (Gorard *et al.* 1999: 442–443). Thus, an achievement gap that decreases from 10 per cent to 9 per cent in one year would likely be reported only as a 1 per cent decrease, when it actually represents a 10 per cent decrease in the gap (one-tenth, or alternatively, 1 percentage point out of 100 possible points). So, achievement gaps at low levels (E, F and G grades) are actually very small in all subjects across stages of schooling. In fact, the biggest gap occurs at the highest grades of any assessment, with more girls obtaining the highest grades (A*, A and B grades); more boys obtain the mid-range grades (C and D grades) (Gorard *et al.* 1999: 444). The notion that the gender gap is 'widening' and that boys are thus underachieving in relation to girls is seen to be based on an erroneous understanding of the term underachievement, as well as the methods used to calculate performance gaps.

Intersectionality

To refocus on gender: a related issue which has been referred to at various points in this chapter, is the problematic nature of viewing 'all' boys and 'all' girls as uniform and unchanging groups. Much research has now been conducted to show the salience of other factors in identity formation, and thus, engagement with school (e.g. Epstein *et al.*, 1998; Gillborn & Gipps, 1996; Skelton, 2001). Socio-economic status and ethnicity have, in particular, been highlighted as significant predictors of achievement. It has been argued that gender may be related to achievement independently of social class and ethnicity; there are thus differences between boys and girls as 'classes' (Delphy, 1993) and these are stable across socio-economic and ethnic groups. This viewpoint has been supported by advocates of biologically rooted arguments regarding the innate nature of 'boys' as different to 'girls' that were discussed earlier in this chapter.

However, contrasting research has found that, while they are stable, overarching gender effects on achievement are relatively small and tend to be eclipsed by the role of social class and ethnicity (e.g. Demack *et al.*, 2000; Gillborn & Mizra, 2000; Smith, 2005). Achievement gaps *within* gender groups are thus larger than *between* boys and girls; for example, the difference in achievement between girls from high socio-economic backgrounds and girls from low socio-economic backgrounds is much greater than the performance difference between 'all' girls and 'all' boys (Connolly, 2006: 14). This type of research has destabilised collective constructions of 'underachieving' boys and 'overachieving' girls, and thus, challenges the notion that innate gender differences are being overlooked by feminised schools, and thus, disadvantaging all boys. We do not escape the problems related to defining terms in this research either: how is underachievement defined; is 'low' achievement actually low; and what is 'low' achievement being compared as 'low' against? Recent research has, however, used multiple measures of achievement, including overall GCSE scores (A*–G), to identify gaps across gender, social class and ethnicity, and similar gaps have been found using several measures (Connolly, 2006).

These findings also contest the notion that all boys (and all girls) behave in identical, or even similar, ways. Boys in primary and secondary schooling adopt a diverse range of masculine identities (Connell, 1989; Davison & Frank, 2006). Under some of these constructions of masculinity, academic success is valued, even if it must be seen as effortlessly won. Similarly, Reay (2001) shows how young girls adopt a variety of feminine identities, including the rejection of conventionally expected feminine behaviour, such as passivity, mild temperament and diligence. These diverse forms of masculinity and femininity rarely exist in isolation from social class and ethnicity. One might ask the question then, if gender identity is so manifold and it explains relatively little of the variation in achievement between pupils, is it useful at all in macro-analysis of educational experiences and outcomes?

A CASE FOR STRUCTURE AND SUBJECTIVITY: THE SALIENCE OF GENDER

Gender identities are diverse and gender itself intersects with other background factors in identity formation. For some young people, as for some adults, gender may not be *the* prominent identifier in their sense of self. Social class, ethnicity, disability, age and faith are all subjective positions that may be more salient in any young person's identity construction at different times. However, just as socio-economic divisions, religion, ethnicity and disability are meaningful in a wider sense beyond individual practice and experience of these, so is gender. It is thus necessary to bridge macro- and micro-analysis in order to understand the – often normalised – connections between human interaction, identity construction and power relations (Norris 2005: 184). In other words, how does the societal, structural and cultural macro context influence identity construction at the individual level?

Jackson (2005) argues that gender is constituted at a number of levels, so while the content of gender categories may be fluid (subjective gender identities may be diverse) the existence of the categories themselves is fixed. Gender as a hierarchical social division between men and women is thus embedded in social structure, institutions and practice, although individuals possess the agency to resist and subvert conventional gender expectations in everyday interactions. This conceptualisation of gender enables us to analyse social inequality as institutionalised at a number of levels, while acknowledging individuals' capability for resisting hegemonic identities and behaviours. This understanding also acknowledges interactions between individual pupils, their peers, families, neighbourhoods and wider society in identity construction and behaviour. Emphasising the constitution of gender at the structural level avoids a neo-liberal approach in which responsibility for identification and action is left solely up to the individual.

Gender hierarchy may thus be maintained and reinforced by schools as social institutions. The structure, practices and dynamics of schools may reproduce binary stereotypes about gender difference. While individual girls and boys possess the agency to subvert stereotypical gender identities, the models of masculinity and femininity that develop amongst pupils and their peer groups are consistently observed in research on educational experience. Indeed, when girls actively reject conventional norms for femininity, this may serve to uphold existing gender relations in their own identification of masculine or 'boyish' behaviour as superior to 'girlie' behaviour, as something to aspire to. This dual 'deval[uation] of the female world' (Reay, 2001: 126) and policing of strict gender norms by individuals, social practices and structures may thus reinforce the oppositional and hierarchical nature of gender categories.

SUMMARY

In this chapter, we have considered the relevance of gender to education, with a particular focus on achievement, learner identities and behaviour, and teaching. Gender has been emphasised as a social division, which is often naturalised in educational and social discourse and practice. The chapter has discussed the power of gender norms to shape behaviour (participation) in education, as well as current concerns about boys' and girls' learning experiences and outcomes. There is an emerging recognition that factors other than gender are salient to educational experience, and that blanket strategies to address the needs of 'all' girls and 'all' boys are untenable. Gender equality (sameness) is therefore not always possible, nor desirable, given the multitude of differences existing between and within gender categories. Thus, a social justice framework which acknowledges multiple subjective positions and advocates equality of opportunity for all may be favourable. However, we must be wary of foregrounding individual responsibility and prioritising the salience of micro-level over macro context; the power of 'gender' in regulating young people's educational experiences must be recognised.

KEY QUESTIONS

1. What does 'gender' mean?
2. Is gender a useful concept in explaining differential achievement between boys and girls?
3. Is there a need for more male teachers in primary and secondary schools? Justify your answer.

FURTHER READING

Carrington, B., & McPhee, A., 2008. Boys' 'underachievement' and the feminization of teaching. *Journal of Education for Teaching*, 34(2), pp. 109–120.

Jackson, S., 2005. Sexuality, heterosexuality and gender hierarchy: getting our priorities straight. In C. Ingraham, ed. *Thinking Straight: New Work in Critical Heterosexuality Studies.* London: Routledge. pp. 15–38.

Skelton, C., Francis, B., & Smulyan, L., eds. 2006. *The SAGE Handbook of Gender and Education*. London: Routledge.

Smith, E., 2005. *Analysing Underachievement.* London: Continuum.

NOTES

1 This apparent greater success in compulsory schooling is not reflected in subject choices made at higher levels of education, however. In 2004, only 37 per cent of A-level Maths students were female, and around 46 per cent of maths undergraduate students in the UK were female.

2 Recruitment targets have similarly been set for black and ethnic minority (BME) teacher trainees, based often on a comparable essentialising argument that BME teachers are inherently better positioned to respond to the universalised needs of minority ethnic pupils.

This chapter links with reading 9 of *The Routledge Education Studies Reader.*

CHAPTER 5

EDUCATION AND SOCIAL CLASS

Jon Davison

The rationale for this chapter is:

- to consider the nature of cultural capital and cultural reproduction and the part these play in maintaining inequalities in society;
- to consider some of the reasons for the underachievement of working class children as a group in school;
- to examine the discourse of official educational reports and documentation to determine whether the values, attitudes, language and preferences of dominant social groups have influenced the discourse of these documents to the disadvantage of working class children.

INTRODUCTION

The last decade of the twentieth century began with a Conservative prime minister announcing that society did not exist and drew to a close with a New Labour prime minister announcing that we are now all members of the middle class. In recent years it has become unfashionable to discuss education and social class. There appears to be an underlying assumption that it is now passé to do so: the debate has moved on; social class is an irrelevance. Today, the closest allusion to the relationship between education and social class appears to be found in the discussions relating to: social and economic contexts of high-quality primary and secondary education; access to, and participation in, higher education; social mobility, and the educational life chances of children related to their postcodes.

It could be argued that the issues of social class and equality of educational opportunity have never been properly tackled in the UK: neither at a national level by government policy, nor at a local level in local authority education policy and practice. In the early 1980s the Inner London Education Authority (ILEA), noted for its development of equal opportunities policy and practice, launched its 'Sex, Race and Class' initiative. However, although the ILEA did much excellent work relating to the first two issues, for all its egalitarian zeal, it shied away from grasping the nettle of social class.

Consistently, reports have shown that academic attainment tends to be low in schools with high proportions of pupils from low-income homes: 'In 2001, only a fifth of pupils in schools with the poorest intakes achieved five GCSE passes at grades A*–C, compared with 50% nationally' (Lupton 2004). Poor examination results at the end of secondary schooling preclude the opportunity to engage in further and higher education by attending college or university. UK Government figures produced in 1991 showed that only 5 per cent of children from skilled manual home backgrounds attended university and despite a claimed 30 per cent increase in access to university, in 1998 only approximately 5 per cent of those at university came from the poorest post-coded areas (Halsey 1998). And data in *The Widening Socio-Economic Gap in UK Higher Education* shows that matters, far from improving, are actually getting worse:

> . . . the gap between rich and poor, in terms of HE participation, has widened during the 1990s. Children from poor neighbourhoods have become relatively less likely to participate in HE since 1994/5, as compared to children from richer neighbourhoods. This trend started before the introduction of tuition fees. Much of the class difference in HE participation seems to reflect inequalities at earlier stages of the education system.
>
> (Galindo-Rueda, Marcenaro-Gutierrez and Vignoles 2004)

Furthermore, while the New Labour Government's Widening Access and Increasing Participation initiative since 1997 has aimed at reaching a target of 50 per cent university attendance from all social groups, '[i]nequalities in degree acquisition meanwhile persist across different income groups. While 44 per cent of young people from the richest 20 per cent of households acquired a degree in 2002, only 10 per cent from the poorest 20 per cent of households did so' (Blanden and Machin 2007: 3).

Despite the inception of a National Curriculum in England, Wales and Northern Ireland, designed to ensure an equal curricular entitlement for all pupils, children from working class backgrounds have continued to underachieve compared to children of the middle classes. 'Parental background continues to exert a significant influence on the academic progress of recent generations of children' (Blanden and Machin 2007: 4).

CULTURAL CAPITAL AND CULTURAL REPRODUCTION

The terms 'cultural capital' and 'cultural reproduction' stem from the work of Bourdieu (see for example Bourdieu 2007). Put simply, cultural reproduction is the process through which existing cultural values and norms are transmitted from generation to generation thereby ensuring continuity of cultural experience across time. Cultural reproduction, therefore, often results in 'social reproduction' – the process through which facets of society, such as class, are transferred from generation to generation.

Bourdieu proposes that different social groups have different 'cultural capital', which may be seen as the knowledge, experience and connections an individual has, and develops, over time that enable a person to succeed more than someone with knowledge, experience and connections that is seen in society as being of less value. Further, particular groups of people, notably social classes, act to reproduce the existing social structure in order to legitimate and preserve their social and cultural advantage.

Education as an agent of cultural reproduction

Brown (1973), Bourdieu (1973) and Bowles and Gintis (1976) propose that it is the stratification of school knowledge that reproduces inequalities in 'cultural capital'. Bourdieu argues that the structural reproduction of disadvantages and inequalities is caused by cultural reproduction and is recycled through the education system, as well as through other social institutions. The education system, therefore, is an agent of cultural reproduction biased towards those of higher social class, not only in the curricular content of subjects taught, but also through what is known as the 'hidden curriculum', which includes the language, values and attitudes located in, and which an individual acquires from, the discourse of curricular subjects and all aspects of school life that contribute to an individual's socialisation through the education process. An individual's success or failure within the formal education system is determined by the ability to achieve formal educational qualifications *and* to acquire the appropriate language, values, attitudes and qualities through the process of socialisation within the system. The ability to complete successfully all aspects of schooling correlates strongly to an individual's capacity subsequently to enjoy high cultural capital such as adequate pay, occupational prestige and social status in adult life. Lankshear sums up:

> Dominant social and cultural groups have been able to establish their language, and their knowledge priorities, learning styles, pedagogical preferences, etc., as the 'official examinable culture' of school. Their notions of important and useful knowledge, their ways of presenting truth, their ways of arguing and establishing correctness, and their logics, grammars and language as institutional norms by which academic and scholastic success is defined and assessed.
>
> (Lankshear 1997: 30)

At this point it would seem appropriate to consider some specific causes of educational underachievement related to social class.

SOCIAL CLASS AND UNDERACHIEVEMENT

In the latter half of the twentieth century a variety of aspects of school life were examined in order to identify the causes of pupil underachievement, such as access, institutional structures, the nature of school knowledge. For example, in the latter half of the twentieth century Hargreaves (1967), Lacey (1970) and Ball (1981) cited the institutional structures of schools, such as streaming and banding, as being influential in determining the performance of working class pupils: a disproportionate number of whom were found to be represented in the lower streams and bands.

It is well documented that, despite the intentions of Education Acts from 1944 to 1988, children from the working class in the UK have continued to underachieve at school. The '11 plus' test was created by the 1944 Education Act, which proposed the establishment of a tripartite system of secondary schooling comprising modern, technical and grammar schools. Success or failure in the '11 plus' determined the type of school an individual attended. The test became the cornerstone of educational progress. Floud, Halsey and Martin (1966) exposed massive under-representation of working class boys at grammar schools. A key filter in the process of selection for grammar school places was the '11 plus' examination, which included an Intelligence Quotient (IQ) test (see below). Douglas (1964) showed how working class pupils with the same IQ scores as middle class children were failing to gain grammar school places, because of the class bias of teachers in primary schools.

Of equal concern is how both working class and middle class girls were institutionally discriminated against in the '11 plus' examination. It is now well known that the '11 plus' examination scores of all girls were adjusted down because they were far outstripping boys' achievement. Thousands of girls who passed the '11 plus' and should have, therefore, attended grammar schools were prevented from doing so because their scores were downgraded. It was feared that all grammar schools were otherwise going to be filled with far more girls than boys (see *The Report of the Task Group on Assessment and Testing* (TGAT) (DES 1987: 40–53) for a discussion of these issues in relation to the establishment of the National Curriculum).

IQ TESTING

Psychologist Sir Cyril Burt (1883–1971) was a leading proponent in the development of the '11 plus' and the inclusion of IQ testing. Burt had a background in research in behaviour genetics, which included twin studies focusing on the heritability of intelligence. During his career he was professor at University College London, a school psychologist and a leading consultant on the development of the '11 plus'. Elsewhere, in a radio interview in the late 1940s he proposed setting up a society for very intelligent people, which today is known as *Mensa*. From this brief outline of Burt's career it might seem that he was an ideal person to be consulted on the nature and content of the '11 plus'.

However, seven years after Burt's death, on 29 November 1978, the *Sunday Times* newspaper carried the headline 'Crucial data faked by eminent psychologist'. Reporters had uncovered evidence that Burt had falsified his data in his twin studies and in the academic papers he had published – papers that had led to his involvement in the development of the '11 plus'. Furthermore, it was maintained that two of Burt's research collaborators, Margaret Howard and J. Conway, with whom Burt had supposedly undertaken work and published in prestigious journals, did not exist: they had been made up by Burt.

Harvard palaeontologist Stephen J. Gould is heavily critical of biological determinism and IQ testing *per se* (see Gould 1981). According to Gould psychological testing suffers from two deep fallacies: the first is *reification*: the tendency to convert abstract concepts into entities. These entities include IQ (the intelligence quotient) and g (the general intelligence factor), which have been the cornerstone of much intelligence research. The second fallacy is that of *ranking*, or the propensity for ordering complex variation as a gradual ascending scale. The ramifications have clear implications for any discussion of social class and underachievement, as Gould is highly critical of the ends to which such testing is put:

> The abstraction of intelligence as a single entity, its location within the brain, its quantification as one number for each individual, and the use of these numbers to rank people in a single series of worthiness, invariably to find that oppressed and disadvantaged groups, races, classes, or sexes, are innately inferior and deserve their status.
>
> (Gould 1981: 24–25)

Within '. . . societies like our own there is a tendency for forms of literacy to prevail which effectively maintain patterned inequalities of power within the social structure' (Lankshear 1987: 79–80).

The '11 plus' and IQ tests were criticised for a middle class bias in their content, their use of middle class cultural references, their vocabulary and language register. The '11 plus' was seen as culturally biased towards the middle class children (for example a question might be related to classical composers, something a middle class child would be more likely to answer correctly than would a child from the working class because of social and cultural differences in their home backgrounds). Additionally, Basil Bernstein (1971) showed marked differences in the language use of members of different social classes, with middle class children having access in their language to a more formal 'elaborated code' while working class language was characterised as operating within a simple 'restricted code'. However, many researchers, including Trudgill (1974), Boocock (1980), and DeMarrais and LeCompte (1990), criticised Bernstein as a proponent of 'deficit theory'.

> Bernstein's theory of codes does not suggest that the academically successful are merely *perceived* as smarter or more capable, due to the marketability of their particular talents. Rather, it implies that the academically successful really are smarter, ready to engage in a discourse capable of expressing 'universal meaning,' eschewing the fragmentation and 'logical simplicity' of the underclass. . . . In such a society, the oppressed are required to climb the ladder of 'equal opportunity.' The higher they get, the more they resemble the oppressors and the more their efforts are rewarded.
>
> (MacSwan & McLaren 1997: 334–340)

This is not to say that working class pupils are simply passive recipients of a dominant culture, for studies by Gaskell (1985) and Willis (1977, 1981) for example, have shown how pupils resist school culture – although Abraham's (1993) study reveals that resistance comes more from 'anti-school' pupils whatever their social background. Abraham (1993: 136) goes on to argue that: '. . . the organising and processing of school knowledge provides a setting which is not sufficiently critical of social class and gender divisions to discourage their reproduction in further schooling and out into the occupational structure'.

SOCIAL CLASS AND EDUCATIONAL POLICY MAKERS

If there are such determinants that militate against success of working class children in the education system, how were these structures and systems put in place? The answer, of course, is that they are, *inter alia*, the results of a combination of national and local education policy, which is espoused in the discourse of dominant social and cultural groups.

The quotation earlier from Colin Lankshear's exploration of sociolinguistics states that dominant social and cultural groups have been able to establish the 'official examinable culture of school' (Lankshear 1997: 30). However, he goes on to say that the determination of the official examinable culture of the school by dominant social and cultural groups is not necessarily a conscious process and far less a conspiracy:

> It is simply what tends to happen, with the result that discourse and discourses of dominant groups become those which dominate education, and become established as major legitimate routes to securing social goods (like wealth and status). As a result, educational success is patterned along distinct lines of prior discursive experience associated with membership of particular social groups.
>
> (Lankshear 1997: 30)

Whilst one might agree with Lankshear's observations regarding conspiracy, there is, nevertheless, a question of power relations to be answered when discussing dominant discourses. Gee (1991: 21) defines discourse as: 'a socially accepted association among ways of using language, of thinking, and of acting that can be used to identify oneself as a member of a socially meaningful group or "social network"'. In order to test these assertions, this chapter will now briefly explore the development of one curriculum subject as a case study, in this case English. On examining official government documents it is difficult not to be struck by the antipathetic attitudes to the working class displayed by educational policy makers throughout the twentieth century. Baldick (1983), Davison and Dowson (2009), Eagleton (1983) and Palmer (1965) consider in detail how beliefs about working class pupils shaped education policy and practice in the English classroom during the twentieth century and here it is useful, briefly, to consider what these attitudes were.

> Many persons, most prominently social and economic leaders and social reformers, grasped the uses of schooling and the vehicle of literacy for the promotion of values, attitudes and habits considered essential to the maintenance of social order and the persistence of integration and cohesion.
>
> (Graff 1987: 7)

For Gossman (1981: 82) state education and the importance of English were 'advocated in a hard-headed way as a means of social control'. Poet and HMI, Matthew Arnold (1869: 105), saw the 'raw and half developed' working class living 'amidst poverty and squalor' as a threat to social stability, which would be averted by a high cultural, pure-English-as-civilising-agent approach to education.

Concerns about the level of literacy among working class children were addressed by the Board of Education (BoE) (1910) *Circular 753*, which was instrumental in establishing the nature of English as it came to be in school, '. . . instruction in English in the secondary school aims at training the mind to appreciate English Literature and at cultivating the power of using the English Language in speech and writing . . .' (par. 2). With the founding of the Board of Education and the establishment of what was, in reality, a national curriculum during the first twenty years of the twentieth century, successive government circulars and reports promulgated beliefs in the power of English to civilise the masses. 'Pure English is not merely an accomplishment, but an index to and a formative influence over character' (BoE 1910: par. 2).

ATTITUDES TO SOCIAL CLASS IN GOVERNMENT REPORTS

The first major report into *The Teaching of English in England* (the Newbolt Report) was published in 1921 and it, too, was suspicious of the growing working class. The Newbolt Report (BoE 1921) was sympathetic to elementary school teachers who had 'to fight against *evil* habits of speech contracted in home and street' [this author's emphasis] and pupils' spoken English is referred to as 'disfigured' (par 67). The Report's hostility to working class children is confirmed when it describes the teacher's battle, which is 'not with ignorance but with a *perverted* power' (par 59) [this author's emphasis]. Working class children who do not use standard English are more than just untutored, in the discourse of the document, they are characterised as being 'evil' and 'perverted'.

Similar attitudes are found in subsequent Goverment reports produced throughout the twentieth century. In the early years of the century, *Circular 753* lamented that pupils 'fall helplessly back on slang, the base coin of the language' (BoE 1910: par. 2). A 'base coin' is a forgery. Therefore, the use of this metaphor in relation to working class pupils' language associates them with criminality through reference to the crime of counterfeiting. A quarter of a century after this circular and 15 years after the Newbolt Report, the *Report on Secondary Education* [the Spens Report] (BoE 1938), described pupils' spoken English as 'slovenly, ungrammatical, and often incomprehensible to a stranger' (p. 220) – presumably a middle class stranger, for one assumes that the working class children would understand each other perfectly. In a notable echo of the Spens Report, nearly 50 years later, a report designed to contribute to the establishment of the National Curriculum – *English from 5 to 16* – believed that pupils should '[s]peak clearly, audibly and pleasantly, in an accent intelligible to the listener(s)' (HMI 1984: 10). In relation to the spoken language of working class children it is clear that for almost 100 years there has been considerable continuity in the attitudes expressed and that they have all been negative.

Furthermore, three years after the inception of the National Curriculum, the draft proposals for a rewritten National Curriculum for English 5–16 (DES 1993) stated that, from Key Stage 1, pupils 'should speak clearly using Standard English' and 'should be taught to speak accurately, precisely, and with clear diction'. Examples of spoken accuracy and precision cited in the proposals include: 'We were (not was) late back from the trip'; 'We won (not winned) at cricket'; 'Pass me those (not them) books'; 'Clive and I (not me) are going to Wembley'; 'We haven't seen anybody (not nobody)' (1993: 9–23). Once again, it is entirely appropriate to assume that working class children would understand the meaning of the incorrect forms perfectly if their peers were using them. What is at issue here is not that the children using the incorrect form would not be understood by anyone of the working class, or indeed the middle class; rather it is the case that the incorrect form offends middle class sensibilities and therefore needs to be corrected. And it should be remembered that while we might write accurately and precisely, no one – whether they be working class or middle class – speaks in standard English: with the possible exceptions of Her Majesty the Queen, and a notable art critic.

THE THREAT OF THE UNIONS

Not only were working class children perceived as potentially dangerous in governmental education reports, so too were members of 'organised labour movements', because they 'were antagonistic to, and contemptuous of literature . . . a subject to be despised by really virile men' (BoE 1921: par 233). The writers of the Newbolt Report stated that 'a large number of thinking working men' believed literature to be as useful and relevant to their lives as 'antimacassars, fish-knives and other unintelligible and futile trivialities of middle-class culture' and that it was taught in schools only 'to side-track the working movement' (par 233). Writing elsewhere, Newbolt Committee member George Sampson (1921) further stereotypes 'the extravagant British workman' and his 'moral, intellectual and emotional level', whose habits lead him to 'the newest and nudest revues' and who ends by 'being divorced'. Sampson believed that working class children would only be saved by the correct teaching of English because it would serve to educate them intellectually, morally and spiritually and 'very especially it will cover all that we at present leave naked and barbarous' (Sampson 1921: 104–105). The teaching of correct English would do nothing to address the glaring social inequalities in society other than 'cover' them: an attitude that re-emerged in the *Report on Secondary Education*, the Spens Report, '. . . it should be possible for the spread of a common habit of English teaching to *soften the distinctions* which separate men and classes in later life' (BoE 1938: 222) [this author's emphasis].

(UN)POPULAR CULTURE

Central to the teaching and learning of English is the study of the literature of the 'Great Literary Tradition', which is, of course, a high-cultural model of English. The texts within the curriculum are drawn from the 'Canon' of great texts. The Canon is constructed and traditionally has been based on the values, preferences and choices of academics, writers, poets and so on – few, if any, of whom would come from the working class. A selected elite agree the Canon of great works into which educated members of society are inducted. The Canon is so ingrained in schooling that it is easily possible to list the writers without thinking: Chaucer, Shakespeare, Milton, Wordsworth, Shelley, Dickens, etc, etc. The great texts speak of the divine nature of human kind, the virtues and duty. It is the literacy of morality. The great writers and the great texts are believed to cultivate the intellectual, emotional and moral aspects of life. In this version of English there is also an emphasis on correctness, on grammar and standard English, because the 'standard form is identified with cultivation and national identity and acts as a form of social closure and social exclusion' (Ball *et al.* 1990: 79). These texts did not get into the curriculum by accident, they were chosen based on the high-cultural attitudes central to the discourse of dominant social groups. The antithesis of high culture is seen to be 'popular culture' – the culture of social groups that are not dominant, namely the working class.

The majority of official education policy documents in the twentieth century are hugely antipathetic to popular culture: so, too, the educational press, which decries the adverse effects of cinema: '. . . the mental effect upon the children was to make them more fond of noise, ostentatious display, self-advertisement and change. The pictures excited their minds and created a love of pleasure and disinclination for steady work and effort' (*Times Educational Supplement* 1915). Hostile attitudes towards cinema, advertising, comics, tabloid newspapers, radio, television, and so on may also be found in official education documentation throughout the twentieth century: 'The pervading influences of the hoarding, the cinema, and a large section of the public press, are (in this respect as in others) subtly corrupting the taste and habits of the rising generation' (BoE 1938: 222–3). Once again a government report raises fears of 'corruption' in respect of 'taste' and 'habits' – both of which may safely be assumed to be middle class. Not only is the working class corrupt, its popular culture is 'subtly corrupting' young people of the middle class. So corrupting is popular culture that it affects not lone individuals, but the entire 'rising generation' of the middle class.

This antipathy to the indulgence of working class children in facets of popular culture may be traced to the present day in educational documents: from cinema through radio, television and video, to personal computers and video games. Although the Bullock Report, *A Language for Life* (DES 1975), helped to pave the way for media education, it contains the same attitudes displayed by dominant social groups half a century earlier: 'Between them, radio and television spread the catch-phrase, the advertising jingle, and the frenetic trivia of the disc-jockey . . . it is clear that the content and form of much radio and television utterance makes the teacher's job a great deal more difficult' (par. 2.8).

Twenty years later, at the Conservative Party conference on 7 October 1992, Secretary of State for Education John Patten railed against '1960s theorists', 'the trendy left', and 'teachers' union bosses', who were destroying 'our great literary heritage'. In a speech that decried working class cultural attitudes by attacking not only the trade unions but also popular culture, he warned: 'They'd give us chips with Chaucer. Milton with mayonnaise. Mr Chairman, I want William Shakespeare in our classrooms, not Ronald McDonald' (Patten 1992). It needs to be borne in mind that the man speaking was not just any government minister, but the Secretary of State for Education – the man with ultimate responsibility for the nation's schools and the National Curriculum and his rhetoric is filled with dominant values and attitudes which will define and maintain the 'official examinable culture' of the school.

Similar hostility to popular culture came from Her Majesty's Chief Inspector for Schools (HMCI), Mr Chris Woodhead. Although the Bullock Report began (some would argue) the rather slow process that led to the establishment of the fast-growing curriculum subject, Media Studies, Woodhead has been resolute in his criticism of the study of popular culture and of Media Studies: 'Media Studies has always been a nonsense – now it has degenerated into a farce. Students ought to be exposed to interesting and worthwhile figures and issues' (Woodhead 2008). Elsewhere his comments mirror educational documents almost 100 years previously: 'The best schools struggle to outdo the influence of peer pressure, and the teenage culture created by the pop and fashion industries, but struggle they must' (Woodhead 2000). Alan Smithers (2000), director of the Centre for Education and Employment Research at Liverpool University, said: 'I agree with Mr Woodhead . . . so far there are not things like Shakespeare and Chaucer on some of the media being studied. I don't think it's the same having someone watch all 57 episodes of *The Sweeney*'. Dominant high-cultural criticisms of working class culture are very much evident in the twenty-first century.

THE PROBLEM OF 'NATURALISATION'

Even from this cursory examination of the development of the subject it would appear that Lankshear's and others' assertions are correct. Throughout the twentieth century, and in the 20 years of the National Curriculum dominant, high-cultural values and views about the nature of English as a school subject have held sway to the detriment of working class children. An exploration of the development of other subjects would provide similar evidence of the influence of dominant cultural values affecting the development of those curricula. Particular 'notions of important and useful knowledge', clearly defined 'ways of arguing and establishing correctness' have formed the basis of school curricula, examination syllabuses, and the National Curriculum for English, which, in their assessment methodology, have established the 'institutional norms by which academic and scholastic success is defined and assessed'.

With the passing of time, the reiteration of a dominant view leads to the belief that the status quo is the natural order of things by some universal right: particular curricular content, attitudes, values and practices are accepted as the very 'nature' of curriculum subjects, rather than interrogated to determine the underpinning value systems: 'A particular set of discourse practices and conventions may achieve a high degree of *naturalisation* – they may come to be seen as simply "there" in a common-sense way, rather than socially put there' (Fairclough 1992: 9).

LITERACIES

State education acts on behalf of employers and manufacturers by providing a functionally literate workforce of active consumers. There is a strong link here with the perceived needs of industry and commerce for individuals who are able to function in the workplace and earn an income.

An Organisation of Economic Cooperation and Development (OECD) report statistics found eight million adults in the United Kingdom to be 'functionally illiterate': 'one in five of all adults had poor literacy and numeracy skills. The proportions were around 10% higher for women than men' (UNESCO 2003). Therefore, much of the drive for the introduction of the National Literacy Strategy came from a belief that workers in the UK were less literate than their European counterparts – most notably those in Germany – and were, as a consequence, not only a symptom, but also part of the cause, of the decline in British manufacturing industries.

There were many cries from employers that the level of literacy among school leavers has been in steady decline. This perception is, however, hardly surprising, considering the social changes that have occurred since, say 1960, and the growth in the literacy demands on individuals: for example, exponential growth in advertising has led to a need to decode sophisticated, complex advertisements in print alone; increasingly, the demands made upon applicants for even the lowest status jobs have increased during periods of high unemployment; as a consumer, the individual has had to develop complex skills brought about by the transition of corner grocery shops into out-of-town supermarkets filled with a plethora of signs and aisle guides, with shelves containing an abundance of groceries in sophisticated packaging bearing complex instructions. Similarly, the 'packaging' of political messages in the 'infomercial' on television, increasing delivery into the home of political pamphlets through the use of the mail-shot (both print-based and electronically via email) and sophisticated enigmatic poster campaigns, all have placed increasing literacy demands on the individual. Meanwhile in the home, every major electrical appliance comes complete with its 48-page installation and user guide in six languages. Lankshear (1987: 135) observes:

> Even if schools improved their current performance to the point where they matched the functional demands of the present day, changes occurring *outside* the school – in technology, economic production, commerce, communications, consumerism, cultural life, etc., – would tend towards creating a rate of illiteracy in the future by simply continuing to raise the minimum required level of print competence.

SUMMARY

Social class and education are inextricably linked. From Bourdieu's perspective the structural reproduction of societal social and cultural disadvantages and inequalities are caused by cultural reproduction and are recycled through the education system, as well as through other social institutions.

In over 100 years of state education in the UK various aspects of schooling have disadvantaged children from the working class: access, institutional structures, the nature of school knowledge, testing and examining; cultural contexts; language and discourse, as a result of the fact that the discourse of dominant social and cultural groups determines the nature of schooling and the curriculum. The language, the cultural references, attitudes and values of the middle class underpin the official examinable culture of the school.

Furthermore, the dominant discourse of government documents that established and maintain the education system in England and Wales was, and remains, high cultural and has displayed an antipathy to working class children and to popular culture. Since 1990 the central metaphor of the National Curriculum has been 'delivery'. Eisner (1984) reminds us that the metaphors we use shape our understanding of the concepts we study. A curriculum to be 'delivered' by a teacher is disempowering of pupils and teachers alike. It is a view of knowledge that is hierarchical, top-down and is characterised by prescription and direction. Consequently, it is unsurprising that the 'official examinable culture' of school – the language, knowledge priorities, learning styles, pedagogical preferences – is that of dominant social and cultural groups. The New Labour Government has announced that the school leaving age is to be raised to 18 years of age. Without a radical change to the curricula and structures of state schooling it is likely that children from the working class will continue to underachieve as a group compared to middle class children. In January 2009, in the introduction to the Runnymede Trust report *Who Cares about the White Working Class?*, the Trust's vice chair Dr Kate Gavron provides an overview of the report's findings:

> . . . working-class people of whatever ethnic background, roughly the poorest fifth of the population, are increasingly separated from the more prosperous majority by inequalities of income, housing and education. By emphasizing the virtues of individual self-determination and the exercising of 'choice', recent governments have in fact entrenched the ability of the middle and upper classes to avoid downward social mobility and preserve the best of life's goods for their own children. . . . life chances for today's children are overwhelmingly linked to parental income, occupations and educational qualifications – in other words, class.
>
> (Gavron 2009)

KEY QUESTIONS

1. What is social class?
2. To what extent does social class explain patterns of educational achievement?
3. Should schools be reformed to take account of social class? If so, why and what sort of reforms would be undertaken? (If not, why not?)

FURTHER READING

Freire, P. (2000) *Pedagogy of the Oppressed* [Trans M. Ramos]. London: Continuum

Jenkins, R. (2002) *Pierre Bourdieu*, 2nd ed. London: Routledge

Lupton, R. (2004) *Do Poor Neighbourhoods Mean Poor Schools?* London: Centre for Analysis of Social Exclusion/ESRC

Runnymede Trust (2009) *Who Cares about the White Working Class?* London: Runnymede Trust

This chapter links with reading 7 of *The Routledge Education Studies Reader.*

CHAPTER 6

CITIZENSHIP EDUCATION AND BLACK AND MINORITY ETHNIC COMMUNITIES

Bela Arora

The rationale for this chapter is:

- to highlight the centrality of addressing diversity within a context of Citizenship Education;
- to highlight the value of embracing diversity rather than something to be 'managed';
- to highlight that the Majorite 'colour-blind' approach to the delivery of education does not ensure equality or meet the needs of a diverse student body.

INTRODUCTION

The educational performance of members of black and minority ethnic (BME) communities has regularly come under scrutiny and there have been serious concerns about the failure of the education system to deliver equal access and success to all members of society, regardless of cultural background. Citizenship Education, in part, aimed to address government concerns over declining levels of political participation and civil engagement; however, it is evident that a universal, 'one size fits all' approach to the teaching of the subject area will risk solidifying the status quo and reinforcing marginalisation. This chapter highlights the need to place diversity at the heart of Citizenship Education and inclusive teaching practice.

There have been countless terms that have been used in reference to ethnic minority groups in Britain. Many of the terms have been used interchangeably, however, and there is a significant amount of ambiguity about usage. Clearly, one of the key challenges is that many of the terms imply a sense of homogeneity and fail to acknowledge that there may be significant diversity within cultures. Some would take a position at the other extreme by advocating the abandonment of terms that group ethnic minorities in favour of only making reference to constituent groups (Aspinall, 2002). This may in some ways be a logical way forward, however it can in some cases be rather cumbersome in reality, particularly in cases when it is possible to identify certain common themes that may span national, cultural and religious boundaries. A second criticism of the term ethnic minority is that the word 'minority' may have connotations of 'less important' or 'marginalised'; however, one could argue that this is an issue that relates to false perceptions of the term rather than a problem with the term per se. For this reason, I have chosen to adopt the term black and minority ethnic (BME) as there are a range of common themes that can be highlighted in the context of citizenship. Clearly, although there may be a degree of commonality in the challenges, there will be significant differentiation in approaches that seek to address the very same challenges.

Within the post-industrial societies of the twentieth century, the national education systems are looked upon as avenues for the economic and civil incorporation of ethnic minority groups into the host societies. As a result, they are also areas of continued tension. Tensions here are mostly centred around the question of the type and level of education needed for minority groups to function effectively in society, whilst still retaining an appropriate level of cultural autonomy (Tomlinson, 1998). In the 1985 Swann Report in Britain, the Committee of Enquiry into the Education of Children of Ethnic Minority Groups recommended that British education should enable all children to understand the multicultural nature of British society, with schools taking a direct approach to tackling racism and stereotyping. The report encouraged Local Education Authorities (LEAs), to commit to the ethos of 'education for all' and to adopt a pluralist curriculum (Blair, 2001). Since this time there has been extensive interest in the educational achievements of ethnic minorities and various theoretical and empirical explanations have been forwarded concerning the diverse educational experiences of ethnic minority pupils (Abbas, 2002).

DIVERSE PERCEPTIONS AND THE CHALLENGE OF INCLUSIVE TEACHING PRACTICE

The qualitative data gathered, during the course of the research that has underpinned this chapter, from educators, students, community group representatives and community group members provided a valuable resource with which to examine the understandings and perceptions of Citizenship Education among young members of BME communities. All four groups of participants harboured very positive outlooks towards Citizenship Education in terms of its importance and purpose and its potential to inform pivotal everyday issues, however, it was clear from the responses gathered, that there was a strong sense of ambivalence surrounding Citizenship Education as it currently stands. Young members of BME communities who took part in the study felt that issues relating to race and identity were not necessarily given due prominence in Citizenship Education. In some cases teachers were able to corroborate this view, but the reasons behind this were varied. For some, it was due to lack of confidence whereas others voiced concern about opening a Pandora's box that could be difficult to control.

Education, and more specifically the delivery of education, is clearly a political issue. Indeed when the issue of race is added into the equation it becomes near impossible to disentangle the political dynamics. Whether for better or for worse, the classroom environment and its activities have become highly structured. The progression towards an audit culture has resulted in a focus on targets and league tables that often constrain the teaching setting. The danger here is that teachers may feel that a standardised and universalistic approach, whereby the same activities are used from class to class and sometimes from year to year, is the most efficient and practical route to take. However, there is a growing realisation that teaching has to be tailored to meet the demographic needs of the class. The demographic make-up of society has evolved, but it seems as though the education system has been slower to respond to the changing environment. Tomlinson highlights how education policy priorities have changed at higher echelons. She argues that there has been a move away from John Major's vision of 'colour blind' policies that failed to recognise racial inequalities in education (Tomlinson, 2005). Such a positivist view of the world, which suggests the existence of one objective reality for all regardless of race, does not acknowledge marginalisation. Moreover, as Lukes points out, this would constitute what he refers to as the second face of power or the ability to set the agenda (Lukes, 1974). That is to say, by removing race as a key dimension in education, removes it from the table of discussion, which is neither healthy nor legitimate. The 1997 New Labour government, in contrast, was keen to step away from universalistic language and towards a discourse of diversity, difference and inclusion. Policies can easily be changed; however, shifts in the delivery of subjects are more difficult to implement.

The classroom environment needs to undergo radical change at all levels. Teachers do not always feel that they have the training or resources to teach in a truly inclusive manner, students do not always feel that they relate to the issues that are being presented to them, and beyond the classroom BME parents have concerns about the way their children are being educated. Tomlinson makes reference to research conducted by Warren and Gillborn (for Birmingham City Council Equalities Division, 2004), which highlights concerns by parents about what they saw as a 'distant and unresponsive education system' (Tomlinson, 2005). Clearly, substantive changes need to be made across the board. It is evident that a paradigm shift is needed in many cases in order to meet the needs of an increasingly diverse student population.

From a theoretical viewpoint, the constructivist approach to learning is thought to effectively facilitate inclusive teaching practice because of its emphasis on students playing an active role in the construction and development of their own learning. This perspective stands in stark contrast to traditionalist views of students as passive empty vessels in need of the infilling of knowledge by teachers. In the constructivist viewpoint, the student endeavours to make sense of the curriculum presented whilst the teacher facilitates this sense-making process. Constructivists also believe that the curriculum is socially negotiated. This suggests that knowledge is both subjective and evolving as opposed to being fixed (Cordeiro *et al.*, 1994). Within constructivism, teachers are required to assist students in the critical analysis of the views contained with textbooks instead of presenting them as absolute truth. This perspective allows for the integration of student experiences from beyond the confines of the school (Cordeiro *et al.*, 1994).

During research on learning experiences within a multi-ethnic setting, Moll (1988) discovered that the most effective classes for Latino students were those in which they were encouraged to use their personal experience to make sense of school experiences. Moll's research highlighted the fact that in most classrooms, home and community experiences are avoided. However when this area of knowledge is valued, positive effects often result. The integration of personal and cultural knowledge within the classroom can increase the cultural relevance of learning (Cordeiro *et al.*, 1994), thus engaging Black and minority ethnic students more effectively. These suggestions are further substantiated by Gay (2004) who stresses the importance of intercultural, multicultural education, which encompasses the exploration of information concerning a range of diverse ethnic groups (Codjoe, 2006). According to Codjoe, this will allow schools to become more effective and relevant learning environments for minority students (Codjoe, 2006). The constructivist approach to learning is particularly relevant within inclusive education because it allows the effects of diversity on learning to feature predominantly in dialogues concerning professional development and teacher training. It also requires schools to focus on the improvement of the sensitivity to, and recognition of, diversity within the school organisation (Cordeiro *et al.*, 1994).

PROMOTING DIFFERENCE

Clearly, British society has become more diverse over the years and it is important for teachers to embrace that diversity. However, it is worth noting that differing positions on diversity do exist, which can lead to further ambiguity. Some see diversity as a challenge to social cohesion and therefore something that has to be 'managed' whereas others see it as something to be celebrated and recognised. Such extremes of position will undoubtedly impact upon the student learning experience when in the classroom. In terms of Citizenship Education, the Crick Report does not particularly accommodate ethnic or religious diversity (Kiwan, 2008), but does allude to political diversity. Diversity is presented as a barrier to citizenship rather than an integral part of citizenship. Moreover, the Crick Report provides a rather unhelpful assessment of the link between citizenship and diversity. Given that the report has formed the basis of the citizenship curriculum, such an omission is both stark and problematic.

Many schools are not only ethnically diverse but also have a proportion of refugees and asylum seekers who have come from challenging backgrounds. The fear of difference can be one of the greatest obstacles to learning in the classroom and therefore it is critical that educators facilitate activities that celebrate difference. Research that I have undertaken highlights the dangers of addressing issues relating to different cultures in a tokenistic way. Furthermore, Carrington and Short (1997) have also argued that simply passing on knowledge about different cultures or religions does not necessarily mean that students will think positively about those cultures and religions. Rather, this may serve to merely reinforce the sense of 'otherness'. They suggest that cultural variations need to be taught in a way that demonstrates that there is no challenge to social cohesion. Undoubtedly, this involves illustrating that there is no single model of citizenship. Rather, one must emphasise that there are multiple forms of citizenship and a multitude of ways of expressing active citizenship. Lawson (2001) argues that 'different standpoints thus influence beliefs about which activities carried out by individuals can be characterised by individuals as "active citizenship" and therefore contribute towards the fulfilment of citizenship obligations.'

However, one cannot understate how challenging it can be to address difference in the classroom, let alone embrace difference. My research highlighted an illuminating mix of perspectives on how Citizenship co-ordinators view teaching in a multi-ethnic environment. Co-ordinators all recognised the need for students to be exposed to different cultures, yet in a number of cases Citizenship co-ordinators conceded that there is often limited interaction between students of different communities. Teachers felt that there was a real need to broaden the outlook of students through wider exposure to different communities but they did not always know how to achieve this. Furthermore, one of the teachers suggested that there is an opportunity for Citizenship Education to play a part in strengthening social cohesion and argued for the 'raising of the status and knowledge about the different communities that are living in the country'. He continued:

> And that, in itself, paradoxically, might raise people's belief in being British, if they feel that their culture is accepted and they are accepted as people they might be a bit willing to become part of what is here, because I believe that there is a non-welcoming aspect to how we live in this country, and if you're new from anywhere it is quite difficult and Citizenship should take that into consideration.

Not all respondents, however, accepted the notion of BME-specific needs, and the research interestingly signalled how problematic the term 'equality' is in practice. This in some respects maps onto a longstanding distinction between BME needs for the same treatment as their counterparts in some contexts and a different range of considerations in other contexts. Moreover, there appeared to be a deficiency in the degree of training that teachers have been given on issues relating to equality and diversity. The research highlighted that a number of teachers in the sample believed that adopting the Majorite 'colour-blind' approach to the delivery of education is a way of ensuring equality. That is to say, in a number of cases, teachers believed a universal approach would ensure that all students are treated equally and fairly. One teacher asserted that the suggestion that BME students may have particular needs stands in opposition to the school ethos of equality which recognises all students as having the same learning and teaching needs. The research did not probe into questions about teachers' interpretations of different levels of academic attainment cut along the lines of cultural groupings and how this can be tackled, however this might have been an interesting line of argument to explore. Clearly, these findings are a stark contrast to research that suggests the cultural background and life experiences of children will determine their values and may impact upon their level of engagement in the classroom.

A proportion of the teachers in the sample made the specific point that it was possible to engage all students in the same way and that there was little or no need to distinguish between groups. In fact, the notion of conscious efforts being made in order to engage particular groups of students was seen to be somewhat problematic in some cases.

> I think a lot of it is to do with, in terms of Citizenship point of view, the key to me is once we come to school we are on a level platform and I don't think we should necessarily be starting to do too much focusing on this group and focusing on that group and making it that it's a big issue and big problems with certain groups of people in this area. For me it would be much better to deliver this is how it is.

In the extract above, the respondent begins by commenting that in school all students are on a 'level platform'. If we place this comment in the context of the whole extract, we see that there is a clear suggestion that 'too much focusing on this group and focusing on that group' may distort this level platform, causing inequalities amongst students. Here it is suggested that the conscious effort to engage students from BME groups could potentially cause problems instead of solving them. It is also suggested that in focusing on certain groups, big issues and problems could possibly be created in relation to those groups. The last sentence of this extract additionally suggests that there is a standard way of delivering Citizenship Education and that it is best to deliver it in this way, rather than in a way that attempts to engage different groups. One respondent emphasised that it would not be practical to teach Citizenship Education in a way that takes into account difference; however, they further justified their stance by suggesting that black students who live in white communities are somehow less 'influenced' by their cultural background.

> Talking about our black pupils, they aren't necessarily involved in the black community because they may live not in a 'black' community, because often pupils here . . . often aren't in the communities, they are in a predominantly white area that the black pupils might live in who come into school . . . At school you are limited, you only have a certain amount of time. I would love to start looking at and be able to look at all the differences – this is the issue to do with black pupils, this is the issue to do with Asian pupils and how they perceive their role in this and that. If you started to look at every single thing you would never get anything done, you would be talking about the same topic for months.

In the extract above, this respondent further suggests that conscious efforts to engage particular BME groups are not always necessary; using the example of their own school, this teacher assumes that since most of the black students who attend the school do not live in 'black' areas they do not face the same community-specific issues as other black people who live alongside other black people within a 'black' area. There is a clear assumption here that those students who do not live in 'black' areas are somehow disconnected from their ethnic communities both geographically and physiologically.

This respondent also raises the issue of time and that there is not enough time in the school context to consider differences between groups.

Clearly, addressing differences, rather than simply focusing on the similarities, can only serve to enhance the learning and teaching experience. Furthermore, by bringing to the fore the differences, one must also be open to debates about various forms of expressing citizenship, political participation and civic engagement. If one suggests that there is only one model of civic and political engagement, i.e. in terms of taking part in traditional structures such as elections, political parties, interest groups and so on, one risks alienating students from the very processes that the citizenship agenda seeks to highlight. Unfortunately, the media often highlight recurring debates about proposals in certain circles to teach classes on 'British values', whatever they may be. This is arguably counter-productive and fails to recognise that there does not even exist a unified body of British values that the English, Irish, Scottish and Welsh would all subscribe to in equal measure. The New Labour government have regularly re-ignited debates about British identity and the relentless drive to establish what it means to be British seems by its very nature to be exclusionary rather than inclusive. Once the elusive characteristics of 'Britishness' are identified, this will unquestionably reinforce a sense of 'otherness'. The focus, therefore, should be the nurturing of broader and more fluid notions of nationhood as opposed to constructs that are divisive. The concept of citizenship is heavily contested and therefore the teaching of the subject area can be highly sensitive. However, the aim, clearly, must be to teach students how to think critically rather than what to think (Lawson, 2001).

It is impossible to be flawlessly objective in the teaching process and it is even more unreasonable to assume that all students will gain in the same way from one single class. Some students may relate to the issue being discussed more than others. Therefore, we need to develop mechanisms of teaching subjects such as citizenship that are inclusive and recognise the impact of the cultural context upon the learning experience. The challenge of inclusion clearly goes hand in hand with that of engagement and is a critical part of teaching in a multi-ethnic environment. The Labour government has been keen to tackle what appears to be a faltering social, or community, cohesion, and therefore, ensuring that all students feel engaged with the national curriculum is imperative. However, it has become clear from the research undertaken that some teachers interpret inclusion as being merely the physical presence of students in class, rather than taking into account the degree of engagement. Respondents highlighted an indicator of engagement as being the inclusion of all students or the absence of exclusion. Some teachers assumed that if everyone was included then this was an indicator that all students were being engaged.

Respondents in the research pointed to a number of factors that they perceived to be constituents of inclusion, particularly within the context of BME students. They highlighted aspects that they regarded as being evidence that the Citizenship curriculum or Citizenship Education within the school was inclusive. The most common factor of inclusion related to the easy or open access that students have to Citizenship Education.

> Everyone has equal access, nobody is left out, special needs are taken into consideration so I think it is totally inclusive. There are no special dispensations for anybody and kids do not get left out of things or brought specifically into things.
>
> It's inclusive in that no-one is excluded from them, so everyone is involved in Citizenship, and everyone is involved in tutorial time, and in the mornings.

Clearly, the language of inclusion and, more specifically, exclusion in schools is quite different to the socio-political discourse. Once again, this reveals a worrying lack of training in this area on equality and diversity. It is vital that Citizenship educators develop more complex conceptions of inclusion and inclusive education and that they develop a sufficient sensitivity towards the possible differences between students from differing ethnic communities. Moreover, there is a clear role for Continuing Professional Development in ensuring that educators are competent and confident in the tackling of race and diversity topics within Citizenship, as there is a real danger that students who sense a lack in these areas will become disillusioned.

However, as previously stated, the picture is very mixed and there are interesting examples of how teachers have recognised the importance of different cultural experiences and how that has an impact in the classroom. In such cases there is a drive to nurture an environment where there is equality of voice in the classroom. The research highlighted that teachers recognise that the inclusiveness of Citizenship Education was dependent upon the relevance of the subjects or issues covered and whether or not they related to the everyday lives of students. One respondent related the inclusiveness of Citizenship to the tailoring of Citizenship Education to meet the needs of students. The respondent also suggested that this involves looking at the 'real issues' as opposed to shying away and only focusing on issues that are 'easy to handle'. There was recognition of the importance of students being able to relate to the issues covered in Citizenship Education and the importance of covering issues that affect students' everyday lives. The research showed that one of the specific ways in which lessons were made relevant to students was through the exploration of key dates and events connected to black and minority ethnic communities. These dates and events were both current and historical. One respondent provided the following example:

> I always try and make things as relevant as I can do, so for example, one thing I did last year, when there was the England v Spain match and the awful chanting against Shaun Wright-Philips, we were doing racism at the time so I did a lesson on that and tried to pose some questions to the kids about what did they think should happen there . . . and we have done things in history, and in the history provision when we look at the war effort and the number of black troops that were involved in that. When I've taught history I've tried to do bits about that as well. So always trying to make sure things are relevant, but I'm sure I could do more like everything else.

There is a growing movement in schools to organise citizenship days as part of the curriculum and undoubtedly there is an opportunity to incorporate activities that reflect the wider dimensions of civic engagement and political participation as well as cultural difference. By working with wider community groups, schools have the potential to provide students with invaluable experience in active citizenship. Such activities not only embed Citizenship Education into a schoolwide setting but additionally integrate the curriculum into the community by bringing the issues to life. In this regard, Potter (1999) argues that the syllabus 'links personal development with community benefit', which ultimately reinforces the government's vision of citizenship which is based on mutual obligation. Learning by doing has become an increasingly popular approach in the classroom and therefore the more learning activities that are student-led, the richer the learning experience will be. Through a student-led approach, the students themselves are able to make contributions based on their own experiences. By harnessing the diversity within a class it becomes possible to use personal experiences of BME students as a springboard for further discussion. Moreover, by relating the issues to the life experiences of students, the issues become more relevant to a wider audience and have greater meaning.

THE CENTRALITY OF CPD

As demographic changes take place, teaching methods should adapt. However, Tomlinson (2005) argues that '[t]here have been no educational policies designed to counter a xenophobic nationalism exacerbated after 11 September 2001, which resulted in enhanced hostility towards Muslims and media-fed hostility towards economic migrants and refugees'. She argues that the government has been far from proactive in guiding the relevant agencies towards moulding a curriculum that addresses racism and ignorance. Furthermore, she points out that there is a disconnect between rhetoric and the challenges in the field. She highlights that although the Teacher Training Agency (TTA) issued guidelines in 2000 regarding the need for trainee teachers to 'prepare all students to play a part in a culturally diverse democratic society which values everybody and accords them equal rights', there is minimal guidance on how this can be achieved in practice. Following the Stephen Lawrence Enquiry, the Macpherson Report (1999) also put forward a number of recommendations of changes that should be made to the national curriculum in order to promote cultural diversity and prevent racism; however, once again there was little direction on achieving this aim.

It is clear that unless teachers are provided with adequate and meaningful training, the current situation will not be resolved. In May 2006 the Department for Education and Skills (DfES) established the Diversity and Citizenship Curriculum Review Group, headed by Keith Ajegbo, which signalled a recognition of this key educational axis. The research investigated how diversity is promoted across the curriculum and whether 'Modern British Cultural and Social History' can be embedded into the programme of study. The research emphasised that further guidance is needed in delivering a diverse curriculum and this is an area that is certainly an imperative in terms of Continuing Professional Development (CPD). The review concluded that a great deal more work needs to be done through the curriculum to enable students to understand diversity in Britain and the contribution of ethnic minority communities to British society. Furthermore, the report argues that common citizenship values and collective British identities cannot be promoted without such a foundation being in place.

Citizenship Education is in its formative stages and is one of the most challenging subjects on the curriculum. The Diversity and Citizenship Curriculum Review Group undoubtedly recognises the value of and need to embed learning opportunities relating to diversity throughout the curriculum; however, there is certainly an opportunity for issues to be explored more fully in Citizenship classes specifically. The pressure is certainly on teachers to tackle issues that have not always been addressed explicitly. However, in schools where Citizenship is taught as a stand-alone subject, there is real scope for in-depth debate of challenging topics, which allows students to explore issues and reach their own conclusions.

One of the greatest assets in Citizenship Education is the flexibility that is offered to teachers in interpreting the syllabus. Teachers have the scope to be creative and innovative; however, conversations with trainee teachers suggest that this can be more of a challenge than a gift. Furthermore, in cases where there is lack of institutional support for the subject area, the challenge of innovative teaching is clearly greater. The aim must be to enhance the teaching and learning experience in a way that is mutually beneficial in a classroom setting. Clearly, in assessing the teaching and learning experience, one has to take into account the difference in perceptions of the delivery of Citizenship Education. Perceptions will vary radically between groups such as headteachers, active teachers of citizenship, Heads of Citizenship, students and even parents. Leighton (2004) highlights that 'teachers and students have different views about what they are offering and being offered'. For this reason it is imperative to take into account all groups in order to get a more complete picture of the subject delivery.

The DfES Diversity and Citizenship Report recommended that schools should audit and evaluate the extent to which they teach students issues relating to diversity (Ajegbo *et al.*, 2007) and this is undoubtedly one way of identifying the differing perceptions of provision in addition to highlighting whether and how teaching issues relating to diversity are being embedded throughout the curriculum. By undertaking an audit of diversity provision this will provide an opportunity to initially raise awareness of this key policy area within the school itself, but will ultimately be a springboard for developing new resources and even be a way of identifying and sharing innovative practice.

SUMMARY

There has been a heightened policy focus on the inter-relationship between citizenship, integration and diversity. The government has been keen to explore all approaches to community cohesion and therefore has undertaken reviews of diversity and citizenship, through the lens of identity, 'shared values' and 'Britishness' (Kiwan, 2008). Until recent years, the literature on diversity has not been integrated fully into analyses of Citizenship Education; however, the 2006 DfES-commissioned report examining the overlap of the two spheres has provided a frank, meaningful and timely contribution. Clearly, teachers cannot afford to adopt a one-size-fits-all approach to the teaching of Citizenship and furthermore, issues relating to equality and diversity need to be reinforced throughout the curriculum. Disappointingly, the Crick Report, upon which Citizenship Education was founded, clearly omitted references to tackling racism head-on and presented a very clinical and sanitised view of issues that were deemed relevant. There are suggestions that the omission was necessary for political reasons at the time; however, this only goes partway in justifying such a significant void. Indeed, there is the potential to alienate those who may feel marginalised in society, but the danger is that this can be mistaken for apathy. Citizenship Education promotes a social contract based on rights and responsibilities and mutual respect, and equality needs to be at its very core. There is limited room in the school curriculum to directly address issues of marginalisation and this can clearly have implications and repercussions. Inequality and discrimination along lines of race, gender, age and disability have sadly been an enduring characteristic in all societies. The issues are rarely addressed in a meaningful way in the national curriculum; however, teachers now have the opportunity through Citizenship Education to raise awareness about diversity and to empower students to create positive change. A universal model of citizenship is idealistic; however, a model of citizenship characterised by differentiation is more inclusive and realistic.

Olssen (2004) argues that '[t]o make all peoples, irrespective of ethnicity, gender, sexuality, race, class, or culture, adhere to the same norms or standards of citizenship, is to fail to respect each particular group's own distinctive cultural values, attitudes and practices'.

Difference should not merely be tolerated as this perpetuates the discourse of 'otherness'. Difference should be actively embraced. Johnson and Lollar (2002) highlight that Aristotle believed in a model of democracy that was based on equality among citizens who hold diverse perspectives. That is to say, unity can embody diversity, and furthermore it is more likely to produce a thriving democracy compared to one based on homogeneity.

However, it is unfortunate that diversity has become a term that is overused, particularly in policy-making circles, and it seems to have become one of a long list of buzzwords that can mean anything to anybody. The demographics of society are fluid and constantly changing and it is imperative that the teaching community is empowered and given room to take on board the changes. Newly Qualified Teachers in some ways have greater awareness and energy to adapt their teaching practices and not fall into the trap of using the same methods year after year, but they do not always have the confidence to work with a subject that may seem at first sight to be lacking in a firm structure.

It is clear that ongoing learning can ultimately only take place in an environment that is supportive and prioritises professional development. CPD is imperative in order to raise the quality of delivery of Citizenship Education to the same level as more established subjects. By investing time and resources into CPD, teachers will be better prepared to meet the needs of a diverse body of students and teach in a more inclusive and holistic way. Some may argue that there is a vacuum between the policy process and the practitioner experience in classroom. CPD would help fill this vacuum by raising awareness relating to the context of many of the government's societal and educational concerns. A vast number of educators are highly committed and enthusiastic about teaching Citizenship, but there is also a great deal of inconsistency. Some teachers simply do not feel that they have adequate support from within their schools and the students pick up on this very easily. Clearly, the danger in such cases is that the lack of value being placed on the subject negatively impacts upon the learning and teaching process.

CPD in the area of diversity should not only be aimed at Citizenship educators, but should be seen as an essential part of teaching across the board. If diversity is merely treated as a silo that is confined to the teaching and learning experience in Citizenship Education, then we are failing our students. The needs of a diverse student body can only be met through a sustained and integrated approach that is reinforced across the curriculum. CPD programmes are crucial in that they support teachers by ensuring that the subjects are presented confidently, accurately and in a way that engages all students. CPD will only be effective, in this context, if an overt commitment towards diversity and Citizenship Education is driven forward in a meaningful way from above.

KEY QUESTIONS

1. What is the meaning of 'race'?
2. Are schools currently inclusive communities?
3. Are teachers, in their working lives as teachers, necessarily politically active?

FURTHER READING

Ajegbo, K., Kiwan, D. and Sharma, S. (2007) *Curriculum Review: Diversity and Citizenship*, London: DfES

Osler, A. and Starky, H. (2005) *Changing Citizenship: Democracy and Inclusion in Education*, Maidenhead: Open University Press

Parekh, B. (2000) *Rethinking Multiculturalism*, Basingstoke and London: Macmillan Press

This chapter links with reading 8 of *The Routledge Education Studies Reader.*

DEBATE 2

SHOULD THE LIBERAL STATE SUPPORT RELIGIOUS SCHOOLING?

James C. Conroy and Tony Gallagher

Dr James C. Conroy is Professor of Religious and Philosophical Education and Dean of the Faculty of Education at the University of Glasgow. He has written widely on politics, education and the imagination, the politics and practices of religious schooling and religious education. Dr Tony Gallagher is Professor of Education and Head of School at Queen's University, Belfast where he has conducted research into and written about education in divided societies.

JAMES C. CONROY

Why the liberal state should support religious schooling

In 2002 the Labour government of the United Kingdom passed legislation designed to effect the expansion of faith based schools in England and Wales. The impulse for doing so has, at best, appeared somewhat transitory and ephemeral as the same government, albeit under somewhat different leadership, has begun the process of reversing a policy which, on the face of things, seemed somewhat odd. Why might it be suggested that such a policy was or appeared to be somewhat odd? Despite the privileged position afforded the established (Anglican) Church, Britain is generally deemed to be a secular liberal polity where religion plays only a peripheral part in the day to day deliberations of both public political and individual personal life. The 2000 Survey of European Values indicated that while 41.6 per cent (valid percentage) of those surveyed (n=1000) considered themselves to be religious, a significantly larger group (53.4 per cent) thought of themselves as not religious, with a further 5.1 per cent declaring themselves convinced atheists. Interestingly these figures show a marked decline on the comparable statistics for 1990 (European Values Study 2009) where 56.1 per cent (valid percentage) declared themselves to be religious, and only 39.3 per cent not religious and 4.5 per cent avowed atheist (http://www.jdsurvey.net/bdasepjds/QuestionMarginals.jsp, accessed 23 February 2009). Against such a background it would appear to be remarkable that any liberal democratic government, reliant on voter approval, would adopt a course of action which, prima facie at least, appeared to be so at odds with the general timbre of the time. It is of course precisely to these sorts of statistics that opponents of religious schooling have recourse in declaring religious schooling to be injurious to a secular liberal democracy. How can we seriously countenance the public (governmental) support for schools whose agency would appear to be at best of no consequence, and at worst inimical to the interests of the population at large? Presumably it is on something like these grounds that a concerted and orchestrated opposition has grown up, organised by, among others, the British Humanist Society. This opposition has been underpinned by a number of normative considerations articulated by philosophers and popular pundits such as Anthony Grayling and Polly Toynbee. Such normative objections have tended to rest upon a particular conception of social inclusion, which, it is argued, is furthered by the project of common schooling and undermined by provision for separate schooling. They have also been grounded in claims about the need to cultivate student autonomy. Recently a group of humanist philosophers have argued that

1. In a free and open society, beliefs about fundamental religious and value commitments should be adopted autonomously and voluntarily.
2. Neither parents nor faith communities have a right to call upon the state to help them inculcate their particular religious beliefs in their children, nor further their own projects, customs or values through their children.
3. In a pluralist, multi-cultural society, the state must promote the tolerance and recognition of different values, religious beliefs and non-religious beliefs.

(British Humanist Association 2009)

In the course of this exchange I have no doubt that my interlocutor, Tony Gallagher, and I will both come back to address, in rather more detail, the issues raised by these claims to principle. Before doing so it might be helpful to delineate some particular empirically and normatively grounded reasons why the liberal state might wish to support religious schooling. Firstly, it might be something of a mistake to assume, as many sociologists of religion (Bruce 2002) do, that the statistics from surveys and studies of religious attachment are all that they seem. While it is undoubtedly the case that religious attachment has diminished over the decades since the end of the Second World War this refers largely to active institutional attachment. The dearth of such affiliation does not necessarily imply that people no longer see themselves as religious nor that they are antipathetic to religious expression and the institutions that embody such expressions. A rather different set of figures emerges from the 2001 UK Census than from the European Values survey (which, after all is a rather more truncated snapshot than a national survey) whereby a much higher pattern of religious self-declaration endures, with 76 per cent of the population self identifying as belonging to a major religious tradition. Given that the figure in 1975 was 78 per cent the decline is modest indeed. The figure in the 2001 Census for those claiming to have no religion was 15.56 per cent and there has been little shift since then (see Brierly 2004). It is remarkable that the decline is so marginal given how much is made of the claims to secularisation. Of course it is reasonable to argue that religious attachment in the 2001 Census is not the same thing as religious attachment in the 1950s or 1960s or 1970s and that religious practice as a marker of attachment has declined much more substantially. Indeed as Voas (2006) argues, the framing of the questions may have much to do with the wide gap between the very high level of Christian affiliation in England and Wales, which produced a very different result from Scotland. Nevertheless if part of the argument against the continuation of support for religious schools is that they no longer reflect the landscape of religious facts then some of these statistics should at least give us pause for reflection.

Much is made of the notion that religious schools are an anachronism in a late industrial liberal democracy but let us suppose, for the sake of argument, that a majority of the population are in favour of state support for religious schools – would this be a ground for continuing such state funding? Or, if this appears to be too big a leap we might adopt a rather more modest claim, 'what should we do if the majority of the population are either in favour of state support for such schools or have no opinion either way?' Can we justify such support on the basis of majority opinion? This is of course a difficult question but liberal democratic governments, especially in an age of hyper-mass communication, are often acutely responsive to public opinion. How then are they to decide in which matters they will act on public opinion and in which they will ignore such opinion, opting instead for a principled course of action, which is deemed to be in the larger public interest? The answer may lie in the very slippery notion of 'judgement'. Politicians are elected on the basis that they will bring to bear their capacity to make 'wise' judgements but it is perfectly clear that politicians often come to very different judgements from each other, even from colleagues in their own party, and indeed from what the population in general might deem to be axiomatically in the public interest. Moreover, politicians' judgements about the particular value of a given social institution such as schooling are often determined by a range of factors including their particular ideological attachments. They are also, at least in part, conditioned by their biography. Perhaps even more significantly, political attitudes to the funding of state schools are not infrequently shaped by the particularities and peculiarities of context. So it is that in the three political jurisdictions of the United Kingdom quite different political and public attitudes have prevailed. In England and Wales there was, until the government revisited faith-based schooling, little enough discussion whereas in Northern Ireland and Scotland there has been rather more angst. In the case of England and Wales such schools are deemed to offer both educational and social advantages but in Northern Ireland and Scotland these advantages are often deemed less important than the disadvantages of appearing to undermine social cohesion or indeed becoming a source of social conflict.

Now it is often argued that the good of the state as representative of the people as a whole, must take precedence over the desires and wishes of the sub-group or individual when determining such matters as the permissibility or desirability of faith schooling. However, as I have suggested above, such decisions are hardly straightforwardly objective but emerge out of a complex range of social and personal interests and dispositions. It is for this reason that it is not at all clear that the state should be the sole determinant of the availability of particular forms of schooling. If there is ambiguity in the state's actual capability to determine such matters according to a single coherent set of principles then surely it is not unreasonable that the state should at the very least be open to the possibility that other voices might be appropriately reflected in running and organising schools.

Given some of the difficulties with the mainstream political voice we might want to ask who these other voices might be. Certainly a significant voice has to be that of the parents. After all, parents have bonds of affiliation and affection, and obligations of concern for the welfare and well-being of the child that have, in important respects, primacy over those of the State. If, for example, a parent wishes to educate their child in a manner which they believe to be most conducive to their child's flourishing then surely they should be enabled and facilitated in doing so. If that entails educating them in a particular intellectual/practical tradition, for example, in a City Technology College, then we might suggest that is a reasonable thing to do. If my daughter displays particular musical abilities, which I think are in her interests, might I not wish to send her to a specialist school? Or again, if I want to retain my linguistic and cultural heritage in Scotland, might it not be desirable to send my child to a Gaelic school?

Indeed, this last example is particularly interesting given that Gaelic schools in Scotland have been created and nurtured to preserve and revivify a part of Scottish history and identity that has been marginalised and peripheral to everyday life. Gaelic language and culture has, until more recent revivals, been assigned a marginal (largely kitsch) role in Scottish mainstream identity. What is the difference between a linguistic culture and a religious culture given that both shape particular groups in their particularity and distinctiveness? Gaelic was itself subject to the erasing forces of a more generalised UK (dominant lowland Scottish) culture in the eighteenth and nineteenth centuries. This leads us to ask whether or not its state-sponsored resurgence undermines the unity of the United Kingdom, since it is funded precisely to assert the distinctive constitutive belief systems of Scots. On such grounds it might be argued that these schools should not be state supported. Such a view would certainly not be acceptable to the wide range of politicians, academics and commentators (see Conroy 2004, 2008) who are eager to challenge the claim that the state should support faith-based schools. If the issue is that schools should unite rather than divide then those opposed to faith schools need to be more consistent. It is unreasonable to support some forms of educational division and discrimination on the grounds that they happen to accord with one's particular interests or dispositions and oppose others on the grounds that they do not fit one's prejudices and predilections.

So it is that, in this opening section, I have demonstrated that the argument in favour of state-supported faith schools is not about numbers but about the locus of care and responsibility. Moreover, I have suggested that the state is not self-evidently consistent and coherent in its claims and legislative imperatives. The liberal state needs to provide for a variety of interest groups and, unless it itself is to be charged with unjustifiable discrimination, then it cannot pick and choose arbitrarily between these. Consistency in a liberal democracy requires that we treat different constituencies similarly unless there are clear relevant grounds for not doing so.

TONY GALLAGHER

Why the liberal state should discourage separate religious schools

Galston (2003) makes a useful distinction between theocratic states, in which a specific religion is part of the state apparatus; civic republic states, in which the involvement of denominational interests in public institutions is specifically, and often aggressively, opposed by the state; and liberal democratic states. For the present purposes the main interest lies in examples of the third type, if only because it is in these examples that the question of religious schools remains open. It should also be noted that no liberal democratic state that I am aware of specifically bans religious schools. Rather, the attitude of the state towards religious schools is based on varying degrees of tolerance. The most tolerant approach is not only to permit religious schools, but to provide full public funding of these schools once they have met some defined viability criteria (which themselves might be more or less restrictive). The least tolerant approach is to permit religious schools, but to deny them access to any public funds so that they are entirely private institutions funded by fees or other external income. In practice many liberal democratic states operate within these boundaries of these polarities and provide partial public funding of religious schools.

The legal basis for this is provided by the conditions established by various human rights conventions and standards. Thus, for example, Article 2 of the First Protocol of the European Convention on Human Rights states that:

> No person shall be denied the right to education. In the exercise of any functions which it assumes in relation to education and to teaching, the State shall respect the right of parents to ensure such education and teaching in conformity with their own religions and philosophical convictions.

Under this article it is legal for denominational interests to establish their own schools alongside state-run systems; it is also permissible for states to set viability criteria which denominational schools must meet before they are entitled to receive any public funds; and it is permissible for states to provide partial funding for denominational schools and thereby require the denominational interest to part-fund the schools in recognition of the distinctiveness of the school's offering. All this has been established by the European Court of Human Rights (see Neill *versus* United Kingdom (Cormack *et al.* 1991)).

Thus, the question here is not whether religious schools should be permitted or not. Rather, the key questions are whether states should use their power to set viability criteria and provide whole or partial funding in ways which encourages or discourages separate religious schools. I want to argue that the default condition should be to discourage separate religious schools.

A core principle in the development of mass education was to encourage a stronger sense of commonality within a community and promote social integration. In many places the original predominant model was based on assimilationist principles in which a common cultural identity was assumed and these values were inculcated through schools. Over time there has been an increased recognition of the reality of diversity, so a key priority for public policy for schools is the achievement of a balance between the importance of social integration, and the recognition of diversity within society. In practice the balance of priority varies across countries, with some placing higher priority on promoting aspects of a common identity or citizenship, while others seek to promote social harmony by permitting, even encouraging, diversity. Obviously this has implications for state policy towards separate religious schools: the former position might lead a state to discourage separate schools and address societal diversity within schools, while the latter approach may favour public funding of separate religious schools. Thus, one way to assess the impact of either strategy might be to examine the outcomes for states at either end of this continuum to see if this provides any insight into the consequences of approaches based on commonality or diversity respectively.

Two such contrasting cases can, in fact, be found in the United States and the Netherlands. The United States constitution disallows the state from endowing any denominational interest, while at the same time permitting virtually unrestrained freedom of religion. The consequence for US Public Schools is that they are avowedly secular institutions in which people sometimes go to what appears to be absurd lengths not to privilege specific denominational symbols. More specifically, this also means that while denominational interests can and do establish private schools, those schools have to rely on fee income for their survival and do not receive public funding. Indeed, the major educational debate in the USA over the allocation of vouchers to parents was controversial not only because it involved the marketisation of school choice, but also because it could lead to the diversion of funds from public schools to denominational schools if the former were deemed to be 'failing' and parents opted to use their vouchers to subsidise the cost of fees in denominational schools. A key aspect of this debate has revolved around the preservation of the integrationist role of the common school (Berube 1994; Postman 1996; Goodlad 1997).

At the other end of the continuum lies the Netherlands, where the Constitution of 1848 established the right of private organisations to found schools. The historical basis for this is linked to the withdrawal of Belgium from the Kingdom of the Netherlands in 1839, a split which left the Netherlands as a religiously plural, but linguistically homogeneous, society. Further divisions within the Protestant community, and the link between religion and politics, meant that all communities were minorities, and none could realistically aspire to majority status.

The political compromises created by this situation led to the model of 'pillarisation' whereby each community could aspire to establish its own distinctive social services and networks. For the Catholic community, for example, this included at one point separate schools, hospitals, newspapers, universities, trade unions and employers' organisations (Walford 1995: 250). Segmentation at the mass level allied to co-operation at the elite level provided a model of consociational democracy that, according to Lijphart (1975), provided the basis for stability in the Netherlands and, it has been suggested, other divided societies.

This means that while state schools are founded and managed by the local authorities, groups of citizens can found a school based on particular orientations including 'religious beliefs, ideological principles or educational views'. In addition, schools are free in their choice of teaching materials and the appointment of teaching staff, thereby allowing them to give tangible form to their own identity. The Ministry of Education, Culture and Science does not prescribe – or produce – specific teaching materials, but does however prescribe the ultimate educational level which has to be attained, although the way in which pupils achieve that level is left to the schools themselves. The Inspectorate maintains minimum standards, and the same salary and pension rules apply to teachers in public and private schools. In addition, all final examinations taken in publicly funded schools are set and supervised by the government which means that diplomas from all schools are equivalent and mobility between them is relatively unproblematic. Beyond these organisational features, however, the model of consociationalism is based on the claim that intergroup harmony can be best maintained by allowing each community to have its own institutions in order to give them confidence that their identity will not be threatened.

What have been the consequences of the different paths followed by these two examples and what might that suggest in relation to the issue of separate religious schools? If the United States is, in Postman's (1996) terms, a social experiment to see if it is possible to make it work, then there have been many moments when the rhetoric of the common good, as embodied in the public schools, has sounded a little thin. Up to 1954 the equality claims of the constitution were seen to be compatible with racial segregation, and while the 1960s saw a rapid period of desegregation, by the fiftieth anniversary of Brown *versus* Board of Education a definite pattern of re-segregation had been established (Gallagher 2007); there remains a vibrant defence of the progressive voice in education (Wells 2009) and the case for the common school (Goodlad *et al.* 2008). Furthermore, the recent election of Barack Obama marked the first time a majority-white society had elected a black president. For all the challenges to the idea of the common school, there would appear to be life in the idea still.

Contrast this with the experience of the Netherlands. For years the consociational model was acclaimed as the 'magic bullet' that transformed a society beset by religious divisions into one of liberal tolerance, to the extent that in the immediate aftermath of democracy in South Africa, the model of pillarisation was offered as a panacea to post-apartheid divisions (Sturm *et al.* 1999). However, the fragility of pillarisation has been laid bare by the apparent inability of Dutch society to cope with an extension of religious diversity and the growth of an Islamic minority. The Netherlands witnessed the theocratisation of migration and a level of racial and ethnic intolerance which rendered what had widely been perceived as one of the most liberal of European states into the one struggling least successfully to cope with societal and religious diversity (Buruma, 2007; Sniderman and Hagendoorn, 2009).

This is but a brief survey, of only two examples with the wider category of liberal democratic states. Both examples have been subject to change over time and will, no doubt, continue to be so. But both offer contrasting models of how we should engage with difference and on which side of the commonality/difference scale we should tip the balance. The evidence seems to me to point clearly towards the path of common schools, and on that basis I would conclude that liberal democratic states should, on balance, discourage separate religious schools.

JAMES C. CONROY

Response to Tony Gallagher

Gallagher offers a careful analysis of two possible ways to understand the principled relationship between the liberal state and the religiously denominated school. On the one hand the state could encourage religiously denominated schooling as a way of foregrounding the importance of links to the individual's religious or cultural grouping and of valorising the European Convention on Human Rights. On the other it could discourage the existence of such schools given that the principle of self-determination in such matters is considered to be subordinate to that of social cohesion with its claims to the common good. Weighing these two principled positions in the balance he opts for the latter presumably on the grounds that it secures the greater good. Indeed he suggests that a, if not the, key central purpose of modern schooling is the cultivation of social harmony. But is this necessarily the case? Does educating people in common schools mean that social harmony is the likely outcome? Much of his case rests on suggesting that the development of a pillarised society, as was the case in the Netherlands until the 1960s, has not led to sustained social harmony. The evidence for this is that Dutch society, often regarded as an exemplar of liberal tolerance, has come under increased pressure from what Gallagher refers to as the theocratisation (that is that Muslims freely assent to the law of Allah as pre-eminent in their lives) of migration. By this I presume he means that many migrants from Islamic backgrounds have become increasingly conscious of their Islamic background, freely submitting to the law of Allah in their everyday lives, and that this religious affiliation has been or become a proximate cause of social disharmony. There are a few difficulties with this line of argument which I shall discuss below.

Gallagher's analysis of the social purposes of education on the one hand and the Dutch experience of liberal tolerance on the other lack a necessary sense of historical context. Let me take these two instances of historical amnesia separately. In the case of the former, it is true that under the guidance of major figures in the United States, such as Horace Mann (Judge 2002), the late nineteenth/early twentieth-century impulse for universal education was partly derived from the desire to establish nationhood. Equally importantly, however, was the need to create minimal education achievement in order to serve the burgeoning industrial and commercial interests of the time. Choosing which of these imperatives is to be accorded priority is not easy but, since Gallagher opts somewhat arbitrarily for the former, I will opt for the latter. In Britain at least, the key driver for universal elementary education was largely the needs of the economy. Today the economic imperative has become even more strident and one only has to look at a number of contemporary political statements on education, such as 'No Child Left Behind' (United States Government 2004), to appreciate the primacy afforded to the needs of the economy, even in the United States.

The supposed separation of powers in the United States between church and state is often cited as an example of a successful liberal state where people live together in relative harmony as a consequence of common social projects. It is often claimed that one of the sources of this supposed social harmony is the common school. Certainly Gallagher implies that this is the case. He suggests that racial desegregation has been a consequence of the common school and that this vindicates his claim that the state should discourage separate schools. But this is something of a romantic trap given that there is no coherent account of cause and effect. It is not at all clear that the improvement in the economic and social conditions in the drive for equality of African American, Latino/a and other racial groups has been a consequence of the common school. It is just as (or more) likely to have been the offspring of general shifts in beliefs and attitudes precipitated by changes in economic, industrial and communication technologies. More than this it is clear that the life chances of what are often marginalised communities in the United States are enhanced by religious schooling. Indeed, for example, contemporary Catholic schools in a number of inner cities in the United States have disproportionately contributed to the education of disadvantaged communities (Greeley 2002; O'Keefe *et al.* 2004). Surely schools which serve to raise aspiration, hope and possibility for racially or religiously downtrodden and often marginalised groups offer a substantial and important contribution to the kind of social cohesion which Gallagher claims to support unless of course he would wish to suggest that social and economic progress and social cohesion are unrelated. Such a claim would, I think, be unsustainable.

Perhaps more importantly, in the Dutch case cited, Gallagher neglects to consider that from the 1960s onwards the pillarisation of Dutch society gradually disappeared and the only residue might be said to be schooling. However, since pillarisation applied only to two religious communities, Catholics and the Reformed Church, and the availability of schooling of choice is available to any community with sufficient numbers it is unclear what connection is being made. The legendary tolerance of Dutch society may or may not have anything to do with pillarisation but a more likely explanation is the complete dependence of the Dutch economy on trading. The success of a trading nation may well be dependent upon its capacity to 'rub along' with cultures quite different from its own. In other words, the existence of separate religiously denominated schools may have absolutely nothing whatsoever to do with intolerance or indeed with the historic existence of pillarisation. In pointing out that immigrant Islamic communities have been theocratised Gallagher neglects to suggest that this is more likely to have been a consequence of the fraught political relations between Islamic nations and Western post-Christian societies. One can only presume that he cites this example because he believes that it shows that separate schooling is injurious to the task of drawing people together. However, as I have shown, the examples he cites cannot carry the particular burden of establishing that liberal states 'should on balance discourage separate religious schools'. But this may not be the end of the story.

If Gallagher's examples won't do the work he desires what about his general point that separate schools undermine the common social project of bringing people together in a liberal democratic project? This is a much-discussed question (see especially,Haydon and Halstead 2007) in the literature on common schooling. While for Gallagher schooling must be primarily concerned with some form of nation building nowhere in his argument does he articulate the kind of society it is into which pupils are to be inducted. It is perfectly possible to conceive of a society where students are all schooled together in common schools and believe that it is not the kind of society one wished to live in. This may be the case most especially if it is not a society which upholds certain values to which liberal societies are deeply attached including, for example, free speech; the freedom to offer opinions that are unpopular or difficult; and the freedom to lay claim to and act upon certain values not generally held by society as a whole (with certain caveats). Surely Gallagher wishes for more than a society that rests on commonality as its core value. While the kind of liberal consensus around a thin (very limited) set of common values mediated by the state may be desirable for many it is ultimately unsustainable in its own terms. Last year I visited a non-democratic country where everything was neat and ordered, where the streets were clean and the services worked (where they existed) but where there was neither freedom of expression nor any deliberative engagement by the people who were deemed subjects and not citizens. The question I asked myself then as now was, 'would I wish to live in a place where I might eat but not live fully, where I would not be free to believe what I wish and speak my mind?'

The argument for supporting religious schools in a liberal democracy is one based on the desirability, indeed the necessity, of freedom of expression. Religious schools offer or should offer a different analysis of the relationship between persons and the world than the common school. The common school offers what it claims on the tin! – the commonly agreed values of the state. Hence, if the government dictates a particular policy on, say, a particular form of education for economic literacy, the common state school has little option but to enact the policy in its social structures and pedagogical practices. However, a school which lays claim to an alternative view of economic relations, may legitimately defend this since it is not fully required to entirely align all its values to those of the state. This liminal (threshold) position is necessary for the liberal state's health and vitality (Conroy

2004). If schools are as important as Gallagher believes in shaping a common citizenship then surely that must entail the capacity to be different and to express those differences in major social investments such as education and schooling. Citizenship itself, as it has come to be understood in Western liberal democracies, is a child of our historical (and indeed religious) culture. To abandon, or as Scruton (2009) has it, to repudiate this heritage in favour of a pared down notion of commonality is to abandon the very ground of our beliefs. The drift towards doing so has had inescapable consequences for the very project of social commonality desired by its protagonists. As he suggests,

> The culture of repudiation has transmitted itself, through the media and the schools, across the terrain of Western civilization, leaving behind it a sense of emptiness and defeat, a sense that nothing is left to believe in or endorse, save only the freedom to believe.
>
> (Scruton 2009: 2)

The kind of citizenship in which Gallagher would have us invest is so stripped out and reduced that it would be difficult to know what it was we were signing up to that was worthy of such an investment in commonality.

One other problem persists with Gallagher's analysis: nowhere, it would appear, do parents have any say in the education of their children. As active citizens who are as likely as other citizens to pay their taxes are they not entitled, in a liberal democracy, to have their choices about their own children's education supported by the state just so long as those choices are injurious to neither the well-being of the children nor the stability of the State? Parents have certain rights and responsibilities with respect to their children and the liberal state has, in turn, an obligation to support parents in discharging such a combination of rights and responsibilities. While these rights may not be absolute – a parent does not have a right to abuse their child – they are substantial and may offer grounds to challenge a state's desire to discourage separate schooling where such schooling is deemed by the parent to be in the child's interests. Brighouse (2006) construes the justification for state support for parental rights somewhat differently. He argues that, negatively construed, the consequence of separation of church and state in the United States has been to drive parents into making educational choices and engaging in educational practices that lie entirely outwith the purview of the liberal state. The consequence of doing so may be to destabilise and disrupt the very commonality which Gallagher seeks to secure.

Here I have argued that Gallagher's account of the relationship between the state and parents, and between the state and religious communities is inadequate and that this calls into question his claim that the State should discourage the existence and sustainability of separate religious schooling. It is in the liberal state's interest in self-preservation to facilitate a certain amount of *dissensus* within and on the borders of its own existence.

TONY GALLAGHER

Response to James C. Conroy

Jim Conroy offers a number of important arguments in his paper, but seems to think that the main argument against separate religious schools is that religion is less important than it once was, therefore the idea of separate religious schools is an anachronism. To counteract this he suggests that while participation in religious institutions may have declined, there is less evidence that religious belief itself has diminished. Because of this he suggests that the state should continue to take religion seriously. And in the absence of any coherent principle by which a decision can be made in favour or against separate religious schools his general argument seems to be that assent should be the default condition.

The weakness in his argument is that there is, in fact, a clear principled basis on which to discourage separate religious schools, regardless of whether religion is important in society or not. The essential principle is based on the need to promote social cohesion and a sense of a common good across society as a whole. Picking up on one of the cases I used in the original contributions to this discussion, for example, most of the drafters of the US Constitution believed in God, yet nevertheless decided to separate church and state. We were most recently reminded of the principled basis upon which this decision was made by Barack Obama in his manifesto *The Audacity of Hope*:

> Jefferson and Madison in particular argued for what Jefferson called a "wall of separation" between church and state, as a means of protecting individual liberty in religious belief and practice, guarding the state against sectarian strife, and defending organized religion against the state's encroachment or undue influence.
>
> (Obama 2008: 217)

Conroy goes on to suggest that politicians are inconsistent in their views on separate schools, with some supporting particular types of separation, while at the same time opposing separate religious schools. To coin a phrase, heaven forfend that I deny the inconsistency, or lack of principle, of politicians. Some politicians, perhaps many, all too readily abandon principle in favour of the prevailing whims of what they believe to be popular opinion. But not all politicians are so promiscuous in their favours, and not all display promiscuity all the time. The examples of separation highlighted by Conroy do not, in fact, serve to strengthen his case.

It is the case that the Labour government under Tony Blair was favourably inclined towards faith schools, although this seemed to be predicated on the claim that faith schools somehow or other seemed to achieve higher added-value in academic outcomes, as compared with their secular peer institutions (Cairns *et al.* 2005). A significant basis for this claim lies in the experience of Catholic schools in the United States where it is claimed they achieve significantly higher performance, at lower cost, than public schools, even with (perhaps especially with) socially disadvantaged pupil profiles (Coleman *et al.* 1982; Bryk *et al.* 1993). Bryk *et al.* (1993) attributed this added-value to social capital effects, although it is possible that it is in fact related to the intake factors, that is motivated parents, rather than school factors. Blair's interest was more related to the supposed performance effects, rather than the value of religious schools per se. To that extent the enthusiasm for faith schools was the latest in a line of imagined 'magic bullets' that would solve the problem of underperformance. The enthusiasm has, of course, since waned and the search for 'magic bullets' has moved onto other terrain.

Conroy's reference to city technology colleges is perhaps more unusual. These were established after the 1988 Education Reform Act in order to provide choice to parents in the newly created educational market, while contributing to two other Conservative targets by encouraging private investment in education while weakening the position of local authorities. The neoliberal basis upon which city technology colleges were created – which assumed that market competition between diverse schools for pupils would ratchet up standards generally – may well have been thoroughly misguided, but a rationale did exist (Walford and Miller 1991) and was based on political ideology rather than educational philosophy. And with the passing of the Conservative government in 1997, so, too, passed the city technology colleges and (some) of the neoliberal market principles upon which they had been based.

His third example may be more apposite, but not as he intended. A decision to permit separate schools where the medium of instruction is through a minority language – the case he cites being Gaelic schools in Scotland – may or may not be problematic, depending on the context within which it is taken. In some contexts it may be seen as the last remaining measure available in an attempt to save a linguistic resource which has a cultural value to the society as a whole: this is clearly the context within which he suggests Gaelic schools should be supported. In other contexts, however, separate linguistic schools may mark a form of separatist assertion which has the effect, whether intended or not, of challenging social cohesion. This is what appears to have happened in Belgium where a seemingly inexorable shift in power away from the central state to the language communities has created a situation where Belgium, as a unified entity, barely exists (Fitzmaurice 1996). Similar processes may be in play in Northern Ireland: the Good Friday/Belfast Agreement which established shared political institutions also included measures supporting the developing of Irish-medium schools. While this might be seen as a laudable recognition of linguistic diversity it adds a futher sectoral division into a school system that is already very divided. Furthermore, in the political talks up to the Agreement it became necessary, as a quid pro quo, to provide official recognition of and support for Ulster-Scots as a distinctive linguistic resource of the Protestant community in Northern Ireland, but this was a decision that seemed to owe more to political trade-offs than anything else and some question whether Ulster-Scots is more than a dialect of English, as opposed to a distinctive language (NicCraith 2003). The point is that once we go down the separatist path then it can quickly lead to a plethora of divisions as more and more claims for separate schools emerge. And the more general point is that social cohesion is the key principle.

When Conroy moves to the specific issue of separate religious schools he nowhere offers any positive reason why a liberal democratic state should encourage separate religious schools; rather most of his arguments are aimed at suggesting why the state should not discourage them: 'Consistency in a liberal democracy requires that we treat different constituencies similarly unless there are clear relevant grounds for not doing so.' But if we were to let Conroy's pragmatism prevail, then, in the light of the previous example of language diversity, we might ask where it would all end. All other things being equal, if one religious community is to be permitted to run its own separate schools, then, why not others? In the British context, for example, if Anglican, Catholic, Methodist or Jewish schools were to be permitted and publicly funded, then why should separate Muslim or Sikh schools or any other variation not have access to exactly the same treatment? It is difficult to believe that, under normal circumstances, such slicing-and-dicing of the schools system would do little more than encourage particularistic identities and affiliation, and create a silo-society in which communities lived their lives separately.

This issue was, in fact, directly addressed by the Swann Report (1985) which had been established to consider reasons for the apparent underachievement of ethnic minority children in Britain. Part of this enquiry examined the case for separate schools, but concluded that the needs and interests of minority communities would be best served by ensuring that all schools reflected pluralism in their curriculum and practice, rather than through the provision of separate schools for separate communities, even though it was recognised that the right to pursue this option did exist in law. The overall philosophy underlying the Swann Report, Education for All, reflected this pluralist ambition.

It is possible to see connections to more recent debates on multiculturalism where the prior privileging of difference is now being questioned by some. Traditional multiculturalists tend to prioritise measures which help preserve cultural autonomy and integrity, but sometimes find themselves giving primacy to groups over individuals (Parekh 2000; Banks 2004a), whereas liberal egalitarians tend to the view that social justice is best achieved through giving primacy to individual rights over the rights of communities (Barry 2001; Kelly 2002). However, even multiculturalists who tend to favour giving primacy to community interests over individual interests accept that there are limits to recognition and that that not all identity claims can or should be accorded a special place in schools (Banks 2004b, c; Gutmann 2004).

The principle of cohesion remains the key, as does the conclusion that, all other things being equal, a liberal-democratic state should seek to discourage the development of separate religious schools, but rather seek to reflect, as far as is practicable, the diversity of society within a set of common schools committed to an inclusive, common good.

CONCLUSION FROM JAMES C. CONROY AND TONY GALLAGHER

In this discussion we have attempted to articulate some of the key arguments in favour of and against the claim that the government should encourage the development of separate religious schools. On one account, the contest is between two important principles of liberal democracy: living together in tolerance and freedom to be different. Gallagher believes that the common bonds of citizenship are made stronger where the presumption is in favour of the common school. Conroy, on the other hand, holds that liberal democracy depends on and therefore must support diversity of opinion and the right to be different. Schools, he wishes to argue are integral to this drive. Neither of us believes that we have exhausted the arguments but have merely opened up a debate with very particular salience at a time where the relationship between religious communities and the liberal state is both fraught and uncertain.

KEY QUESTIONS

1. Should faith schools be supported on the grounds of the right in a democratic society to express one's beliefs?
2. Should faith schools be supported on the grounds that they are wanted by significant numbers of families?
3. Should faith schools be supported in light of data about educational achievement?

FURTHER READING

Cairns, J., Gardner, R. and Lawton, D. (eds) (2005) *Faith schools: consensus or conflict*, London: Routledge

Gutmann, A. (2004) Unity and diversity in democratic multicultural education: creative and destructive tensions, in Banks, J. (ed.) *Diversity and Citizenship Education: global perspectives*, California: Jossey-Bass

Walford, G. (1995) Faith-based grant-maintained schools: selective international policy borrowing from the Netherlands. *Journal of Education Policy*, 10(3), 245–257.

This debate links with readings 4, 11 and 19 of *The Routledge Education Studies Reader.*

CHAPTER 7

VIEWS OF INTELLIGENCE

János Gordon-Győri and Márta Fülöp

The rationale for this chapter is:

- to introduce how the notion of intelligence, as one of the most important constructs of psychology, was scientifically conceptualised and then reconceptualised many times since the seminal work of Francis Galton 150 years ago;
- to introduce some of the most important controversies related to intelligence: the nature/nurture debate; the role of society, family and education in the development of intelligence; and the relationship between intelligence and sex/gender, ethnicity, culture and other factors;
- to present the interrelated nature of intelligence and education.

INTRODUCTION

Intelligence is probably the most successful construct of psychology. Only 150 years after the first pioneer scientists in the field of intelligence (e.g. Galton, 1869), it would be hard to find anybody without at least some idea of what intelligence is. Even children of elementary school age are able to tell *something* about intelligence (whether one person is smarter than another). They are also able to differentiate between people according to their assumed quality of intelligence (Räty & Snellman, 1997).

However, intelligence is also one of the most controversial construals of psychology. The foremost problem with the notion of intelligence is that nobody has been able to define this phenomenon in a scientifically satisfactory way since the middle of the nineteenth century. A great number of definitions have been constructed but experts are still very far from finding any kind of agreement (Sternberg & Detterman, 1986). Another serious problem with the notion of intelligence is that it has always been an ideologically, politically and emotionally overheated concept. Consequently, it has been almost impossible to approach in a pure scientific way.

Since intelligence is a multifaceted phenomenon, it is extremely difficult to grasp. To build it up as a scientific construct, experts should understand and probably agree on at least the following (Demetriou & Papadopoulos, 2004):

- *What is the general nature of intelligence?* What are its basic biological foundations? How do these basic biological elements function and how are they able to function as a stable, cogent, still immensely flexible and adaptive system? How are the brain, mind, intelligence, and thinking interconnected with each other? What are the social foundations of intelligence? How is it socially, culturally constructed? How does it change with time? And how are all these biological and social elements orchestrated with each other?

- *How can we conceptualise the architecture of intelligence?* What are the main elements – abilities, functions and processes – of intelligence? What are its different levels and parts? How do these levels and parts of intelligence interact with each other?
- *What are the developmental aspects of intelligence?* Which ones are universal and which ones are special? What are the social, cultural and individual factors in the development of human intelligence? Is intelligence changeable, malleable? Is education an effective tool for fostering intelligence development?
- *What would be the most effective way of measuring intelligence?* Is intelligence *one entity* that we could measure with a particular type of tool, or do we have to measure all these different aspects of intelligence with different tools?
- *What is the social relevance of intelligence?* Is intelligence – in a Darwinian sense – the biological basis of social selective systems? Does a small difference in intelligence level lead to broad gaps among people in social life? Is it true that smarter people statistically have a better chance to become wealthier and reach higher social status easier than others – and why?

Unfortunately, during the last 100 years nobody has been able to build a comprehensive, scientifically coherent construct of intelligence. There is still a lot of work to do on such a theory. Despite an infinite number of instructive research results, many of which seem to have real scientific explanatory value, the fact is that many results are controversial. Furthermore, all these results are based on a very fragmented and therefore very fragile basis of knowledge of human intelligence.

A CONTEMPORARY DEFINITION OF INTELLIGENCE

There are dozens, if not hundreds, of definitions of intelligence (Sternberg & Detterman, 1986). In their seminal article on the 'state of the art' of the science of human intelligence, Neisser and his colleagues (Neisser *et al.*, 1996: 77) state: 'Individuals differ from each other in their ability to understand complex ideas, to adapt effectively to the environment, to learn from experience, to engage in various forms of reasoning, to overcome obstacles by taking thought'. Although the authors do not state it explicitly, we can interpret this statement as their definition of human intelligence. It states that: a) intelligence is one of the abilities of humans; b) intelligence is a cognitive function; c) intelligence leads to effective adaptation to the environment by understanding (complex ideas), reasoning (various forms), problem solving (obstacles), and learning (from experience); and d) people differ in their intelligence.

A SHORT HISTORY OF VIEWS OF INTELLIGENCE

Francis Galton and the modern approach to intelligence investigation

The very first person who directly focused on intelligence with a scientific approach was Darwin's uncle, Francis Galton (1822–1911). He wanted to unfold the nature of intelligence and its hereditary aspects. Galton measured his participants' reaction time, their perceptual speed and how precisely they reacted to different kinds of stimulus. He assumed the faster a person's reaction time, the faster and more effective were his mental processes, and the faster his mental processes, the more intelligent was the person. He found that mental effectiveness or intelligence is highly hereditary – more intelligent parents have more intelligent children – and he also found that there are only very few exceptionally intelligent geniuses on the top of the intellectual pyramid (Galton, 1869).

Alfred Binet, Theodore Simon and their Intelligence Scale

Some decades later, in 1904, a group of French developmental psychologists was asked by the education department of the French government to develop a method to distinguish weak students who needed special education because of their low level of mental abilities, from those students who were poor achievers because of their adverse environment. Binet (1857–1911), an active member of this group of French experts, became interested in developing a scale to estimate children's intelligence. In 1905, in collaboration with Theodore Simon (1873–1961), he published their tool as a measurement for mental abilities. They put together 30 tasks of increasing complexity. Because their tool had practical goals of educational placement, they invented a simple scale that combined the child's actual chronological age (CA) with the level of intelligence called mental age (MA), i.e. the actual ability to solve problems. Comparing MA with CA gave the child's position relative to their age mates. Somewhat later, in 1912, William Stern started to use mental age as a denominator of actual age and called the score 'intelligence quotient'. In 1916, to get a more 'user-friendly' number, Terman multiplied this quotient by 100, and this is the IQ-score which is so familiar nowadays.

Charles Spearman and General Intelligence or 'g'

In 1904 – interestingly at the same time when Binet and Simon started to develop their measurement – Charles Spearman (1863–1945), an English psychologist, published his paper titled 'General Intelligence, Objectively Determined and Measured' (Spearman, 1904).

Spearman tried to unfold the correlations among intelligence tests. He wanted to understand how consistent a given person's results are on different tests – or from another aspect – how consistent the intelligence tests are with each other. To this end, Spearman invented a statistical method called *factor analysis*. Deeply influenced by Francis Galton's idea on the heredity of intelligence, Spearman used factor analysis to discover that scores of mental ability tests correlate with each other at a high level: i.e., when a person reaches high scores in an intelligence test or in subtest/s, he has a good chance of reaching something similar in another test or subtest. Therefore he believed that a common source of variance accounted for the correlations among all the mental tests and he called this the 'general factor', or 'g'. He argued that people with a higher level of 'g' can be expected to achieve better in intellectual tasks.

Although it is widely believed that 'g' defines a person's general intelligence, it is no more than a quantity derived from statistical operations. 'G' is not equal to a general mean of different tasks in a given intelligence test or in different intelligence tests, but it does represent intelligence in general: a kind of statistical artefact that expresses the correlation among the results of different intelligence tests.

However, he argued that there are also other factors that cover specific abilities in intelligence tests and he called them 's' (specific) factors. Since he used 'g' and 's' factors for explaining the structure of human intelligence, we describe his system as 'two-factor theory'.

The educational aspects of 'g' theory

'G' shows a high correlation with academic school performance and also with the level of a person's yearly income later in life (Gottfredson, 1997). Although 'g' seems to be the most precise single predictor of school performance, it is still not able to explain more than 25 per cent of overall variance (Neisser *et al.*, 1996).

David Wechsler and measuring intelligence in adulthood

Binet's tool did not measure adult intelligence. In 1939 David Wechsler (1896–1981) published the first intelligence test that was explicitly designed for an adult population (Wechsler Adult Intelligence Scale, or WAIS). After the publication of the WAIS, Wechsler extended his scale to create the Wechsler Intelligence Scale for Children, or WISC, for children between six and 16 years of age. (His revised tests are: WAIS-R (standardised in 1981), and WISC-R (standardised in 1974). There are also newer versions of both scales.) The Wechsler scales contain separate sub-scores for verbal and performance IQ – thus being less dependent on overall verbal ability than early versions of the Stanford-Binet scale – and was the first intelligence measurement to base scores on a standardised normal distribution rather than an age-based quotient. Since the publication of the WAIS, almost all intelligence scales have adopted the normal distribution method of scoring, making the term 'intelligence quotient' an inaccurate description of the intelligence measurement. However, 'IQ' is colloquially still used to describe all scores on intelligence scales currently in use.

Louis L. Thurstone and the theory of primary abilities

While European psychologists were influenced by Spearman's g-theory, experts in the United States tended to reject this approach and focus more on specialised mental abilities. Thurstone (1887–1955) challenged Spearman's theory on unitary human intelligence, stating that 'g' was no more than a statistical artifact. Like Spearman, Thurstone also used factor analysis but a different version of it. He found 'g' to be not one single major factor but a set of *primary mental abilities* or cognitive modules (Thurstone, 1938), of which he distinguished seven: word fluency, verbal comprehension, spatial visualisation, number facility, associative memory, reasoning, and perceptual speed (Thurstone, 1957).

However, after several investigations Thurstone realised that he could not explain differences in human intelligence by primary mental abilities in themselves, so he, too, had to introduce general mental factors. The 'double failure' of these two prominent researchers – Spearman having to introduce 's' in addition to 'g' and Thurstone having to introduce 'g' in addition to 's' – shows that intelligence is a very complex, multifaceted phenomenon and is hard to explain or describe with one simple category.

Educational aspects of the primary mental abilities theory

Thurstone's theory had an indirect influence on education. He rejected Spearman's unilateral, entity view of cognitive abilities and stressed the significance of a set of mental abilities. This encouraged teachers to believe that their students' achievement does not depend necessarily on a single unitary quality of the mind, i.e. a kind of inherited mental strength, but on different, quite independent cognitive abilities.

Raymond B. Cattell and John Horn and the theory of fluid and crystallised intelligence

Raymond B. Cattell (1905–1998) and his student John Horn (1928–2006) proposed that 'g' is actually not one single mental entity but a cumulative conglomerate of two broad sets of mental abilities, *fluid* and *crystallised* intelligence (Cattell, 1971). Abstract, non-verbal tests load strongly onto a factor labelled by Cattell and Horn as fluid intelligence factor (*Gf*), while those tests that measure knowledge, language and acquired skills load strongly onto a factor called crystallised intelligence (or *Gc*). Cattell and Horn described Gf and Gc as two really different sets of mental abilities with largely different developmental courses. Gf shows a stronger effect in childhood and adolescence, reaches its peak during young adulthood and then gradually and irresistibly declines (Horn, 1985). In contrast to this, Gc is that part of intelligence that develops gradually during the whole life course.

Cattell and Horn state that fluid intelligence – what refers to general information processing, reasoning abilities, the mental ability to deal with new and unusual problems, working memory, and other cognitive processes that play a major role in Spearman's 'g' – is inherited, while crystallised intelligence is connected to learning, since it refers to knowledge, and information shaped by social environment. However, as it later became clear, the heredity of Gf is not stronger than the heredity of Gc, and Gc is not influenced more by the environmental factors than Gf (Mackintosh, 1998).

One explanation of this may be the fact that crystallised intelligence is the product of fluid intelligence (the correlation between a person's Gf and Gc is .60). In other words, although crystallised intelligence is a result of cultural activities (learning, different life experiences and so on), it is constrained by fluid intelligence, i.e. with a lower level of Gf we have less of a chance to learn from education and other experiences, and the opposite is true for a higher level of Gf (Mackintosh, 1998).

Educational aspects of the Gf/Gc theory

It is very important that Cattell and Horn distinguished Gc as an intelligence that refers to learning experiences and that can develop throughout a person's whole life span. If intelligence is a constantly developing human phenomenon, then it can also be deliberately developed by education. So the Cattell-Horn theory leaves room for educational influence, and establishes a theoretical basis for the notion of life-long learning. This concept is crucially important in modern societies in which life expectancy is growing rapidly and there are more and more elderly people. Despite the fact that our intelligence declines irresistibly after its early peak, the theory of Gc says that not *all* of our intelligence is declining and that a part of it is gradually developing during our whole life. Paul Baltes (1939–2006) a German psychologist conceptualised intelligence as a changing cognitive phenomenon during a person's life span; he stated that wisdom means gaining expertise in the fundamental pragmatics of everyday life (Baltes & Kunzmann, 2003).

Howard Gardner and his theory of multiple intelligence

In the 1980s, a new theory of intelligence was proposed. Howard Gardner in his *Frames of Mind: Theory of Multiple Intelligences* (1983) suggests that intelligence is not one single entity – nor a hierarchical system of abilities – but is rather a composition of seven frames (later, eight or hypothetically more, Gardner, 1999a): linguistic, musical, logical-mathematical, spatial, bodily kinaesthetic, interpersonal, intrapersonal and naturalist intelligence. According to Gardner's theory, these frames are independent of each other in their development and in their functioning. They process different information specific to the given frame and they also operate separately by themselves. According to his explanation, this is why people with severe local brain damage may have serious problems with specific mental tasks while they do not have any achievement problems with other types of tasks. This is also why some autistic children with severe verbal and communication difficulties are still able to play music at the highest artistic level or solve difficult mathematical problems.

Although Gardner's theory offers new approaches to human intelligence and also became very popular among psychologists, educators and everyday people, his multiple intelligence theory is seriously questioned by many experts (Schaler, 2006). One of the most problematic aspects is that he never developed any kind of tool with which we could measure these intelligences. Also, he never explained the way these independent intelligences harmonises with each other in the case of a given mental process, for example during problem solving, nor could he explain whether these 'intelligences' are really cognitive functions or rather important cultural domains related to specific talents.

The impact of Gardner's multiple intelligence theory on education

Gardner's theory had a huge impact on everyday practice in schools (mainly in the United States). There are hundreds of schools which base their teaching programmes or at least a part of their education on Gardner's multiple intelligence theory. The reason is that Gardner himself translated his ideas into the language of education and published many articles and chapters on the relevance of multiple intelligence theory to education (Gardner, 1999b; Gardner & Hatch, 1989). Many educators believe that traditional education is too verbal, abstract, and analytical – what may be effective for some groups of students may not be for many others who have different strengths. Teaching in schools influenced by Gardner's multiple intelligence theory is very colourful, as teachers try to stimulate their students' intelligences with different kinds of tasks. Students in a class can be more sensitive and responsive to different kinds of stimuli, e.g. verbal, numerical, or musical. However, it is frequently mentioned that Gardner's theory does not have any predictive validity for human behaviour or intellectual development, so it is not a good idea to build ambitious educational programmes on it. It is also mentioned that with the multiple intelligence approach, the general academic level of education is decreasing rather than increasing.

Robert Sternberg and the triarchic theory of intelligence

Another contemporary approach in the field of multiple forms of intelligence is R. J. Sternberg's 'triarchic theory of intelligence' (Sternberg, 1985) and successful intelligence (1996). According to triarchic theory, human intelligence is built up from three fundamental aspects of intelligence: componential/analytic, experiential/creative and contextual/practical intelligence. Componential intelligence includes the analytical abilities that enable us to analyse, compare, plan, carry out strategies, acquire knowledge and so on; these are the abilities typically measured by traditional intelligence tests. Experiential intelligence is the ability to use former experiences for discovering new, creative solutions to novel problems. Contextual intelligence involves three types of mental processes that help a person fit into her environment: adaptation to the environment, shaping one's environment and selection of the environment. This practical intelligence enables a person to perform intelligently in her outside world. The knowledge base of this intelligence strongly differs from the knowledge base of componential intelligence, since this so-called *tacit knowledge* is rather non-academic and not directly taught in formal education (it is informal).

Tacit knowledge is relatively independent of scores on traditional intelligence tests, but it is a key element of *successful intelligence* because it significantly correlates with different types of indices of job performance (Sternberg & Wagner, 1986). For a successful life, a person must synchronise his analytical, creative and practical intelligence in an effective way, and has to compensate for his mental weaknesses with his strengths.

John B. Carroll and the three-stratum model of intelligence

Since Galton's first steps in the field, the most remarkable effort to synthesise the many trends in intelligence research was probably made by the American psychologist John B. Carroll (1916–2003). Carroll reanalysed more than 400 research studies on intelligence carried out with more than 100,000 participants. He presented his results in his famous book: *Human Cognitive Abilities: A Survey of Factor Analytic Studies* (1993). Based on this huge amount of data, he proposed a new, hierarchical model of intelligence, called the Three-stratum Model of Human Cognitive Abilities.

In this model he differentiates three strata: the lowest strata contains many task-specific, narrow, contextually bound cognitive abilities, for example reasoning, speed of processing and memory in different specific, scientific or other areas. The second strata contains a set of broad – less specific – cognitive modules that play a crucial role in thinking and problem solving in different broad fields. The third, highest strata is general intelligence, or 'g'.

ENVIRONMENTAL EFFECTS ON INTELLIGENCE AND EDUCATION

Since Galton, *nature vs. nurture* has been an ongoing debate among academicians as well as among politicians and other members of modern societies. Nowadays even the most devoted environmentalists or hereditarians admit that both nature and nurture play an obvious role in the development and functioning of human intelligence and because of their mutual interactions, their impact is complex. However, the *ratio* of their impact is problematic in the assumption that *there is one given 'eternal' number, or one given 'stable' ratio* that would explain the relationship and impact of nature and nurture on human intelligence.

This assumption is evidently false because the relationship between the environment and a given person is in constant change. The impact of the environment on the person can be minimal or can be decisive, and it can be changed in very short periods of time. Also, people differ as to how much the same environment can psychologically influence them. The same environment can be mentally very fascinating for one and totally boring for another. For a child with high abilities in mathematics, a special class organised for mathematically talented children can foster development because s/he is intellectually involved and motivated in learning mathematics. But in the case of another child with the same mathematical abilities, it can have a neutral or harmful effect, simply because this second child – despite his/her abilities in mathematics – is more involved in art, sports or leadership than in solving challenging academic tasks.

The Flynn effect

One of the most remarkable proofs of environmental impact is that intelligence test performance is continuously rising. Although this phenomenon was already noticed and partly described by many psychometricians, it was not systematically investigated before the work of James Flynn (1984, 1987). Because of his major contribution to the understanding of this effect, the phenomenon is now called the 'Flynn effect'.

Because of this steady increase, intelligence tests must be periodically re-standardised. If not, a person who scored 100 points in a test 20 years ago would score approximately 106 nowadays.

Since this evident increase has been present in all industrial and post-industrial societies in the past 75 years, most experts agree that it is a clear result of the developing social environment.

However, there are some doubts too. For example Flynn argues that the fact that intelligence *test scores* are constantly rising, does not mean that *intelligence itself* is also rising. He states that it could be a cumulative effect since people are more and more familiar with these kinds of mental tests (Mackintosh, 1998).

The correlation between a person's social class of origin and his/her IQ

It may be surprising that there is only a modest correlation between parental socio-economic status (SES) and children's IQ. In his meta-analysis of a large number of American studies, White (1982) found a correlation of only 0.33. In another meta-analysis, Bouchard and Segal (1985) also could not find a correlation stronger than 0.28. Generally we can state that the correlation between parental SES and their children's IQ is statistically not stronger than 0.30–0.35. White (1982) and Caldwell and Bradley (1978) however suggest that family atmosphere, family interactions as mediators of culture and the parents' positive response to their children's (intellectual) needs are better indicators of children's IQ than SES by itself. This means that personal communication and emotional elements of the environment might have as important an impact on children's intellectual development as their social circumstances, if not more so.

Family

Home environment

Although we do know that the lack of a minimum level of attention in a family toward a child can cause a severe deficit in the child's intellectual development, we cannot be sure if a supportive family environment has a real additional value on the children's intellectual development. A correlation was found with the richness of intellectual resources at home (e.g. Gottfried, 1984) and the parents' use of language (Bernstein, 1971; Hart & Risley, 1992) but we do not have enough evidence to decide whether this is only a correlation or a causal relationship. For example, genetic background can be a mediator between family influence and intelligence development of children. Much contemporary research on the development of siblings, twins and adopted children shows that the influence of family environment on intelligence development decreases with the age of the child (Mackintosh, 1998).

Family size and birth order

Later born siblings statistically tend to have lower level of IQ than earlier born siblings (Mackintosh, 1998). Zajonc's 'confluence model' (Zajonc, 1983) implies that the more time a parent spends with a child – the more (intellectual) attention s/he pays to the child – the higher the child's IQ. Zajonc also states that elder siblings are themselves intellectually stimulated by regularly teaching younger ones. Also it is well known that the average IQ level of a family is lower with more children than with one or two (Belmont & Marolla, 1973).

However, with some exceptions (mainly in some religious communities), there is a strong correlation between the number of the children in a family and the economical status of the family; all over the industrialised world there are more children in families with lower SES. In these families there is a higher chance of having children with lower IQs, not because of any kind of genetic reason, but because the parents cannot provide as rich and stimulating an environment for their children as parents in middle class families.

Parental behaviour

The intellectually stimulating attitude and behaviour of parents correlate with their children's IQ more than factors like parental income (Mackintosh, 1998). Although it could be taken for granted that stimulating parents have a beneficial effect on their children's intellectual development, a different explanation is also possible: the more intelligent – curious, open-minded – a child is, the more stimulating his/her effect on the adults. As a consequence, this triggers a more inspiring intellectual reaction in the social environment. Without taking the contribution of genes into consideration, it would be hard to explain intellectual development and individual differences (Scarr, 1997).

Education

There is a strong correlation between education and intelligence. Although intelligence tests are the best predictors of school success, there are many other very important factors – for example motivation, interest, persistence, etc. – that play determining factors in school achievement. It is therefore important for teachers to pay attention not only to their students' intellectual development but also to the development of their personalities.

Intelligence and the length of education

People with a higher level of intelligence spend more time in education than those with lower levels of IQ. In the United States this correlation is .55, which means that intelligence is responsible for about 30 per cent of the variance that may influence the total length of education (Neisser *et al.*, 1996). However, social factors are also decisive. For example a given student's social background, the family SES and the parents' values, and their visions of the child's future also play a determining role in the decision to pursue higher education. Still, intelligence is the strongest *single* predictor of school achievement.

Formal schooling and intelligence development

One of the main tasks of education is to foster children's development of intelligence. It is not easy to confirm whether education is able to fulfil this task effectively or not. However, some cases show – e.g. during a war – that in the long run children's IQ decreases without education (Mackintosh, 1998). Also, there is evidence that with education children gain some intelligence points. For example Ceci's (1990) meta analysis shows that one year of education counts in intelligence development: one year in age difference clearly counts, but one year of educational difference counts much more (mainly in verbal abilities).

Early compensatory education and direct intervention for developing children's intelligence

Growing up in a deprived environment is a special problem from the aspect of intelligence development. The ratio between the effects of nature and nurture differs in disadvantaged and advantaged families. Turkheimer and his colleagues (2003) found that environmental factors have determinative – constraining – effects on children's intelligence development in families with lower SES, while inherited intelligence has a much bigger chance to manifest itself in a family with better SES.

In the last decades a large number of educational programmes were designed to compensate for this 'unjust' and continuous fallback of students with impoverished family backgrounds and to foster their intelligence development. These programmes typically focus on enhancing children's intelligence before and during their early years of education. Although many of these short- and long-term pre-school or early-education programmes, like Head Start in the USA or Sure Start in the UK, were and are very promising, they have had rather short-term positive effects on children's intelligence development. Those children with a deprived family environment who took part in an effective pre-school compensatory education programme and gained some extra points in their intelligence, statistically lost all or a large part of their gains by the age of 12 to 14. Their results were similar to children with similar family backgrounds but without pre-educational compensatory programmes (Neisser *et al.*, 1996; Zigler & Muenchow, 1992). It seems that the

> lesson to be learned from these programmes is that long periods of cultural and educational deprivation cannot be cancelled by short term intervention programmes, however well they are designed. Thus, boosting the intelligence of underprivileged populations requires permanently enriching their cultural and educational environment rather than trying to compensate for deprivation.
>
> (Demetriou & Papadopoulos, 2004: 459)

Self-theories on the modifiable nature of intelligence

The development of intelligence is not isolated from self-fulfilling ideological factors. If a student or his teacher believes that intelligence is not malleable at all, they will tend to relate to intelligence development with a kind of fatalism or learned helplessness (Seligman, 1975). For example Carol Dweck (2002, 2006) has proven that self-theories of intellectual achievement have a strong impact on actual academic achievement.

GROUP CHARACTERISTICS OF INTELLIGENCE

Although intelligence is strictly an individual human trait, both lay people and experts have always been interested in its hypothetical 'collective' levels. A group of people cannot possess anything like 'intelligence'; still, people have always wanted to determine the 'intelligence' of a group of people. Two kinds of 'group aspects' of intelligence, sex and ethnic differences, will be introduced in this section, but it has to be kept in mind that '[t]he reasons for IQ differences between groups may be markedly different from the reasons for why individuals differ among themselves within any particular group (whites or blacks or Asians)' (Gottfredson, 1994).

Sex differences

Sex differences in general intelligence

There are hundreds of research studies on sex differences or similarities in general intelligence. And as could be expected, they are controversial. Probably the most relevant research, carried out with the Raven Matrices (the more frequently used non-verbal test) in Britain and Ireland, shows no differences in general intelligence between the sexes (Mackintosh, 1998). Others – like the revisited Wechsler tests (WISC-R and WAIS-R) – show at least slight differences (Mackintosh, 1998). Some experts like Lynn (1994) state that there is approximately a five-point difference in

IQ-tests favouring males. His explanation is that men's brain size is comparatively bigger than women's. But as Mackintosh (1998) warns, his argument is very weak and full of scientific misunderstandings.

Sex differences in specific parts of intelligence

It is widely known that women generally have better verbal abilities than men, while men are statistically better in solving spatial-transforming or mental rotation type of problems. However, results of verbal ability tests are very controversial, showing some advantage in females, for example in naming tasks (Gordon & Lee, 1986). Visio-spatial tests seem to be more consistent in their results: men statistically outscore women in this field. Also, after puberty, math scores and scores on mechanical reasoning tasks show substantial advantages in men (Halpern *et al.*, 2007).

Ethnic group differences

Asian Americans

For a long time, many East and South-East Asian countries have excelled in large international comparative educational studies (Gonzales *et al.*, 2008) and, also since World War II, many immigrant students with Asian backgrounds have scored outstanding achievements in the American educational system (National Center for Education Statistics, 2008). We could therefore assume a higher intelligence level among them than among Caucasian Americans. Stevenson and his colleagues (Stevenson, Lee & Stigler, 1986) did not find any pronounced differences among Chinese, Japanese and American students' intelligence in China, in Japan, and the United States respectively, but did find some slight differences among their spatial abilities (in favour of Asians). Spatial abilities play an important role in math learning, so it can be one factor resulting in achievement differences between Asian(-American) and American students. However, when the school achievement of the Asian-American and Anglo-American students with the same level of intelligence is compared, Asian Americans' school achievement is statistically better. So we can assume that cultural factors – like motivation, fulfilling social obligations, spending more time in non-formal out-of-school education, etc. – play at least as important a role in the achievement differences as intelligence differences. As Mackintosh states: 'IQ is not the only predictor of educational and occupational attainment. Hard work, diligence, and ambition may be equally important ingredients of success' (Mackintosh, 1998: 168).

African Americans

Probably the more frequently mentioned ethnic difference in the United States is the fact that the black population's IQ score is statistically 10 to 15 points lower than that of the white population (Thorndike, Hagen & Stattler, 1986; mentioned by Neisser *et al.*, 1996). There are three typical explanations for this fact: the hereditarian explanation which ascribes these differences to inherited genes; the environmental argument, that this difference goes back to the different social backgrounds of the two populations; and last but not least, the statement that the difference may emerge from test biases (Jensen, 1980). Despite the widely prevalent lay and sometimes also (biased) professional explanation, which says that this black/white IQ-difference may come from some genetic factors, *there is no reasonable research which could ever prove this explanation* (Mackintosh, 1998).

Jewish people

In a recent study Lynn and Longley (2006) summarised the results of the most relevant studies on the Jewish population's intelligence in the United States and in Britain. According to their analysis, Jewish people have a mean IQ of approximately 109–110, higher than the white gentiles' average in the two countries. They also found that in relation to their population, scientists and artists with a Jewish background are overrepresented in the Royal Society in Britain and among Nobel prize-winners in both societies. They state that this can be partly explained by the higher average of the IQ among the Jewish population; however 'partly' means here that there is also a very complex set of other – social and environmental – factors behind these results.

CULTURE AND INTELLIGENCE

For a long time intelligence seemed to be a universal concept: the same phenomenon – only possessed to a different degree by everybody. However, Alexander Luria (1902–1977), a Soviet researcher in intelligence, was very much surprised when some peasant participants from central Asia were incapable of an obvious reasoning that Luria was sure they should have been able to do (Luria, 1976). Luria reasoned the explanation could be that the way his participants were socialised to think about things differed totally from his expectations. Their intelligence was intact but *culturally different*.

Luria's anecdotal story was probably the first sign for the scientists that there is no way to understand such a complex human phenomenon like intelligence meaningfully without understanding its cultural aspects. The conceptualisation, development and assessment of intelligence are all socially/culturally constructed phenomena (Sternberg, 2007).

Culture and the conceptualisation of intelligence

Everyday people's concept of 'intelligence' and their idea of an 'intelligent person' – what Robert Sternberg labels the implicit theories of intelligence (Sternberg, 2007) – can be constructed in very different ways in different cultures (Sternberg & Kaufman, 1998), since in different cultures different aspects of intelligence are considered important and meaningful. For example, while Western cultures emphasise the value of mental speed, other cultures rather prefer depth of reasoning (Sternberg *et al*., 1981). While for Western people intelligence is only a kind of mental ability built up of different functions of cognition like recognising, comprehending and the similar, in the East it also includes determination, mental effort and even feeling (Das, 1994).

Culture and the development of intelligence

Naturally, parents and educational institutions all over the world try to develop their children's intelligence as effectively as they can. However, as we have already seen, the concepts of intelligence and the intelligent person are constructed in culturally different ways in different human communities. Also children try to develop contextually relevant cognitive skills, according to their own understanding of their cultural contexts.

For example, Western formal education socialises students to be fast in solving intellectually difficult problems and to find unequivocal answers; standardised intelligence tests also prefer quick and unambiguous answers. However, Native Americans rather prefer to give a right than a quick answer to a question. Also, without being absolutely certain in an answer, these children are socialised to say wisely, 'I am not sure.' – an answer that would be hardly rewarded by any intelligence test constructed by Western scientists (Sinha, 1983; Triandis, 1989).

Culture and the assessment of intelligence

One of the main discussions about measuring intelligence is whether intelligence tests are culturally fair or not, or whether it is possible to measure intelligence in a culture-fair way.

As a result of many scientific investigations carried out in the last decades, we now know that it is impossible to construct culture-fair measuring or testing of intelligence. The reason is partly the fact that in some ways all intelligence tests measure at least some kinds of knowledge; and knowledge is culturally constructed, culturally bound. For example any kind of verbal testing has serious difficulties from the perspective of culture. Verbal reasoning, story telling and similar tasks are deeply culturally contextualised. For example, although Harkness and Super (2008) tried to carry out some simple storytelling tasks with intellectually intact three- and six-year-old Kipsigis (Kenyan) tribe children, the participants did surprisingly poorly: only 10 per cent of the three-year-olds and less than 50 per cent of ten-year-olds could repeat *any portion* of a story of ten sentences about a boy who got a stick to herd his family's cows. As it was revealed by the research, there were several cultural factors behind this poor result. For example, the testing situation itself, i.e. a white adult asking black children, was so strange for Kenyan children that Harkness and Super concluded the best 'testers for traditional African children might be other [African] children' (Harkness & Super, 2008: 185).

For a long time non-verbal, strictly visual-abstract tests like Raven Matrices were believed to be culturally fair tests – meaning the same for anybody all over the world, equally solvable by anybody independent of the participant's culture. Although the Raven Matrices does not try to investigate any kind of cultural knowledge directly, it is also a culturally biased test in a more subtle way. These kinds of abstract visual reasoning tasks are easier to solve for children familiar with visual tasks (i.e. they are used to solving this type of task in school) than for children who have never come across similar tasks. As Sternberg summarises: 'all tests of intelligence require knowledge, even if it is only knowing how to take the tests and to maximize one's score on them' (Sternberg, 2007: 557). Because of this, Sternberg suggests the development of a new generation of intelligence tests which are culture-relevant, instead of trying to develop culture-fair tests – which is impossible.

SUMMARY

The concept of intelligence has been defined and redefined many times in its 150-year history, and it is important to understand the issues at stake within each way of measuring and defining it. The five basic questions that each theory should address are:

- What is the general nature of intelligence?
- How can we conceptualise the architecture of intelligence?
- What are the developmental aspects of intelligence?
- What would be the most effective way of measuring intelligence?
- What is the social relevance of intelligence?

This chapter took a short tour of the history of views of intelligence, and how each view affects the way we approach education, from the initial attempts to measure it by Francis Galton, to the birth of the IQ-score and its modifications, to John B. Carroll's attempt at some form of synthesis of concepts in his model of a three-stratum intelligence. Each theory approached the effects of the environment on intelligence in a different way. These effects can come about in myriad ways, and there have been ongoing controversies as to the importance of each influence, and whether or not it can be modified by education. Various studies have looked at the correlations between a person's intelligence and:

- their family – their home environment, social class, family size and birth order, and their parental behaviour;
- their education – how, for how long, and from how early a person is educated;
- their group – whether and how sex or ethnicity makes a difference;
- their culture – how their own and other cultures assess intelligence, and how this modifies behaviour.

In short, students should now have a guide to the controversies and issues surrounding the concept of intelligence and the various ways this may and should affect their approach to studying education.

KEY QUESTIONS

1. How has intelligence been conceptualised and reconceptualised since the nineteenth century?
2. To what extent is intelligence dependent on physiological or sociological factors?
3. How can those involved in schooling best attempt to develop intelligence?

FURTHER READING

Demetriou, A. & Papadopoulos, T.C. (2004). Human intelligence: From local models to universal theory. In R.J. Sternberg (Ed.), *International handbook of intelligence* (pp. 445–474). Cambridge: Cambridge University Press.

Mackintosh, N.J. (1998). *IQ and human intelligence.* Oxford: Oxford University Press.

Neisser, U.N., Boodoo, G., Bouchard, T.J., Boykin, A.W., Brody, N., Ceci, S.J., Halpern, D.F., Loehlin, J.C., Perloff, R., Sternberg, R.J. & Urbina, S. (1996). Intelligence: Knowns and unknowns. *American Psychologist*, *51*(2), 77–101.

Sternberg, R.J. (2007). Intelligence and culture. In S. Kitayama & D. Cohen (Eds.), *Handbook of cultural psychology* (pp. 547–568). New York: The Guilford Press.

This chapter links with reading 6 of *The Routledge Education Studies Reader.*

CHAPTER 8

HOW DO PEOPLE LEARN?

Des Hewitt

The rationale for this chapter is:

- to enable you to reflect on everyday views of learning in a more systematic way;
- to help you address how our views of the way we learn has changed over the centuries and what the different theories are of how we learn;
- to explain how learning differs between home and school and whether younger and older children learn in the same way;
- to explore why some people are better at learning than others;
- to explore the link between learning and teaching.

INTRODUCTION

Learning is a defining characteristic of human beings. Few people would disagree that learning happens everywhere and all people are capable of learning. Sometimes learning is a pleasurable experience, but it can also be dull and dire. Whilst we may all have had such experiences, we may not have reflected on what is actually involved in learning and the process by which we learn. A whole book on this area alone would not do justice to the complexity of the subject. Learning is complex and problematic. Despite all the research into learning, there is still much which we do not fully understand. The rationale for this chapter will be reviewed and explained in the context of wider theoretical accounts of learning in the following sections:

Traditions and models of learning

- learning through the ages;
- learning theory;
- constructivism and information processing;
- self-regulated learning;
- neuro-sciences.

Learning in different contexts

- early years learning;
- school learning.

TRADITIONS AND MODELS OF LEARNING

Learning through the ages

It is fascinating to compare learning and views about learning through the ages. For instance, in Ancient Greece, there was a system of formal education; but this was generally only available to boys and men. Reading and writing skills were widespread, but the oral tradition for learning was dominant. Teachers were generally despised and boys had to be accompanied to their place of learning by a slave, so as to provide moral protection from the undue influence of their teacher.

Boys started school at seven years of age. Their education was divided into literature, physical education and music. Learning about knowledge and moral development were seen as being intertwined; and poetry was seen as an important vehicle for moral development. Whilst prose authors were not studied; rhetoric (the art of argument) was seen as an important skill. It is interesting to compare views of the 'Sophists' and Socrates, one of the important teachers/ philosophers of the time:

> They (the Sophists) profess knowledge of all sorts, he (Socrates) professes ignorance; they parade skills in public speaking; he can only ask questions, and rejects the prepared answer; they offer to teach, to make men better, he merely offers to confirm man's ignorance; they charge high fees, his teaching is free.
>
> (Boardman, Griffin & Murray 1986: 229)

From the distance of the twenty-first century, you might be forgiven for questioning the relevance of the Ancient Greek education to how we learn now. Whilst the Sophists made a virtue of learning forms of argument, Socrates employed a method of approaching learning as a dialogue in which the teacher, through carefully crafted questions, helped the learner towards greater understanding. These approaches to learning have their twenty-first century equivalents. Learning by heart (rote learning) can be seen in the way children learn to recite their 'times tables'. Alexander (2005) talks about dialogic teaching as a way of promoting greater understanding in learners: this mirrors Socrates' approach. Teacher questions are seen as an important tool for developing learning in general. What constitutes good questioning though is the subject of much debate:

> More worryingly, in a heavily accountable teaching culture, highly instructional, objectives-based pedagogy seems to be required, and well-paced, teacher-directed learning are considered valuable, safe approaches. Interaction in whole class settings is, for many, currently equated with discourse patterns where pupils take part mainly in response to the teachers' questions and invitations to respond, with little extension of opportunities for use of talk to actively work on their own thinking and learning experiences. In this evidence whole class talk is being used by the teacher for 'teaching' rather than being an instrument for learning. The emphasis on transmission of information and factual questions reflects the concern with content and the awareness of the need to meet objectives.
>
> (Burns and Myhill 2004: 47)

Whilst the church played an extraordinarily important role in learning in medieval times, this was by no means the only place of learning. Schools were not friendly places of learning. Birching was the common and regularly administered form of punishment for the mainly male scholars of the fifteenth century. Some views at the time seem to reflect more contemporary approaches to learning: 'children should not be "inforced by violence to lerne but sweetly allured with praises and such praty gyftes as (they) delite in"' (Sir Thomas Elyot 1541, quoted by Hibbert 1986: 114).

The Inns for learning in Law were seen as important alternative establishments for a broader education in 'manners', partly reflecting the particularly upper class contempt for a University education reflected in the quip 'a Mayster of Arte is not worth a Farte' (Jestes of Sloggin quoted by Hibbert 1986: 121). Learning a trade was seen as a worthy goal for any young man in medieval times. Whilst a young man could learn what we now call a vocational education, this also provided a wider education and preparation for life:

> The craftsman . . . had usually served out his apprenticeship in the house of a master who undertook to teach him his trade, and who might additionally be required to give him a general education, as well as bed, board and clothing, in return for a complete subservience and a hard day's work as soon as he was qualified to provide it . . . If skilful and ambitious he might then submit an example of his craft to his guild which would decide upon its merits whether or not he could become a master himself.
>
> (Hibbert 1986: 105)

It is important to recognise that learning has always been provided beyond the walls of the formal classroom. The links between commerce, trade and education are as important today as they ever were. Perhaps the experience of the medieval apprentice reflects the focus on training rather than education which is currently a point of debate in the twenty-first century.

Whilst a history of our education system provides a context for contemporary perspectives in learning, theories of learning help to explain how people learn. Education theory tends to be grouped around a few high-profile models from the second half of the twentieth century.

MODELS OF LEARNING

Learning theory

For a large part of the twentieth century, the ideas and experimental approach to learning of a Russian, Pavlov, and an American, Skinner, were dominant in the field of education. This approach focused on observable events: seeking no less than the determination of general laws and ultimately a scientific theory of learning. For this reason, the approach was called 'Learning Theory'. Pavlov's famous experiment measured the production of saliva in dogs following a bell rung at feeding time. Like many experiments in this field, the research sought to examine the necessary conditions (the sound of the bell) which resulted in expected outcomes (production of saliva). Skinner explained that the best way to ensure consistency of response to a stimulus, involved a schedule of selective reinforcement such that the learner did not always receive an expected reward. This led to an alternative name of 'Stimulus-Response' theory.

Skinner argued that much of the education approaches of the 1950s and 1960s ran counter to learning theory, due to the perceived emphasis on aversion (use of sanctions and negative feedback) in the classroom. However, teachers may recognise elements of this theory in the early approaches to classroom behaviour management called 'assertive discipline':

> Assertive teachers react confidently and quickly in situations that require behaviour management. They have a few clearly stated classroom rules and give firm, clear, concise directions to students who are in need of outside control. Students who comply are reinforced, whereas those who disobey rules and directions receive negative consequences.
>
> (Canter and Canter 1976)

Psychologists often talk about an emphasis on instrumental motivation in learning theory. In learning theory, the view is that learners are motivated to learn because of what they can get, rather than for the intrinsic and unobservable features of learning. This focus on the observable features of learning was seen to be a significant problem; and especially due to the growing recognition of another theory of learning known as cognitivism (Wood 1998).

Constructivism

Constructivism is a collective term for different theories of learning, which include cognitivism. They have the following features in common:

- the learner is seen as an active participant in the process of learning with more or less prominence given to the teacher, parent or more able peer depending on the particular branch of this approach to learning;
- learning involves changes to the way we organise our knowledge and thinking as a learner;
- learning involves adaptation by the learner to the world through:
  - *assimilation*: taking in new experiences and fitting these to current patterns of thinking; and
  - *accommodation*: a process of changing existing patterns of thinking in response to new experience.

Jean Piaget had an immense and continuing influence on our understanding of how we learn (Smith, Cowie and Blades 2003). Through learning experiments often involving young children, he developed a theory of how we learn which depicted learning as a journey through certain stages of development. From the early so-called egocentric stage, in which children only saw the world from their own perspective, they developed increasingly more abstract forms of thinking and learning by moving through the stages of development. Piaget viewed the stages of development as relatively fixed.

Readiness to pass to another stage of learning was an influential factor in the view that children should only be taught to read from a certain age at which they were ready to read. Formal methods for teaching reading in some European countries routinely only start from about the age of six to seven years of age, whilst four to five years is the common starting age range in England in 2008.

Piaget wrote about his scientific approach to learning from the 1920s onwards. Ultimately, he sought to combine logic and mathematics in his explanation of the evolution of mind (Wood 1998). The focus here was on the child, especially, as learner. At the same time, Lev Vygotsky was developing a theory of learning which sought to combine a view of the development of learning and instruction. Piaget and Vygotsky did discuss their findings and each heaped praise upon the other's work. Whilst Piaget's career continued into the latter part of the twentieth century, Vygotsky died in 1934; his work was only brought to the attention of the West by a group of American psychologists of the 1950s. Prominent among these was Jerome Bruner.

Vygotsky saw learning as constructing new knowledge on the basis of the learner's experience of action in a social context. For this reason, Vygotsky's theory of learning is called 'social constructivism'. Vygotsky (1978: 89) explained how teachers develop 'learning potential' in the concept of the 'zone of proximal development': 'the distance between the actual developmental level as determined by independent problem solving and the level of potential development as determined through problem solving under adult guidance or in collaboration with more able peers' (Vygotsky 1978: 89).

Many educational programmes over recent years have attempted to focus on the process of instruction by prescribing pedagogical structures and routines, which focus on how the tutor raises the level of skill, understanding and knowledge expected of the pupil. Vygotsky (1962) explains that the role of the teacher or more able peer is to model skilled performance, which the learner appropriates through a process of internal reconstruction; though they are not always successful in achieving this.

Vygotsky (1978) famously stated that that which exists on the 'inter-psychological plane' will go on to exist on the 'intra-psychological plane'. Hence external social processes go on to become the templates for internal psychological processes. Furthermore, the external control of learning initially exerted by the tutor or more able peer will pass to the learner by a process in which regulation of the learning is 'handed over' by the tutor to the learner. Self-regulation by the learner is an important aim for most curricula.

Bruner, like Vygotsky, emphasised the importance of language as central to the development of thinking. Dialogue is not only a mechanism for developing learning and supporting new forms of thinking, but different languages and varieties of language actually mould and influence different forms of thinking. Bruner (1983) went further to explain that language was a tool and like other cultural tools enables the learner to achieve ever more sophisticated forms of thinking and learning. For instance, the written language has provided a way of representing incredibly complex scientific ideas (Darwin's theory of evolution) and artistic works of great beauty and complex emotional force (e.g. Mark Haddon's *The Curious Incident of the Dog in the Night-time*), which would have been impossible in a purely oral form.

Whilst Bruner was a loyal and prolific supporter of the work of Vygotsky, his own theoretical model of learning was highly influential. For instance, he explained that the role of the teacher or more able peer was to scaffold learning in those aspects of an activity, the learner was unable at that point to do on their own. This includes, for instance:

- physical manipulation of objects on behalf of the learner;
- formulating approaches to problem solving to support the learner;
- remembering steps in a task;
- emotional support for a learner during a task to maintain their attention, interest or participation in the task.

Both Vygotsky and Bruner disagreed with Piaget's concept of readiness for learning. Margaret Donaldson (1978) proved that children could understand quite sophisticated and abstract concepts, so long as learning was presented in an appropriate context. For instance, up to about the age of seven, learners were unable to understand concepts presented in so-called 'disembedded' abstract contexts.

Piaget described a task to prove that children were unable to see from the perspectives of others: this involved asking young children to describe what different figures could see on a model of a mountain. However, when Donaldson (1978) presented the same task in a different context involving a naughty policeman and different characters in a model of a high street, the children were able to describe what other characters could see. This is an important factor in current approaches to education which seek to accelerate children's learning. Donaldson suggests that by presenting or explaining learning activities in a way which the learner can understand, more sophisticated and abstract concepts than were predicted by Piaget are indeed possible. Such views are highly influential in the area of early years education: play-based child-led activities are suggested to be more effective than formal forms of learning in the early years, because learners approach tasks in a more contextually appropriate way.

Whilst our understanding of how people learn is still dominated by theorists such as Bruner, Vygotsky and Piaget, technological advances have provided alternative evidence to enhance our understanding of learning. These include the development of computers and models of artificial intelligence. The explanations of learning in Skinner's learning theory and Piaget's depiction of thinking in schema theory both employed elements of logical and mathematical symbolism.

Ultimately, Information Processing theory uses an analysis of actions, their goals and the means by which these are achieved and evaluated as a framework for understanding how we learn (Wood 1998). What are the basic components of this learning system? Whilst the reality is much more complex, all learning involves:

- *sensory perception:* auditory and visual processing of information, for example, received in the form of spoken or written language which we hear or read;
- *attention:* strategies for maintaining an efficient focus on the most relevant information in a task;
- *memory:* storage of information of different forms – short-term working memory whilst a task is completed; and long-term memory to store previously processed information which can be accessed at a later point;
- *metacognition:* strategies for reflecting on learning;
- *production:* verbal or non-verbal response following information received.

It is important to recognise that each of the above aspects of learning may be more or less successful. Likewise these develop throughout childhood – in many cases continue to develop (for instance, our ability to reflect on learning) – whilst for many as we grow older other features, such as short-term memory, diminish.

Self-regulated learning

Claire Weinstein and her colleagues (2000) provide an example of this approach in action. It is important to recognise that her model, like many in this area, goes beyond learning as merely a cognitive skill to recognise that emotions and the ability to regulate one's own behaviour are important aspects of how we learn.

An emphasis on the use of learning strategies to support self-regulated learning has been shown to support an increase in the outcomes of learning (Pintrich and Schunk 1996). Weinstein *et al.* (2000) identified three critically important characteristics in learning strategies: they must be goal-directed, intentionally invoked and effortful.

Weinstein *et al.* (2000) are emphatic that cognitive learning strategies do not work in isolation. Thus just as it is important that learners know the what, how and when of using learning strategies, so it is also important to know why a strategy is important, and therefore to understand and to want to use it. Weinstein *et al.* (2000) describe a model of learning strategies which includes both affective and cognitive factors. At the core is the learner: a unique individual who brings to each learning situation a critical set of variables, including his or her personality, prior knowledge and school achievement history. Around this core are three broad components that focus on factors that, in interaction, can tremendously influence the degree to which students set and reach learning and achievement goals. Weinstein *et al.* (2000) suggested a model of learning with three components, referred to as 'skill', 'will' and 'self-regulation'.

Skill includes:

- using learning strategies;
- finding the main idea/information;
- reading and listening comprehension;

- listening and note-taking;
- preparing for and taking a test;
- using reasoning and problem-solving skills.

Will includes:

- setting, analysing and using goals;
- motivation for achievement;
- affect towards learning;
- beliefs about learning;
- volition;
- creating and maintaining a positive mind-set towards learning.

Self-regulation includes:

- time management;
- concentration;
- comprehension monitoring;
- a systematic approach to learning and accomplishing academic tasks;
- coping with academic stress;
- managing motivation for learning and achievement.

Guy Claxton (1990) emphasises the social dimension to learning. He viewed learning as the development of informal mini-theories of learning, which developed in response to real life learning: not dissimilar to Piaget's idea of 'accommodation'. Claxton thus offers a constructivist interpretation of learning, in which children's problem-solving capacities develop from their experience of dealing with problems in real situations. Claxton suggests that play itself incorporates potential ways of enhancing learning; play-based learning in the early years, for instance, once developed for the purpose of having fun, can develop into a more generalised learning strategy for self-empowerment. The development from mini-theories to learning strategies is contingent on both successful and unsuccessful application in varying contexts. Application of the theory in differing contexts allows the activity or procedure to become more adaptable and generalisable. Unsuccessful application of the mini-theory, according to Fisher (1990), can be used by the learner to develop a tool-kit for repairing learning in future similar situations. This is a feature commonly identified in the literature of self-regulation. For example, Wood (1998) identifies strategies to repair communication breakdown as an important high-level skill.

Claxton summarises his position in the following: 'Every learning experience is not only an invitation to improve our theories about the world; it is also an opportunity to improve our implicit theories about theory-building: to become a better learner' (Claxton 1990: 101). Claxton's evidence of how we learn is very much located in the classroom and reflects on learning in an authentic setting.

Neuro-sciences

A major problem for research into learning lies in the lack of the potentially observable evidence. Many aspects of thinking and learning are neither concrete nor observable. On the one hand thinking takes place in an observable social context, but the activities of the brain are not observable by the average professional. We can see the products of learning, but it is not so easy to observe the processes of thinking. It is true that new technologies allow scientists and medical professionals to observe the brain in operation, but we are still far from being able to link specific neurological events and specific words or concepts.

Goswami (2004) highlights some facts and myths linked to neuroscience and education. For instance, certain physical facts can be linked to learning and child development. Children with a high level of one particular gene (monoamine oxidise A) seem to be protected from developing antisocial behaviour as a result of maltreatment and poor family environments. The gene seems to limit the brain's response to stress (Caspi *et al.* 2002). Likewise, use of a medication called Ritalin has been shown to improve the attention of children with ADHD (Attention Deficit Hyperactivity Disorder) for visual and auditory stimulus (Seifert *et al.* 2003). This however has been seen as a controversial step by some people.

The brain is made up of two major parts, commonly called the 'right brain' or 'right hemisphere' and 'left brain' or 'left hemisphere'. Though it is not controversial to say that for many people certain skills can be said to be 'localised' in certain parts or 'hemispheres' of the brain, this is not universal. For instance, language and grammatical skills in particular are said to be located in the left brain, whilst this is not the case for blind people or for those who learn a language later in childhood in a new linguistic community (Goswami 2004). The evidence from neuroimaging research suggests that both sides of the brain are employed in all cognitive tasks. In spoken language both right and left brain are involved in processing and producing language: left for vocabulary and right for use of intonation. Another brain myth surrounds the notion of a 'male' or 'female' brain to distinguish between so-called differences in neurological construction (Goswami 2004). Here the terms were used to talk about particular styles or approaches to learning and were not meant to represent significantly different physical entities. As Goswami says, the terms are used as 'psychological shorthand'.

Goswami (2004) explains that there are optimal periods in a child's life for certain types of learning. However, these periods are by no means 'critical' and no forms of learning are 'lost' if children do not develop at certain stages. Even the extreme cases of child maltreatment such as 'Genie' demonstrate that development can still take place later in life, albeit in a much less developed way. Genie was deprived of any human contact or stimulation for a substantial part of her childhood, locked away from society in the most cruel of circumstances. Her experience shows the resilience of children. Whilst this experience understandably had a dramatic impact on the rest of her life, she did develop some communication skills and was able to develop aspects of her learning denied her earlier in life. But cognitive impairment can ensue from severe and sustained social and emotional abuse. Rutter (1975) gives the example of a girl teased about her foreign accent by her peers in school who chose not to speak at all in the classroom over a long period of time ('elective mutism'). One would think that the lack of spoken communication by this child in the classroom would severely impact on her development. That was not the case and in fact her learning and intelligence were measured as developing at normal rates.

The evidence from brain-damaged patients as well as experiments to map how the brain works when we learn, have been very helpful in clarifying our understanding. However, there still remains significant uncertainty about the physical activity of the brain in different people: 'The brain is composed of about 50 billion interconnected neurons. Therefore, even complex cognitive functions for which a modular description seems apt rely on a number of interconnected brain regions or systems' (Banich 1997: 52).

Whilst recent research in cognitive neuropsychology and computational cognitive science seeks to map or replicate the system of connections between different parts of the brain, this is a world away from learning in everyday life (Eysenck and Keane 2005: 9). Much of this evidence is based on learning in quite decontextualised experiments which do not reflect the complex psychological, social and emotional settings of everyday life. An analysis of learning in authentic settings will help us to understand this reality.

LEARNING IN DIFFERENT CONTEXTS

In a sense, all learning happens in a context; but here we will review learning outside the experimental setting. Eraut (2000) explains that our understanding of learning should not be limited to just formal or conscious forms of learning. For instance, he considers various forms of informal learning:

- implicit learning, where learning is not undertaken in any conscious way, and there is no conscious knowledge of what has been learned;
- reactive learning, which is seen as being near spontaneous in its development. The knowledge from this type of learning is only marginally open to conscious interrogation;
- deliberative learning, which takes place in a planned context, and is the most open of informal learning to conscious reflection.

So much of what we focus on in the classroom relates to Eraut's description of 'deliberative learning'. Hargreaves (2003) identifies the predominance of an 'objectives model of learning' in English schools. This involves an approach to the curriculum and teaching in which the teacher defines learning objectives in planning, which break down complex activities into a range of objectives which are 'taught' by the teacher to encourage 'learning' by the children. She explains that the National Curriculum (QCA 1999) and national testing arrangements in England have driven this. An 'objectives model of learning' and teaching tends to ignore implicit and reactive learning. Such learning is not necessarily measurable and naturally can deviate from the programme of objectives outlined in any curriculum. Quoting Dann, she says:

> Children are expected to demonstrate the objectives identified. They have no scope to shape, negotiate or deviate from these objectives. Together these theories underpin the role of the pupil as a mechanical agent who will react to the contexts and information given to him/her.
>
> (Dann 2002: 12–13)

Tacit knowledge is the understanding of people, situations, and routines which develops from implicit learning. Eraut (2000) points out the dilemma in investigating any forms of tacit knowledge. Although children's abilities to discuss informal learning increase, the more they are asked to do this, with younger learners, the problem is compounded by their inexperience in reflection, and their limited vocabulary for discussing learning. It should not however be dismissed as being unimportant: as Eraut (2000: 118) says that a person may be socialised into the norms of a school or the classroom without being aware either of the learning or of what the norms of the class are. This is a very important point. Teachers and learners need to be aware of the wider view of learning. Teaching and learning operates at an explicit level in the traditional classroom activities which we see in school, such as whole class activities to promote reading or writing in primary school, but also in the so-called 'hidden curriculum' (Pollard 1997). Teachers communicate their intentions as to the type of learning and goals of the classroom in both implicit and explicit ways.

Whilst learning happens beyond the formal setting of the nursery or school, these are very important contexts for learning. What characterises learning at the first stage of formal education?

Learning in the early years

Much learning in the early years is of a less formal, play-based form, often led by the interests of the child (Smith, Cowie and Blades 2003). It allows children to build on their first experiences of learning and development at home, and provides them with the opportunity to explore the physical, social and emotional world of the nursery or playgroup. Play contributes to learning in many different ways:

- *physical activity:* as a young baby rhythmical kicking and bodily movements are an early form of play;
- *rough and tumble play:* play fighting between children is common from the age of three years – for children who have less well-developed social skills, this can turn into real fighting;
- *games with rules:* for example, games like 'tig' where you have to catch someone;
- *practice play*: acting out a situation in preparation for or in response to a real life event;
- *fantasy and pretend play:* for example, playing out stories or variations of stories based on a TV or computer game. At early stages of development, pretend play relies heavily on realistic objects, but as children grow older, they are able to use less realistic objects to imagine real life situations. This very much mirrors what we said early about the importance of disembedded or decontextualised learning later in childhood (Donaldson 1978);
- *language play:* if there is evidence of simple language development from about the age of 12 months, it is clear that play has an important role in enabling children to experiment with new sounds, ways of combining words and making meaning. Whilst it might serve as an opportunity to practice language, playing with sounds and words also has an important role in entertaining and bonding with others. Of course, language of a social or exploratory nature may accompany any of the above forms of play.

Long before Vygotsky's original writings, other European theorists had re-evaluated the educational significance of play. Learning can of course be different in different cultures; but Froebel saw development from within the child as important. The 'kindergarten' or 'child garden' reflected Froebel's views of the child: 'Play, truly recognized and rightly fostered, unites the germinating life of the child attentively with the ripe life of experiences of the adult and thus fosters the one through the other' (Froebel 1906).

Maria Montessori is still hugely influential in the field of early years learning (Smith, Cowie and Blades 2003). Whilst she saw the value of self-initiated learning, it was her belief that children should be encouraged to learn about real life through real activities rather than pretending through socio-dramatic play. Thus children in a Montessori early years setting will be encouraged to take ownership of their own learning in as authentic a way as possible. In the earliest traditions of Montessori, children would be encouraged to serve food themselves, rather than just play at serving food.

Play is widely considered amongst early years' institutions as an important way for children to learn. However, it is not without its critics. Brian Sutton-Smith (1986) for instance argues that many theories of play are merely an 'idealisation' of the needs of the child. He sees theories of play as reflecting more the needs of adults in organising and controlling children, rather than the actualities of children's behaviour (Smith, Cowie and Blades 2003: 232). Sylva, Roy and Painter (1980) highlight that different forms of play can be more or less effective in helping young children to learn:

- high-yield play is structured with some kind of goal and a means to achieve it (e.g. building, drawing or solving puzzles);
- low-yield play is informal and involves unstructured social playing (e.g. rough and tumble games).

(Smith, Cowie and Blades 2003: 233)

This view is in itself controversial, as Sylva *et al.* define 'yield' in cognitive terms, whilst social, emotional and affective aspects are no less important in children's learning. In a sense, the 'higher yield' activities are those which resemble more closely the cognitive demands of the later more formal curriculum of schools.

School learning

Learning in school is rather paradoxical. At home, children generally ask questions and adults try to answer them. Whilst in school, children answer questions posed by their teachers who generally know the answers:

> The young child is often thought of as a little scientist exploring the world and discovering the principles of its operation. We often forget that while the scientist is working on the border of human knowledge and is finding out things that nobody else yet knows, the child is finding out precisely what everybody already knows.
>
> (Newman 1982: 26)

If the child is seen to be at the centre of learning in the early years' philosophy (Smith, Cowie and Blades 2003), then the aims of state mainstream education in England seem to be more balanced between development of the child as an individual and socialisation of the child into the norms of society and the particular culture of the school community. Of course, the patterns of socialisation of the home may be different to those in school. This can create conflict and educational success or failure, according to the relationship between home and school. If the culture and patterns of socialisation between home and school are different, should the responsibility for change lie with the school or home? Or should the 'learner' move to a school setting where the patterns of socialisation are nearer to that of the home?

What do pupils bring to the learning process? How can teachers be responsive to this? In English, even more than other subjects, these are particularly important questions, since pupils are required to demonstrate knowledge and understanding of texts and issues which are open to interpretation. Opinions must be justified with evidence, and arguments must be well-founded with a logical sequence of thought. Their interpretations of and responses to texts, though mediated by the pedagogical support of the teacher, will nevertheless be further mediated by the prior knowledge, attitudes and skills which the learners bring to the activity.

The traditional conception of the passage through the 'zone of proximal development', is of a teacher leading a learner by the hand down an avenue, and at a certain point when they are able to find their own way to the destination, the teacher lets go and the pupil makes their own way to the end of the road. The pupil comes on the journey sometimes with an idea of how to get to the destination, maybe with a compass, a map or the ability to ask passing people the right direction. The pupil may be a willing traveller. They may like and respect the person they are travelling with, or indeed they may be so scared of that person that they are only travelling under coercion. Their intention may be to shoot off down a side alley, as soon as the opportunity arises! Others may accompany the child on the journey, happy to enjoy the social interaction.

Alternatively, as the teacher and pupil walk down this road of learning, there may be a gang of kids jeering mockingly at the pupil. For some pupils this may be enough to deter them, others may be resilient enough to ignore such distractions, and others may have to weigh up the choice between popularity within the peer group, and a successful trip along the road to learning. Of course, this metaphor can be taken further – what if the local community is hostile to those who walk the road of learning?

Pupils bring skills, knowledge and attitudes, which can facilitate or indeed block their passage through the zone of proximal development. This is the pupils' learning journey.

In school learning and instruction take various forms. Teachers have a range of routines to encourage learning through instruction:

Rote learning

This involves learning facts or routines by heart. This may be helpful in certain areas of knowledge (numerical facts and laws, for example); but not in others (learning about characters in literature, for example, where the skills of interpretation and the development of empathy are important).

Investigations

Learners will carry out an activity to further develop their understanding of a topic, either with or without a firm indication of how to approach the task from the teacher. This can be a very effective way of supporting learning in both sciences (for example, investigating the properties of different materials) and the arts (for example, investigating patterns of spelling in English).

Group learning

Whilst this is a way of organising learners and the classroom, small groups of four to five learners can be a very effective way of supporting dialogue. Variations of this involve learners moving between groups to share information.

Paired learning

Pairing learners can develop dialogue and interactive learning in a way which is impossible where the teacher is teaching a whole class. For instance, asking pairs of learners to discuss a question before sharing individual responses in the whole class can promote a greater degree of pupil involvement and talk for learning of a higher quality.

E-learning and the use of technology

University teachers have been using Virtual Learning Environments (VLEs) for the last decade in their taught programme. These involve a range of tools to support learning: learning objects (such as multiple-choice questions for self-testing), discussion boards, documents (text, graphics, sound and film) to support learning and various ways of communicating with learners (e-mail announcements, etc.). Such technologies are now being developed for schools as we move towards the end of the first decade of the twenty-first century. Schools, on the other hand, have already made significant use of different presentation (interactive whiteboards and projectors) and response tools (voting systems).

Whilst this list is not exhaustive, it is important to recognise that there are a range of teaching and learning strategies which learners will experience in school.

The relationship between teaching strategies and pupil self-support learning strategies is a dynamic one. Wood (1998) proposed a 'principle of contingency' by which teachers help children to construct local expertise (connected with that particular task or group of tasks) by focusing their attention on relevant and timely aspects of the task, and by highlighting things they need to take account of. This principle also encourages teachers to break the task down into a sequence of smaller tasks that children can manage to perform. Wood (1988) suggests that effective teaching through the zone of proximal development gives only that level of support which enables the learner to accomplish it successfully: combining a suitable level of challenge and support. Wood further stated, however, that in the real world of the classroom achieving contingent instruction is far more difficult than is suggested by the largely 'experimental' evidence of constructive activities between adults and one or two children. Wood considered that many lessons taught in school often involve tasks that do not have a clear, obvious structure and may not yield single 'right answers'. As Pollard (1985) would say, this reflects the dilemma that pupils and teachers face in the classroom, leading to the development of coping strategies in order to balance the competing and often irreconcilable issues.

Andrew Pollard (1988) describes the process of learning from a sociological as well as a psychological point of view. Whereas teachers are under the spotlight to achieve certain outcomes with their pupils, regardless of the background or starting point of the learner, the students themselves may be disengaged and demotivated as a result of an irrelevant state curriculum or prescribed teaching methods. In such situations there can be a gap of relevance between the school curriculum and the priorities of the learner. Whilst there are several options open to the learner and teacher in such situations, all ultimately provide a means for both the teacher and learner to survive in a challenging and potentially irreconcilable context. For instance, many teachers and learners report the importance of humour and banter in the secondary school (Hewitt 2008) as a way of getting through the lesson. Whilst most teachers and pupils would argue for the importance of an interesting curriculum in itself, most would also agree that the particular demands of the school learning context provide considerable pressures and 'coping' itself may be a positive outcome.

Learning is a complex, controversial and problematic process. Research into how people learn has produced as many theories as there are learners. How we learn reflects society in general. We very often focus on thinking and so-called cognitive skills in learning; but social and emotional factors are equally part of thinking and learning. The reality of classroom learning suggests that learning itself may be more a vehicle for socialisation as ultimately what we learn becomes less important than how we learn. The journey of learning is therefore more important than its destination (Hewitt 2008).

SUMMARY

Learning through the ages

Whilst conceptions of how we learn have changed through the ages, current views seem similar to that of nearly a century ago:

> 'A good school is a community of young and old, learning together,' and that 'the curriculum of the primary school is to be thought of in terms of activity and experience rather than knowledge to be acquired and facts to be stored'
>
> Haddow Report (1931)

Learning theory

Skinner explained that the best way to ensure consistency of response to a stimulus involved a schedule of selective reinforcement such that the learner did not always receive an expected reward. This led to an alternative name for learning theory of 'Stimulus-Response' theory for this tradition.

Constructivism

The learner is seen as an active participant in the process of learning with more or less prominence given to the teacher, parent or more able peer, depending on the particular branch of this approach to learning. Donaldson (1978) proved that children could understand quite sophisticated and abstract concepts, so long as learning was presented in an appropriate context.

Information processing theory

Cognitive psychology represents learning in different individuals as involving more or less successful use of: sensory perception (including understanding of language); attention; memory; metacognition; and production strategies (including production of language).

Self-regulated learning

Weinstein *et al.* (2000) describe a model of learning strategies which includes both affective and cognitive factors. At the core is the learner: a unique individual who brings to each learning situation a critical set of variables, including his or her personality, prior knowledge and school achievement history. Around this core are three broad components (skill, will and self-regulation) that focus on factors that, in interaction, can tremendously influence the degree to which students set and reach learning and achievement goals. This accounts for different outcomes in learning.

Learning in the early years

Learning always takes place in a social context (Vygotsky 1978). Much of learning in the early years is of a less formal, play-based form, often led by the interests of the child.

School learning

Vygotsky (1978) sees learning as taking place in a 'zone of proximal development'. The teacher supports the learner in the early stages of learning new skills or performing a new activity. As the latter becomes more able to take on responsibility for the action, control will be handed over to the latter. The learner will at some point take full control, regulating their own performance. In an attempt to balance the competing demands of the classroom and the priorities of learning, both teacher and learner develop 'coping strategies' as ways of surviving a potentially irreconcilable situation (Pollard 1985).

KEY QUESTIONS

1. How would you describe the relationship between teaching and learning? (Can teaching be said to have taken place if learning did not occur?)
2. In another chapter in this book you have read and answered questions about the work of Piaget and Vygotsky. How does the work of Bruner differ and how is it similar?
3. Compare learning through play and school-based learning – what are the pros and cons of each, and is one approach more suitable for a specific group than another?

FURTHER READING

Donaldson, M. (1978): *Children's Minds*. London: Fontana.
Hewitt, D. (2008): *Understanding Effective Learning*. London: OUP.
Wood, D. (1998): *How Children Think and Learn*, second edition. London: Blackwell.

This chapter links with readings 3 and 6 of *The Routledge Education Studies Reader.*

SECTION 2

CONTEXTS

Making education work

CHAPTER 9

UNDERSTANDING UNDERACHIEVEMENT IN SCHOOL

Emma Smith

The rationale for this chapter is:

- to examine the evidence for 'underachievement' in school;
- to consider what it is that we mean by the term 'underachievement';
- to look at alternative accounts for boys' 'underachievement' in literacy-based subjects.

INTRODUCTION

If you were to make a list of the issues that concern those who teach, research or seek to change education, it would not be long before you came to 'underachievement'. 'Underachievement' is a familiar word to those who work with young people, however the term itself is not unproblematic. Indeed, for such a widely reported phenomenon, it is perhaps surprising that very different perspectives as to the nature and importance of the concept exist. It is these different perspectives on a seemingly well-established discourse, along with an examination of the concept we call 'underachievement', that form the focus of this chapter.

Today, underachievement is a synonym for much that is perceived to be wrong in today's society, from low scores on international children's reading tests to the social consequences of underachievement such as criminal behaviour, social exclusion and unsuccessful relationships and marriages. Increased scrutiny of examination performance as the most tangible outcome of schooling has led to sections of the school population being labelled as failing or underachieving. Sophisticated international comparative tests such as the Programme for International Student Assessment (PISA) and the Trends International Maths and Science Study (TIMSS) enable nations to look critically at the achievement of their students in the international arena. This has led to many nations re-examining their education systems in light of perceived failings in these comparative assessments. In some countries, this has been used to further justify dissatisfaction with the domestic school system and has led to accusations of underachievement and a 'crisis account' of falling academic standards and failing pupils (Smith 2005). In the United Kingdom, for example, unfavourable international comparisons have contributed to the assertion that the performance of certain groups of students is characterised by a 'long tail' of underachievement. Here recent government policy has its focus firmly on raising standards and eliminating all forms of underachievement, one consequence of which is a system of national testing and target setting that is of unprecedented scale.

Within this discourse of 'falling standards' and 'failing students' sit concerns about the apparent failure or underachievement of large sections of the school population. In the UK, we are concerned about the relative attainment of young people from certain ethnic minority groups, and, to a seemingly lesser extent, the attainment of young people from the least wealthy homes. But, as the quotations below illustrate, it is the underachievement of boys that has received the most attention: in the corridors of Westminster, in the pages of the national newspapers, in the lecture rooms of our universities and in the staffrooms of our schools.

> We face a genuine problem of underachievement among boys, particularly those from working class families. This underachievement is linked to a laddish culture which in many areas has grown out of deprivation, and a lack of both self-confidence and opportunity.
>
> (David Blunkett, Secretary of State for Education, August 2000)

> Boys underachieving at school, says study.
>
> (*The Telegraph* newspaper, 14 August 2007)

WHO GETS WHAT? THE EVIDENCE FOR UNDERACHIEVEMENT OF BOYS

The underachievement of boys has been a key topic in the field of education for many years. Theories have been developed to explain the phenomenon and costly programmes have been put in place to try to raise achievement scores. Indeed, evidence for the differential attainment of the nation's boys is not hard to find and it is easy to see why we might be concerned. For example, examination results, especially at GCSE, show us that the performance of girls is higher than that of boys. The table below shows the proportions of students who achieve five or more GCSE passes at grades A*–C, as well as those who achieve at least a grade C in English language. In both areas, the performance of boys is consistently lower than that of girls. However, notice also that the scores of *both* boys and girls have risen throughout the past decade and that the overall rate of improvement is faster for boys than for girls. For example, the proportion of boys achieving grade C or above in English increased by nearly 20 per cent between 1996 and 2007, compared with around 10 per cent for girls (see also Gorard 2000).

Table 9.1 GCSE achievements according to sex, England (1996–2007)

Year	5+ A*–C grades		English	
	Boys	Girls	Boys	Girls
2007	57	66	56	70
2006	54	64	55	69
2005	51	62	54	69
2004	48	58	53	67
2003	48	58	52	68
2002	46	57	52	67
2001	45	55	51	66
2000	44	55	51	66
1999	43	53	50	66
1998	41	51	48	64
1997	40	50	46	63
1996	40	49	47	64

Source: DfES 1996–2007.

Despite the trends in Table 9.1, relatively little attention has been paid to the improvements in the achievement levels of girls and the fact that the attainment of all pupils has risen steadily over the last 30 years is barely mentioned unless it is to raise concerns over falling standards and a 'dumbing down' of the school curriculum. In short, boys have fallen behind in this one crude measure of success and the dominant view is that something has to be done about it. Numerous feminist researchers have drawn attention to this 'backlash' (see for example, Francis and Skelton 2005) and have made it clear that any attempts to raise the achievement of boys must not lose sight of the work done over the last three decades to improve the lot of girls in school. Several explanations for the apparent 'underachievement' of boys exist; three of the most widely used are summarised here.

Changing masculinities

One explanation frequently offered for the apparent underachievement of boys is that there are innate, natural born differences between the sexes: boys are more likely to suffer from oxygen starvation at birth, they have poorer verbal reasoning skills, they mature later than girls, their parents do not talk to them as much as they do to their sisters and so on (for example, Cohen 1998). In the UK, the collapse in the post-war boom of heavy industry and the replacement (particularly in some working class homes) of the male as the main family breadwinner, has led to what some researchers would call a change in the gender regime of these communities and another explanation for the poor performance of young men in our schools (see for example, Francis and Skelton 2005).

The classroom, the teacher, teaching and learning

Claims about the feminisation of the school curriculum have come hand-in-hand with criticisms of female teachers for imposing female values on our pupils. Despite an uncertain evidence base, these claims are reworked as an explanation for the relatively poor performance of boys and in calls for an increase in the number of male teachers in our schools. The different behaviour and learning cultures of boys and girls is well documented (see for example Younger and Warrington 2005). In the classroom it is the boys who command the 'lion's share' of the teachers' attention and receive a disproportionate amount of the teacher's time compared with the girls. Boys can bring another agenda into the classroom, asserting themselves as jokers and as risk-takers, with a noisy approach to their work and a dislike of the tedium of writing. As a result, they are frequently the focus of classroom activity, whereas the girls are 'marginalised' on the edges.

Assessment and the school curriculum

Achievement gaps between boys and girls in English and other language- and literacy-based examinations is one key piece of evidence supporting the claim that our boys are underachieving. The acquisition of literacy skills is important but is one that can sometimes be seen as a highly gendered activity. For example, research tells us that throughout school, girls are the keener readers who are more likely to be 'devoted' to their books (Millard 1997). When boys do read, their favoured genres – action and adventure and non-fiction – can leave them disadvantaged in the school curriculum, where narrative accounts that emphasise personal responses are favoured. However, although the English curriculum may well disadvantage boys, there is little correlation between achievement in English examinations and success in later life (Millard 1997), but as success in English examinations can act as a gate-keeper to education and employment opportunities, the disadvantage that boys have in acquiring the 'right' literacy skills can be compounded.

Thus, there are three dominant explanations for the apparent 'underachievement' of boys in schools: the conflict of masculinity in contemporary society, the curriculum and its assessment, and finally the everyday experience of both students and teachers within the classroom. In response to concerns about male underachievement, a plethora of strategies and initiatives have emerged. These range from experiments with single-sex teaching to networks of sports clubs aimed at encouraging 'failing' students to do better in school. However, the absence of rigorous trialing means that the efficacy of many of these strategies remains largely unproven (Slavin 2002).

WHAT IS UNDERACHIEVEMENT?

Before continuing our focus on understanding the underachievement debate, it is perhaps worth pausing to consider what it is that we actually mean by the term underachievement. One thing that explanations for the underachievement phenomenon have in common is the tacit acceptance of a common meaning for the term 'underachievement'. However, despite the widespread use of the term there is little consensus over what 'underachievement' actually means. For example, how do you define underachievement and how do you measure it? Simply labelling one group of students, such as boys, as underachieving compared to another group, such as girls, tells us nothing about which boys may be in need of additional support in school and nothing about what the nature of this support might be. Frequently the terms underachievement and low achievement are conflated and the subject becomes even more complex if you were to ask yourself what any underachievement might be relative to. Is it related to some kind of innate ability on the part of the individual or is it achievement relative to that of a larger group? In addition, as we have seen above, the underachievement label is not only confined to describing the relative achievement of groups of students, or indeed individual students, it is frequently offered as an explanation for the relatively poorer academic performance of schools and of nations. Questions and confusions such as these are fundamental to our understanding of the underachievement discourse.

The wider perception of what is understood by the term 'underachievement' has been further complicated with its adoption by the media as a synonym for much of what is perceived to be wrong with education and is exacerbated by its confusion with low achievement. For example, when we read that smaller numbers of boys are achieving minimum proficiency levels compared with girls, it is often suggested that the boys were 'underachieving'. Whether these pupils were underachieving or not, is unclear from these results; what the results might tell us is that the achievement of boys on this particular measure was lower than that of girls. This conflation of underachievement and low achievement is important, as I have argued elsewhere: underachievement and low achievement are not the same thing (Smith 2005).

Consider, for example the student who, despite their best and most sustained efforts, fails to reach minimum proficiency levels on a given assessment. In the current climate of high stakes testing, this individual might arguably be labelled a 'low achiever' but, given their hard work and sustained effort, is surely not an 'underachiever'? Consider another student, whose past achievement has suggested them to be academically very capable but whose relative lack of interest or effort has secured them a B grade, rather than a top scoring A grade. Arguably this individual is 'underachieving' but is surely not a 'low achiever'? Recently the underachievement debate has evolved and become more nuanced to differentiate episodic underachievers, able underachievers, less able underachievers and so on. The fact that there can now be so many possible different types of underachievers should perhaps tell us that if underachievement cannot be adequately defined and measured then it is of little use in helping us understand what is happening in schools. This problem with conceptualising underachievement has led researchers to re-examine what it is that we mean by the terms underachievement and low achievement and so to identifying groups of students who may be underachieving or who may be low achieving. Perhaps unsurprisingly given the multiple types of underachievers, our research suggests that they are a relatively heterogeneous group of individuals who, when they do appear to underachieve, do so for a range of reasons, some transient, others more profound (Smith 2005). Thus, anyone could arguably underachieve at a given point in their school career, whether they are a gifted and talented student, a new arrival to the school, male or of an ethnic minority. Arguably perhaps, underachievement is an individual phenomenon: a behaviour rather than an outcome. Of course this makes it a lot more difficult for schools to identify potential underachievement and to intervene, but underachievement is a complex phenomenon which can manifest itself in a range of behaviours and consequences for the individual.

Low achievers on the other hand, are a clearly defined group of students: they are those who come from the least wealthy homes and who are more likely to be disadvantaged in the school assessment system, in aggregate terms, at every level. For example, if we consider eligibility for free school meals (not a perfect proxy for poverty but the best we have available), we can see achievement gaps between those that can receive free school meals and those that do not at every level of schooling and which extend far beyond the reach of compulsory education: a pattern which is reflected across different nations. Indeed, even though the attainment of students who are eligible for free school meals is improving and often at a faster rate, achievement gaps in the performance of boys and girls are dwarfed by the achievement gaps between young people from the least and most wealthy homes.

Table 9.2 GCSE attainment according to eligibility for free school meals, England (2002–2007)

Year	Percentage of 15-year-old students achieving 5+A*–C grades at GCSE	
	Eligible for free school meals	Not eligible for free school meals
2007	35	63
2006	33	61
2005	30	59
2004	26	56
2003	24	55
2002	23	54

Source: DfES 2002–2007.

So whether you believe that our schools are characterised by falling standards and underachieving students, or that the 'underachievement' discourse tells us little about what is really happening with regard to the relative attainment of students in school; it is clear that certain groups of students do not achieve as well as perhaps they could. As a consequence, one of the key questions to face educators today is how to close the achievement gap.

AN ALTERNATIVE ACCOUNT OF BOYS' UNDERACHIEVEMENT

In this section we will re-examine some of the evidence often presented for the underachievement of boys. Given the complexity of the gender debate and uncertainties over what it is that we actually mean by the term underachievement, it is not surprising that an alternative account of the underachievement phenomenon also exists. For example, Delamont contends that 'it is pointless to be swept away by a moral panic about "failing", anti-school working-class boys. This is not a new problem' (1999: 13). Schools, she argues, have never been able to deal with the working-class boy. According to Delamont, the whole standards debate is surrounded in a 'discourse of derision' (1999: 3), compounded by a lack of understanding of the academic gains made by all pupils, and coupled with the media's resistance to hearing good news. That 'underachievement' is not a new phenomenon has also been demonstrated in an historical study by Cohen (1998). She noted the seventeenth-century academic John Locke's consternation that young men found it difficult to succeed in Latin, while their younger sisters would 'prattle' on in French having had little or no formal instruction. The standard of the young men's English also gave him little joy. In England and Wales, concern over falling standards is well established with influential government-commissioned reports having a long history of criticising school standards as being in crisis. For example the Black Papers, published in the late 1960s, reported that achievement in reading was lower than previously, older children did not know their tables, examiners were appalled at the poor levels of English and the standard of the 11+ intake into grammar schools was in decline (Cox and Dyson 1969). Indeed, in Wales, the 11+ examination results were adjusted so that equal numbers of boys and girls could attend grammar school. If the top 40 per cent had been selected for these schools regardless of sex, two-thirds of the pupils in grammar schools would have been female (Rees and Delamont 1999). Gorard (2000) also disputes the fact that boys have ever attained higher grades than girls in compulsory education at any time over the past 25 years. However, underlying these concerns about gender bias in the way that students are assessed is the assumption that our assessment system is gender-neutral and that boys and girls *ought to* achieve the same levels in school examinations.

As we saw above, one important piece of evidence supporting the underachieving boys claim is the differential performance of boys and girls in English and language examinations. Next I will consider student performance data in literacy-based subjects. Evidence from three sources will be presented: national tests in English Language in England and Wales over a 30-year period; nationally representative longitudinal assessments of reading in the USA; and the results from international comparative tests of reading literacy.

RECONSIDERING THE GENDER GAP IN LITERACY-BASED SUBJECTS

That boys underachieve in literacy-based subjects is of fundamental concern to many who are engaged in the 'underachieving boys' debate. Here the evidence from three assessments will enable us to consider achievement gaps between male and female students in literacy-based subjects across time as well as across different cultural and educational settings.

England and Wales: Achievement in English at age 16

Figure 9.1 shows the achievement gap[1] between the number of 16-year-old students who gained a grade C or above in national tests in English between 1970 and 2007. The results for English show a

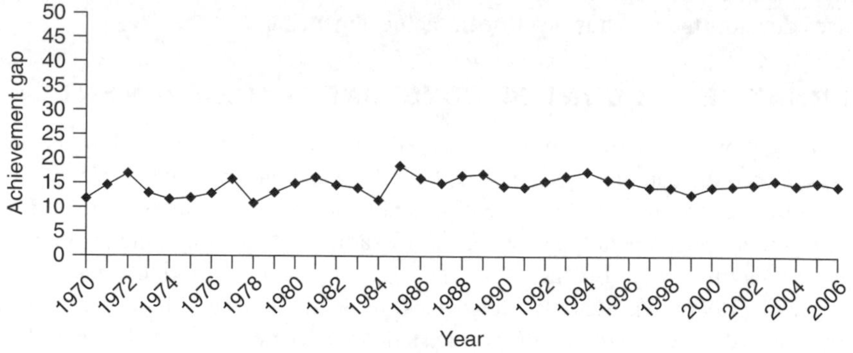

Figure 9.1 Achievement gaps in English language examinations

Source: Welsh Joint Education Committee (WJEC) examination board

steady achievement gap in favour of the girls, but it is a gap that has hardly changed since the early 1970s. There is little evidence here of any differences over time in the relative performance of boys and girls in English, indeed the current gap is the smallest since the early 1980s.

Similar trends have also been noted for other subjects. For example in History, French and Welsh, the performance gap has consistently been in favour of girls, with little fluctuation for almost 30 years. Mathematics was one subject that has seen a decrease in the achievement gap. From favouring the boys in the 1970s and 1980s, the trend changed in the early 1990s and both groups now enjoy almost equal success. What caused this change to a well-established trend is not easy to uncover, but it does appear to coincide with the introduction of compulsory coursework in mathematics during the early 1990s (Smith 2005).

The United States of America: Achievement in the NAEP at age 13

The National Assessment of Educational Progress (NAEP) is a large-scale national test that is used to monitor achievement trends in the United States. Also known as the 'Nation's Report Card', NAEP has been undertaking nationwide annual assessments of student achievement in various subjects since 1969. In addition, the NAEP long-term trends assessment has been administering the same set of tests to 9-, 13- and 17-year-olds since 1971 in reading and since 1973 in mathematics; so making it possible to track educational progress over extended periods of time (NCES 2005). Table 9.3 below shows the trends in average reading scores for 13-year-old students between 1971 and 2004. The same pattern in male/female attainment in reading occurs here as in national examinations at 16 in England and Wales, and reflects an achievement gap in favour of female students that appears to have existed over the last three decades.

Table 9.3 Average reading scores among 13-year-old students, according to sex

Year	Female	Male	Total students
1971	261	250	255
1975	262	250	256
1980	263	254	258
1984	262	253	257
1988	263	252	257
1990	263	251	257
1992	265	254	260
1994	266	251	258
1996	264	251	258
1999	265	254	259
2004	264	254	259

Source: NAEP 2005

International: The Programme for International Student Assessment (PISA)

The Programme for International Student Assessment (PISA) is a series of international comparative tests which are designed to 'assess student performance and collect data on the student, family and institutional factors that can help explain differences in performance' (OECD 2001: 14). To date, there have been three waves of PISA: the first, in 2000 focused mainly on reading, the second, in 2003, focused on mathematics and the most recent wave, in 2006, focused on science. The next wave of PISA is scheduled for 2009 and will again focus on reading. As our concern in this discussion is with differential attainment in literacy, I have presented data from the 2000 wave of PISA. As you can see from Table 9.4, girls are performing consistently higher than boys in the PISA reading assessment: a trend that is replicated not only across all countries presented in Table 9.4, but across all countries participating in PISA 2000.

Table 9.4 Student performance on PISA 2000 combined reading assessment, according to sex

Country	Mean score (boys)	Mean score (girls)	Mean score (all pupils)
Australia	513 (4.0)	546 (4.7)	528 (3.5)
Brazil	388 (3.9)	404 (3.4)	396 (3.1)
Canada	519 (1.8)	551 (1.7)	534 (1.6)
Finland	520 (3.0)	571 (2.8)	546 (2.6)
France	490 (3.5)	519 (2.7)	505 (2.7)
Germany	468 (3.2)	502 (3.9)	484 (2.5)
Japan	507 (6.7)	537 (5.4)	522 (5.2)
Korea	519 (3.8)	533 (3.7)	525 (2.4)
Mexico	411 (4.2)	432 (3.8)	422 (3.3)
United Kingdom	512 (3.0)	537 (3.4)	523 (2.6)
United States	490 (8.4)	518 (6.2)	504 (7.1)

Source: OECD (2001) (standard errors)

Notwithstanding the technical and conceptual problems of comparing test data across different years, cohorts and nations (for example, Bracey 1996, Prais 2003), it does appear that achievement gaps between male and female students in literacy-based subjects are relatively well established across time, as well as appearing resistant to various cultural and educational settings.

SUMMARY

Several issues arise from our re-examination of some of the issues surrounding recent moral panics about the underachievement of boys. They challenge the very nature of the term 'underachievement' and lead us to question the whole phenomenon of 'underachieving boys' in particular. Indeed, one of the enduring 'myths' about standards in education has arisen from 'moral panics' about the perceived underachievement of boys in school examinations. This 'moral panic' has come about largely through interpretations of examination data which suggest that not only are girls outperforming their male peers but also that the performance gap between them is widening. But, as some of the evidence presented here has shown, the reality is not so clear-cut. There is no evidence to suggest that the gap in male/female performance is increasing, that girls are becoming more likely to achieve higher grade passes than boys, or that boys are underachieving in school examinations.

In fact, the very constancy of achievement gaps in literacy-based subjects over time and place suggests that it is a phenomenon that transcends cultures, curricula and education systems. This constancy might make us reconsider some of the explanations given for the apparent underachievement of boys. Indeed, if you consider the present underachievement debate alongside long-standing concerns about falling standards in our schools (as outlined in the 1969 Black Papers, see Delamont 1999, for example), boys never have done as well as girls (remember that entrance to grammar schools was biased in favour of boys) and the evidence for boys' underachievement as being a new phenomenon that requires radical changes to teaching methods and assessment practices, begins to look rather shaky.

Whatever side of the underachievement debate you choose to sit, two things are clear. First, the achievement of all students is improving and long-standing achievement gaps, for example between boys and girls, are becoming smaller. And secondly, despite these improvements, considerable inequities do still exist, most noticeably between the achievement of the most and least economically advantaged students. Therefore, while some of the premises upon which the underachievement discourse are based are open to reinterpretation, inequities in the achievement of certain groups of students remain, and it is clear that strategies that are proven to close these achievement gaps should be developed, refined, or supported in wider practice.

That boys are performing less well than girls in certain literacy-based subjects is indeed a cause for concern: 'the issues surrounding boys' achievement are real and should not be underestimated but the question of gender and performance is more complex, affecting different sub-groups of boys and girls in different ways and often reflecting the influence of class and ethnicity' (Arnot *et al.* 1999: 1). But the focus should be on which (if any) particular group of pupils appears to be failing to reach their potential and why. This would herald a move away from the traditional binary notion of boys versus girls to include an assessment of other variables such as ethnicity and home background which may have a more profound effect on an individual's learning. For example, if it is the case that boys are underachieving in school, then labelling boys as underachieving does little to help explain or remedy the issue – we cannot change the fact that they are boys. Another issue is the assumption that our assessment system is gender neutral and that boys and girls should achieve the same outcomes in school examinations. Of course, it could become gender neutral by ensuring equal success for boys and girls; in much the same way that places in grammar schools in England and Wales were allocated 40 years ago, but is that really what we want from our school assessment system?

In short, that boys are less likely to reach expected proficiency levels in literacy-based subjects should not be taken as evidence for their underachievement. As we have seen, underachievement is itself a concept over which there is much confusion and little consensus. Indeed, underachievement is a term that has probably outlived its usefulness. The lack of clarity in its use has led to multiple meanings that sometimes disguise the true nature of patterns of learning in schools. Its conflation with low achievement presents further complications and obscures the fact that there are clearly defined groups of young people who fail to achieve minimum levels at each stage of their education; these of course are the young people who come from the poorest homes. Perhaps it is here that educational reform programmes ought to first be targeted.

KEY QUESTIONS

1. Is the debate about falling standards really a concern about underachievement? (What, if anything, is the difference between these areas?)
2. Do boys achieve at a lower level than girls?
3. What is the value and disadvantages of large-scale national and international testing?

FURTHER READING

Francis, B. and Skelton, C. (2005), *Reassessing gender and achievement: questioning contemporary key debates*, Abingdon, Oxon: Routledge.

Gorard, S. (2000), *Education and social justice*, Cardiff: University of Wales Press.

Smith, E. (2005), *Analysing underachievement in schools*, London: Continuum.

NOTE

1 The achievement gap is defined as 'an index of the difference in an educational indicator (such as an examination pass rate) between two groups (such as male and female)' (Gorard 2000: 203). It is calculated by analysing the gaps in entry and in performance between two groups as shown in the equation below:

$$\text{Achievement gap} = \underset{\text{gap}}{\text{performance}} - \underset{\text{gap}}{\text{entry}}$$

$$\text{Achievement gap} = \frac{(GP - BP)}{(GP + BP)} \times 100 - \frac{(GE - BE)}{(GE + BE)} \times 100$$

GP = number of girls achieving that grade or better
BP = number of boys achieving that grade or better
GE = number of girls entered
BE = number of boys entered

This chapter links with readings 7, 8, 9, 14 and 22 of *The Routledge Education Studies Reader.*

CHAPTER 10

THE POLITICS OF EDUCATIONAL CHANGE

Alan Reid

The rationale for this chapter is:

- to make an argument that education is a political activity and educational change is a political process;
- to critique dominant approaches to educational change in education systems;
- to propose an alternative democratic model of educational change based on practitioner inquiry.

INTRODUCTION

Education as a political activity

A central feature of politics is that it is a process of decision making involving human beings. There are a few aspects to this deceptively simple statement. First, any decision making involves a consideration of, *inter alia*, values, ideologies, ideas, concepts and priorities. Since people come to decision making with different perspectives and beliefs, politics is invariably a contested process. Second, the people involved in decision making are rarely equal participants. There is always a relationship of power, whether it is based on sex, age, ethnicity, 'race', class, experience or a combination of these. Thus politics is a power-laden activity.

Once these factors are taken into account it becomes clear that it is not only the processes of formal institutions of government that are political – politics is also present in other arenas such as the local sports club, the workplace and the family home, that is, any place where people interact and make and implement decisions relevant to the activities which bring them together.

Armed with this more expansive understanding of politics, it is possible to see that formal education is a political activity. It has all the necessary ingredients, involving people engaged in a common practice and a contest of ideas, values, beliefs, and strategies. Thus education is political in at least two senses. First, it is an object of policy development and implementation in the formal institutions of the state such as Parliament; and second, formal education is a human activity conducted in places like schools and universities where decisions have to be made and implemented on a daily basis. But above all it is the contested nature of education that makes it such a political activity.

If education policy is contested, then the contest often turns upon the different values and beliefs that are held by the participants. These are expressed in education debates, in policy development and implementation, and in educational practice; and they are based on questions as diverse as the type of society we want, the best strategies to promote excellence in education, and the sorts of capabilities that should be developed in students. They are never resolved completely. Rather there is often a sort of policy 'settlement' during which time a dominant view tends to shape – but not monopolise – the parameters of educational discourse.

For example, the dominant contemporary discourse in many countries such as Australia and England is that individual choice and competition is the best way to promote quality and excellence in education. It is assumed that as education 'consumers', parents and students will vote with their feet, bypassing schools that are not up to the mark, so causing all schools to strive to emulate those which are most successful. The logical consequence of such assumptions is strategies which facilitate comparison and competition, such as league tables of schools organised on the basis of test results, or naming and shaming schools and then closing those that 'fail' (Gewirtz *et al*., 1995). (Much of this chapter makes points relevant to all sectors of education. However, I use schools as my reference point throughout the chapter, unless otherwise stated.)

But the dominant discourse is not uncontested, and in Australia and England a number of professional groups and associations argue against the contemporary policy trajectory on the basis of an alternative set of assumptions. For example, some claim that the best way to enhance quality is not to promote a culture of competition, comparison and fear of failure. For them, quality is best fostered through processes of collaboration and inquiry where educators feel able to identify and share problems, concerns and dilemmas in their practices and to explore them collectively, rather than put up smoke screens to cover problems in order to look good.

Clearly then, education is a political activity which goes far beyond the level of policy making. It follows then that the processes of educational change, at all levels of education, are political processes. These processes have a number of dimensions, including the following:

The location

It is important to recognise the political interconnections between the various arenas of education. Many writers focus a study of the politics of education on the state and its institutions such as Parliament or education departments, since these are the places where education policies and associated strategies are formulated, debated and decided upon. But the formulation of policy is, as Stephen Ball (1994) points out, only one point in the policy trajectory. Education policy is designed to shape the practices of educational institutions and the extent to which it is implemented, distorted or rejected in schools and classrooms constitutes another political process and point in the policy cycle. In these ways the various political arenas intersect. In addition, there is a micro-politics (Ball, 1987) of these institutions, where decisions are made on a daily basis as the participants engage in their ongoing work. These are as political as any engagement in the public sphere.

The participants

In each of the locations where the political process is unfolding there are participants who stand in a particular relationship to each other. Sometimes, the participants are acting individually, and sometimes in groups which are organised – formally or informally – to protect and/or promote a particular set of interests and commitments. For example, at the level of the state these individuals and groups include politicians from competing political parties, bureaucrats in education departments, lobby groups, trade unions, and professional associations; and at the level of the institution they might include teachers, parents, and students. In addition to the affiliation of interest of individuals and groups, the participants also stand in a power relationship. The extent of power is usually constructed through such factors as hierarchical position, age, sex, ethnicity, class and 'race' – individually or multiply held. Although socially constructed, these power relationships operate to maintain and extend the interests of those who hold the most power, and marginalise those who don't.

The issues and perspectives

While the ongoing practices of organisations and institutions constitute a political process, the politics of education is usually at its starkest when it is focused on a specific issue. Although the dimensions of an issue may vary according to the arena(s) in which it is being handled or discussed, educational issues invariably relate to education policy and/or practice. These can cover any number of topics such as curriculum, teaching and learning, assessment and reporting, behaviour management, funding, school and system organisation, human resources, and so on. One question that needs to be asked in any study of the politics of education is how an issue gets on the agenda: that is, for whom this is an issue or problem. It is also important to recognise that the stance on any issue is influenced by the perspectives of the participants. These perspectives are shaped by the values, beliefs, ideologies, interests, experiences and backgrounds of those involved in the issue, and can be conscious and explicit or subconscious and implicit. In either case, an understanding of any issue in education demands that the perspectives and interests of the participant are laid bare and scrutinised.

The political processes

A study of the politics of education must involve an examination not only of the substantive issues around which there is political activity, but also the processes that are being used to engage with the issues and to arrive at a decision. Of particular interest here are questions about which voices are being heard and which muted, marginalised or silenced; the methods through which issues are discussed and debated; and the processes by which decisions are made and monitored. There are many approaches to governance and ongoing decision-making in educational systems and institutions. These range from highly democratic and participative to hierarchical and authoritarian – with any number of variations in between. Just like the issues themselves, the processes employed reflect particular ideologies, values and beliefs – this time about the management and governance of human affairs.

These four dimensions suggest that understanding the politics of education and educational change involves asking a range of questions, including:

- Where are decisions being made? Why here? To what extent are these arenas autonomous?
- Who is involved? Why are they involved? Who has the most power in this situation?
- What is the issue here? Why is it an issue now and for whom?
- How is the issue understood by the various participants? What are the values, beliefs, assumptions, ideologies and concepts that are in dispute?
- What are the processes being employed for discussion and decision-making? Whose voices are being heard and whose are being marginalised or silenced?
- What are the processes by which decisions are monitored and evaluated?

I have argued that education and politics are intimately connected, and that the processes of educational change are political processes. And yet much of the literature about educational change, as well as the processes of change employed by most education systems, ignore this obvious fact (Hargreaves and Goodson, 2006). They tend to treat change as an apolitical phenomenon, free of the messiness of politics. In my view this blind spot impoverishes not only our understanding of educational change but also weakens educational decision making and practice. If education is a political activity involving a contest of ideas, values and beliefs, then there should be structures and processes which enable the political process to function effectively; and those involved – practising educators as well as policy makers – need to understand not only the process but also have the skills to engage as active participants in it.

In the rest of this chapter I want to pick up on this aspect of the politics of education by exploring it from the perspective of educational change. In so doing I will make the argument that the structures and processes extant in most education system are inadequate to meeting the challenges of contemporary times and I will propose an alternative model of educational change.

Educators and processes of educational change: the dominant model[1]

Although practising educators are central to the implementation of education policy, they have not always been important participants in the development of education policy. That is, in many, even most, education systems, teachers are treated as classroom technicians whose task it is to put in place the ideas and plans of 'experts' such as policy makers in education bureaucracies, rather than as professionals with important knowledge and insights. This approach is institutionalised in the structures and processes of education systems (Smyth *et al.*, 2000).

In the dominant organisational model a policy, plan or product is developed in central office – usually as a response to emerging needs or a government priority – and the task of schools is to implement that policy. The extent to which this happens in isolation from schools varies depending on the system. In some education systems there is a history of widespread consultation in relation to major policy developments. This contrasts with other jurisdictions where consultation is limited and where there is a high level of central prescription. Nonetheless, in both cases consultation about a policy or product is invariably about the detail – it rarely involves input into the process of conceptualisation. The sorts of questions that teachers ask in this model are: how do we implement this? How do we achieve these targets? In addition, the consultation process itself is usually in relation to the 'product' or 'policy' at a particular point in time: it stops when the development phase is over.

There are a number of problems with this dominant model. First, the model impoverishes the knowledge base for educational policy making. By foregrounding bureaucratic knowledge, the model marginalises arguably the most consequential knowledge in an education system – school-based knowledge-in-action, that is the knowledge produced by educators in the context of working with children and young people.

Second, the model promotes a façade of change. All that has been discovered about educational change over the past 20 years tells us that change occurs when those whose practice is the focus of change are involved in the process of challenging and rethinking the assumptions and theories upon which their practice is based (e.g., Fullan, 1999, 2001, 2003). Unless this happens, imposed change in the form of a new 'product' is simply filtered through the lens of established beliefs and practices, and is colonised by that practice. The same things are done but with new labels.

Third, the model limits the possibilities for real improvement, because it does not encourage educators to focus on deepening their understanding about teaching and learning. Indeed the model promotes superficial forms of external accountability. It understands accountability to mean closing the gap between what is developed (or aspired to) centrally and the 'outcomes' in schools. When the gap refuses to close, the fault is invariably located with schools. This is a spurious form of accountability because it encourages educators to hide issues and problems, rather than discuss them openly. In so doing, it contributes to the privatisation of professional practice. Real accountability comes from genuine attempts to deepen understandings about teaching and learning through inquiry and research, discussion and debate, in an atmosphere of collaboration and trust. Imposed accountability encourages smoke screens; real accountability is transparent.

Finally, the model fails to recognise the rapidly changing contexts in which schools operate and for which they are preparing students. Contemporary times have been labelled as the end of certainty (e.g., Kelly, 1992). That is, the confident twentieth-century belief that scientific rationality can solve all our social and environmental problems has been replaced by a recognition of the greater complexity and ambiguity of late modern times. In all countries, economic, political and cultural globalisation, accompanied by new communication technologies are affecting every aspect of our lives, including work, family, communities, citizenship and identities. The nature and speed of this change have significant implications for education because it redefines the sorts of capabilities that are needed to live in the twenty-first century.

Kress (2000), for example, maintains that the scale of change calls for an 'education for instability' by which he means that education for the stabilities of well-defined citizenship or participation in stable economies must be replaced by education for creativity, innovativeness, adaptability, and ease with difference and change. This form of education would seek to promote in children and young people the capabilities to generate new ideas, insights and explanations to meet the challenges of the changing contexts in which they live.

In the twenty-first century educators must have the capacity to question their routine practices and assumptions and to investigate the effects of their teaching on student learning. Many of the issues facing educators today are context-bound: they are not amenable to universal solutions. That is, educators face the considerable challenge of designing curricula for local contexts that are flexible enough to address the rapid growth of knowledge, and that recognise the increasing religious, cultural and ethnic diversity in their student populations. Educators must have the capacity to be always deepening their understandings of teaching and learning through *reflection and inquiry*. After all, if the task of educators is to develop in children and young people the learning dispositions and capacities to think critically, flexibly and creatively, then educators too must possess and model these capacities.

This argument suggests that the dominant model of educational change where educators are excluded from the politics of the policy process and expected simply to implement policy and programs developed by others, is no longer tenable. From this perspective, educators are professionals who are able to theorise systematically and rigorously in different learning contexts about their professional practices – including the issues, problems, concerns, dilemmas, contradictions and interesting situations that confront them in their daily professional lives; and can develop, implement and evaluate strategies to address these. That is, educators are understood as people who learn *from* teaching rather than as people who have finished learning how to teach (Darling-Hammond, 2000).

If being an educator in the twenty-first century centrally involves the capacity to inquire into professional practice, then the notion of inquiry is not a project or the latest fad. *It is a way of professional being.* The question that needs to be asked is not whether educators should be inquirers into professional practice, but how they can become more so and how they can continue to build their inquiry capacities throughout their professional lives.

Unfortunately, the dominant model of educational change creates its own logic and dynamic and entrenches the view of educators as technicians whose job it is to implement policy and curriculum products designed by others. Ironically one of the responses to the speed of change has been to strengthen this view. Thus, often the reaction to the challenges of the new environment has been to devise and implement more policy, produce more packages and construct more accountability mechanisms. It is an old response to a new challenge.

Rethinking the role of educators in decision making

One alternative to the dominant approach is to establish a system that organises its practices upon and around *inquiry and research*. This would mean moving from the well-worn path of producing and imposing more products as a response to new challenges, to an approach that focuses on the strengthening of professional capacity and agency. This does not mean that educational resources and policies are not needed. Rather, it suggests that these should be more responsive to the insights and issues that emerge from a process of inquiry and research. That is a very different dynamic. But before explaining how this might work, it is important to briefly sketch out what I mean by inquiry.

There is a wealth of research and professional literature that focuses on inquiry, also referred to as reflective practice. Its beginnings can be traced back to the work of John Dewey (1933/1958), but it is in the last 20 years that the literature has burgeoned through the writing of scholars such as Schon (1983, 1990), Goodman (1984), Cochran-Smith and Lytle (1993), Zeichner and Liston (1996) and Farrell (2004). Elsewhere, I define inquiry as a 'process of systematic, rigorous and critical reflection about professional practice, and the contexts in which it occurs, in ways that question taken-for-granted assumptions' (Reid, 2004, p. 4). Its purpose is to inform decision-making for action. Inquiry can be undertaken individually, but it is most powerful when it is collaborative. It involves educators pursuing their 'wonderings' (Hubbard & Power, 1993), seeking answers to questions or puzzles that come from real-world observations and dilemmas.

Inquiry is not just a technical activity, focusing only on how to make existing practices more efficient. It has two other important dimensions. The first – a conceptual dimension – involves educators analysing the reasons for actions taken, such as examining the theory behind their practices and exploring alternatives. And the second – a critical dimension – involves justifying what is done in relation to the moral, ethical and socio-political issues associated with practice and looking at the external forces and broader social conditions that frame it, in order to gain greater understanding (Farrell, 2004). Critical forms of inquiry are centred on a commitment to equity and social justice. Thus inquiry involves the following sorts of reflective questioning:

- What am I/we doing in relation to this practice/issue/question/puzzle? (e.g. in the classroom/school/district/central office);
- Why am I/we doing this? (e.g. what theories are expressed in my/our practices, and whose interests do these represent?);
- What are the effects of these practices? Who is most advantaged/least advantaged?;
- What alternatives are there to my/our current practice? Are these likely to result in more just outcomes? What will I/we do? How will I/we monitor these changes in order to assess their outcomes?

I have argued that all those involved in education systems – those whose main role it is to support educators as well as those directly engaged with children and young people – should be inquirers into their professional practices. Given the interdependence of these roles, the question of who is involved in specific processes of inquiry will vary according to the context and circumstances.

As a general rule, those who are most affected by the focus of the inquiry will be involved. In education this is seldom easy to determine and it does raise some interesting questions. For example, a classroom teacher may decide that the focus of her inquiry is a puzzle associated with her teaching. In those circumstances where decisions need to be made in a short space of time she will inquire on her own. In other circumstances where the matter is not as urgent or is complex she will work with others over a longer period of time.

Inquiry is often more powerful when it is conducted with invited others – perhaps other educators who are interested in the same puzzle or who she trusts, or someone outside the site. More than this, however, the puzzle will invariably have some connection to the students in her care. Students can be involved as inquirers, learning about their learning, and about inquiry, as they explore an inquiry question with their teacher. Reflection is best conducted as a social rather than a solitary practice, and our ideas can be better clarified when we talk with others about them. As Osterman and Kottkamp argue:

> Because of the deeply ingrained nature of our behavioural patterns, it is sometimes difficult to develop a critical perspective on our own behaviour. For that reason alone, analysis occurring in a collaborative and cooperative environment is likely to lead to greater learning.
> (Osterman & Kottkamp, 1993: 25, quoted in Zeichner & Lister, 1996: 18)

The wider the question, the wider the scope for involvement of others. An inquiry question that relates to a whole institution demands a much broader involvement. Of course there might be a small number of staff members who lead the inquiry, but they will find ways of involving those who are affected by the issue – such as other staff, students, parents and community members – both in the process of reflection as well as data gathering.

Another way of looking at the question of who is involved in inquiry is to recognise the importance of looking outside the specific workplace for ideas and inspiration. Inquiry can be an exercise in navel gazing, or it can offer a powerful means to look outwards, engaging with the ideas, innovations and research that are circulating in the wider society. Questions such as how do others see this issue?, what are others doing?, what does the research tell us? are all ways of expanding the possibilities of inquiry.

It should be clear from my description that inquiry is not a 'thing', such as a model or series of steps or procedures. While it involves logical problem-solving processes, it also involves intuition, passion and emotion. It is a holistic way of working and responding to the many issues and dilemmas that emerge in any workplace. Educators who are inquirers will never announce that they 'do' inquiry, thus separating the activity from their professional being. Rather they might describe how they work – that is, the ways in which they inquire into their professional practice and how they are always striving to develop and expand their capacity to inquire.

There are a range of ways in which a process of inquiry or reflection can be facilitated. Over the course of their professional careers, educators might develop a suite of inquiry approaches and techniques, a sort of inquiry toolbox. The key characteristic of each approach is that it is designed to facilitate critical reflection. Inquirers will continue to work to sharpen these through practical experience and reflection, and to add to the tool-box by exploring new approaches. The approaches include action research, critical dialogue, systematic observation and reflection, appreciative inquiry and so on.

It is crucial to recognise that each of these approaches to inquiry has a body of research literature behind it. This suggests that an inquiry tool-box needs to be built slowly. It might involve selecting an approach, reading about it, talking with people who have used it, experimenting with it and documenting experiences, and reflecting on the approach itself as well as the focus of the inquiry in which it has been used. No education system or single institution should simply exhort people to engage in inquiry without an acknowledgement that inquiry skills need to built thoughtfully and systematically.

Of course, inquiry will only flourish in conditions that promote it. Since the basis of inquiry involves self and collaborative critical reflection about established practices and routines, it presumes an institutional and system-wide environment of *trust*. That is, educators must feel that they can reveal aspects of their practice about which they have concerns and explore these without it counting against them. A culture of inquiry would also be one that celebrates discussion and debate. However, such an environment demands a number of characteristics, not the least of which is that such debate is civil and respectful, where people are not put down or demeaned for holding different viewpoints, where there is a genuine attempt to listen to all, not just the most powerful, and where there is a plentiful supply of good humour. It also demands that participants are open-minded and willing to subject their beliefs, assumptions and practices to critical scrutiny.

Inquiry is not just a matter for individual teachers. If as I have argued, inquiry is a way of professional being for the educator of the twenty-first century, it is crucial that educational institutions as a whole (such as schools and universities) and the central and regional offices of education systems, model and support inquiry. Unless this happens, inquiry approaches are destined to be constrained at best and fail at worst. Wells (1994) for example, argues that inquiry and research should focus on whole school/centre improvement, not just individual classroom improvement, and that the policies, artefacts and processes of the site should be consistent with inquiry. This is an important step, but in my view going beyond individual educators to the whole school/centre level is still not sufficient.

The operations of education bureaucracies are also fundamental to inquiry and research. Unless they are consistent with inquiry they can actually work against it. This means more than providing support to schools. It also means developing policies and processes relating to such areas as planning and reporting, curriculum, and human resources in ways that both model and sustain inquiry and research. In another context, Fullan (2003) calls this a 'tri-level reform' model where the interaction between the layers of the system mutually reinforce the reform aspirations. This may seem obvious, and yet despite plentiful rhetoric, to my knowledge there are no education systems in the world that have consciously organised their policies and practices such that they are consistent with inquiry and research. So what can be done?

EDUCATORS AND PROCESSES OF EDUCATIONAL CHANGE: AN ALTERNATIVE APPROACH

So far I have argued that if education is a political process at a range of levels, then educators should be involved in the political process. Not only should they have the skills and understandings to be so involved, so too should the organisational structures and processes of education systems promote such involvement, central to which are inquiry and research. However, the dominant model of educational change is at odds with such a view, understanding educators to be passive implementers of policy rather than active agents in policy development. This fails to meet the challenges of education in the twenty-first century.

An alternative model would be based on a system-wide culture of inquiry and research where teachers are engaged in inquiry and research into the issues, problems, puzzles and dilemmas associated with their educational practice; and where the new knowledge and the issues that emerge from this process are fed back into classrooms and schools, deepening learning and reinvigorating professional discussion and debate. But more than this, such a model would ensure that there are structures and processes in place that enable the insights and issues from inquiry to be aggregated and responded to at the various bureaucratic levels such as the regional level (e.g., in the form of professional development support), and the Central Office level (e.g., in the form of changing policy or providing resources to meet emerging demands).

It is important to understand that this model is not a 'bottom-up' approach. Rather, it is constructed upon an understanding that there is an iterative dynamic between the various layers of the system. This dynamic does not obviate the continued need for the central identification of system priorities. The government will continue to express priorities, although they may be affected by the knowledge that is being produced, and the issues that are being identified, by schools. But much of the work of Central and Regional Offices will involve responding to the implications of what is emerging from inquiry and research in relation to these priorities – meeting the needs identified by schools for learning and professional development resources, providing arenas in which the new professional knowledge can be shared and debated, altering policies to reflect new insights, and so on.

It is also important to understand that the model is not suggesting that the only worthwhile knowledge is that produced in schools. Far from it. The sort of inquiry being argued for here will draw upon innovative ideas and the latest research, produced in other contexts and other countries. Indeed, it may be that the system could establish a group, centrally based, whose function it is to keep ideas circulating in the system, challenging established practices and sacred cows. And there would be a close relationship with the educational research community, with a constant and interactive flow of people and ideas. But the difference is that these ideas would not be imposed. They would be treated as part of an inquiry-mix, examined systematically by those engaged in the business of educating.

It will be apparent that the dynamic here is very different from that of the dominant approach. Rather than responding to the challenges of contemporary times by developing new products, this model focuses on the processes of inquiry and research and the development of professional capacity through a dynamic relationship between centre and schools. The products and policies follow. Put another way, the sorts of questions that schools ask in this model are: What is our current practice in relation to this priority? What are the issues? What do we need to know about these and how will we get the information? What support do we need? What should we aim to achieve? How will we know if we get there?

In my view there are a number of advantages of this approach. These are that the model has the potential to:

- foster deeper understandings about teaching and learning and thus enhance student learning outcomes;
- lead to genuine forms of accountability that are based on collaborative efforts to identify problems and their causes;
- make Central Office policy, plans and products responsive to the needs of schools;
- contribute to the breaking down of the 'them and us' culture that has developed in education systems in recent years;

- lead to genuine change because it is consistent with what is known about the factors that promote change;
- ground the idea of a learning organisation and foster powerful professional development (Dana, Gimbert & Silva, 2001);
- provide a much richer source of information for education policy making.

But just as there are many advantages, so too are there dangers. A key one is the danger of superficiality, where the concept of inquiry is embraced enthusiastically but applied uncritically to many activities and issues without a deep understanding of the conditions that are needed for it to flourish. It is crucial that education systems move gradually, thoughtfully and systematically to build a culture of inquiry. So what needs to change if an education system is to move to this approach? What would be the characteristics of a system that was organised around inquiry and research?

An education system that has institutionalised inquiry and research as a way of system being would have a number of characteristics which would be apparent at every layer of the organisation. For example:

1 All staff in the education system would possess, and continue to develop, the skills and dispositions for inquiry and research. This would need to happen in a coherent and systematic way. For example, education systems might undertake a stocktake of the resources and programmes supporting the development of inquiry capabilities, and explore additional ways to refine and expand inquiry capabilities. The latter might include working with the universities and their pre-service teacher education students to explore approaches to linking students to inquiry projects, thus providing an inquiry resource to schools and a valuable learning experience for students (e.g., Reid & O'Donoghue, 2004).
2 There would be structures and processes that model and support inquiry and research. An education system that was organised upon a culture of inquiry would ensure that its structures and processes at every level, from the classroom to Central Office, are consistent with, and promote, inquiry. These would facilitate knowledge exchange, encourage discussion and debate and promote evidence-based policy.
3 The culture of an inquiry-based system would be one that consciously builds an environment that nurtures the conditions within which inquiry and research can flourish and grow. These conditions need to be a common denominator across the system. They include the nature of relationships and the conduct of professional conversations, and they need to be explicit and never taken for granted. The sorts of conditions that foster deep and transparent critical inquiry include ones that encourage discussion and debate involving the widest range of voices possible; reject certainty and dogmatism; are based on trust, where people feel free to talk about difficulties and concerns in their teaching; model inquiry at all layers of the system; and are respectful, tolerant and civil.

Moving to a culture of inquiry will not happen overnight. It will have to be built thoughtfully and systematically, and it needs to be sustainable. Hargreaves and Fink (2003) describe this as moving beyond the notion of implementation of change towards the *institutionalisation* of change. For them, sustainable change involves building long-term capacity for improvement, not squandering resources on glamorous pilot projects that burn brightly for a time and then vanish without a trace. Sustainable change cultivates and recreates an 'educational ecosystem' that promotes diversity and creativity not standardisation. In short, sustainable change:

> . . . is enduring, not evanescent. It does not put its investment dollars into the high profile launch of an initiative and then withdraw them when the glamour has gone. Sustainable improvement demands committed relationships, not fleeting infatuation. It is change for keeps and change for good. Sustainable improvement contributes to the growth and good of everyone, instead of fostering the fortunes of the few at the expense of the rest.
>
> (Hargreaves and Fink, 2003, p. 694)

SUMMARY

In this paper I have argued that education is a political activity because it involves people making decisions about a social practice, the purposes of which are contested on the basis of differences about beliefs, assumptions and values. If the object of educational practice is political because it is disputed, then so too are the processes that lead to decisions about educational enactment in different places, contexts and times. I suggested that an understanding of the politics of education demands a capacity to ask and respond to a number of critical questions about the various dimensions of the political process.

More than this, however, I maintained that since education is a political and therefore contested activity, a key consideration for any democracy is how to establish processes which best foster discussion and debate, do not involve some and exclude others, and are based on the best information available to the decision-makers. In this chapter I have focused on the role of educators, arguing for the need for an alternative to the dominant managerialist and interventionist models of educational change that are so prevalent today. Such approaches have been largely discredited in the educational literature, and yet there have been few, if any, attempts to establish different models of educational change. I have proposed a system-wide approach organised around inquiry and research as a powerful alternative strategy which is more suited to the demands of the contemporary world.

KEY QUESTIONS

1. Do you agree that the broad purposes of schooling are the achievement of democratic equality, social efficiency and social mobility?
2. What would a school look like that was in a good position to achieve these three purposes?
3. What sort of changes, if any, do you think need to be made to the current education system in order to achieve the three purposes mentioned above?

FURTHER READING

Ball, S. (2008) *The education debate*, Bristol, UK: Policy Press.

Fullan, M. (2003) *Change forces with a vengeance*, London & New York: RoutledgeFalmer.

Hargreaves, A. & Goodson, I. (2006) Educational change over time? The sustainability and nonsustainability of three decades of secondary school change and continuity. *Educational Administration Quarterly*, 42, 1, 3–41.

Lankshear, C. & Noble, M. (2004) *A handbook for teacher research: from design to implementation*, Buckingham, UK: Open University Press.

NOTE

1 In 2004, I was seconded to the South Australian Department of Education and Children's Services (DECS) to work on the development of a culture of inquiry across the public education system in South Australia. Some of the ideas in the rest of this chapter were developed during that experience and I would like to acknowledge the many DECS educators with whom I discussed and refined the ideas; and some of the text is based on a paper that I wrote for DECS (Reid, 2004).

This chapter links with readings 4, 10 and 11 of *The Routledge Education Studies Reader.*

DEBATE 3

ARE DEVELOPMENTS IN POST-14 EDUCATION REDUCING THE DIVIDE BETWEEN THE ACADEMIC AND THE VOCATIONAL?

Richard Pring and John Fox

A debate between Richard Pring, Lead Director 14-19 Education and Training England and Wales, and John Fox, Advanced Skills Teacher, Oxfordshire Local Authority. Both Richard Pring and John Fox are hugely experienced in the field of academic and vocational education. Their knowledge, experiences and perceptions allow them to reflect on fundamental questions about the nature of education and schooling that are applied particularly in the context of a highly significant White Paper published in 2005. The contributors to this debate have made use of their overlapping but distinct experiences and show important reactions to the arguments about the purpose of education.

RICHARD PRING

14-19 developments

There are many changes taking place in what is now called the 14-19 phase of education and training. Two are of significance for this paper.

First, there is concern about the number of young people who are 'turned off' education at an early age, leaving school at the first opportunity – many joining those 'not in education, employment or training' (the so-called NEET group). What is needed, so it is argued, is more motivating learning experiences – a different sort of curriculum from the traditionally 'academic' one at which so many fail.

Second, the country needs a much more skilled workforce if it is to compete successfully in a highly competitive world market.

The answer, expressed in many government papers (the most significant being the DfES *Education and Skills 14-19*, referred to from now as the White Paper), would seem to lie in the introduction of vocational studies. The academic suits some, the vocational motivates others as well as producing the skills that the Leitch Report said were lacking for future economic needs.

In one sense, this division of formal learning into the academic and the vocational would not seem to create too divided a system because another arm of government policy is that of creating strong collaborative partnerships between schools, colleges of further education, independent training providers and employers. Already about 150,000 young people aged between 14 and 16 do some of their studies in the more vocationally oriented environment of colleges of further education. There are Centres of Vocational Excellence which students are attending from schools, as well as those from colleges of FE. With the new Diplomas, 'generic learning' (e.g. wider key skills) and specialist learning (which could include an 'academic subject') sit alongside 'principal learning' (which would be occupation-related, for example, in engineering, hairdressing or health and social care). It would seem that 'academic' and 'vocational' are coming together through a wider range of, and greater access to, courses and through the collaborative learning partnerships which are being created.

But is this the case? And if not, what are the problems?

A divided system?

First, the government's rejection of the Tomlinson Report in 2004 led to the maintenance of a divided system, in that, instead of creating a flexible set of tracks through different kinds of courses under the umbrella of a single Diploma, the government chose instead to create a tripartite system based on very different routes beginning at the age of 14: the GCSE route leading on to A-Levels, what was initially called the general vocational Diploma route, and the specifically focused apprenticeship route – very definitely 'vocational'. The Diploma route was at first to replace such popular qualification programmes as the BTEC which attracted many young people into the colleges at 16 to pursue a more practical mode of learning which opened up particular careers.

However, language matters. The vocational diplomas were to lead into both higher education and apprenticeships, but later it was felt that the term 'vocational' might deter potential higher education applicants, and so 'vocational' gave way to 'specialised', and even this has now been dropped. But relevance to the world of employment is preserved through the 'principal learning' plus at least ten days work-based learning each year. And their vocational orientation is maintained through the leadership of 14 Diploma Development Partnerships which are made up mainly of employers. It is difficult to describe the qualifications framework without slipping into the academic/vocational divide.

Second, the apprenticeship route continues to be emphasised as a vocational alternative to the academic for those who know where their working lives should lead and who therefore want the required skills and experience. But apprenticeships have been constantly 'reformed' in content and ownership. Once they were work-based learning routes, involving a contract with an employer, leading to a 'licence to practise', and with some relevant day-release studies in a local college. The creation of 'modern apprenticeships' transformed this so that Level 2 would hardly constitute a licence to practise, even though it counted as a 'completed' apprenticeship, and many even at Level 3 do not involve a contract with an employer.

In effect, those encouraged to progress up the vocational route(s) are those deemed unlikely to succeed academically. They increasingly are directed to institutions which specialise in 'the vocational', or into apprenticeships. Schools' sixth forms, and especially the growing number of sixth-form colleges, look after the 'academic' students, deprived of any opportunity to pick up the practical. We therefore retain a tripartite system, albeit often implemented within a more co-operative institutional environment.

Academic and vocational

However, there is something wrong with this distribution of young people into academic and vocational. The distinction, which permeates policy and practice, between 'academic' and 'vocational', though taken as self-evident, provides a limited view of both. For Dewey (1916, p. 307), 'a vocation means nothing but such a direction of life activities as renders them perceptibly significant to a person, because of the consequences they accomplish, and also useful to his associates'. 'Vocational' in this broad sense embraces all kinds of personally significant learning as the young person contemplates the future direction of his or her life.

Furthermore, partly as a result of that 'false dualism', the importance of 'the practical' (so often confused with the vocational) as a way of knowing and understanding has been undervalued, especially but not exclusively for the so-called academic young people.

'Academic' is never defined, but it is strongly associated with a certain content and mode of learning, a modernised echo of the mid-twentieth-century bias for classics against science, history and geography and the general suspicion of new, slightly dubious subjects like archaeology and geology. The content is largely determined by the theoretical knowledge, which is organised in subjects, which can be transmitted as such to the learner, and which can be written down. Literacy skills are extremely important – to be able to read textbooks and to be able to put on paper what has been learnt. This in turn requires certain forms of assessment and grading and a penchant for writing.

'Vocational', on the other hand, is seen to require the acquisition of practical skills – the ability to do and to make. Such capacities relate eventually to doing a particular job, that of a hairdresser, a mechanic, an electrician, a secretary. There is an emphasis on employment-related 'skills'. As a result, a lot of learning which is associated with the 'academic' (knowledge of principles underlying the practical, understanding of the historical and social context of the vocational skills) is neglected or omitted. Some people are good with their heads, some with their hands, and some simply good – a three-part classification which was embodied in the Norwood Report (1943), which recommended and shaped the post-war tripartite system.

This distinction carries with it a differentiation of status. No declaration of 'equality of esteem' between academic and vocational qualifications will make them so. Indeed, in order to give equal status to vocational qualifications, the General National Vocational Qualifications at Level 3 were renamed Vocational A-Levels and, as with the later development of GNVQs, were supposed to gain respectability through a mode of assessment which would show their comparability with A-Levels. The practical learning at the heart of the vocational qualifications was increasingly to be assessed through the written medium.

However, it is difficult to maintain this distinction and, with it, the differentiated status which it implies. It is difficult, for example, to see where the arts and humanities fit within such a distinction. Is drama (not writing criticism of plays but acting in and directing plays) academic or vocational? Is the exploration, in the humanities, of the controversial issues which divide people in society and which require systematic reflection upon experience, academic or vocational? It is significant that, in the changes which are taking place, the arts and the humanities can be dropped at the age of 14, and practical engagement with them is playing a less significant part in the education of young people.

The practical

It is important to distinguish between 'knowing that' and 'knowing how' – between propositional knowledge and practical know-how. Propositional knowledge is the knowledge of the physical and social world which can be put down in statements, be verified by reference to experience, and give rise to explanatory theories. Practical knowledge, on the other hand, often escapes articulation in 'knowledge that'. Such practical knowledge is gained from practising, albeit often under the correction and guidance of a mentor or trainer. Moreover, it is assessed through the 'successful doing', not through writing about doing.

Such practical knowledge can be more or less intelligent. The recognition of the distinctive quality of practical intelligence was provided by the Manifesto of Capability published by the Royal Society of Arts in 1986. The Manifesto emphasised the capacity for 'intelligent doing', and indeed this notion of 'practical intelligence' or 'capability' has been a hall-mark of the RSA throughout its 250 years of history. That history is distinguished by the advocacy of the integration of theory and practice, of thinking, doing and making, and of the arts, science and commerce. Such a unity is destroyed, to the detriment of all, where the division is made between the academic (the world of abstractions and the transmission of knowledge) and the so-called vocational.

It is, therefore, a mistake to confuse 'practical' with 'vocational'. The practical is a valuable way of knowing and of *intelligent* doing in itself. That is, and has been, reflected, in a wide range of innovative practices, both past and present. The Technical and Vocational Education Initiative launched in 1983, integrated theory and practice through making and designing. That was an attempt to overcome the divide between the academic and the vocational, but it did not survive the introduction of the National Curriculum.

Conclusion

The developments aimed at a reform of the 14-19 phase of education and training are still in danger of assuming a clear distinction between academic and vocational courses, leading to increased selection at 14. Those who are not very good at so-called academic work will be, if they are not already being, directed up the so-called vocational route, which is more practical and employment-related.

The dangers are these. First, the importance of practical learning in general education is not recognised, creating a division therefore between the academic learning (non-practical) and vocational learning which is identified (wrongly) with being practical and which is seen as a poor relation. What were once thriving woodwork and metalwork departments in schools have declined, as indeed has the training of teachers of practical subjects. Where practical courses do exist, the 'successful doings' are so often assessed as if they were theoretical undertakings.

Second, the practical costs much more than the academic which can survive on pen and paper; the rise of Health and Safety protocols has increased the expense of kitting out basic workshops even from what it used to be; the finding of suitably qualified teachers to use such workshops has also become a problem because of the degrees most teachers have to have – a result of the academic/vocational divide!

Third, the confusion of practical learning with 'vocational training' undermines the value of practical learning for all young people, especially the 'academically able'.

JOHN FOX

The following is a reflection from a teacher (who daily witnessed the damage of the academic/vocational divide) on the White Paper *Education and Skills: 14–19*, and on the Tomlinson Report to which it was an answer. The current distinctions between the academic and the vocational, and the developments which are underpinned by those distinctions, are embodied in that Paper and that Report.

'Vocational'?

The new use of 'vocational' is as a catch-all (or bin) for all that is 'not academic'. It is a well-meant, respectful re-tooling of an ancient term to describe that major part of the educational spectrum which has been held in lower esteem than it should have been.

'Vocational' appears to be about attaining 'parity of esteem' against education's built-in academicising tendency. Language lives and changes, but this evolution of the 'vocational' has been induced and accelerated. We may have to accept it, but it brings ambiguities. 'Vocation' was originally taken from the religious way of life, literally a 'calling', and by extension has long been used to describe 'business or profession' as a secular *way of life*. It now seems to be being stretched to cover more of the education spectrum than it should and thereby becoming a synonym for 'practical education' which, however, is a dimension, not a category. 'Vocational GCSEs' are surely *pre*-vocational work – 'practical education' formalised and specialised? If not, then A-Levels in law and psychology should also be called 'vocational qualifications' (which they are patently not).

Both the Tomlinson Report and the White Paper showed awareness of this overstretch and both tried to separate 'vocational' (which they both insisted upon keeping) from 'training' and 'skill specialism' to give it a more general 'educational' level of meaning. However, they do not explain how the newly coined 'vocational *education*' is to be distinguished from the older more recognisable currency 'vocational *training*'? Does it need to be? Is it sending confusing signals?

Am I alone in interpreting education as 'broader, for life' and for its own sake, and training as 'narrower, more utilitarian, for specialist skills', while accepting some overlap?

By 2015 students are to be taught 'by restaurant chefs, not cookery teachers' (White Paper, 7.14). The soundbite is unfortunate for its apparent disdain for teachers, schools and 'cooking', and for its dazzled respect for the restaurant lifestyle. David (a White Paper illustration), who is 'very clever and also enjoys taking things apart', is assumed to be an unusual combination, although his was once called an 'enquiring' rather than a 'clever' mind, the one a description, the other a value claim. Another exemplar obtained a place at Cambridge with '*only* vocational qualifications' (9.2), but the university graduates [with non-vocational, irrelevant degrees] who go on to make bespoke furniture are not mentioned.

The White Paper's chef has his place in fine dining; he may be community-minded enough to help in FE; but he will never cover the nation's schools (revealingly the White Paper intends he should be confined to FE colleges). A curriculum enrichment and teaching resource, however welcome, can never replace the good (but almost extinct) 'cookery teacher' who would generate the 'practical education' dimension in school, drawing on his/her experience.

Cooking – academic or vocational, education or training?

Who enthuses the budding chef? Jamie Oliver lamented the lack of basic knowledge of food, nutrition and food preparation in the youngsters he televised. The domestic science, housecraft and home economics (synonyms 1940–1980) teachers together with their facilities were eliminated from the curriculum in 1988. With them went transmission of basic life and care skills 'from birth to death' and a practical dimension in schooling. Teachers still taught the new 'vocational' GCSEs; in one school I know, a former nurse teaches 'health and social care' and a former business executive teaches 'business'. Students attend FE colleges for other popular 'vocational GCSEs'. Were it not for the particular life experience of the two staff – an accident, not a requirement of their being teachers – and the versatility which marks out so many teachers, no 'vocational' GCSE could be seriously offered in that school. The FE lead providers would provide all. If 'vocational' eclipses the dimension of 'practical education', and if colleges will be the new lead-providers, and if school teachers are marginal to the newly dubbed 'vocational' teaching, the question is, what will be left for schools?

The White Paper's proposal that by 2015 pupils will be taught 'by restaurant chefs not cookery teachers' reveals an ignorance of modern school staffing and facilities, let alone the real role of a good chef. Food and nutrition is so central to life it should not be trivialised in education debates or polarised between fine chefs and the school dinner service. 'Cookery' reflects the mild contempt made explicit to my sister, a lifetime Domestic Science teacher, by one headmistress, 'Any fool can cook'. The trained domestic science teacher was a professional teacher who had a recognised specialism acquired at a recognised institution such as Gloucester or Bath. No one ever questioned the academic respectability of the major sciences because of their practical element, but domestic science even at A-Level did not get the recognition as a science, let alone a life skill, which it deserved. The arbitrary refusal of some universities to accept it as a genuine A-Level did not help, but this was waning before 1987. The subject's demise was partly due to the politics of the curriculum, where new faculties competed for ownership of smaller cross-faculty subjects and haggled over whether domestic science was a technology, an art, a science or, as its teachers argued, a life skill and/or science *sui generis*. It was also relatively expensive in plant and personnel and had a traditional gender slant which could in turn feed a gender prejudice. Interestingly that gender prejudice has evaporated since boys do cook and it is no longer a poncy thing to be seen doing. The National Curriculum almost dealt it a mortal blow. In 'academic' eyes domestic science was caricatured as secondary modern CSE 'cookery' and as non-academic time-filling. This all meant that domestic science was never reformed appropriately.

Current headline concerns about diet, obesity and lack of basic food knowledge show what a gap has been left. It is not nostalgia to ask for revival of the teaching of such real life skills, particularly with Tomlinson's emphasis on skill lists. 'Domestic science' was a genuinely 'practical education', and was never offered as 'vocational training' any more than maths is taught to train mathematicians. It educated all the senses (including, unusually, smell and taste) in courses wider than just practical nutrition (though cookery was a more visible core feature). Budgeting, decorating, home buying, home running, home nursing, first aid, baby care, elderly care, hygiene, textiles and social services were about core life skills in a way that restauranting, however highly starred, can never be. It was 'practical education' par excellence, the *dimension* which provides the excitement, the taster, the enthusiasm, and relevant life skills, but *not a training*.

Through what Tomlinson several times calls 'passion and excitement', and the White Paper once actually calls 'enjoyment' (3.12), many pupils may be inspired by the practical dimension to go on to specialism training, *but later*. Most will not, but all will have had a balanced 'practical and abstract' education (3.3), taken away a life skill, and with good teaching will hopefully have enjoyed it.

Academic?

Popular parlance, shaped by the language of the public debate, increasingly uses 'vocational' as the opposite of 'academic and intellectual'. The White Paper did mention 'vocational training *and* education' in the 14-19 context (2.20), but with no explanation of the difference, or of where one exchanges with the other in the 14-19 spectrum. It adds to the confusion with 'vocational *study*' (3.10), which may be an attempt at academic dress. A prestigious new university in its hotel and catering management-degree course recently required an *essay* on 'crumbing', thereby academicising the removal of crumbs from flat surfaces.

Sir Humphrey could have written the circumlocution in 2.17, which after calling A-Level and GCSE 'well recognised routes to success' goes on to describe 'those who *prefer* to learn in a different way, who would benefit from a greater variety of learning skills . . . or who are more interested by learning in ways with direct practical applicability'. In this thinking style, the 'academic' is the norm, the route to success, a gift. The 'practical' is a condition needing a remedy, a preference, a fad, an 'educational veganism' which needs special provision, rather akin to 'special needs'. It speaks later of 'those whose preference is for more practical learning with obvious relevance and application . . .' (3.3).

The question is surely and seriously begged, what *in*applicable *ir*relevancies are 'academic' youngsters studying now and why? Are we overteaching certain limited subjects to fill statutory school time, and to the exclusion of other areas of experience? David (7.00), who is 'not only academically able [but also] enjoys taking things apart' gets no credit for any ability to *rebuild* (or for having to organise his shed in which he stores all those bits he can't put back). The proposed Skills Level 3 (Advanced) is still primarily about university – 'real stretch . . . for those preparing for a top university' (7.9). By implication, manual skills, brains in fingertips, are *not* stretched or stretching. The White Paper laments 'fewer than 40% of the age cohort take even one A-Level' (8.13); in contrast, Tomlinson noted that 'fewer than one-fifth of our 17-year-olds study an advanced level vocational topic' (133), but *neither* laments this for Skills Levels 1 or 2 which seem not to count, yet which are far more populated and which are the decision-making levels. The elite is still top of both protagonists' agendas in the current debate. Significantly there is no comparable qualification at (Advanced) Skills Level III. The narrower NVQ Level 1 in motor mechanics is only available to students over 16 and in employment.

There is still an academic/vocational divide.

RICHARD PRING

Response to John Fox

The account, just given, points to the elastic use of the word 'vocational', but at the same time its association with 'the practical' and thereby its contrast with the 'academic'. In consequence, it carries with it a lower status than that attributed to the academic. The 'practical' is not valued. Therefore, the academic/vocational divide is retained in the status given to certain courses and learning experiences, rather than others, and in the allocation of learners to them. Whatever the rhetoric about 'equality of status', academic courses lead to the more prestigious higher education and vocational courses lead to lower-paid, lower-status jobs.

The account, however, questions the distinction and so much that hangs on it. And that questioning seeks a re-examination of the tradition of practical intelligence and 'doing', exemplified, as I had said, in the work, over two centuries, of the Royal Society of the Arts and in so many of the achievements in architecture, engineering, medicine and design. John Fox gave the example of 'cooking', as indeed did John Dewey (frequently), in demonstrating how the practical engagement and thoughtfulness opens up a deeper grasp of the concepts, modes of enquiry, theoretical understanding, and intuitive grasp of a problem. He demonstrates, too, how the failure to recognise that has led to the diminishing importance, if not extinction, of practical subjects or practical approaches to subjects within the curriculum. Where are the woodwork and metalwork rooms of previous years?

Within a proper understanding of, and respect for, the 'practical', the questionable distinction between the academic and the vocational would gradually disappear – as would the division of different status courses which that distinction re-enforces.

This is increasingly recognised in a range of initiatives from sponsors, foundations and other outside bodies which are increasingly entering into mainstream education. The RSA's 'Opening Minds Project', drawing upon its own tradition of integrating thinking and doing, intellect and skill, working with brain and hands, is operating in almost 200 schools. Edge Foundation is promoting practical learning in a large number of schools but also in the training of teachers through Lewisham College and South Banks University. The Young Foundation is establishing 'Studio Schools' in which all students will be actively engaged in commercial activities. The Nuffield Foundation has supported the innovative Applied Science courses which have motivated so many young people to continue with science because they see its practical use; the practical engagement embodied in the Paul Hamlyn Foundation's 'Musical Futures' is spreading across the curriculum in many schools. I could go on. But enough has been said to support the view that a quiet revolution has been set in motion in which the divide between the academic and the vocational will disappear – the divide still exists.

JOHN FOX

Response to Richard Pring

Richard Pring's follow-up from my professional reflection on the importance of the 'practical' in overcoming the divide between the academic and the vocational would benefit from a more detailed case study. Good philosophy works through the concrete case.

SKIDZ is one of the '350 projects' said by the White Paper to be working on the Increased Flexibility Programme, which enables young people aged 14–16 to have a more skills-based and occupation-related learning experience. This educational charity has centres in High Wycombe, Aylesbury and Banbury. It is represented on the South Bucks 14–19 Consortium, which includes 26 schools and recently received the entire damages from a high-profile motor racing industry court case in order to found a new centre in London. The average 14–16 pupil sent to SKIDZ works a two-hour 'practical education' slot and has a day's work experience each week in a local garage. The 'practical education' is taught by experienced automotive mechanics in sophisticated garage workshops. Its manager Stephen Godfrey describes SKIDZ as 'learning at work, not about work'. In short, it is serious experiential learning.

Maths can be related to measuring; science to wiring, battery chemicals, friction, metallurgy and corrosion; IT to the writing up and researching required; history of roads and cars is taught as well as basic OS map reading. The incentive to read comes from knowing that real interest lies behind written words in Haynes car manuals, car magazines (among the most numerous in WH Smith) and instructions on packaging. Tutor and IT rooms lead off from the main workshop space.

SKIDZ began in 1998 as a diversionary project for young offenders or those at risk of offending. It is open to all in term-time, evenings and vacations. Activities with cars, motor cycles, quad-bikes and go-carts as well as practical mechanics are offered. Obviously it has expanded greatly into the schools sector, providing 'practical education' which schools cannot do. Its problem is no longer that of having to sell its product – schools requested 500 places for pupils in September 2005.

Is this academic or vocational? The question seems increasingly irrelevant, if not unintelligible.

One major problem is the lack of research on SKIDZ's success and on SKIDZ's pedagogic 'hunches'. Evidence is currently being lost as it flows through and out of SKIDZ hands. This crying need for proper research is true of all 'practical education' providers, particularly the smaller ones unable to invest in serious research.

CONCLUSION FROM RICHARD PRING AND JOHN FOX

In our debate we have reflected on the nature of what is being discussed and implemented in the name of 'academic' and 'vocational education'. We feel that it is unhelpful to establish misleading dichotomies: practice and theory; academic and vocational; thinking and doing. Instead we suggest that such simplistic distinctions hinder the achievement of clearer and better thoughtful practice in schools, colleges and universities. The absence of creative thinking that has led to an emphasis on supposed divisions between the 'academic' and the 'vocational' may be – in theory as well as practice – simply a matter of according status to groups of learners.

KEY QUESTIONS

1. In what ways (if at all) are academic and vocational education separate fields?
2. What is the relationship between schooling and the economy?
3. What three initiatives would you propose to help overcome some of the problems discussed by Richard Pring and John Fox?

FURTHER READING

Dewey, J. (1916/1966) *Democracy and Education*. London, Macmillan Free Press. (chapter 23) Go to the home page of the Department for Children Schools and Families (http://www.dcsf.gov.uk/) and search for the publication titled *Education and Skills 14-19*. This is the White Paper referred to in the above debate.

Go to http://www.14-19reform.gov.uk/ to read the Tomlinson Report.

This debate links with readings 2 and 10 of *The Routledge Education Studies Reader*.

CHAPTER 11

THE HISTORICAL AND SOCIAL CONTEXT OF CURRICULUM

Bob Moon

The rationale for this chapter is:

- to show how the content or curriculum of any educational system is influenced by historical, political and social factors;
- to critically review the way in which a government-regulated National Curriculum has been introduced in parts of the UK (especially England) over the last two decades;
- to analyse the ways in which the organisation of knowledge becomes part of the pedagogic task of all teachers.

INTRODUCTION

There are always controversies around curriculum. The 'what should be taught' question stimulates debate at all levels in any education system. Where governments regulate the structure and content of the curriculum, discussion can be particularly fractious. How important is the teaching of history, for example?

And if history is taught, what content should be included? In Britain, how and when do you include teaching about the Empire and colonialism? In Australia how is the history of the Aboriginal communities, especially the recent history, dealt with? Such questions often spill over into political and media debate.

Few subjects escape controversy. Mathematics might be seen as outside the social controversies associated with History, Social Studies or literature. Not so. The historical record shows that a 'mathematics controversy' has erupted in most of the decades over the last 50 years. In the 1960s and 1970s the attempt by many (including very distinguished university mathematicians) to introduce new or 'modern maths' into the curriculum created, in many countries, the most violent arguments. One French university professor, Roger Apery, apopletically suggested in February 1972 that: '[p]ornography, drugs, the disintegration of the French language, upheavals in mathematics education, all relate to the same process: attacking the central parts of the liberal society' (*L'Express*, 6 February 1972). And in a self-parody, a German teacher's 'new maths' handbook has a cartoon showing two long-haired primary pupils (with average signs on their t-shirts) carrying a banner saying 'Down with Alef!'. Alef was the name given to one new maths programme.

One of the longest running disputes about what should be taught is in the USA where individual states have considerable powers over education. The teaching of biology and evolution in particular has occasioned fierce antagonisms and numerous court cases. In many states, particularly in the south, there have been attempts to ban the teaching of Darwinian ideas and concepts. This has attracted widespread professional and lay involvement. It has even generated a Pulitzer Prize-winning book, Edward Larson's *Summer for the Gods* (1997), a highly readable historical account of 'The Scopes Trial'. At the time this was referred to as 'The Monkey Trial'.

The state of Tennessee had passed a law making it unlawful to teach evolutionary theory in any state-funded educational establishment. John Scopes was a high school teacher who, financed by the American Civil Liberties Union, intentionally violated the Act. At his first trial a jury found Scopes guilty. Eventually on appeal Scopes was cleared on a legal technicality, but the statute remained in place and was not repealed until 1967. Although, in 1968, the Supreme Court of the USA ruled such legislation as illegal, the controversy lingers on.

A similar sort of debate, although with less redress to the law, has more recently been taking place in England around the teaching of creationism. Arguments have been made by some for teaching creationist theories alongside ideas about evolution. In 2008 Professor Michael Reiss, Director of Education of the Royal Society (and an ordained Church of England clergyman), had to resign for advancing such a view.

Textbooks often provide a focus for disagreement. In Japan there have been any number of court cases about the Ministry of Education approach to approving history text books, most specifically in relation to the activities of the Japanese Army in China around and during the time of World War II. History textbooks, inevitably, are a particular focus of debate about differing interpretations of events, especially recent ones. The conflict in the Middle East, the wars in the Balkans, the Turkish treatment of the Armenians and, in England, the interpretations around the Miners Strikes in the early 1980s, have all been subject to disputation.

In one sense there is nothing surprising about this. Democratic debate around 'what should be taught' is perhaps one of the characteristics of a free society. What is more important is who actually makes the final decision about curriculum and in England this has significantly changed from the late 1980s onwards.

For much of the post-World War II period England, and the UK as a whole, was often held up as a highly decentralised model of curriculum decision making. Schools, headteachers in particular, could make decisions about the structure and organisation of the school curriculum. There were, of course, constraints. In primary schools where an 11+ examination existed, the nature of that examination influenced the teaching in the upper primary years. In the secondary school the various 16+ and 18+ examination syllabuses did likewise.

However, there was considerable room for manoeuvre and this grew during the 1960s and early 1970s. The abolition of the 11+ examination in most areas, for example, freed up the primary curriculum. More child-centred, topic-based work was introduced often in newly built open-plan classrooms. This trend was given quasi-official approval with the publication of a report in 1967 on children and their primary schools. This report was produced by a committee chaired by Lady Plowden and it has become enshrined in educational folklore as the Plowden Report. Plowden provided no prescription for curriculum and it has been widely interpreted as legitimating the freedom of teachers to innovate, particularly in respect of progressive approaches to education.

Curriculum is inextricably linked with contemporary social and ideological movements. Plowden, a product of the 1960s, reflected the wish to move away from constrained instructional approaches to primary schooling, especially what many saw as the gradgrind of the 11+ selective process. It is important for teachers, parents and others to understand this historical and sociological dimension to curriculum. If we stand outside the post-war chronology for a moment and go back to the mid-nineteenth century, the distance of history shows this more starkly. The Taunton Report on schools produced 100 years before Plowden, in 1868, was very specific about the link between curriculum and social class:

> 'we shall call these the Third, the Second, and the First Graded education respectively. . . . It is obvious that these distinctions correspond roughly, but by no means exactly, to the gradations of society.
>
> First Grade . . . This class appears to have no wish to displace the classics from their present position in the forefront of English education.
>
> Second Grade . . . though most of these parents would probably consent to give a higher place to Latin, they would only do so on condition that it did not exclude a very thorough knowledge of important modern subjects, and they would hardly give Greek any place at all.
>
> Third Grade . . . belongs to a class distinctly lower in the scale. . . . The need of this class is described briefly by Canon Moseley to be 'very good reading, very good writing, very good arithmetic'.
>
> (Schools Inquiry Royal Commission, The Taunton Report, 1868, pp. 15–21)

In England and Wales, nearly a hundred years later, the 1944 Education Act strongly suggested a similar tripartite system of schooling. The rationale, however, was not social class but psychology. The belief in the ways psychometric testing could identify pupil aptitudes was strong (and only a few people were pointing out the way such aptitudes reflected nineteenth-century ideas of class).

The 1944 Act was significantly influenced by a 1938 report (the Spens Report) which proposed three types of secondary school: grammar, modern and technical. Grammar schools, it was proposed, would have a traditional curriculum, including the classics; technical schools would concentrate on science and technical subjects; and modern schools would have a less academic curriculum for the more practical child.

There was little opportunity to develop the technical school curriculum because few were established. There were, however, curriculum differences between grammar and secondary modern schools. A major part of the argument for a move to a more comprehensive form of secondary schooling was the need to move towards a more common curriculum for all and this idea became increasingly influential through the 1970s and early 1980s.

A number of questions that influence curriculum can be drawn out of these events.

- If all children are to experience a 'common' curriculum, what form should it take?
- What proportion of the school week should the common elements take up?
- At what age would the 'common' curriculum be succeeded by a more diversified approach?
- Who should be making these sorts of decisions?

INTRODUCING A NATIONAL CURRICULUM

In 1988 the Conservative government, led by Margaret Thatcher, intervened to provide answers to each of these questions. The last question was uncompromisingly addressed. It would be the government who decided. A subject-based specification for the curriculum was introduced covering both primary and secondary schools. It was, and remains, decidedly traditionalist.

This was not the first time an English government had decided to legislate for the curriculum. In 1904 a specification for the growing secondary sector had been put in place by the then Board of Education. Robert Morant, head of the Board as Permanent Secretary had been particularly influential in ensuring that the curriculum required was academic in form and structure. Table 11.1 below shows the 1904 and 1935 reviews alongside the 1988 formulation. There are remarkable similarities that demonstrate the hegemony achieved by a curriculum model that had predominated in the private sector (the so-called 'public' schools) of England in the latter part of the nineteenth century.

Table 11.1 Government curriculum regulations for 1904, 1935 and 1988 (England)

1904	1935	1988
English language	English language	English
English literature	English literature	A modern language
One language	One language	Geography
Geography	Geography	History
History	History	Mathematics
Mathematics	Mathematics	Science
Science	Science	Art
Drawing	Drawing	Physical education
Due provision for manual work and physical exercises	Physical exercises and organised games	Music
(Housewifery in girls' schools)	Singing	Technology
	(Manual instruction for boys, dramatic subjects for girls)	

Teachers working in all parts of the UK are required to give significant attention to national requirements set out everywhere except Scotland as a legislated National Curriculum. There has been continuous debate about this. Look, for example, at the two extracts below.

The National Curriculum: Straightjacket or Safety Net

Extracts from a pamphlet written in 1989 by Bob Moon and Peter Mortimore for the Education Reform Group

What are the potential benefits of a National Curriculum?

Strong arguments can be advanced to support the idea of a national curriculum. Many see this as the logical extension of the common comprehensive school principle established painstakingly in the post-war years for primary schools and, in the 1960s and 1970s, for the majority of secondary schools. It has the potential to create an entitlement to learning, giving to pupils and parents a clear agenda for the eleven years of compulsory schooling and beyond. It can also provide the yardstick against which educational inequality can be judged and remedied.

A national curriculum could also provide a framework in which teachers could work co-operatively together in seeking improvement. The evidence of numerous activities – the Records of Achievement Projects and the Technical and Vocational Educational Initiative (TVEI) being recent examples – shows how much there is to be gained from such co-operation. [In the early and mid 1980s significant resources were put into introducing more practical and vocational elements into the school curriculum.] We would also argue, citing TVEI, that a responsive national curriculum could promote the introduction of new knowledge and dispense quickly with outdated subjects or parts of subjects. Sensitively planned, a national curriculum could create a sense of public ownership of education, raise the status of teaching and schooling, and provide sound criteria against which issues of accountability, effectiveness and improvement could be judged.

Are there any problems or limitations in the Government's approach?

In our view, the Government's approach to the National Curriculum reveals some potentially damaging flaws and inconsistencies.

The absence of a carefully reasoned foundation to many of the proposals is a fundamental cause for concern. Plans, sometimes highly complex and technical, are being implemented without due consideration of the issues involved and of the evidence available. During the passage of the Bill one response to criticism was to mount attacks on the views of experts. This atmosphere of anti-intellectualism bodes ill for the introduction of a major Education Reform Act. We believe it important that all the issues be debated in a full and open way, not least if the essential support of teachers is to be enlisted.

We now turn to the proposals for the content of the National Curriculum. The legislation, and the much-criticised consultative document that preceded it, present the curriculum in needlessly rather restricted terms. Thus the primary curriculum was put forward as if it were no more than a pre-secondary preparation (like the worst sort of 'prep school'). All the positive aspects of British primary schooling – so valued by HMI and the Select Committee of the House of Commons and so praised by many foreign commentators – were ignored.

The secondary curriculum, in turn, appears to be based on the curriculum of a typical 1960s grammar school. We would not take issue with the subjects included, but we believe that such a curriculum misses out a great deal. Information technology, electronics, statistics, personal, social and careers education have all been omitted. Yet, surely, these are just the areas that are likely to be of importance for the future lives of many pupils?

Moreover, the emphasis on single subjects ignores the lessons that have been learned from the successful TVEI programmes. The proposal makes coherent planning into the 16–19 curriculum more not less difficult and flies in the face of governmental, HMI and educational opinion as it has developed over the last decade. We believe that a curriculum is more than the sum of its parts and we regret that the advice given by HMI on so many occasions, that schools should embrace the concept of whole curriculum planning, was ignored by those who had the opportunity to make this a reality.

The inadequate conceptual basis for the curriculum proposals, inevitably, will create serious difficulties. Subject working parties have been set up without a clear idea of the curriculum time available or of the relationship of one subject area to another. This has led to the Science Working Group recommending that not less than one-sixth of the curriculum time be devoted to its area and, in years four and five of secondary schooling, up to 20 per cent. The Secretary of State, however, in his proposals suggests that 12.5 per cent will be sufficient for some pupils.

All the evidence from the past indicates that such difficulties will increase as the different Subject Working Groups report. The list of single subjects is likely to prove a straightjacket within which it is impossible to accommodate satisfactorily competing interest groups.

The potential problems of implementation, identified above by Peter Mortimore and myself, did materialise as I set out in the following extract published nearly 15 years later in Demaine (2002).

> . . . if across the pre-school to eighteen curriculum there is a more realistic but restricted core, space opens up for a range of locally based, school-based activities. Schools should be judged on the range of variety of opportunities they provide. Perhaps one of the most dispiriting features of the last decade has been the unwillingness of teachers and schools to 'risk', as they saw it, national curriculum progress by allowing time for other activities. Innovation and experiment as words have almost disappeared from the teaching lexicon.

The best moments of learning often come at unexpected times, outside the bureaucratic, predictable and standardised regime in which far too many schools feel they are working. A sense of exploration unfettered by time limits and age-related tests must be brought back into the curriculum if schools are to contribute significantly to developing articulate, confident and flexible young people. The design of the curriculum and the structures of any measurement of progress must go beyond the world of percentages if we are to boost the self-image, improve standards, and develop positive attitudes towards a future where lifelong learning is taken for granted in the social culture of the times.

To achieve a new sense of innovation and experimentation a final point needs to be made. Curriculum policy in England is far too centralised. Recent in origin, it lacks any of the checks and balances that formally centrally controlled systems display. Across the channel in France we find the archetypal concept of central control. But look at it in practice and you find a healthy corpus of consultative mechanisms for bringing a range of interest groups into the change process. The immature English model, driven initially by authoritarian Secretaries of State, displays all the worst characteristics of overly centralist systems. Decisions made by a few are required to be rapidly implemented by the many. The few are subject to the vagaries of media manipulation and Whitehall politicising. Respect for evidence grows weak. Others have described just how chaotic the national curriculum building process was (Taylor 1995; Barber 1997). But re-establishing a balance between central prescription and the energy and creativity that more localised decisions can make is crucial. It is not restoring the old order. New forms of accountability in curriculum policy are here to stay and government has a crucial role in this. Relentlessly trying to hammer half a million teachers and more than twenty thousand schools into line is failing. The inspiration to find the solutions to the problems facing the educational system must go beyond government. The changing social, economic and technological environment present challenges that require the involvement of everyone within the education service and to achieve this some devolution of responsibilities is absolutely crucial.

These proposals are located within the English context as the last decade of the century draws to a close. Underlying all this, however, is the quest to open up the education system to new forms of creativity and opportunity. The normative quest for standardisation has gone too far. Ironically, the strategies being adopted have more in common with the closing years of the last century than at any time since the 1950s. Thinking the unthinkable, as a fashionable policy option, in education is almost wholly a question of looking back. England is not unique in this, but the particular brew of Thatcherism and some new Labour beliefs is closing down the vision of the more optimistic of the human capacity to learn and understand, to theorise and create, visions that the revolution in our understanding of cognition has done so much to promote. The story is, as I suggested at the outset of this chapter, an old one. John Dewey, writing in the first years of this century, was very clear about the responsibilities that policy-makers bear in education. Word for word the analysis holds good for today:

'It is easy to fall into the habit of regarding the mechanisms of school organization and administration as something comparatively external and indifferent to educational purposes and ideals. We think of the grouping of children in classes, the arrangement of grades, the machinery by which the course of study is made out and laid down, the method by which it is carried into effect, the system of selecting teachers and assigning them to their work, of paying and promoting them, as, in a way, matters of mere practical convenience and expediency. We forget that it is precisely such things as these that really control the whole system, even on its distinctly educational side. No matter what is the accepted precept and theory, no matter what the legislation of the school board or the mandate of the school superintendent, the

> *reality of education is found in the personal and face-to-face contact of teacher and child. The conditions that underlie and regulate this contact dominate the educational situation.'*

THE ORGANISATION OF KNOWLEDGE

The knowledge dimension of pedagogy is manifest in many ways. What types of knowledge, for example, can be introduced or encouraged in a pedagogic setting? A common reference point in responding to this question is the distinction between propositional (knowing that) and procedural (knowing how) knowledge. There have been strong arguments that curriculum planning and teaching focus excessively on the former, particularly in formal school contexts. And the distinction has provoked considerable philosophical controversy. Paul Hirst, for example, has argued that all knowledge is of the 'knowing that' variety and that the distinction cannot be made. 'Knowing how' knowledge, he argued, is essentially 'knowing that' plus experience. Paolo Freire accepted this distinction (Freire, 1998, p. 93):

> In the first moment, that of the experience of and in daily living, my conscious self is exposing itself to facts, to deeds, without, nevertheless, asking itself about them, without looking for their 'reason for being'. I repeat that the knowing 'because' there is also 'knowing' that results from these involvements is that made from pure experience. In the second moment, in which our minds work epistemologically, the methodological rigor with which we come closer to the object, having 'distanced ourselves' from it, that is, having objectified it, offers us another kind of knowing, a knowing whose exactitude gives to the investigator or the thinking subject a margin of security that does not exist in the first kind of knowing, that of common sense.

To us there seems value to the teacher in reflecting on the different categories of types of knowledge that can be constructed. Berieter and Scardamalia (1993) have been influential and central to thinking about the forms of pedagogic settings. They suggest a five-fold distinction:

- formal knowledge;
- procedural knowledge;
- informal knowledge;
- impressionistic knowledge;
- self-regulatory knowledge.

The first two categories repeat the 'knowing that'/'knowing how' distinction. Informal knowledge is somewhere between the two. It represents knowledge used in problem solving but which somehow cannot be formulated in words. Others have referred to this as tacit knowledge. A very experienced teacher may know how to act in a variety of settings but may not always have the words to communicate this to novices. In all sorts of organisations tacit knowledge is increasingly recognised as crucial to achieving goals – hence the importance now being given to the informed guesses and hunches of creative organisations. It is this type of knowledge with its hesitations and uncertainties (what Freire called 'epistemological inquietude') that can cause much misgiving, perhaps to the point of being shut out in formal learning and teaching situations.

Impressionistic knowledge is even more difficult to define. It refers to that background knowledge which can, in an amorphous way, exert a strong influence. Perhaps a few particularly inspiring lessons on the teaching of attitudes to knowledge, Shakespeare, for example.

Self-regulatory knowledge, which may include elements of all the other four, refers to a personal understanding of strengths and weaknesses – those ways in which we personally come to have ideas about what works for us. A well-designed curriculum seeks an appropriate relationship and balance between these different ways of knowing.

The way some kinds of knowledge come to be more valued than others is not a matter of chance, but rather the playing out of power relations in any group. This can work in a formal political way, such as which subjects are included in a national curriculum, or in more informed subtle ways, such as the way senior academic members of a university research group might work to exclude certain ideas and approaches. The choices research councils make about which areas of research to fund illustrate another power dimension. There need not be anything sinister or dysfunctional about this because the exercise of such power relations is part and parcel of the human condition. But this does mean a stratification of knowledge which needs to be seen and understood. This can happen as much within as between subjects. Gary Spruce, for example, looking at the teaching of music, has shown for just how long the guardians of the music curriculum held out against popular and world music displacing the nineteenth-century canon of great composers. And in the same way, just how long it took to allow children to make music before learning the basics of musical notation (Spruce, 1999).

Maps of knowledge constructed by a teacher are not necessarily self-evident to the learner. It is rather obvious to point out that young (or older) children do not have an innate knowledge of the school curriculum. But teachers often assume that the categories of subjects, even the subdivisions within subjects, form an established part of a child's existing knowledge. Some impressions do begin to appear from the earliest of ages (encyclopaedias now exist for the nursery school!). The distinguished American psychologist, Jerome Bruner, has talked of the way children build a model of the world to help them understand their everyday experience (Bruner, 1996). For Bruner curriculum prescription can limit learning. His seminal text published in 1960, entitled *The Process of Education*, argued that schools waste a great deal of people's time by postponing the teaching of important areas because they are deemed 'too difficult'. Bruner began with the hypothesis: 'that any subject can be taught effectively in some intellectually honest form to any child at any stage of development' (p. 33). From this Bruner derived two important ideas. The first was the importance of making structures in learning central to the pedagogic process:

> the learning and teaching of structure, rather than simply the mastering of facts and techniques, is at the centre of the classic problem of transfer. . . . If earlier learning is to render later learning explicit, it must do so by providing a general picture in terms of which the relations between things encountered earlier and later are made as clear as possible.
>
> (p. 12)

The second was the concept of the 'spiral curriculum', whereby a curriculum as it develops should repeatedly revisit the basic ideas that make up the general picture, building upon them until the student has grasped the full formal apparatus that goes with them. For Bruner, therefore, pedagogy involved a process of curriculum creation. The building and constructing of knowledge as a social process, becomes, literally, one of the teacher's most important tasks. The process of identifying the big ideas and working pedagogic strategies around these is central to pedagogy. It might be seen as self-evident, but much curriculum design (including many formal regulatory syllabuses) is often about 'coverage' rather than structure, and coverage is often the enemy of understanding.

By making the organisation of the curriculum central to the pedagogic process, the teacher has to reflect on the structure of knowledge. For many teachers, their very identity is linked to a certain subject, and subjects, disciplines or domains have a very strong hold on the forms of knowledge that schools especially are given the responsibility to teach.

Disciplines, however, are not equal in their structure, power and status. Some appear to have strong boundaries (mathematics), while others are more fluid in the forms they take (social studies).

Some disciplines have a direct titular link to the high-status knowledge of universities (science), while other parts of the curriculum can have a more temporal, even political, form (citizenship, as taught in England, is one example that comes to mind) that would not be accorded the descriptor 'discipline'. Some disciplines also appear to have a more overt, linear, sequential structure (French) than others (art), although how pronounced this sort of juxtaposition really is remains a matter of some dispute.

Over the years the importance of the disciplines of knowledge, as they have been created over the centuries, has been the source of much disputation. The hegemony of the traditional disciplines, for example, as legitimised by traditional and established forms of authority has been frequently challenged. They do, however, provide important points of reference that seep into all the corners of our pedagogic endeavours. Bruner, in a more recent expansion of his ideas, has stressed the importance of knowledge that has been accumulated in the past. This is how he puts it:

> Early on, children encounter the hoary distinction between what is known by 'us' (friends, parents, teachers and so on) and what in some larger sense is simply 'known'. In these post positivist, perhaps 'post modern' times we recognise all too well that the 'known' is neither God-given truths nor, as it were, written irrevocably in the Book of Nature. Knowledge in this dispensation is always putatively revisable. But revisability is not to be confused with free-for-all relativism . . . teaching should help children grasp the distinction between personal knowledge, on the one side, and 'what is taken to be known' by the culture, on the other. But they must not only grasp this distinction, but also understand its basis, as it were in the history of knowledge. How can we incorporate such a perspective in our pedagogy? Stated another way, what have children gained when they begin to distinguish what is known canonically from what they know personally and idiosyncratically?
>
> (1996, p. 61)

Howard Gardner, whose work on multiple understandings of intelligence has been so influential, has adopted a similar stance towards discipline.

> Organised subject matter represents the ripe fruitage of experiences . . . it does not represent perfection or infallible vision; but it is the best at command to further new experiences which may, in some respects at least, surpass the achievements embodied in existing knowledge and works of art.
>
> (1995, p. 61)

The disciplines, therefore, become more than a framing reference for pedagogy, rather they nurture and feed the forms of pedagogy that evolve to serve the sorts of interests Bruner outlines. This is the very knowledge base of teaching – the intersection of content and pedagogy. The main task of teachers then becomes to transpose the context knowledge they possess into forms that are pedagogically powerful.

KNOWLEDGE AND PEDAGOGY

At this point the interrelation of knowledge and pedagogy becomes important. The term transpose is used deliberately. In finding pedagogic ways to present knowledge the teacher is transposing rather than transforming. This can be a difficult task. Teachers have to take their subject knowledge, gained perhaps during undergraduate study and formulate it in ways that could be termed 'school knowledge'. A number of educationalists have argued that the intersection between subject knowledge, or knowledge per se, school knowledge and pedagogy has, in understanding the work of the teacher,

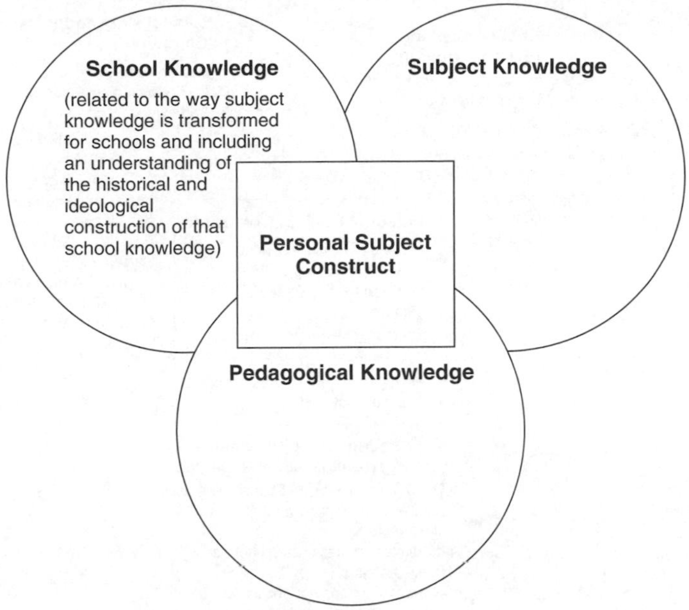

Figure 11.1 Teachers' professional knowledge

been insufficiently explored. Lee Shulman has been one of the leading figures in this debate (see Shulman, 1986, 1987, 2006). But there is also a large body of work in European research, especially from France and Germany, on what one French writer has termed 'la transposition didactique' (Chevellard, 1991).

Jenny Leach and Bob Moon (Leach and Moon, 1999, 2008) drawing on a number of research studies of teachers' professional knowledge, have suggested that a teacher's identity is strongly linked with ideas about knowledge.

Figure 11.1 represents in diagrammatic form their synthesis of professional knowledge based on observations of teachers' overlapping identities. In school, they are 'subject' experts (subject knowledge); subject specialist teachers (school knowledge); and classroom experts (pedagogic knowledge). Beyond and within the school, they are individuals with key commitments to a range of other groups and communities (personal knowledge).

This model has been used in a range of international settings to argue that the development of professional knowledge is a dynamic process. It depends on the interaction of the elements we identify, but is brought into existence by the learning context itself – learners, setting, activity and communication, as well as context in its broadest sense.

Most importantly it emphasises that the personal construct – the identity – of the teacher lies at the heart of this process: a complex amalgam of past knowledge, experiences of learning in a range of communities, a personal view of what constitutes 'good' teaching and a belief in the purposes of the subject. This model holds good for any teacher, novice or expert. A student teacher needs to question their personal beliefs as they work out a rationale for their classroom practice. But so must those teachers who, although more expert, have experienced profound changes in what constitutes subject or pedagogic knowledge during their career.

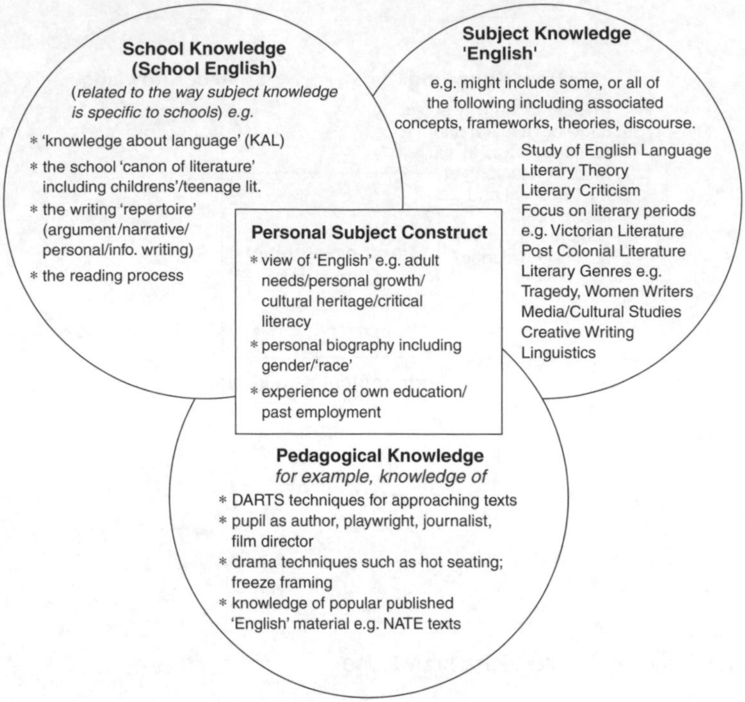

School Knowledge
(School English)
(related to the way subject knowledge is specific to schools) e.g.
* 'knowledge about language' (KAL)
* the school 'canon of literature' including childrens'/teenage lit.
* the writing 'repertoire' (argument/narrative/personal/info. writing)
* the reading process
Subject Knowledge
'English'
e.g. might include some, or all of the following including associated concepts, frameworks, theories, discourse.
Study of English Language
Literary Theory
Literary Criticism
Focus on literary periods e.g. Victorian Literature
Post Colonial Literature
Literary Genres e.g. Tragedy, Women Writers
Media/Cultural Studies
Creative Writing
Linguistics
Personal Subject Construct
* view of 'English' e.g. adult needs/personal growth/cultural heritage/critical literacy
* personal biography including gender/'race'
* experience of own education/past employment
Pedagogical Knowledge
for example, knowledge of
* DARTS techniques for approaching texts
* pupil as author, playwright, journalist, film director
* drama techniques such as hot seating; freeze framing
* knowledge of popular published 'English' material e.g. NATE texts

Figure 11.2 English teachers' professional knowledge

Figure 11.2 illustrates the way in which this model was exemplified by a group of English teachers. They recognised a clear distinction between 'English' as practised, for example, in their university and college communities ('subject' knowledge) and school communities ('school' knowledge). Most school departments, for example, required that members know about authors, themes and styles (mostly texts written for children or teenagers, or deemed suitable for the younger reader) that were distinctively different from the literature they had studied in university and college seminars. Few degree-level communities incorporated knowledge about the reading process in their curriculum, but this was a statutory part of school 'English' in the U.K.

SUMMARY

From this discussion it is possible to identify a number of perspectives on knowledge. First that knowledge creation is a social process, constantly in a state of flux and expansion. As knowledge grows so more and more sub-divisions or specialisations emerge. Science, for example, especially medicine, is constantly forming new fields. The general work of a surgeon 50 years ago would not be recognised by their counterparts today, focusing as they do on very specific parts of the body. New knowledge draws into question the nature of the school curriculum. The passage of new knowledge into the school curriculum, however, as the new maths example showed, can be a fraught process.

This leads to a second perspective. In creating a curriculum, making decisions about what is to be taught, then significant power relations are involved.

These relations of power influence designs. This perspective also works at many levels, including that ever-present human propensity to establish barriers and frontiers of a form and strength that transcend any practical purpose. Take secondary science. Should the curriculum be organised around topics like global warming or environmental problems rather than physics, chemistry or biology or earth sciences? And if the latter, what curriculum weight should be given to each? In England this debate has led to constant changes in the organisation of the science curriculum, with more than one 'Royal Society' representing the traditional sciences weighing in to protect their subject. Such power relations work in other types of knowledge domains. There are ongoing arguments in vocational subjects about the relative weight that can be given to generic skills and understandings (communication skills, numeracy) as opposed to the practical realisation of those skills and understandings in specific vocational domains (plumbing, electrical work, information technology). These sorts of tensions, as has been suggested above, have dogged the development of a National Curriculum in England.

A third perspective suggests that any curriculum can be significantly enriched if knowledge beyond the propositional is acknowledged. This wider conception inevitably opens up a wider process of understanding and a broader array of pedagogic strategies.

A fourth and final perspective is that the initiation of learners into an understanding of the deeper structures that have come to frame knowledge areas is an essential part of the building of meaning. This has led some to argue that the classroom should try to replicate the authentic settings that scientists or mathematicians inhabit. And in this, Vygotsky and Bruner suggest, the pedagogic process rather than trying to develop individual understanding independent of others (too often the implicit, even explicit *modus vivendi* of many classrooms) more appropriately gives due attention to individuals 'as they become fully effective, functioning members of communities'. In other words you do not acquire 'the knowledge'. Rather, knowledge building is a social process which may precede the appropriation of certain skills and understandings into a personal repertoire.

In this way knowledge and learning became inseparable. Different forms of knowledge may presuppose certain forms of pedagogic activity (contrast the work of the science or art teacher). But in general terms knowledge building is a social process. At the heart of the pedagogic process is the space in which the planned, enacted and experienced come together. It presupposes a view that cognition, activity and the world mutually constitute each other.

KEY QUESTIONS

1. The curriculum is now more explicitly regulated by government than it once was. Why?
2. What sorts of disadvantages are there to state regulation of the curriculum?
3. Does a particular arrangement of knowledge in the form of a curriculum subject lead to a particular teaching style?

FURTHER READING

Kelly, V. (2004) *Curriculum: Theory and Practice*, London, Sage Publications.

Leach, J. and Moon, B. (2008) *The Power of Pedagogy*, London, Sage.

Moon, B., Hutchinson, S. and Shelton Mayes, A. (2002) *Teaching, Learning and the Curriculum in Secondary Schools*, London, Routledge.

Peddiwell, J. A. (1939) *The Saber-tooth Curriculum*, New York, McGraw Hill.

Young, M. (2008) *Bringing Knowledge Back In: From Social Constructivism to Social Realism in the Sociology of Education*, London, Routledge.

This chapter links with readings 4, 5, 11 and 12 of *The Routledge Education Studies Reader*.

CHAPTER 12

HOW SHOULD WE TEACH?

Chris Kyriacou

The rationale for this chapter is:

- to consider the key issues involved in the choice of teaching methods to be used in the classroom;
- to illustrate how the context of policy and practice initiatives impacts on teaching methods;
- to explore how teaching methods need to take account of pupil characteristics (age, ability, knowledge, social context, self-perceptions, motivation, and previous experience of learning).

INTRODUCTION

In considering how teachers should teach in the classroom, it is useful to make a distinction between three aspects of teaching: (i) the use of particular teaching methods and learning activities; (ii) the relationship between the teacher and pupils and how the teacher maintains authority and discipline during lessons; and (iii) how teaching and learning in the classroom enables each pupil to feel challenged, engaged and motivated by their experiences. These three aspects of teaching will be addressed in this chapter. Particular reference will be made to how teaching needs to take account of the ages and different abilities of pupils.

The wealth of writing and research on teaching methods and pupil learning in schools has provided us with a solid foundation upon which to consider how teachers should teach (Kyriacou, 2009; Muijs and Reynolds, 2005; Wilen *et al.*, 2008). However, it needs to be stated at the outset that the complexities involved in teaching are such that effective teaching cannot be reduced simply to requiring teachers to mechanistically adopt a set of practices that will successfully enable all pupils to learn to the best of their ability.

On the contrary, effective teaching requires teachers to adapt what and how they teach in sophisticated and skilful ways that take account of pupils, the subject matter, what they want pupils to learn ('the learning outcomes'), and the context within which the lesson takes place. Teaching methods and learning activities that might work well for one pupil for one set of learning outcomes in one context, may not work well for another pupil for another set of learning outcomes in another context. Expertise as a teacher is based on being able to make high-quality judgements about teaching and being able to put these into effect in a skilful manner.

The word 'pedagogy' when used in the UK refers to the practice of teaching, with a particular focus on teaching methods. A number of government policy guidelines and research studies in the

UK dealing with teaching have used this word. It is interesting, however, to note that in mainland Europe, the word 'pedagogy' has a broader meaning that is much closer to what we might mean when we use the word 'education'.

In recent years a great deal of attention has been given to commissioning reviews of the research literature to evaluate the best available research evidence concerning the relative effectiveness of different ways of teaching. This has given rise to the term 'evidence-based teaching' – that is, teaching which is guided by taking account of the best available research evidence concerning 'what works'. Whilst such reviews have shortcomings, they have usefully added to our understanding of how we should teach. At the same time, they highlight the difficulties involved in moving from a statement that begins "research shows . . ." to a sentence that begins "teachers should . . .". Again, this highlights the importance of teachers being allowed to critically access for themselves how policy guidelines on teaching based on research evidence can help inform their classroom practice. Numerous review reports dealing with aspects of 'how we should teach' are available online at the Evidence for Policy and Practice Information and Coordinating Centre (EPPI Centre) website (see: http://eppi.ioe.ac.uk); other relevant reviews together with research reports commissioned by the Department for Children, Schools and Families (DCSF) are also available online at the DCSF website (see: www.dcsf.gov.uk).

TEACHING METHODS AND LEARNING ACTIVITIES

Before considering teaching methods and learning activities two important theoretical frameworks need to be outlined. The first is the *constructivist view of teaching and learning*, developed by Piaget, in which children are seen as active learners who continually explore the world by comparing and contrasting new experiences with their current understanding (cognitive schema), which either confirms their current understanding (i.e. assimilates the new experiences into their cognitive schema – existing schema remain the same), or changes their current understanding (i.e. accommodates their schema to the new experience – existing schema change). It is through continuous cycles of assimilation and accommodation in the light of new experiences, that Piaget argues the child's understanding develops. In the context of schooling this means that teachers need to take careful account of what pupils already know in order to plan a lesson that will be successful in advancing their understanding.

The second important theoretical framework is Vygotsky's notion of the *Zone of Proximal Development*, which refers to the difference between the level of learning that a pupil reaches in undertaking a task on their own and the (higher) level that a pupil can reach when another person (normally the teacher) guides their understanding. This notion is particularly important in considering how a teacher can intervene when it appears that a pupil or small group of pupils is having a problem, to probe their understanding and offer guidance. A useful technique to use here is *scaffolding*. This refers to ways in which the teacher can use questions to help guide pupils to solve the problem they face, rather than just telling them how to solve the problem. Scaffolding thereby promotes higher-quality thinking on the part of pupils, and gives pupils a greater sense of ownership over their progress in learning. The term scaffolding was coined by Bruner based on the writings of Vygotsky, and is now widely recognised as an effective teaching technique.

The ideas developed by Piaget, Vygotsky and Bruner in the twentieth century regarding cognitive development have had a major impact on our thinking about teaching methods and learning activities, and accounts of their work and how their ideas apply to teaching are widely available (e.g. Goswami, 2008; Smith *et al.*, 2003). Such research has also highlighted the importance of taking account of the pupil's age and ability when teaching.

Teaching methods and learning activities can generally speaking be divided into two broad categories. The first category deals with methods and activities in which the teacher takes centre-stage in explaining, demonstrating, directing and questioning, and can loosely be referred to as *whole-class interactive teaching*. The second category deals with teaching methods and learning activities where pupils are set tasks and where the teacher's role is to monitor, support and facilitate pupils in carrying out these tasks successfully, and can loosely be referred to as *academic tasks*.

Whole-class interactive teaching

Whole-class interactive teaching can be regarded as the main teaching method used in UK schools, and features in a variety of government guidelines on pedagogy in schools, including the National Strategies that deal with teaching in primary and secondary schools (DCSF, 2008a; DfES, 2003, 2007; Hayes, 2006). The word 'interactive' refers to the notion that teaching should not be one-way transmission from a teacher (as the holder of knowledge) to pupils (as receivers of knowledge). Rather, the interactive quality is there for teachers to make use of questioning strategies to encourage pupils to engage in high-quality thinking and the sharing and discussion of ideas.

Studies of how well teachers make use of whole-class interactive teaching, however, have highlighted that whilst all teachers make frequent use of whole-class teaching, the 'interactive' quality advocated in government guidelines is frequently absent or occurs at a very low level (Galton, 2007; Smith *et al.*, 2004). Teacher–pupil interactions all too often take the form of a low-level Initiation–Response–Feedback chain of events: Initiation (teacher asks pupil a question), Response (pupil replies), and Feedback (teacher comments on the reply).

Part of the problem is that teachers still ask too many *closed questions* (questions where there is one right answer) rather than *open questions* (where they may be several right answers or no right answer as such), and too many *lower-order questions* (requiring simple recall of facts) rather than *higher-order questions* (requiring conceptual analysis). Training materials aimed at student teachers typically illustrate questioning techniques that teachers use which encourage pupils to explain and develop their ideas, and engage in high-quality dialogue with the teacher and with other pupils (Mercer and Littleton, 2007).

Academic tasks

There are a variety of different tasks pupils can be set. These include small-group work activities, individualised tasks, reading tasks, writing tasks, investigations, projects, experiential learning, role play activities, and ICT-based tasks. Here, the role of the teacher is to circulate around the classroom and monitor the way the pupils are working on these tasks. This is likely to involve giving focused support to an individual pupil or to a small group of pupils as and when appropriate. In particular, the teacher can intervene when it appears that a pupil or small group of pupils is having a problem, to probe their understanding and offer guidance and, if appropriate, use scaffolding. It is also important to probe the understanding of pupils who appear not to be having problems, in order to enrich the learning experiences of more able pupils and those pupils adept at avoiding attention.

Given the increasing use of ICT-based activities in the classroom, it is important to note here that teaching using ICT offers benefits and challenges to pupils and teachers. On the one hand, using ICT is often experienced by pupils as enjoyable and motivating, and will often engage pupils in learning who would otherwise be disinterested. However, pupils and teachers sometimes lack the skills and expertise in using ICT to raise their learning experiences to a higher level in which the use of ICT genuinely enhances the quality of the learning taking place and leads to deeper understanding of the work at hand. Whilst the motivating effect of using ICT has major benefits and also helps pupils develop ICT skills, effective teaching using ICT only reaches its full potential when it is used to develop a deeper understanding of the topic under study.

Taking account of age and abilities

Relating teaching methods and learning activities to pupils' age and abilities requires teachers to take account of pupils' cognitive and social development and the relevance of their learning to their out of school experiences and interests. We know, for example, that younger children have shorter attention spans and are more reliant on feedback to sustain their engagement in a task. Moreover, more able children are able to work at a faster speed and to show more initiative. In developmental terms, we also know that primary school children generally require concrete examples and experiences, whilst secondary school pupils become increasingly able to work with abstract concepts and to generalise. The programmes of study for pupils as they move through primary and secondary schools are designed to take account of differences in ages and abilities. This is particularly the case where knowledge and understanding is cumulative (i.e. where new knowledge and understanding can only occur if it builds upon previous knowledge and understanding which is sound and secure). This is why taking account of prior learning is so important, and led to Ausubel's famous dictum that 'The most important single factor influencing learning is what the learner knows already. Ascertain this and teach him accordingly.' (Ausubel, 1968, p. iv).

In cases where previous knowledge and understanding is not sound and secure, Ausubel argues that the teacher must focus their learning on rectifying this. This has given rise to an approach called 'mastery learning' where an emphasis is placed on ensuring that learning objectives for a lesson are mastered before moving on to new learning objectives. Research on the effectiveness of mastery learning, however, is mixed (Schunk, 2008). One of the drawbacks of the mastery learning approach to teaching is that it tends to focus overmuch on preparing pupils for the tests of learning, such that there is too much 'teaching for the test' at the expense of other activities. This can lead to short-term gains in the knowledge and understanding being tested, but evidence of long-term gains are mixed. This issue has been applied to explaining why pupils appear to have done better at standardised tests of performance in literacy and numeracy in the first few years of the twenty-first century compared with the first few years of the 1990s, but why the attainment displayed by pupils does not appear to be sustained after the tests.

RELATIONSHIPS, AUTHORITY AND DISCIPLINE

One of the major challenges facing teachers is to establish positive relationships with pupils that will both maintain discipline in the classroom (so that learning can take place in an orderly working environment) and maintain pupils' engagement in their work (taking care to avoid alienating pupils through aggressiveness). This is no mean feat, as the classroom climate needs to be experienced by pupils as, on the one hand, supportive and conducive to learning, and on the other hand, controlled to the extent that pupil misbehaviour is minimised. At the heart of doing this successfully lies the ability of teachers to establish their authority based on mutual respect.

Minimising misbehaviour

Much have been written about teacher–pupil relationships and establishing discipline in the classroom (Evertson and Weinstein, 2006; Kyriacou, 2007). These include a number of interesting studies in which pupils are asked about the type of teacher they would like. The following five attributes are fairly typical of such research findings:

- explains things well;
- can keep control;
- will help you if you are having problems;
- makes lessons interesting;
- is friendly and has a sense of humour.

There is a danger in such studies, however, of assuming that pupils are a homogeneous group and that they will hold similar views. In fact, each class contains pupils with a range of needs and attitudes, and the type of teacher that will suit one pupil best may not suit another. Teacher expertise lies in part in being able to cater for such pupil diversity. It is also important to note that different types of teachers can be highly successful – i.e. there is no blueprint that all teachers need to model themselves on. What we do know, from research studies, is that certain practices are more likely than others to establish the classroom climate that combines both order and support. For example, a study by Opdenakker and Van Damme (2006) surveyed the views of pupils in 132 secondary school mathematics classes taught by 78 mathematics teachers in Belgium regarding the teaching style of their mathematics teacher and the classroom climate of their lessons. Opdenakker and Van Damme identified a number of features of lessons of the teaching which were associated with establishing a positive classroom climate. These included:

- the use of differentiated activities and material;
- undertaking activities to help problem pupils;
- active pupil participation in lessons;
- an orientation towards the development of the personality of the pupils;
- establishing a personal relationship with pupils based on trust.

The picture that emerges from research and writings on discipline is that discipline needs to be seen as something that naturally arises when good teaching is taking place, rather than as something that is imposed by how the teacher deals with pupil misbehaviour. A seminal study by Kounin (1970) compared videotapes of lessons given by teachers who had good discipline with those by teachers who had discipline problems. Kounin expected that this comparison would show how the teachers with good discipline dealt more effectively with pupil misbehaviour. To his surprise he found there were no differences between the two groups of teachers in how they dealt with pupil misbehaviour. However, what he did find was that the teachers with good discipline actually organised and managed pupils' learning in a very effective manner so that pupil misbehaviour rarely arose, whilst the latter group's management of pupils' learning was much less effective, thereby creating opportunities for pupil misbehaviour to occur. His conclusion was that teachers who have discipline problems need to think primarily about how to improve their teaching practices so that pupils remain fully engaged in the work, rather than about how to deal with pupil misbehaviour. The strategies Kounin identified that sustained pupils' engagement are widely cited in texts dealing with effective classroom teaching (Kyriacou, 2009; Wilen *et al.*, 2008) and include such features as with-it-ness (an awareness of what is happening throughout the class so that opportunities for misbehaviour are avoided by appropriate interventions), overlapping (being able to carry out various tasks simultaneously) and smoothness (being able to move the pupils on smoothly from one task or activity to the next).

In addition, having clear and consistent rules and expectations regarding what counts as good behaviour in the classroom and what types of behaviour are regarded as unacceptable, are also important for minimising pupil misbehaviour.

Exerting discipline

Even the most skilled teachers will have to deal with pupil misbehaviour from time to time, and in these circumstances they need to exert discipline. Some writers have developed a set of strategies that can be adopted when misbehaviour occurs (e.g. Rogers, 2006). There are four main strategies that teachers can employ in exerting discipline when pupil misbehaviour occurs: getting pupils back on task; counselling; reprimands; and punishing.

Getting pupils back on task refers to a strategy where the teacher's intervention focuses on the work that needs to be done, so that the misbehaviour is not mentioned or dealt with explicitly. For example, if two pupils are talking, the teacher asks one of the pupils a task-related question. The key here is to get the pupils re-engaged in doing academic work with as little fuss as possible. It might appear that this implicitly condones the pupil misbehaviour, but in fact pupils will be very much aware that the timing and nature of the teacher intervention is in part triggered by the teacher's awareness of them not working.

Counselling refers to a strategy where the teacher takes a neutral (rather than hostile) stance towards investigating why the pupil is misbehaving rather than working and counsels the pupil towards behaving better. For example, if two pupils were talking, the teacher might walk up to the two pupils and ask 'What's going on here – is there a problem?'. Questions such as this are seeking information about the situation without being accusatory. So, for example, if the pupil says they are not sure what to do, or are stuck, or find the work boring, these responses give the teacher an opportunity to encourage the pupils to refocus on the work at hand and to provide appropriate support or guidance to help them on their way. Because such strategies are non-accusatory, they are unlikely to produce a hostile reaction from the pupil which may enhance their disaffection and undermine their feeling of having a positive relationship with the teacher.

Reprimanding refers to admonishing misbehaviour. This may take the form of rule-reminders, such as 'put your hand up if you want something', or 'you shouldn't be out of your seat without permission'. In general, it is regarded as better to criticise the behaviour rather than the pupil (i.e. it is better to say, 'you need to spend more time working than talking' rather than 'you are an idle pupil') as this emphasises that it is the pupil's behaviour you disapprove of rather than the pupil. It is also better to issue reprimands privately (one-to-one) and quietly, rather than to shout across the class, so as not to disturb other pupils or expose pupils in front of their peers (although there are circumstances when a public reprimand is appropriate, particularly when a teacher wants to signal to the whole class what is unacceptable behaviour).

Punishing refers to formal sanctions, such as detentions, extra work, or being sent out of the lesson. Whilst punishments are the most severe action that a teacher can take, paradoxically they are also the most ineffective. Punishments are a last resort, and their frequent use will almost certainly alienate pupils. In some circumstances, however, they can indicate that the teacher views the misbehaviour with such gravity that the punishment is given to provide the pupil with an indication of this. As such, it is always important to combine a punishment with a discussion of why the punishment has been given and for the pupil to agree to improve their behaviour in future.

It is interesting to note that most student teachers, experienced teachers, and pupils view 'getting pupils back to work' strategies and counselling strategies as more effective than reprimanding and punishing when pupil misbehaviour occurs, but there is a tendency for teachers to use reprimanding and punishing more frequently than their espoused views on their effectiveness would lead one to expect (Evertson and Weinstein, 2006; Wilen *et al.*, 2008).

Taking account of age and abilities

The type of relationship you can establish with pupils and the way in which you establish and exert discipline needs to take account of differences in age and abilities.

With younger (primary school) pupils, the relationship with a teacher is very likely to be respectful, with the teacher taking on a role that is close to being parental. One difference, however, is that teachers need to be more assertive and less tolerant than many parents in how they deal with pupils' wishes and misbehaviour. In many ways, dealing with young children can be seen to be very much part of socialising children into the norms and expectations of society. Misbehaviour can often be regarded as simply a lack of self-discipline. The sanctions available to teachers in primary school tend to be quite soft – an admonishment can often be more than sufficient.

With older (secondary school) pupils, teachers can view pupil misbehaviour as more wilful and expect pupils to take more responsibility for their actions. The sanctions available to teachers in secondary school, particularly when dealing with disaffected pupils, tend to be less effective, and there is more of a need to convince pupils to behave better. Relationships with pupils in secondary schools are also much more complex. Adolescence is a time of rebellion, turmoil, puberty, sexual awakening, and developing a sense of identity and how one relates to others. Secondary school teachers need to be very sensitive to such complexities.

Differences in abilities are important here, in part because dealing with misbehaviour needs to take account of how a pupil's level of ability may have played a part in the misbehaviour (for example, not being able to do the work but feeling this might be ridiculed by other pupils if this was evident may lead the pupil to simply engage in endless social conversation with other pupils). High-ability pupils may also need and expect to have a more mature, adult-like, relationship with their teachers.

CHALLENGING, ENGAGING AND MOTIVATING PUPILS

The need to use teaching methods and learning activities which challenge, engage and motivate pupils has been highlighted in many policy statements and research writings. All too often pupils report that they find lessons boring, and there is a continuing concern about pupils who become disaffected and leave school with few, if any, academic qualifications. The need to challenge, engage and motivate pupils is also a recurrent theme in the DCSF guidelines dealing with pedagogy (e.g. DCSF, 2008a; DfES, 2003) and in the annual report by the Office for Standards in Education and Children's Services and Skills (Ofsted) on standards in schools based on the school inspections it conducts (e.g. Ofsted, 2007). Ofsted's reports are available on the web (www.ofsted.gov.uk) and give Ofsted's views on what features of teaching they regard as desirable. The features highlighted by the DCSF and Ofsted typically include:

- the teacher has good subject knowledge;
- the teacher has high expectations for pupils' work;
- the work is challenging for pupils;
- the teacher has established good relations with pupils;
- the teacher manages the class well;
- the lesson is well planned;

- the teacher adopts a variety of teaching methods, including ICT;
- the needs of the different ability groups within the class are catered for;
- the teacher makes good use of a variety of questioning techniques;
- classroom dialogue is used to extend pupils' thinking.

The notion of 'challenge' is sometimes referred to as setting a task 'which is difficult, but achievable with effort'. In other words, a challenging task requires pupils to feel that the task is not one that can be done easily, nor it is one that is so difficult that if they try hard it is still unlikely they will succeed. There is a tendency amongst beginning teachers, particularly when teaching pupils who are low attainers, to think that giving pupils plenty of easy work to do in a lesson is a good way of keeping them occupied and under control. In fact, this is often not the case, as pupils will quickly get bored, or feel insulted, if the work they are given is easy.

The notions of 'engagement' and 'motivation' overlap somewhat, but the former tends to refer to pupils being and feeling 'involved' in their academic work, whilst motivation tends to refer to their general attitudes towards doing academic work and the degree of effort they are prepared to exert.

Raising pupil motivation and engagement

Kyriacou and Goulding (2006) conducted a review of research studies looking at ways in which teachers could employ strategies that would raise and sustain pupils' motivation and engagement in mathematics in secondary schools. The following three key findings, whilst focused on mathematics, apply equally well to other curriculum areas.

First, it is important for pupils to develop a self-identity of being able to succeed in the subject. In some subjects, pupils will say 'I am no good at . . .'. The task of the teacher is to ensure that pupils are given opportunities to succeed so that they do not feel making an effort will be a waste of time and that they lack the aptitude or ability to make any worthwhile progress in a particular subject.

Second, pupils enjoy the opportunity to talk with other pupils, to discuss and share ideas, and to engage in hands-on activities, particularly activities involving the use of ICT. Opportunities to take part in small group activities, investigational tasks, and ICT-based activities are likely to engage pupils in the work and increase their motivation.

Third, the relationship with the teacher needs to be one where the teacher is seen as supportive and where pupils' views and efforts are treated with respect. Instead of the teacher being seen as the font of all knowledge, who simply transmits this knowledge to pupils and evaluates what pupils have to say as simply right or wrong, the teacher should develop a more equal relationship with pupils in which the lesson is seen as an opportunity for the teacher and pupils to co-construct knowledge and understanding. This means the teacher will listen carefully to what pupils have to say and enter into a dialogue with them in which the pupils are given opportunities to explain their ideas.

In thinking about how to make use of teaching methods and learning activities which challenge, engage and motivate pupils, teachers have to balance two considerations: first, the intellectual integrity of the academic work (does the task genuinely lead to worthwhile learning outcomes in terms of pupils' understanding?); and second, the motivational impact of the academic work (does this task lead to pupils enjoying the work and finding it interesting?). On the one hand, there are times when a task is set that is enjoyable and interesting, but where the teacher might wonder about the quality of the learning taking place. On the other hand, there are times when a task set is hard, and pupils are struggling to make sense of it, but where the teacher feels the learning that takes place will lead to the development of important knowledge and understanding.

Teachers can take a great deal of satisfaction from a lesson which achieves both high-quality cognitive outcomes and is experienced by pupils as enjoyable and interesting, but all too often teaching involves trying one's best to achieving a balance between cognitive and affective outcomes.

Learning styles and personalised learning

One important development in recent years has been the increased attention given to pupils' learning styles. It is argued that pupils differ in their preferred ways of learning, and that some pupils find it easier, more effective or more enjoyable, to learn using some types of activities (e.g. group work discussion) rather than other types of activities (e.g. finding things out for themselves). Where pupils have a strong preference for certain activities, they can be identified as having a particular learning style.

It may be argued that for pupils who have a particular learning style, it might be advantageous for a teacher to take account of this by allowing them to make frequent use of learning activities that fit their preferred learning style. However, it would be a mistake for teachers to do this. All pupils need to develop the skills to learn in different ways from different learning activities. As such, what is important is not that teachers should attempt to match learning activities to particular pupils, but rather that teachers should make use of a range of learning activities so that all pupils have regular opportunities to learn in both their preferred and non-preferred ways. Policy guidelines on pedagogy often advocate the importance of teachers making regular use of a range of learning activities (e.g. DfES, 2003, 2007).

Nevertheless, writing on learning styles has prompted a closer look at how teachers can best meet the learning needs of pupils by taking careful account of each pupil's circumstances. This has given rise to the notion of 'personalised learning', which refers to how a school can tailor the curriculum and teaching methods to the specific learning needs of each pupil, and offer each pupil the type of personalised support that will enable them to develop the skills needed to access learning activities to better effect. Personalised learning has featured heavily in a range of DCSF policy statements dealing with the need to raise the level of pupil engagement in schools, particularly amongst pupils who are disaffected (e.g. DCSF, 2008b; DfES, 2007). The DCSF also notes that personalised learning needs to be based on the regular assessment of pupil progress to identify each pupil's learning needs in order to teach them accordingly ('assessment for learning'). The essence of personalised learning is for the pupil to experience learning as something that is relevant to their needs and which they can readily engage in with success. Key features of personalised learning include:

- personalising content, sources and resources;
- providing pathways through content that are personalised to individual pupils' needs;
- presenting a range of activities appropriate to individual pupils' level and ability;
- using assessment to guide each pupil's future learning;
- providing flexibility regarding when, where and with whom pupils learn.

Taking account of age and abilities

Challenging, engaging and motivating pupils of different ages and abilities presents teachers with a number of challenges, particularly when there is a wide range of ages and abilities in the same class, as can occur in small rural primary schools where a class can often include pupils across two or three year groups. The key to the teacher's ability to meet these challenges lies in the use of differentiation – which refers to how teaching methods and learning activities can be organised so that they allow for pupils of different ages and abilities in the same class to do work that is challenging, engaging and motivating. Research on teachers' use of differentiation in the classroom has highlighted seven types:

1. *differentiation by task*, where pupils cover the same content but at different levels;
2. *differentiation by outcome*, where the same general task is set, but they are flexible enough for pupils to work at their own level;
3. *differentiation by learning activity*, where pupils are required to address the same task at the same level, but in a different way;
4. *differentiation by pace*, where pupils can cover the same content at the same level but at a different rate;
5. *differentiation by dialogue*, where the teacher discusses the work with individual pupils in order to tailor the work to their needs;
6. *differentiation by support*, where the degree of support is tailored to the needs of individual pupils, with less support offering more challenge and opportunity for initiative;
7. *differentiation by resource*, where the type of resource used (worksheets, internet, graphical calculator) is tailored to the pupil's ability and skills.

SUMMARY

In this chapter we have focused on issues facing teachers in employing teaching methods and learning activities effectively. Whilst there exists a plethora of writings, research studies and policy statements to guide our thinking, there is not, nor will there ever be, an unequivocal list of teaching methods and learning activities that teachers can be instructed to use which will lead unproblematically to pupil learning. We know a lot about the nature of teaching and learning, but successful teaching relies heavily on teachers understanding how to make the best use of teaching methods and learning activities that take proper account of the precise classroom circumstances within which they are working.

KEY QUESTIONS

1. What is the 'constructivist view of teaching and learning'?
2. What is meant by the 'zone of proximal development'?
3. In your experience of schooling to what extent are the ideas of Piaget and Vygotsky influential?

FURTHER READING

Hayes, D. (2006) *Inspiring Primary Teaching: Insights into Excellent Primary Practice.* Exeter: Learning Matters.
Kyriacou, C. (2009) *Effective Teaching in Schools*, 3rd edn. Cheltenham: Nelson Thornes.
Muijs, D. and Reynolds, D. (2005) *Effective Teaching: Evidence and Practice*, 2nd edn. London: Paul Chapman.

This chapter links with readings 12 and 13 of *The Routledge Education Studies Reader.*

CHAPTER 13

ASSESSMENT

Lee Jerome

The rationale for this chapter is:

- to introduce the reader to some of the main issues and concepts which underpin debates about assessment;
- to provide a critical account of assessment policy in England, considering the implications for equity in education;
- to discuss Assessment for Learning as a key development in policy and practice.

THINKING ABOUT ASSESSMENT

Students' experiences of assessment play an important part in how they view their schooling and how they perceive themselves as learners. The same assessment system will produce both failures and successes, but assessment is not a neutral process which simply measures success or failure. The particular form of assessment adopted in schools plays a part in the active production of success and failure. This chapter aims to provide an insight into the evidence and various arguments that inform the debate about the ways in which assessment has developed in England, and its impact on students.

Some key concepts

In order to engage with the debate about the development of assessment policy it is useful to establish some basic concepts. In this introductory section we consider some of the key terms that have shaped the academic and policy debates about assessment, consider the interests of different audiences for assessment information and finally outline the role of assessment in the overall education system, focusing on the ways in which assessment data have been used to pursue school improvement.

There are two concepts which are fundamental when considering the extent to which assessment is accurate or effective. The first is *reliability*, which refers to the extent to which the assessment, if repeated, would give the same results, i.e. that the measurement is accurate and replicable. An exam is reliable to the extent that the same learner gets the same result, regardless of extraneous circumstances, such as the identity of the marker. This is crucial if learners, parents, schools, employers and government are to have confidence in the outcome of assessment (Black and Wiliam, 2006: 119). This is less important if the assessment is not intended for publication or for comparative purposes, for example assessment that forms part of a relatively informal and personal exchange between a learner and teacher, which is designed to help the learner make progress (ASF, undated: 8). The second key concept is *validity*, which refers to the extent to which an assessment actually measures what it claims to measure. A tape measure provides a valid measure of the width of a desk; a history teacher's classroom test is valid to the extent that it measures the learner's historical understanding, rather than, for example, skills of memorisation or comprehension.

Validity can also relate to the way in which assessment data are used, for example, a maths test may be valid as a measure of mathematical ability but be rendered invalid if used to determine suitability for an art course (Stobart, 2006: 133–4). When commentators question whether more key stage 2 learners in England achieving level 4 in their standard assessment tests (SATS) reflects better learning in literacy and numeracy, or merely better 'test taking skills', this is a question about the validity of the SATS (Stobart, 2006: 135–6). When an assessment is high in reliability and validity we might say, in less technical terminology, that it is 'dependable' or 'trustworthy' (Black and Wiliam, 2006: 130).

The pursuit of reliability and validity can lead to assessment processes becoming increasingly complex and time-consuming, but effective assessment also has to be practical. This means some measures that might enhance reliability or validity may prove to be prohibitively expensive. For example, double marking all scripts may improve reliability, but would cost much more than simply moderating samples. There is often a trade-off between reliability and validity when making decisions about practicability, for example computerised marking of multiple choice papers might increase reliability, but will also reduce validity by narrowing the range of skills and understanding measured within a subject (ASF, undated: 8).

We also have to be clear what we are measuring, for example whether we want to assess people in relation to others, or in relation to a common agreed standard. *Norm referencing* might be used where an examination is used as a selection tool for an institution with a limited number of places; for example if the civil service organised an entrance examination for new recruits but had only 50 vacancies a year, the score a 'successful' applicant would have to get in order to be accepted would vary year on year, depending on how well the others in the top 50 performed. The 11-plus examination in practice included an element of norm-referencing, because the exact score an individual needed to gain access to a grammar school depended on the relative performance of the other learners in the local area and the number of grammar places available. On the other hand, *criteria-referenced* assessment involves establishing what is required of a learner in order to pass a test, or gain a grade, before the test has been taken. A basic example of such assessment is a swimming certificate which requires the candidate to swim 50 metres unaided in a given time. A more familiar example from school is the use of assessment criteria from exam boards, or national curriculum levels in subject-specific attainment targets. Establishing clear and concise criteria for assessment requires the careful definition of areas of subject knowledge/skills (referred to as domains) to be assessed (Lambert & Lines, 2000: 17).

The purposes of assessment

As is already clear from the examples discussed above, the decisions we make about the most appropriate form of assessment often relate to the purpose of that assessment. Sometimes we may design a *diagnostic* assessment to identify specific learning difficulties, for example learners may be referred to an educational psychologist to identify dyslexia. More broadly construed the term can also overlap with formative assessment, in the sense that assessment is concerned with identifying where the learner is at, in order to plan future teaching and learning. The term *formative* assessment has been popularised by the Assessment Reform Group (ARG) (Black *et al*., 2003) to refer to any assessment activity which feeds back into learning. The purpose of this form of assessment is to enhance learning and it is therefore known as *assessment for learning* (AfL); this will be discussed in greater detail below.

Formative assessment is often contrasted with *summative* assessment, which refers to any assessment that takes place at the end of a period of learning. In schools this is typified by end of unit tests or examinations. Such assessment is not intended to feed directly back into learning, but rather provides some measure of learning that has already taken place. This information may lead to some level of certification or accreditation of learning; it may also be used to inform the transition from one institution to another, or within an institution to inform decisions about streaming or setting. These data are used to report on an individual's achievements but are also used to *evaluate* school/teacher effectiveness (Black, 2001: 31). This is exemplified in England by the publication of league tables, which are intended to hold schools to account for the performance of their pupils by enabling parents and other interested parties to compare schools. The policy has come under sustained criticism and has been refined to incorporate more subtle statistical measures of 'value added' and subsequently 'contextualised value added'. We will explore this dimension to assessment below, but here it is enough to note the additional purpose for which summative data are used.

It is also useful to remind ourselves of the range of audiences for assessment information. Obviously learners want to know how they are doing and are often motivated by the assessment process itself, where this is represented by certificates, qualifications, and access to further opportunities. Parents and guardians also form a significant audience for school assessment, through regular reports home and opportunities to discuss progress with teachers. Teachers themselves will use information from assessments, in their day-to-day planning, to track learners' progress over time, and also when managing the transition from one school to another. School managers use data on assessment to look for patterns of underachievement, or to inform judgements about the quality of teaching. Finally, outside of the school, the local authority will analyse data, comparing school performance year on year and in relation to other schools in the local area, central government generates league tables and monitors progress towards targets, and of course the media runs detailed coverage of these assessment data. In the discussion that follows we need to think about how each of these assessment 'consumer' groups engages with the assessment system, and whose needs are best being met by different aspects of the system.

Characteristics of the assessment system in England

First though we need to appreciate quite what the 'system' is – what is the assessment framework for England? David Miliband, in a speech as Minister of State for School Standards (2004), argued that data were central to the project of raising achievement; the following extract reflects the list of 'consumers of assessment' above, but also explains how data are supposed to lead to improvement:

> It starts with data: the strengths and weaknesses of every child, in every class. It extends to every teacher: their performance management, their professional development. It reaches every school: how it is doing, where it is trying to do better, where it needs support. And it demands action from LEAs [Local Education Authorities] and DfES [Department for Education and Skills]: a synchronised engagement between public bodies and the schools they serve.

Miliband argued that national testing provides national benchmarks for everyone to aim for, and against which performance can be judged. Through such a system of common standards, educational inequalities can be challenged. He explained that 'we shall only reap the rewards, in terms of raised standards of pupil attainment, if we get performance management right', by which he meant 'effective monitoring, observation and review', which in his speech should be linked to effective professional development for teachers, but is also obviously linked to the possibility of weeding out ineffective teachers. Put simply:

> Performance management is an approach where teachers' understanding of pupil progress is informed by rich sources of data on pupil performance. Where everyone in the school is homing in on why particular pupils are doing well or are doing not so well.
>
> (Miliband, 2004)

Since the early 1990s the data have essentially been generated by a system of national assessment at the end of each key stage (7, 11 and 14 years of age) and exam scores at 16 and 18 (Gipps & Murphy, 1994: Ch.7). Core subjects have been assessed through externally set and marked tests for 11- and 14-year-olds. From 2003 this has been complemented by a Foundation Stage Profile, which provides some form of baseline measure at the start of an individual's education, although this is solely reliant on teacher assessment (Gillborn, 2008). Following the failure of a new contractor to complete the 2008 SATS satisfactorily (there were questions about reliability as well as problems with delays and lost tests), the Department for Children, Schools and Families (DCSF) announced the end of the key stage 3 SATS. In the same year the DCSF's evidence to the House of Commons Committee enquiry into assessment had been unequivocal about the benfits of the system:

> The aspirations and expectations of pupils and their teachers have been raised. . . . And for the education system as a whole, standards of achievement have been put in the spotlight, teachers' efforts have been directed to make a difference and performance has improved.
>
> (Children, Schools and Families Committee, 2008: 10).

A recurrent theme, discussed in the same Committee report, is that tests reveal the depths of inequality and challenge schools and teachers to tackle these. Just four years earlier, Miliband (2004) had argued that: 'When the vigour brought by national testing is lost, the evidence from the history of the English education system is that pupils in the poorest communities suffer most.'

In the next section we will consider the impact of this testing regime to ascertain the validity of the assumption that testing has indeed challenged inequalities and the specific warning about the possible effects of changes to the testing system.

TESTING, TESTING

The SATS were piloted in 1990–1991 and they revealed an interesting insight in relation to patterns of inequality. The key stage 1 and 3 tests revealed that girls outperformed boys, minority ethnic groups generally did less well than white children, and those for whom English is an additional language did less well than others (Gipps & Murphy, 1994: 205). Gipps and Murphy concluded their discussion of the introduction of SATS with the warning that the speed of change in test design, the speed of implementation and the temptation to move to more easily administered traditional timed tests should give cause for concern as there was insufficient attention being given to assessing the impact on learners, especially in relation to equity issues (Gipps & Murphy, 1994: 209).

Fifteen years on and there are some serious concerns about the operation of the national assessment system. Whilst there has been improvement overall, the gender gap has continued, and there are still disparities in how learners from different ethnic groups fare. David Gillborn's *Racism and Education* (2008) and *Rationing Education* (Gillborn & Youdell, 2000) explore some of the ways in which the assessment system in its current form exacerbates and even causes some of these inequalities. Assessment data are used to make decisions about streaming, which has been vigorously promoted by the Labour government since 1997. In a group of 30 secondary schools piloting *Aiming High*, an initiative intended to tackle black underachievement, Gillborn found that 88 per cent of the schools streamed classes by ability in key stage 3 (11–14 years of age) and 100 per cent of the schools did so in key stage 4 (14–16 years) (Gillborn, 2008: 94). According to Gillborn, the streaming process is one of the main mechanisms through which black children are discriminated against. In this *Aiming High* pilot project, 10.5 per cent of black Caribbean boys in the year group were placed in top sets for maths, whereas 24.9 per cent of white boys and 31 per cent of white girls achieved this (and remember these schools were focusing on ways in which they could *overcome* black underachievement) (Gillborn, 2008: 95).

This streaming has severe effects, given that GCSE papers are tiered, so top grades are only available to those registered for the top tier. When Gillborn completed his research, the maths papers were organised into three tiers and the bottom tier denied access to a grade C, which condemned all learners registered for that paper to achieve less than the commonly accepted pass grade (Gillborn, 2008: 96). Whilst this particular problem has been overcome by changes in maths tiers, the more general point holds that, in the 'A–C economy' (Gillborn & Youdell, 2000), the effects of streaming can therefore be very significant on future access to further and higher education and certain careers (applicants for teacher training for example must have a grade C in English and maths).

As well as using past assessment data to allocate black students to lower streams, with less access to examination success, this pressure to organise learners by ability works in other ways, for example, by 2005 only 2 per cent of black African learners and 4 per cent of black Caribbean learners had been identified as 'gifted and talented' under the government's initiative to cater for the most able, whereas 10 per cent of white children had been registered (Gillborn, 2008: 115). Interestingly, whilst Indian children as a group regularly outperform white children in examinations (Gillborn & Mirza, 2000), the gifted and talented programme only recognised 6 per cent of Indian children.

Through the establishment of performance management data systems, Gillborn argues that many schools have come to build in lower expectations for black students. By buying in to a system of cognitive ability tests (CATs) and predictive software packages that provide personal target grades for individual students, schools have come to rely on the assumption that it is possible to measure some form of innate capacity for learning, which predicts future performance. The danger is that tests which may be valid for assessing current performance in maths or English, are being rendered invalid because they are used as proxy measures for general ability or potential (Gillborn & Youdell, 2000). In fact, this elaborate statistical package achieves little more than the reinforcing of the view that low achievers at key stage 2 or 3 will remain low achievers at key stage 4. This process is not the neutral application of performance management techniques it purports to be, in fact it represents a not so subtle labelling process through which expectations and aspirations are controlled.

Labelling and low aspirations are not the only way in which the formal assessment system works to the detriment of some learners. The Assessment Reform Group (2002) reviewed 19 reliable studies (selected from 183 potential sources of evidence) to consider the impact of high-stakes assessment, such as SATS. They concluded that the introduction of SATS led to a reduction in self esteem for many of those children who did not achieve well (ARG, 2002a: 4). Whilst regular test-taking provides some higher-achieving learners with opportunities to improve their self-perception, lower achievers can become overwhelmed by assessments and demotivated. Three studies provided evidence that this process increased the gap between low- and high-achieving learners (ARG, 2000a: 4). In addition, the curriculum has narrowed, as teachers provide increasing time for test preparation and practice, a phenomenon known as 'teaching to the test' (Davies, 1999). A curriculum which is driven by the nature of SATS is less likely to respond to the needs and interests of the children themselves and the ARG report demonstrated that this phenomenon of curriculum narrowing is experienced consciously by learners.

This focus on tests also means that, as learners proceed through their schooling, they tend to become increasingly focused on performance outcomes rather than learning processes, and also experience more resentment and anxiety (ARG, 2002a: 5). There is some evidence to suggest that girls experience this anxiety more acutely than boys and also that they are more likely to take personal responsibility for their grades (as opposed to attributing success to external factors), which in turn makes some girls more vulnerable to low self esteem (ARG, 2002a: 5). Gillborn and Youdell (2000) conducted their research in two secondary schools and described some of the ways in which a focus on high-stakes testing in a climate of performance management and league tables can lead to counterproductive policies. In one school, the key stage 4 cohort was regularly re-assessed for their predicted GCSE points score. The students were ranked from top to bottom and this list was published in order to create a competitive climate. This kind of feedback was identified by the ARG report as being most likely to foster a focus on improving grades, rather than encouraging deeper understanding (ARG, 2002a: 6). But of course that is only likely to be the case for those who are at the top of the list. The school in Gillborn and Youdell's case study sought to solve the problem of labelling those at the bottom by removing the last few names, so no-one knew who was last out of the whole year, but in terms of motivation one can only wonder what effect the system had on those students whose names did not appear at all on the regularly updated list. The ARG survey indicates this is likely to decrease motivation and self esteem and foster a lower sense of self-efficacy (the extent to which individuals feel they are capable of undertaking a task successfully) (ARG, 2002a: 5–6).

The report found evidence that for all types of learners, regular test practice reinforced test-taking strategies, rather than deeper learning or higher-order thinking (ARG, 2002a: 4). This results in the accusation that the numbers of learners achieving level 4 in their key stage 2 SATS is a reflection of the teachers' increasing competence in teaching test-taking skills rather than representing any significant improvement in depth of subject understanding (Davies, 1999: 18; Broadfoot, 2007: 33). This is one of the key flaws in the system which links individual learner assessment with school accountability measures (Stobart, 2008: 116).

In 2008, the House of Commons Committee for Children, Schools and Families issued a report into their investigation of these matters. The committee concluded that: 'A variety of classroom practices aimed at improving test results has distorted the education of some children, which may leave them unprepared for higher education and employment' (Children, Schools and Families Committee, 2008: 3). Overall the Committee argued that the continued linking of individual learner's assessment and school accountability data had narrowed the curriculum; led to resources in some schools being focused on grade D candidates to achieve more A–C grades overall; and actually led to questionable data as improved grades are as likely to reflect enhanced test-taking strategies as actual improvements in education. Their conclusion was that the government should seek alternative ways to measure performance for accountability purposes.

So, there are some powerful reasons for questioning the system of assessment that has developed in England. Here we have briefly seen how the system itself may feasibly be implicated in distorting the curriculum and encouraging decisions in schools which have detrimental effects on some learners – especially those already at risk of relative educational failure. To end this section I return to three of the key terms defined at the beginning of this chapter – reliability, validity and practicability.

There is an obvious problem with high-stakes examinations in that they measure one-off performances. We are all familiar with the problem of 'exam nerves' which may limit an individual's performance in an examination, even though they have done well through the course to date. In fact the problems with over-relying on relatively short and structured examinations or tests are more significant than just performance anxiety. First, the tests themselves are unlikely to assess the whole range of skills, simply because some areas of the curriculum do not fit easily into the test format, for example, speaking and listening in English, and enquiry in science. Second, there is a technical consideration related to gathering sufficient evidence to make an accurate judgement about overall performance – just as in social science research we would question anyone who came to firm conclusions based on a sample of one, there is some variation in how individuals respond to individual tasks on specific occasions and so a larger sample of work than one or two tests helps make a more accurate overall judgement. Black, Wiliam and Dylan have estimated that, whilst the individual exam and test papers are largely accurately marked, the effect of this narrow evidence base is likely to generate a margin of error of up to 30 per cent (Children, Schools and Families Committee, 2008: 22). That is to say, almost one in three exam or SATS grades do not accurately reflect the overall ability or level of attainment of a learner in that subject, although the grade may well accurately reflect what the learner did on that particular occasion. Third, as we have seen, the effect of teaching to the test may well indicate that the test performance reflects increased test-taking ability, rather than improvements in subject understanding. Clearly, this poses a challenge to the reliability and validity of high-stakes testing for all the purposes they have been used for.

In terms of practicability, the high-stakes system clearly has a narrowing impact on the curriculum and accounts for large amounts of time for preparation in some schools; there are thus hidden costs in addition to the actual costs of administering the system. Whilst introducing even more tests may go some way to tackling some of the inadequacies noted in the previous paragraph, it seems likely that one of the more practicable ways to address some of these problems is to use the information that teachers gain about individuals, to provide a broader picture of learners' attainment (Children, Schools and Families Committee, 2008: 25).

None of the arguments considered in this section provides unequivocal support for scrapping national tests, but they do indicate that there are some dangers, which teachers must try to guard against, and some weaknesses that should be addressed. The Assessment Reform Group's (2002) review of research included evidence that almost all of the negative effects of testing they had discussed could be ameliorated by sensitive teachers, school systems and parental support. It is against this backdrop that we turn next to consider the rise of assessment for learning, which at least in part, might be seen as a balancing force to the external testing regime, and which places teacher and learner relationships at the heart of its vision of assessment.

ASSESSMENT FOR LEARNING

The principles of Assessment for Learning (AfL) might be described essentially as the principles of effective teaching and learning, but they have become especially significant precisely because of the high-stakes testing regime, which provides the backdrop for the rise of AfL.

> In an era dominated by summative accountability testing, this [AfL] can be seen as an attempt to rebalance the uses to which assessments are put, by making it *part* of the learning process, rather than standing outside it and checking what has been learned.
>
> (Stobart, 2008: 146)

This positioning of the AfL movement is justified by the Assessment Reform Group's own analysis of the situation in their influential pamphlet, *Inside the Black Box,* which criticised the government's 'failure to perceive the need for substantial support for formative assessment' in the face of the 'new and mountainous burdens of the National Curriculum' (Black & Wiliam, 1998: 8).

Assessment for Learning is essentially the process by which learners gain feedback on their learning to date, to improve their subsequent performance. The Assessment Reform Group (2002b) summarises AfL through the following ten principles:

1. It is part of effective planning;
2. It focuses on how students learn;
3. It is central to classroom practice;
4. It is a key professional skill;
5. It is sensitive and constructive;
6. It fosters motivation;
7. It promotes understanding of goals and criteria;
8. It helps learners know how to improve;
9. It develops the capacity for self assessment;
10. It recognises all educational achievement.

These principles may be used to review and inform many aspects of teachers' practice, for example by improving the use of questioning in class to promote deeper understanding; by enhancing the quality of feedback and marking and providing learners with opportunities to respond; and by encouraging learners to develop their understanding of tasks by assessing their own work and that of their peers (Black *et al.*, 2003). We can see therefore, that AfL does not simply represent an approach to assessment, but is actually an

> [i]nteractive pedagogy based on constructivist ideas about learning and integrated into a wide range of teaching and learning activities. Unless formative assessment involves learners actively, it is little more than conscientious summative feedback and target setting.
>
> (Ecclestone & Pryor, 2001: 2).

In relation to the key terms discussed at the beginning of this chapter, AfL tends to promote diagnostic marking, focusing on what has been achieved and what is required next, and to favour ipsative and criteria-referenced assessment, which comments on individual progress in relation to their own previous performance or explicit success criteria, rather than focusing on comparisons with other learners.

Members of the Assessment Reform Group built on their original analysis of AfL and established an implementation project to support teachers who wanted to develop their practice in line with these principles (Black *et al.*, 2002). One participant summed up the positive impact across a range of factors:

> The project has raised my awareness of the many ways that I assess students in the classroom and has underlined the importance of sharing the assessment process with them and, indeed, inviting them to participate in it. . . . This has encouraged the students to become more independent learners. . . . We have learnt that in order to implement peer and self-marking we have to share assessment criteria . . . the students really enjoy the challenge of such an activity and, by becoming so involved in the assessment process, what they learn tends to stay with them. . . . The results [of comment only marking] were especially noticeable in lower attainers, since grades can often have a de-motivating effect.
>
> (teacher quoted in Black *et al.*, 2003: 85).

Many of the participants initially struggled to incorporate the full range of AfL techniques in their practice, precisely because they had become used to working with assessment for narrower purposes (summative assessment and record-keeping). Once they had begun to make the recommended adjustments to their practice however, they came to understand how relatively small changes to classroom practice (such as combining 'thinking time' with the 'no hands up' rule) can bring about substantial changes to the levels of learner engagement and the depth of understanding achieved (Black *et al.*, 2003: 80–99).

Because of this link to improving classroom practice, AfL has been largely accepted by the Qualifications and Curriculum Authority (QCA) and the DCSF, and it features on the QCA website and in Primary and Secondary Strategy materials for schools on the DCSF Standards website. Although it may be seen as being bound up with a critique of the summative assessment system, it has, more importantly, also been accepted as part of an overall strategy for counter-balancing some of the negative effects of summative assessment. If, as the teacher quoted above indicated, these simple strategies could be developed to overcome some of the problems discussed above then AfL becomes a natural addition to the assessment system.

The implementation problems experienced in the initial stages of some of the ARG work indicate a problem with the roll out of AfL though. In this regard Smith and Gorard's (2005) case study of AfL implementation is revealing. They studied a school which was introducing comment-only marking for one year 7 class (out of four classes in the year group). The evaluation showed that the results for the AfL implementation group were actually worse than the control groups. Teachers reported that students were "gagging" for their marks, and students reported frustration that they did not know how well they were doing. There was also evidence that the teachers had been unable to refocus their comments sufficiently in response to the loss of grades. In other words, the students felt they were simply receiving half the feedback the other classes were getting – which left them with some rather bland comments about neatness, completion and effort, with few clear indications of achievement or next steps. The researchers concluded that the intervention in this case was ineffective and actually created 'dis-improvement' (Smith & Gorard, 2005: 37). Such research indicates that we may need to be cautious about the extent to which AfL offers an easy solution to the problems of working under a high-stakes assessment regime, and it is to these concerns that we now turn.

CAN AFL WORK IN A SYSTEM OF HIGH-STAKES SUMMATIVE EXAMS?

In this section we briefly consider two categories of problem associated with the development of AfL. The first sub-section relates to the role of teachers, and the difficulties they experience incorporating AfL in their practice. The second sub-section considers the ways in which AfL may be becoming the 'junior partner' to summative assessment, with the effect that AfL becomes distorted to the demands of high-stakes assessment rather than mitigating its worst side-effects.

Developing teacher skills

The above example of teachers struggling to make the AfL strategies work is more than simply a case of inadequate teaching or poor project design. Stobart (2008: 160–69) reviews research into feedback and discusses the complexity at the heart of this deceptively simple concept. There is evidence to suggest that much feedback is ineffective and that its effectiveness is related to four dimensions: (i) feedback about the task, (ii) feedback about the processes that were undertaken, (iii) the learner's understanding and ability to respond to feedback, and (iv) feedback which is interpreted as personal. Getting the balance right requires demanding and subtle judgement about how the teacher relates their own deep understanding of the subject to the learner, their level of motivation and their current level of understanding. In this task, one can appreciate how demanding the shift to AfL really is and we can begin to think about the demands for professional development.

The second way in which the role of the teacher should make us cautious relates to the renewed focus on the quality of interactions between teacher and learner. This is one feature of AfL which seems especially attractive when contrasted with the impersonal summative assessment system that dominates much of education, however, we should also remember that the classroom is itself a site of intense and complex social processes, which are likely to influence the ways in which teachers form judgements about individuals. Elwood (2006: 228) argues that this is an under-researched area of AfL implementation and, drawing on research into gender, argues that we should anticipate that gender is likely to influence teacher assessment. There is no reason to think that other significant sources of social difference (religion, ethnicity, social class) will not also be important in influencing the assessment process. In other words, AfL is likely to be implicated in perpetuating whatever existing patterns of classroom inequality currently operate.

The uses of AfL

There is a fine line between on the one hand knowing enough to achieve clarity about a task and the expectations of learners in successfully completing it, and on the other hand knowing so much that the activity becomes little more than following directions – an exercise in compliance (Stobart, 2008: 155). If the learning outcomes themselves are merely delivered to the teacher by the examination board or the QCA, through curricular guidance, then AfL becomes little more than what Stobart calls a 'mechanism for sweetening the "delivery"' (2008: 157). Torrance has examined the use of such strategies in Further Education settings and concluded that:

> the practice of assessment has moved from assessment *of* learning, through assessment *for* learning, to assessment *as* learning, with assessment procedures and practices coming completely to dominate the learning experience and 'criteria compliance' replacing 'learning'.
>
> (Torrance, 2007: 281).

Torrance describes a situation in which classroom practice involves excessive discussion of assessment criteria, multiple opportunities to revise work for assessment, and intensive coaching to achieve the required criteria. This in turn leads to an instrumentalist view of schooling, with the ultimate goal being the achievement of specific criteria, as opposed to deep learning (Torrance, 2007: 283). In fact this is not very far from the phenomenon of 'teaching to the test' which has been so roundly criticised (section 2, above). This tendency is exacerbated by the trend towards ever smaller chunks of specified learning, which make it easier to coach learners through each part, but which moves us collectively further from deep and connected understanding of an area and autonomy in applying what has been learned (Sadler, 2007).

SUMMARY

Assessment for Learning is part of the answer to the problems created by an unwieldy and overpowering summative assessment system but we must be realistic about what it can achieve. The future of assessment is unlikely to involve the whole-scale replacement of one system by another, and so educators and policy makers must start from where they are and develop sensitive solutions which respond to the conflicting demands placed on the assessment system as a whole. At the time of writing (2008) it seems that the tide is beginning to turn, away from the myth that a single test can provide all things to all interested parties, and towards a more creative mix of assessment strategies that addresses the learning needs of learners as well as it does their need for certification. At the same time, the government will continue to want to hold schools to account for their results, and so teachers will need to develop assessment strategies within some externally imposed parameters. In developing these strategies we need to maintain a focus on the need for valid, reliable and practical assessment, but we should also judge it against two additional criteria – fairness and the promotion of learning. The fact that our current system falls short on both counts should remind us to take nothing for granted.

KEY QUESTIONS

1. What are the purposes of assessment?
2. Do you think that there are some purposes of assessment that should be emphasised more than others?
3. Do you think that assessment data show that standards have risen in the last decade?

FURTHER READING

Black, P., Harrison, C., Lee, C., Marshall, B. & Wiliam, D. (2003) *Assessment for Learning: Putting it into practice*, Maidenhead: Open University Press

Broadfoot, P. (2007) *An Introduction to Assessment*, London: Continuum

Stobart, G. (2008) *Testing Times: The uses and abuses of assessment*, Abingdon: Routledge

This chapter links with readings 10 and 14 of *The Routledge Education Studies Reader.*

DEBATE 4

DO SCHOOLS CONTRIBUTE TO SOCIAL AND COMMUNITY COHESION?

John Preston and Namita Chakrabarty

In this debate John Preston (Professor of Education at the University of East London) provides a sociological perspective on issues of social cohesion, drawing attention to the contested nature of the term and the importance of equitable education in enhancing cohesion. In contrast, Namita Chakrabarty (Senior Lecturer at the Cass School of Education, University of East London) considers psychoanalytical and literary perspectives. She considers the possible emancipatory potential of schooling but also its inherent contradictions as both a site of liberation and aggression. John's response considers that cohesion is a multi-level and multi-faceted phenomenon. For some major educational theorists cohesion (as currently envisaged) is incompatible with human rights and development. Namita's response focuses on ways in which cohesion protects forms of privilege. The neutrality of cohesion is disputed as processes of assimilation obscure power relations. Rather than being seen as fostering value consensus, assimilation marks certain categories (heterosexuality, whiteness) as normative and others as abject. The debate reveals not only the complexity of the relationship between education and cohesion but the need for educators to reflect on and challenge dominant notions of social order.

JOHN PRESTON

Schools have become the most overburdened institutions of the welfare state. Whilst the purposes of hospitals (to promote health) and the army (to defend the nation) are clear, schools are now responsible for far more than education. Fighting obesity, combating extremism and reducing crime are, in various DfES and DCSF mandates, objectives of British schooling. However, these objectives pale into insignificance when the sheer rate of DfES / DCFS discourse on promoting 'cohesion' is taken into account. In this respect schools, as a major component of secondary socialisation, are given a literal role in bringing together divided communities and societies. This is not a new role for schools, indeed in classical writings on education, schooling is emphasised as being centrally important in promoting the sorts of citizenship which would encourage conservative forms of social integration (Rousseau, 1991). However, what is new is the role in which schools are playing in promoting particular forms of community and social cohesion to meet societal goals. Schools can certainly promote certain types of community and social cohesion, but the bigger question is whether we would want them to or not. 'Cohesion' in itself is not a meaningful social goal for schools and is always overlaid with political ideologies, or what could be described as regimes of social cohesion.

It is very important at the outset to distinguish between social and community cohesion as these concepts operate at different levels of aggregation and emerge from quite different historical contexts. Social cohesion is a concept with a long lineage in classical sociology in the work of Durkheim, Spencer and Marx who were writing in a context where there was grave concern about the impact of capitalism on social order. For Durkheim, social cohesion in the modern world was associated with organic solidarity or the types of cohesion that are built through the integration of individuals into work or other social groupings such as voluntary associations. However, social cohesion was a property of societies, not individuals, and societies could be 'sick' or 'anomic' with corresponding social dysfunction, such as higher suicide rates. Some interpretations of Durkheim have stressed this functionalism and critiques from both Marxists (on the basis that societies within capitalism are internally divided due to the dialectic between capital/labour) and conservatives (who stress the importance of traditional ties: mechanical rather than organic solidarity) have cut against Durkheimian functionalism. However, Durkheim also stressed not just integration but the importance of equalities in solidarity. From Durkheim, contemporary writers on social cohesion have stressed the ways in which different systems of integration might pull towards and against cohesion. For example, Lockwood (1964) has stressed social and system integration as sometimes supportive and sometimes contradictory elements of social cohesion.

Moving away from a normative sense of cohesion as always beneficial for society, social cohesion regimes can be understood as ways in which practices and discourses of social cohesion can act as forms of power. In rethinking social cohesion in this way there has been a 'return' to social cohesion but it maintains its roots as a classical sociological concept. Community cohesion, on the other hand, is not grounded in classical sociology and is more of a reactive concept: born of a perceived crisis in community relations: than a productive one. Community cohesion is based on individualistic notions of social capital (Putnam, 2000), that bonding rather than bridging capital means that communities have become not only isolated but hostile to each other. Differences in race, ethnicity and faith are foregrounded as essential differences between communities. Community cohesion is thus ideological, emphasising discourses of 'difference' and 'othering' in an updated form of community relations. Internally cohesive ethnic or faith communities in this discourse do not make for community cohesion (quite the contrary) nor does community cohesion necessarily make for social cohesion.

Although social and community cohesion appear to be somewhat reactionary concepts, policy makers have considered that there are indicators of cohesion that most would agree are normatively 'good' for society (OECD, 2006). For example, lower crime, greater social trust and improved civil and political liberties are often considered to be positive social cohesion outcomes. Much current thinking on social and community cohesion considers that the improvement of educational levels or achievement is key to achieving higher levels of these so-called social 'indicators'. Indeed, at an individual level there seem to be associations between education and these social 'benefits' of learning (Schuller *et al*., 2004). However, what holds true for individuals does not necessarily hold true for societies and there are vast differences between levels of these variables between countries. Empirical analysis, using data for 30 countries over a period of 25 years shows that societal educational *equality*, rather than economic growth/educational levels, is associated with improved 'social cohesion' indicators (Green, Preston and Janmaat, 2006). This would correspond with Durkheim's suggestions concerning the relation between equality and cohesion. In turn, the factors that appear to be associated with improved social cohesion indicators are comprehensive schools, a small (or highly regulated) system of private schools, limited or no school choice and low levels of school segregation. A social democratic, even socialist, education system is therefore more likely to produce more socially cohesive outcomes as compared to a neo-liberal one. In short, although individual schools can do little to promote social cohesion measured crudely by these indicators, the system of schooling does have a role in terms of mitigating against educational inequalities. This is because streaming, selection, choice and privatisation are anathema to educational equality and hence social cohesion.

Before we become passionate advocates of the Scandinavian welfare model (where educational outcomes are relatively equal), though, let us take a step back from the idea of social cohesion as a normative concept and rather interrogate it as a system of power – that is, as a social cohesion regime. In this articulation cohesion is a non-normative term which implies many forms of hidden exclusions and relations of domination. As discussed earlier, schools are becoming increasingly responsible for the maintenance of various forms of community cohesion. Directing schools towards 'community cohesion' and 'combating extremism' may appear to be worthy and neutral discourses but these are often code for racialisation of certain groups of students. For example, in combating extremism or building community cohesion the focus is normally on Asian and/or Muslim students who are the focus of such initiatives. Predominantly white schools in white areas are encoded as 'non problematic' in terms of community cohesion and hence white homogeneity is taken to be the least problematic situation in terms of school cohesion. Other work which I have conducted has shown that since the Cold War schools have been articulated as sites of 'national security' in which whiteness has been equated with security and cohesion. In the Cold War, for example, schoolchildren in the USA were involved in civil defence exercises in schools (such as 'Duck and Cover'), the emphasis of which was the protection of white children and families in the suburbs rather than on BME children in the inner cities (Preston, 2008). More recently, teachers and pupils in schools have been instructed to monitor (implicitly) Asian and Muslim students (as shown in the 'Extremism toolkit' recently issued to schools; DCSF, 2008). Through such discourses security and cohesion become associated with 'whiteness'.

In conclusion, for some 'indicators' of social cohesion, although individual schools can't necessarily contribute, more equitable education systems are associated with improved outcomes. These are, in turn, those education systems within which neo-liberal policies of choice and privatisation are limited. They are comprehensive systems with few branching points where students can be ejected from the system to lower-status educational routes. These are associated with social cohesion regimes, primarily in the Scandinavian countries, where education (and income) are relatively evenly distributed. Although appealing to policy makers, we must remember that these are homogeneous countries in terms of the 'whiteness' of the native population with pernicious immigration policies and relatively low levels of racial tolerance. Therefore the 'cohesion' that is achieved is one in which the 'rights' of native white citizens are guaranteed at the expense of BME citizens and immigrants. Similarly, community cohesion policies of schools are aimed at racialised 'others' rather than the white majority. Whilst it is possible for schools (or at least school systems) to contribute towards social and community cohesion the question is whose interests these types of cohesion serve. A worrying (although methodologically problematic) set of studies suggest social cohesion is associated with (white) ethnic homogeneity and community cohesion is therefore implicitly associated with whiteness (Putnam, 2007). Although we might like schools to be engines of social and community cohesion we should ask whose interests such prescriptions serve. Remember that in Nazi Germany, schools were very effective engines in creating forms of community and social cohesion but one would hardly wish to support the use of schooling in 'ethnic regimes' of cohesion.

NAMITA CHAKRABARTY

My starting point, before we can question the ideals of curriculum and assessment, is to address the role of the institutions where organised teaching and learning is supposed to happen, schools. Education, the process by which we learn, is seen by organised society as happening in schools, however it is something that happens to us – through culture – in the immediate locality in which we live and the wider culture around us which now stretches globally via the internet. Thus education happens in a vast range of locations, through parenting in the home, places of organised religion, youth clubs, friendship groups, the 'street', and through the media. One of the issues raised by the 7 July 2005 bombings in central London was the issue of the British-born Asian bombers' education and culture; Rai examines the 'turning points' for the 7/7 bombers from rejection of parental culture, a temporal integration within mainstream local culture, and then, after 9/11 and the invasion of Iraq, immersal, through a local gym, into the tight-knit network of al-Qaeda supporters and activists (2006, pp. 82–83). In a later chapter Rai addresses 'The Myth of Control', the stereotyping of Asian youths as being under the tight control of their community, citing Raminder Singh from the appendix to the Bradford Race Review: 'it is wrong to assume that the community leaders are losing control over the youth. The existence of any such control has been a myth' (2006, p. 99). The example of the 7/7 bombers and Singh's latter assertion point to the need to examine the role of schools in contributing to community cohesion despite the conflicting and competing social messages from diverse locations of education.

There is great potential for schools to contribute to social and community cohesion given the nature of the length of the school day and week and the obligations of schooling for young people under law. However the reality is stained by the nature of uncannily aggressive paternalism, of all institutions, and the social hierarchies implicit in organised society constructed through a fear of the other. *Civilization and its Discontents* (Freud 2001) addresses the latter psychoanalytically and Freud points out how education fails to address the needs of young people by promoting a false picture of society: Freud's main reference to education in the latter paper is as a footnote to the phrase: 'the price we pay for our advance in civilization is a loss of happiness through the heightening of the sense of guilt' (2001, p. 134). In the footnote Freud addresses the failure of education:

> . . . Its other sin is that it does not prepare them for the aggressiveness of which they are destined to become the objects . . . the young are made to believe that everyone else fulfils these ethical demands – that is, that everyone else is virtuous.
>
> (2001, p. 134)

Freud's point is that schools, rather than fostering guilt regarding human compulsions, could deal instead with facilitating young people's needs in learning how to deal with the aggression of society. Instead schools generally, like the countries in which they are situated, produce barriers against cultural exchange and thereby prevent social cohesion.

A post-modern awareness of schools as performances of majority culture would echo the theatrical alienation theory of Brecht. Peter Brook writes of Brechtian theatre as '. . . serving the purpose of leading its audience to a juster understanding of the society in which it lived, and so learning in what ways that society was capable of change' (1972, p. 82). In other words a school shining a light on the inadequacies of schools as complete educational institutions could empower teachers and learners: in the very acknowledgement of the limitations of schools would be the beginning of the schools of the future. To develop autonomous learners, confident speakers and intelligent readers, schools would need to learn from elements of other successful non-hierarchical organisations, for example the work of A.S. Neill at Summerhill School in developing democratic schools, or in the workings of other educational techniques such as Open Space Technology (Owen 2008) or the use of other theories such as the use of activist counter-narratives in Critical Race Theory to critique society. One of the ways that high-functioning schools foster safe learning environments is by developing respect, where it is due, in the positive relationships between staff, between staff and students, and between students. In acknowledging difference and simultaneously fostering equality, these schools develop coherence of policy and a workable cohesion in the school community through school and student charters; an example is the use of anti-bullying charters. Used well, an anti-bullying charter, explored through dissemination in the drama, history, geography and citizenship curriculum, would generate student knowledge of structures of bullying on the macro and micro scale, and through creating their own policy, would explore democratic procedures and explore the complexities of social integration.

The foregoing suggestions acknowledge the uneasy and unfinished nature of any sense of community cohesion; this is why fundamentally schools should be safe environments away from the world and yet of them too. Royle writes of 'haunted teaching' (2003, p. 51); writing of the uncanny nature of education, and of Derrida's exploration of the contradictory readings of Nietszche's work, he posits that '[t]he ear is an unspoken key to the future of education' (2003, p. 64), a metaphor for the necessity of multiple readings. Within the question of the role of schools towards social cohesion we could ask who is listening, to whose policies, and for whose benefit. Royle's reading of education and the curriculum uses the uncanny as a means to define both the limits and the lack of limits of what may be possible within education as he alludes to pleasure and to how 'Death, then, is strangely at the heart of life, of writing and of teaching' (2003, p. 66). The twentieth century demonstrated examples of what social cohesion might start to look like, and interestingly these examples all have the death of the other as historical catalysts and as symbolism for change: the 1960s and 1970s civil rights movements for ethnic minorities, gay rights, the women's movement, the peace movement, and later, in the 1980s and 1980s, the Ecstasy generation promoted young people perceiving themselves as equal and cohesive (if on drugs). What all these movements have in common is the desperate urge for equality and without it the death of social cohesion.

Curricular exploration of issues of social cohesion, for example the teaching of the history of the Third Reich, needs to expose the meta-narratives of cohesion; in this case cohesion of one group via state policy produces annihilation of the other. The narratives of traditional teaching promote specific cause and effect; for example, questions of the type 'The five causes of World War II' direct students to a reading of culture that can only lead to war and social disintegration. Introducing young people to the philosophy behind concepts of community and cohesion might be a method of addressing this; another might be the deconstruction of the language of cohesion policy. In particular, the term 'community' has come to be used by those in charge of the status quo to define those qualified to speak on behalf of minority groups. During the aftermath of the 7/7 bombings it was obvious in the media that although pictorially Muslims were seen as of both genders, in terms of voicing concerns airtime was given to predominantly male speakers. The community was defined by the government, local governmental bodies, and the media; and the view projected was that this was a group where the women were subservient and traditionally dressed and the men were traditional and conservative or young and led astray by radical preachers. Another picture of the Muslim community might be more accurately taken from sitting on a London tube train – like all communities, the 'community' of Muslims is made up of diverse individuals.

Cohesion, the sticking together of substances hitherto separate, is a process which has to be formally constructed. Historically many givens that now seem reasonable, like votes for women and for all people over a certain age, once seemed totally unbelievable. The process by which common political suffrage came about was through political activism and education. Who chooses what we learn, how it is taught, at what age, and how it is assessed are matters of importance in the forging of social cohesion within schools. The National Curriculum in English has started to address other cultures and traditions in literature, and social and community cohesion would welcome the development of this as long as it is not supplementary but integral to the curriculum. A teacher body that reflects the student body, in terms of ethnicity, gender, and class, is essential in continuing to address issues of community and social cohesion (Callender 1997). It is however in the ghostly educational trinity, the curriculum, teachers and schools, and the necessity of its fragmentation that a movement towards real cohesion might develop. The possibility of a meaningful cohesion is there in futurity – when the spectres of the historical past and the present are examined within the curriculum, when the uncanny body of the teaching profession becomes a mirror to society, and when the spectral institutions beyond schools are judged within the iron gates.

JOHN PRESTON

Response to Namita Chakrabarty

The challenge of post-modernist, post-structuralist and psychoanalytic perspectives to 'functionalist' theories of social cohesion is a welcome one. The problem with social cohesion as an idiom is that it almost invites a functionalist interpretation. That is, cohesion is inevitably good and that institutions, particularly schools, can contribute towards a more cohesive society. Alternative 'post' perspectives certainly have a lot to offer in terms of questioning not only official discourses of social cohesion but also examining how resistances can be built at the level of the individual. In much of the work on education and social/community cohesion, these phenomena are believed to exist at the 'macro' or 'meso' level and, almost by definition, this limits the type of response that one might make to problems of cohesion. Social cohesion, if considered to be a 'macro' or societal phenomena, invites responses at the 'macro' level in terms of welfare states or education systems. Community cohesion, if considered to be a 'meso' or intermediate-level phenomenon, invites responses at the level of organisation or social group. In either case, the individual level of analysis is neglected. Certainly, there is a need to go beyond analysis at just one level and to look at the interactions between levels. Even if we understand social cohesion to be ultimately a macro-level phenomenon then we need to understand how various levels of analysis can help us to comprehend a macro-sociological outcome – for example, how individual values and attitudes and resistances and meso-level social movements and institutions ultimately resolve into macro-level social cohesion. There are already theories which enable us to understand these different levels of interaction. Rather than asking how 'schools' contribute to cohesion we could understand this through more complex processes of how schooling systems, individual schools and teachers and pupils work together (or not) to produce different cohesion 'regimes'.

However, talking about the need to integrate various 'levels' of analysis is rather abstract and another key theme which emerged from the above is how the present context nature of schooling is 'haunted' by past social movements and struggles: 'the 1960s and 1970s civil rights movements for ethnic minorities, gay rights, the women's movement. . . . What all these movements have in common is the desperate urge for equality and without it the *death of social cohesion*' (my italics). Here rather than equality contributing towards social cohesion (which is implicit in the analysis which I have undertaken previously: Green, Preston and Janmaat, 2006) equality cannot be attained without destroying the current regime of cohesion. This resonates powerfully with many current theories in the sociology of education concerning not only the compatibility of schooling with abhorrent societal regimes but also of the unique place of schooling in overturning those relations. For example, from Marxist theories McLaren's (2005) discussion of education not only as providing 'labour power' in capitalist social relations but the possibility of teachers using revolutionary critical pedagogy in overthrowing it. Analogously, from critical race theory, Gillborn (2008) discussed education as providing support for white supremacy but also as being a space where resistance may be built. 'Social' and 'community' cohesion are premised on notions of societies and communities that are not aberrant, and when they are why should we want schools to promote them?

NAMITA CHAKRABARTY

Response to John Preston

Schools are without doubt burdened by the state agenda on cohesion but this work is also contradicted by legislation: this is shown in recent policies regarding the role of educators in combating student extremism. This latter example is fundamentally divisive and heralds a less cohesive society as the policy is aimed at Islamic extremism rather than white fascism and also assumes a homogeneous teaching body. The recent (November 2008) controversy over the internet publication of the membership list of the British National Party is an interesting critical moment through which to consider issues of cohesion, naming, and education. The BNP will inevitably make use of the very human rights legislation that politically they are against in seeking privacy for their members who may lose their jobs as a result of publication. Publication has exposed the fact that espousal of racist ideology pervades many professions, including education at all levels, and is spread through many areas in the UK. Legislative issues arising from the publication have included the contrasting of the prohibition of membership of the BNP for the police whereas teachers, and other public servants such as health workers, have no such prohibition despite working under the same Equal Opportunities and Race Relations legislation. There is inevitably a conflict between Data Protection legislation and the Human Rights Act when considering the ramifications of a social cohesion agenda in the age of equality of opportunities. A way of looking at this for the future is to consider the new American era of Obama and its impact on the UK.

The build-up to the election of Obama was the material of Hollywood movies; the parallel headlines in the UK media questioned the possibility of a similar outcome in a UK election (Siddique 2008). The opinion pieces published make useful reading in addressing the issue of schools' ability to foster social cohesion. The theme of equality is fundamental both to the issue of minority political representation as it is to the question of cohesion and education. Obama's privileged and diverse education, besides his race, was seen as a factor in his rise to power in embracing difference and uniting voters, and yet also being nominated by a political elite. An ethnic minority candidate who had not graduated through the same educational channels would not have stood a chance within that system due to the social capital that needs to be accrued for nomination. As Preston points out, educational systems which work towards equality of opportunity like the comprehensive system, which focuses on mixed ability teaching rather than streaming or setting, are shown to increase 'some indicators of social cohesion'. The main problem in the ideal of educational social cohesion is the lack of acknowledgement of the complexity of the term cohesion. Generally it is read as an equal coming together and melding of ideas, whereas in practice it involves compulsory assimilation for minority groups and dominance by the majority. This affects teachers, pupils and communities alike. Like the compulsory heterosexuality explored by Adrienne Rich (1981) the emphasis should be directed at those who withhold equality rather than those who are negated by it.

CONCLUSION FROM JOHN PRESTON AND NAMITA CHAKRABARTY

In policy terms social and community cohesion are likely to remain as priorities of the state. In particular, in times of economic crisis, inequalities of income and education will widen. Education (and particularly training) will be seen as a panacea for social inclusion, combating extremism and promoting civil society. In these circumstances, education could become increasingly concerned with socialisation and work, and other areas of society (such as the community) will become increasingly pedagogical. Both authors consider that in certain regimes of social cohesion, education has the potential to be reactionary and to promote the normative. This pessimistic assessment must be tempered by the paradoxical nature of education in subverting categories even as it creates them. For example, an initial response to the economic crisis has been the explosion of 'social unrest' by young and highly educated people throughout Europe but in particular in France and Greece. Social unrest is anathema to the types of social cohesion promoted by the OECD but the role of students in these demonstrations (and the role of pupils in demonstrations against the Iraq war in the UK) points not towards anomie but to critique.

KEY QUESTIONS

1. What is meant by 'social cohesion' and is it different from 'community cohesion'?
2. Is an emphasis on cohesion likely to restrict or emancipate?
3. What could schools do in order to work appropriately with communities (within and beyond the school – locally, nationally, globally)?

FURTHER READING

Callender, C. (1997). *Education for Empowerment: Practice and Philosophies of Black Teachers*. London: Trentham.

Green, A., Preston, J. and Janmaat, G. (2006). *Education, Equality and Social Cohesion*. London: Palgrave.

Putnam, R. (1995). *Bowling Alone: The Collapse and Revival of American Community*. New York: Simon and Schuster.

Schuller, T., Preston, J., Hammond, C., Brassett-Grundy, A. and Bynner, J. (2004). *The Benefits of Learning: The Impact of Education on Health, Family Life and Social Capital*. London: RoutledgeFalmer.

This debate links with readings 7, 8, 9, 10, 11, 19 and 20 of *The Routledge Education Studies Reader.*

CHAPTER 14

PROFESSIONAL LEARNING

Liam Gearon

The rationale for this chapter is to provide an overview of initial teacher education through the prism of four key and interrelated aspects of the profession:

- the gatekeepers: initial teacher training;
- the inspectors: monitoring and reporting on the standards;
- the new professionals: the Universities Council for the Education of Teachers (UCET) and the General Teaching Council for England (GTC);
- the researchers: knowledge and professional practice.

INTRODUCTION

An indirect consequence of democratic political revolutions in the eighteenth century was national education systems in the nineteenth. In England, this can be dated from the 1870 Education Act which made elementary education compulsory, marking too the period when formal teacher training became a pragmatic necessary (Aldrich, 1990, 2006; Coppock, 1997; Dombkowski, 2002; Dyhouse, 1997; Ellis, 1979; Heafford, 1979; Heward, 1993; Vrocdc, 1981; Williams, 1971; Willis, 1997). Political and economic theorists have been historically divided over the state's role in education. A century before compulsory schooling in England, Adam Smith's (2008 [1776]) *An Inquiry into the Nature and Causes of the Wealth of Nations* argued that education should be private and competitive. Only a decade before the 1870 Education Act, John Stuart Mill's (2008 [1859]) *On Liberty* argued for education and not schooling to be compulsory. The strongest case for state intervention in nineteenth-century political theory arguably comes from Karl Marx and Friedrich Engels's *Manifesto of the Communist Party* which saw education as part of the advancement of the masses (see West, 1979, 1991, 1994; see also Dewey, 1916). The modern-day context of initial teacher education has come a long way since the 1870 Education Act and this chapter outlines aspects of the complex bureaucratic and multi-agency system into which the new teacher is inducted, organisational structures which now help define teaching as a profession.

THE GATEKEEPERS: INITIAL TEACHER TRAINING

The Graduate Teacher Training Registry (GTTR)

If you want to teach in state schools in England, Wales, Scotland or Northern Ireland, you are required to undertake a course of Initial Teacher Training (ITT) in order to be able to achieve

Qualified Teacher Status (QTS), or the devolved equivalent such as the Teaching Qualification (TQ) in Wales. Although not a Government requirement, many independent schools also stipulate QTS or equivalent. The body responsible for the majority of admissions into the teaching profession in England, Scotland and Wales but not Northern Ireland is the Graduate Teacher Training Registry (GTTR).

Applications are generally made to achieve QTS with a specific age range: three- to seven-year-olds; three- or five- to 11-year-olds; seven- to 11-year-olds; seven- or nine- to 14-year-olds; 11- to 14-year-olds; 11- or 16- to 19-year-olds; or 14- to 19-year-olds.. Each relates to different sectors of schooling:

- *Primary:* Primary courses generally train you to teach all the subjects in the primary school curriculum to children in the age ranges three to seven, five to 11, or seven to 11 years old.. Some primary courses allow you to specialise in one subject, while learning to teach all the other curriculum subjects.
- *Middle years:* Middle years courses train you to teach children in the age ranges seven or nine to 14 years old. Most middle years courses require you to specialise in teaching one or two subjects. There are no training providers in Wales that offer middle years courses.
- *Secondary:* Secondary courses normally require you to specialise in teaching one or two subjects in the secondary school curriculum to students in the age ranges 11 to 16, 11 to 18 or 14 to 19 years old.
- *Post-compulsory or further education:* Training providers normally offer a general course for teaching in further education. The range of subjects that a training provider can offer may vary from year to year depending on the teaching placements they can arrange in FE colleges. Post-compulsory and further education courses do not normally provide Qualified Teacher Status (QTS) for teaching in state schools (www.gttr.ac.uk).

As its name implies, the GTTR is a graduate registry and thus deals only with those applicants with a university or higher education degree. Non-graduate entrants to teaching need to apply through UCAS and undertake a three- or four-year undergraduate degree course which can also provide QTS. The most common application route for graduates is a Postgraduate Certificate in Education (PGCE), or in Scotland the Professional Graduate Diploma of Education (PGDE). The majority of applications for QTS are to universities and colleges of higher education, and in England only to school-centred initial teacher training (SCITT) consortia. The latter focus predominantly upon school-based training, often with a lead school and school-based (as opposed to university) mentors though there is likely to be some university involvement in both the input and validation of the SCITT courses, with some research questioning the contribution of school-based initial teacher training to secondary school performance (Hurd, 2008; Hurd *et al.*, 2007).

Another not unrelated Government initiative has been the creation of 'training schools' which take a lead in teacher training within local consortia of schools. Brooks (2006) presents five different models of partnership: 'collaborative, complementary, HEI-led, school-led and partnership within a partnership' and identifies ways 'in which Training Schools represent a break with established practice considered together with their implications for the dominant mode of partnership led by higher education institutions (HEIs)'.

All forms of university or college teacher training presently involve a partnership between schools and universities, usually following a pattern of placements in partner schools (18 weeks for primary and 24 for secondary); the status of one section of the partnership in terms of importance is a matter for occasional tensions (Mutton and Butcher, 2007; Mutton, 2008). In any of these contexts, the relationship between the trainee and the school-based mentor is almost invariably regarded as a key to the success of the trainee, a high proportion of whose course will be spent in schools (Edwards and Mutton, 2007; Hobson *et al*., 2008).

One of the most significant and large-scale research projects on initial teacher education is *Becoming a Teacher: Student Teachers' Experiences of Initial Teacher Training in England* (Hobson *et al*., 2006), a comprehensive analysis of these and related issues, including student teachers' accounts of their school-based experiences, and their experiences of initial teacher training in Higher Education Institutions (HEIs). The wide-ranging findings cover a number of areas, including:

- student teachers' experiences of, and feelings about, the overall content of their ITT programme;
- trainees' accounts of their school-based experiences during their ITT;
- their accounts of the HEI-based elements of their initial teacher preparation;
- trainees' perceptions of the outcomes of their ITT programmes;
- student teachers' experiences of obtaining a teaching post, factors affecting their choice of school/teaching post and their expectations for their professional teaching careers upon completion of training;
- the characteristics and experiences of trainees who withdrew from, or deferred completion of, their training programme, and the reasons for the non-take-up of a teaching post among those who did complete their ITT;
- the perceptions of ITT programme personnel regarding different aspects of initial teacher training.

(Hobson *et al*., 2006: ii)

While SCITT courses, training schools, and the increased emphasis placed upon school-based experience for trainees might seem to suggest a less than optimistic perspective about the role of universities in the process of initial teacher training (Furlong, 2008), the findings of *Becoming a Teacher* are in many ways ambivalent. Reported high levels of satisfaction (84 per cent) of students across all routes into teaching do not give a clear indication of the superiority of one route over another, except, since the majority of trainees follow the traditional university-based PGCE route to QTS, there is an argument to suggest that this route is numerically not only more popular but more successful in generating satisfied teachers. Initiatives like the Masters in Teaching and Learning and the introduction of Masters level qualification into the PGCE would also indicate an increased emphasis upon the continuing professional development of teachers as graduates. This would surely entail not only a continued but an enhanced profile for the contribution of universities to initial teacher education and to a formal and more systematic contribution of universities to the continuing professional development of teachers.

When, as part of the then Teacher Training Agency (now TDA) funded research, Smith and Gorard (2006) asked the question 'Who succeeds in teacher training?', examining factors that 'support high quality initial teacher training in England', the findings were surprising:

> The study had two chief aims. The first was to characterise successful trainees in terms of data already known about them as a dataset of all 72,881 postgraduate trainees from 1998–2001. The second was to relate these findings to potential determinants of the effectiveness of different kinds of institutions and routes in their training of teachers. There was little variation in success rates of trainees with different entry qualifications, background or areas of subject specialism. Almost 90% of trainees were successful in achieving qualified teacher status and

> 95% of these were able to secure a teaching post within six months of finishing training. This varied little according to one type of institution that was attended, its level of research activity, or its quality as determined by the Office for Standards in Education (OFSTED) inspections. This leads us to conclude that there is no evidence, on these existing data, of a differential institutional effect in determining the success rates of trainees in ITT.

The study might indirectly show, of course, that the imposition of standards for initial teacher training has had a levelling effect in terms of ensuring consistency across the field of initial teacher education and training, but what the findings do not illustrate is the extent of career progression of entrants to the teaching profession from different institutions.

Furlong (2005) argues too that while New Labour have 'significantly moved away from a concern with individual professional formation; individual professional formation has been seen as far less critical than it was, especially at the level of training' and in 'the lives of young teachers, the state now provides far greater direct guidance than ever before in the definition of effective teaching, learning and assessment in both primary and secondary schools'. In this context the centralised, Government-directed emphasis upon Professional Standards at all stages of teachers' careers means that 'teacher education is no longer accorded the key political significance that it had', principally because these Professional Standards originate outside the Academy, and arguably limit the autonomy of university-based initial teacher education. This is perhaps reinforced by the inspection framework of OFSTED that focuses almost entirely on the delivery of the Standards as a benchmark for good-quality initial teacher education.

Noting but reserving judgement on the shifting and possible transitional balance of significance between universities and schools in initial teacher training, the remainder of this chapter can at least provide some definitive evidence of the increasingly interrelated bureaucratic systems and structures into which new teachers are inducted. This might lead one to question the actual extent of professional autonomy aspired to and treasured within the teaching profession (Furlong *et al.*, 2008; cf. Hughes, Jewson and Unwin, 2007; Schon, 1995; Wenger, 1998).

The Standards and Accountability: Qualifying to Teach and the Frameworks for Initial Teacher Training

Overarching responsibility for all aspects of compulsory education in England falls to the Department for Children, Schools and Families (DCSF). The DCSF defines its purpose in immensely wide terms: 'to make England the best place in the world for children and young people to grow up'. The Department for Education has in the past few decades variously been named the Department for Education and Employment (DfEE) and the Department for Education and Skills (DfES). The present Department for Children, Schools and Families indicates the orientation of Government education policy as centring not only upon the well-being of children and young people but also encompassing wider strategic policy moves which look to the integration of services for children. This shift was marked by the 2003 *Every Child Matters*, a green or discussion paper published in response to the death of Victoria Climbié. Its four themes represent an attempt to consolidate provision of services for children, young people and families:

- increasing the focus on supporting families and carers – the most critical influence on children's lives;
- ensuring necessary intervention takes place before children reach crisis point and protecting children from falling through the net;

- addressing the underlying problems identified in the report into the death of Victoria Climbié – weak accountability and poor integration;
- ensuring that the people working with children are valued, rewarded and trained.

Every Child Matters: Change for Children was subsequently published in 2004, identifying five outcomes for education and related provision for children and young people:

1 Be healthy;
2 Stay safe;
3 Enjoy and achieve;
4 Make a positive contribution;
5 Achieve economic well-being.

The same year Parliament passed the Children's Act 2004, the legislative framework which would ensure that such policy objectives were enshrined in law, including the formation of Children's Trusts, which offer an overview and monitoring of cooperation between the multiple numbers of agencies involved in the welfare of children and young people, or as the DCSF state, a 'key element in the implementation of Children's Trusts is the development, by the local authority and its partners, of a single, strategic, overarching plan for all services affecting children and young people – the Children and Young People's Plan' (see section 17 of the Children's Act 2004; also the revised framework for *Every Child Matters 2008*).

Every Child Matters: Change for Children – An Overview of Cross Government Guidance 'provides details of all the cross-government guidance supporting *Every Child Matters*'. As the DCSF express this:

> This means that the organisations involved with providing services to children – from hospitals and schools, to police and voluntary groups – will be teaming up in new ways, sharing information and working together, to protect children and young people from harm and help them achieve what they want in life. Children and young people will have far more say about issues that affect them as individuals and collectively.
>
> Over the next few years, every local authority will be working with its partners, through children's trusts, to find out what works best for children and young people in its area and act on it. They will need to involve children and young people in this process, and when inspectors assess how local areas are doing, they will listen especially to the views of children and young people themselves.

Such initiatives were also supported by the creation in 2005 of a Children's Commissioner for England 'to give children and young people a voice in government and in public life'.

The Children's Plan is the strategy in which the DCSF sets out the means by which such goals can be achieved. The Children's Plan specifically aims to:

- strengthen support for all families during the formative early years of their children's lives;
- take the next steps in achieving world-class schools and an excellent education for every child;
- involve parents fully in their children's learning;
- help to make sure that young people have interesting and exciting things to do outside of school; and
- provide more places for children to play safely.

The Qualifications and Curriculum Authority (QCA)

The Qualifications and Curriculum Authority (QCA) is responsible for the development of the national curriculum, the overarching framework for teaching, learning and assessment in school 'which defines the knowledge, understanding and skills to which children and young people are entitled'. The national curriculum is kept under review 'to evaluate its appropriateness and relevance to the changing needs of learners and society'. The National Qualifications Framework 'enables us to accredit qualifications at appropriate levels to meet the needs of employers and learners', with 'the suitability and availability of qualifications' kept regularly under review. In 2008, the Government established Ofqual, a new regulator for qualifications and assessment in England.

At a level appropriate to an early stage of their professional careers, the effectiveness of a teacher will depend on their ability to deliver the National Curriculum to an appropriate age phase at an appropriate level. Increasingly, however, teachers are required to attend to much wider policy initiatives designed for the welfare of children and young people, and teachers at all stages of their career are increasingly involved in a complex multi-agency system.

The Training and Development Agency (TDA)

The Teacher Training and Development Agency (TDA), formerly the Teacher Training Agency (TTA) is the agency specifically responsible for providing the frameworks for the training and professional development of teachers at all stages of their career. The change in title of the agency is indeed indicative of this wider remit. Much in the same way as the DCSF has shifted to a wider remit of welfare for children, schools and families, and Ofsted has widened its remit to be an inspectorate for more than educational establishments, the TDA now concerns itself not simply with the training of teachers but the professional development of the teaching profession. This includes too the professional development of support staff such as teaching assistants. The TDA defines support staff as 'everyone who works in a school [and] has a part to play in raising standards and giving children a better start in life'; the TDA sets out advice on 'training and development opportunities that will help you work more effectively, and open up new career opportunities'.

The TDA's guidance on QTS standards and ITT requirements are the benchmark by which entrants to the profession are judged as trainees in both university–school partnerships and SCITT schemes. The standards are also extended into a framework by which teachers can demonstrate different levels of professional proficiency, related to different levels of a teacher's career: Q – qualified teacher status; C – core standards for main scale teachers who have successfully completed their induction; P – post-threshold teachers on the upper pay scale; E – excellent teachers; and A – advanced skills teachers (ASTs). The standards are arranged in three inter-related sections: professional attributes; professional knowledge and understanding; and professional skills.

The standards show clearly what is expected at each career stage. Each set of standards builds on the previous set, so that a teacher being considered for the threshold would need to satisfy the threshold standards (P) and meet the core standards (C); a teacher aspiring to become an excellent teacher would need to satisfy the standards that are specific to that status (E) and meet the preceding standards (C and P); and a teacher aspiring to become an AST would need to satisfy the standards that are specific to that status (A) as well as meeting the preceding standards (C, P and E) – although they can apply for an AST post before going through the threshold.

With an increased emphasis upon the connectivity between people, systems, agencies, the TDA provides a useful range of means by which those within the teaching profession can advance their knowledge, understanding and skills in order to benefit those in their care and as a means of advancing their own career. The ITT Professional Resource Networks (IPRNs) offer specialist professional expertise for teachers at any stage of their career.

THE INSPECTORS: MONITORING AND REPORTING ON THE STANDARDS

The Office for Standards in Education (Ofsted) was formed in 1992 to monitor, report on and improve standards across a variety of educational provision within England, as defined by Education (Schools) Act 1992. In 2007 Ofsted was reconstituted in line with the broader remit of the DCSF and related multi-agency initiatives such as the Child Plan, to form the Office for Standards in Education, Children's Services and Skills. The Education and Inspections Act established the new inspectorate, mandating it to:

- promote service improvement;
- ensure services focus on the interests of their users;
- see that services are efficient, effective and promote value for money.

Services inspected or regulated by Ofsted in England now include:

- childminders;
- full and sessional day-care providers;
- out of school care;
- crèches;
- adoption and fostering agencies;
- residential schools, family centres and homes for children;
- all state-maintained schools;
- some independent schools;
- Pupil Referral Units;
- the Children and Family Courts Advisory Service;
- the overall level of services for children in local authority areas (these are called Joint Area Reviews);
- further education;
- Initial Teacher Training;
- publicly funded adult skills and employment-based training.

In its own terms, as with the DCSF, we note the new Ofsted's broader socio- and even politico-economic ambitions 'to raise aspirations and contribute to the long term achievement of ambitious standards and better life chances for service users' so that 'their educational, economic and social well-being will in turn promote England's national success'; 'To achieve this we will report fairly and truthfully; we will listen to service users and providers; and we will communicate our findings with all who share our vision, from service providers to policy-makers'. The inspections which Ofsted carry out claim to 'report impartially, without fear or favour, demonstrating integrity in all we do' but working 'closely with partners and stakeholders, including government departments and other agencies, to make sure that our inspection and regulation are used to realise our vision'.

The judgements of school mentors and university tutors are ultimately inspected and validated by Ofsted, and Ofsted remains a critical source of quality assurance throughout the teaching profession, from initial teacher training through all aspects of school life. The following documents are particularly relevant to the inspection of initial teacher training and related continued professional development:

- *Professional standards for Qualified Teacher Status and requirements for ITT* (Training and Development Agency for Schools);
- *New professional standards for teacher/tutor/trainer education in the lifelong learning sector*;
- *Grade criteria for the inspection of initial teacher education 2008–11*;
- *Inspections of ITE 2008–11: A guide for providers on the organisation and management of inspections*.

For the inspection of schools:

- *Every child matters: Framework for the inspection of school in England* (2008).

THE NEW PROFESSIONALS: THE UNIVERSITIES COUNCIL FOR THE EDUCATION OF TEACHERS (UCET) AND THE GENERAL TEACHING COUNCIL FOR ENGLAND (GTC)

The Universities Council for the Education of Teachers (UCET)

University-based partnerships with schools through the PGCE remain the most common route into teaching. The professional network of universities involved in teacher education is the Universities Council for the Education of Teachers (UCET). UCET is committed to the support of university-based providers of the education and training of teachers. UCET defines itself as 'an independent, professional organisation funded solely by its member institutions, i.e., universities and university-sector colleges in the UK involved in teacher education' which acts 'as a national forum for the discussion of matters relating to the education of teachers and to the study of education and educational research in the university sector'.

UCET's core mission is to 'represent the UK's higher education based professional educators providing research-informed and formally accredited education, training and development opportunities', seeking specifically to:

- facilitate communication and co-operation between member institutions;
- provide a forum for sharing information across the UK and internationally;
- enhance the quality and impact of education through the application and championing of research;
- influence the development and implementation of policy by working in partnership with other agencies and by undertaking campaigning and lobbying activities;
- champion the professional status of educators throughout the UK;
- articulate the role of education as an interdisciplinary-based subject that adds value to the creation and communication of knowledge within the higher education community.

Investigations into changes of identity from undergraduate to professional, and the wider issues of teachers' professional identities have received some attention (Goodson and Hargreaves, 1996; Goodson, 2005). One of the distinctive challenges met by new teacher educators is not only specific pedagogies for teaching in higher education but also obligations to be 'research active' (Raffo and Hall, 2006). In specific relation to initial teacher training, research indicates tensions and uncertainty about the current effectiveness and future direction of school- and university-based training; one of the prevalent features of uncertainty in the teaching profession in both schools and universities is over the nature and identity of professionalism itself. Arguably the major issue here is related to the increasingly transnational emphasis upon prescriptive Government-directed standards in initial teacher training – and teaching more generally – driven by neo-liberal thinking. In other words, in a globalised economy of free market economics education, nation states need to constantly enhance performance to maintain competitiveness, and for education this has meant an increasingly universal emphasis upon standards by which to benchmark performativity as a global neo-liberal agenda (see Harris, 2005; Hill, 2007). In the context of initial training Menter, Brisard and Smith (2006) argue that standards fail to reflect the complexity of effective teaching and learning:

> There is an apparent contradiction between the widespread moves towards a uniform and instrumentalist standards-based approach to teaching on the one hand and recent research-based insights into the complexity of effective pedagogies. The former tendency reflects a politically driven agenda, the latter is more professionally driven.

Examining the contexts of England and Scotland, the researchers suggest:

> . . . while features of national culture, tradition and institutional politics have a significant role to play in the details of the approaches taken, there is nevertheless evidence of a significant convergence between both countries in one aspect of the determination of initial teacher education, the definition of teaching through the prescription of standards, which set official parameters on professional knowledge required for entry into the profession. This, it is suggested, reflects trends associated with neoliberal 'globalisation'.
>
> (Menter, Brisard and Smith, 2006: 269)

Wider sociological analyses argue, however, that the notion of teachers' professional autonomy is itself contradictory since the relationship between society and schooling generally is almost inevitably driven by the agendas of any given state (Meyer and Rowan, 2007).

The General Teaching Council for England (GTC)

The General Teaching Council for England (GTC) is a high-profile example of a body formed to enhance the professional identity of teachers. The GTC places a strong emphasis upon continuing professional development for teachers, ensuring through this that the quality of teaching in the profession is maintained. The GTC's Connect Network ensures a collaborative structure which brings 'CPD coordinators, advisors and leaders together to share, stimulate and support good practice in leading professional learning', giving 'access to research and resources on supporting teacher learning'. The GTC places high importance upon research as 'crucial to the development of teaching and the quality of learning: both education policy and educational practice should be informed by the best available evidence': 'Research includes scholarship and theory as well as empirical evidence. The GTC's research activity includes appraising and utilising the fruits of others' research, as well as sponsoring or directly commissioning new studies'. Its research (in 2008) is focused upon three strategic areas: CPD; pupil learning; and workforce.

THE RESEARCHERS: KNOWLEDGE AND PROFESSIONAL PRACTICE

Some research has been undertaken into the shift of identity when school teachers take on a new role as university-based tutors, particularly through the uncertain paths of induction into higher education (Murray, 2005), including the need for a pedagogy suitable for higher education, and as critical, the need to be research active (Murray and Male, 2005). Yet this too raises issues about the breaking down of traditional boundaries between universities and other sectors of education. All of the organisations reviewed in this chapter place a strong emphasis upon research in order to improve the professional practice of teachers, though while some of the research is conducted by Government agencies like the DCSF, most remains conducted by universities (for example, cited above, Hobson *et al.*, 2006). More widely, one of the many criticisms of contemporary educational research in the late 1990s had been the lack of involvement of practitioners in the design, implementation, evaluation and use of research (Oancea, 2005; Pring, 2004). As a result of such criticisms there is increasing emphasis placed upon the involvement of teaching and related professionals within research communities, including the British Educational Research Association (BERA), the Collaborative Action Research Network (CARN), the Evidence for Policy and Practice Information (EPPI), and the Evidence-Based Education Network, and Teacher Research. BERA for example developed a series of research briefings which aimed to disseminate research to practitioners, its Professional User Reviews. The EPPI initiatives have involved practitioners at every level of their systematic reviews of research. The Higher Education Academy subject centre, ESCalate, has a research remit but one directly related to policy, for example, supporting the implementation of the Professional Standards Framework across institutions.

The largest research initiative ever undertaken in the UK into education – the ESRC funded Teaching and Learning Research Programme (TLRP) – is evidence of the high public importance given to practitioner and professional involvement in educational research. The programme was designed to 'increase the volume, quality and use of UK education research' across all sectors of education, from early years through primary, secondary, further, higher and lifelong learning. The TLRP's director, Professor Andrew Pollard, suggests:

> The TLRP's uniquely broad range of evidence on improving teaching and learning means that future policy can be based on real knowledge about how people make sense of the world around them, and can move beyond the current policies. We now have an opportunity to build an education system which is based on genuine evidence about how people learn.

With funding from the Higher Education Funding Council for England (HEFCE), Department for Children, Schools and Families (DCSF), the Welsh Assembly Government, Northern Ireland Executive and the Scottish Government, some of the high-profile findings of the research are:

- development of better ways to teach reading to address the difficulty of spelling words when the spelling cannot be predicted from the way the word sounds;
- genuine engagement with students will help them to feel valued and part of the learning process, as well as respected as individuals;
- learning how to learn is crucial to improved standards – this area focused on developing the skills to allow pupils to become autonomous learners;
- the first study of group work in the UK to show positive attainment gains in comparison to other forms of classroom pedagogy;
- how to smooth children's transition between schools, and between home and school.

Among the major implications of the research regarding the transition from university to employment are the challenges to current policies regarding the employability and skills agenda:

- early career learning followed a group of graduates in their first jobs to investigate informal and short semi-formal learning episodes;
- research to provide a quantitative description of who goes into higher education, the experiences of different students and their subsequent success in the labour market;
- ground-breaking research in collaboration with multinational corporations around the world suggests that policy makers have yet to appreciate the fundament shifts in the way companies use skilled people.

In specific terms of research into teacher education, one of the strands of the TLRP highlights how professional standards, so prevalent a mark of a new professionalism, may 'pay too little attention to what "becoming" a teacher is really like'. McNally (2008) presents findings that

> existing standards ignore the emotional, relationship and personal issues which are the real challenge for teachers starting out in their careers, focussing instead on the acquisition of skills and knowledge. Resulting from the study, researchers propose a new model which aims to improve existing standards by capturing the multi-dimensional experience of new teachers.

As one of the one research team comments: 'Professional standards are clearly vital in terms of public accountability'.

> The existing standards are a step forward but we believe they fail to capture the complexities, demands and difficulties of the first year of teaching. Our new model encompasses a fuller appreciation of the learning process that statutory standards neglect through a more sophisticated recognition of early professional learning (EPL).

The research team outlined seven dimensions of EPL:

- *emotional*: range and intensity of feeling from anxiety/despair to delight/fulfilment that permeate new teachers' descriptions of their experiences;
- *relational*: social interactions, mainly with pupils and colleagues, which produce the relationships crucial and central to the new teachers' professional identity and role;
- *structural*: organisational aspects of the school and the educational system, including roles and procedures, that govern entry into the profession and also education within society;
- *material*: resources, rooms, etc.;
- *cognitive*: explicit understandings applied in professional practice, e.g. curriculum knowledge, assessment, differentiated teaching, including the professional standard itself;
- *ethical*: new teachers' expressed sense of commitment and care;
- *temporal*: recognition that the above dimensions change over the induction year.

Researchers

> spent three years tracking these seven dimensions among different groups of new teachers in their first year, discovering that the emotional and relational aspects proved more important than the cognitive in the first few months of induction, and that the multidimensional nature of

early professional development is key to understanding how new teachers develop their identities in the profession. [. . .]': 'Based on the seven dimensions and with the aim of enhancing existing professional standards, researchers have developed five quantitative indicators: job satisfaction, children's views on their learning environment, interaction with colleagues, teaching ability as judged by an external expert; and the development of the new teacher's pupils over the year as judged by colleagues.

SUMMARY

In modern times, teaching has been seeking enhanced levels of professionalism since the nineteenth-century development of compulsory education (Johnson and McClean, 2008). Today such professionalism has been marked by the creation of formal associations of and for teachers such as the General Teaching Council for England and in initial teacher education the Universities Council for the Education of Teachers. With such professionalism has come, for a variety of reasons, an immensely developed sense of accountability measured by initiatives such as the Professional Standards designed by the Training and Development Agency, and inspected by the Office for Standards in Education. These Professional Standards are evident not only on entry to the profession but mark all stages of development up to the advanced skills teacher. It might thus be suggested that there is an irony here. As has been shown, with enhanced notions of professionalism has come a greatly increased determination of standards and accountability beyond the teaching profession, invariably determined directly by Government or its agencies, and this, it might be argued, has led to a loss of professional autonomy with which professionalism might ordinarily be associated.

KEY QUESTIONS

1. Define or characterise an educational professional.
2. Is professionalism a positive force in education?
3. How should beginning teachers be prepared for entry to the profession?

FURTHER READING

Dewey, J. (1916) *Democracy and Education*, online http://www.ilt.columbia.edu/publications/dewey.html, retrieved 24 July 2009.

Hobson, A.J., Malderez, A., Tracey, L., Marina, G., Pell, G. and Tomlinson, P.D. (2008) 'Student teachers' experiences of initial teacher preparation in England: core themes and variation'. *Research Papers in Education* 23 (4), 407–433.

Pring, R. (2004) *Philosophy of Education Research*, 2nd ed., London and New York: Continuum.

This chapter links with reading 15 of *The Routledge Education Studies Reader.*

CHAPTER 15

RADICAL EDUCATION

The past?

Ralph Leighton

The rationale for this chapter is:

- the scrutiny of a range of ideas, insights and actions which might constitute 'radical education';
- the development of an understanding of differences between 'change' and 'radical change';
- to consider whether radical education is a thing of the past, and only of the past.

INTRODUCTION

There is an ambivalence to the title of this chapter which raises further questions. Is radical education all in the past? Indeed, is it realistic to characterise the history of education as radical? Principally, what is 'radical education'?

For the purposes of this chapter I have taken 'radical education' to include those educational ideas, actions or legislative Acts which have been significantly different to the historical or political context in which they have occurred, and which have had some identifiable impact. That impact might be on the thinking and practice of some educators rather than demonstrably on the daily experiences of school pupils and their teachers, or it could be something which causes a major shift in either theory or practice. Some radical ideas have flourished temporarily then died away, others have been adapted and adopted so that they remain with us in different forms, while yet other radical developments have become part of the mainstream. It can be a challenge at times to identify what was ever radical about the last of these but, as we shall see as the chapter develops, it is the context which dictates the nature and extent of radicalism.

An illustration of the significance of context can be seen in the proposals to introduce free and secular education for all between the ages of 6 and 13, to be administered by locally elected school boards, in late nineteenth-century England. This is not something which current mores might view as radical but which was far removed from the prevailing provision.

Until this time, the provision of education had largely been the preserve of the Church, independently financed institutions, governesses and tutors, with a few 'enlightened' factory owners providing some schooling in those skills they wished to see developed in their workforce. To a background of political and social reforms in the 1850s and 1860s which recognised the growing strength of identity and power of the emerging industrial proletariat, and which attempted to stem any movement towards revolution by allowing limited involvement by some of the members of that class who were perceived as more responsible, came the 1870 Education Act. During the 1867 debate on an early draft of the Bill, Robert Lowe, Chancellor of the Exchequer, argued in favour of the legislation on the grounds that 'we must educate our masters' (Jarman, 1966: 264). In other words, having given some power to the masses, government viewed it as essential that those masses be informed and directed to think in ways which would not unsettle the status quo. Such a strategy, when considered in the light of Lukes' (1974) 'Three-Dimensional View of Power', demonstrates control over the political agenda and over decision making – the Weberian concept of normative power (Weber, 2009) – and is far from radical. Although it brought about significant changes, these were changes *within* the system rather than *to* the system; the curriculum, the organisation and management of schools, the purpose and focus of education, pupil/teacher relationships – none were radically altered. It was more of the same for a lot more people, tailored to ensure that the working classes developed the skills and attitudes desired of them by the ruling class. The purpose of extending education was to ensure that how and what people thought and what they thought about was under state control. Indeed, perhaps the only truly radical aspect of this legislation was that it allowed women to stand and vote for the education boards it established.

If we consider other major educational reforms in England since the 1870 Act – the legislation of 1944 and 1988 are perhaps the most important examples – we can apply the same insights and come to very similar conclusions. 1944 saw the reorganisation of school provision, and formalised concepts of measuring 'ability', within a parcel of reforms derived from the recommendations of the Beveridge Report; this was the attack on the 'evil' of ignorance, just as other legislation attacked the evils of idleness, need, poverty, and squalor. There were no attacks on disempowerment, inequality, injustice, discrimination or social inequality. The 1988 Act brought about the National Curriculum in order to bring education more explicitly under state control, in a response to Thatcherite concerns about 'trendy' teaching methods and perceived moves (by whom is not clear) to use education as a vehicle for social engineering. It had – and continues to have – a major impact on teaching and learning, but was inherently reactionary rather than radical.

This is not to say that there have been no radical ideas, movements or moments in education, but that they are unlikely to be found in state legislation under a capitalist system. To identify whether ideas or actions are radical, we have to view them in their political and historical contexts – which is what this chapter endeavours to do. As such ideas and actions are identified and discussed we will go on to look at their impact, to discover whether the radical past of education has had any lasting effect, and whether there is any likelihood of a radical future.

RADICAL IDEAS LEADING TO RADICAL ACTIONS

One of the first educators to propose that education should be about developing the whole person rather than simply about what Bowles and Gintis (1976) later called 'role allocation' was JH Pestalozzi (1746–1827). He placed the emphasis of learning on self-directed inquiry, arguing that an environment should exist where children follow their natural inquisitiveness rather than learning by rote those things which teachers or legislators consider important. With his emphasis on 'head, heart and hands' – that children needed to learn how to do things, to feel compassion for the natural world, and to be able to think for themselves – he was one of the first educators to consider holistic or child-centred education as valuable. He was clearly out of step with the ideas of his time which emphasised highly didactic fact processing and the training of young people to fit their preordained places in the social structure, and he saw education as an essential step in improving social conditions at a time when those with power had no interest in doing this.

Several subsequent educators have been heavily influenced by Pestalozzi's principles, most notably Steiner (1861–1925) and Montessori (1870–1952). One aspect at least in common to all three is the continuation of their ideas through international networks of schools, each tradition bearing its founders name. AS Neill (1883–1973) founded Summerhill School on the basis of similar principles. These schools might often now be viewed as middle-class enclaves, but that should not prevent us from considering their 'radical' credentials.

Although more than simply a few variations around a common theme, these approaches to schooling have much in common. Neill (1960), for example, believed that children learn best when they are happy, and are more committed to learning when they have some say in how it is managed and delivered. All shared a commitment to developing emotions and skills in children, as well as intellect. By emphasising that education is about learning and development rather than training and repetition, about personal fulfilment rather than economic expedience, that children's talents should be nurtured rather than being replaced by externally imposed knowledge, and that they should be encouraged to pursue their interests under adult guidance rather than being forced to follow adults' perception of what is important, those who follow these educators' principles clearly challenge an economic needs driven perspective on education.

Many current developments in education clearly owe much to the radicalism of these ideas and actions. The emphasis on 'child-centred learning', Gardner's (1983) work on multiple intelligences and regarding a range of learning styles, individual learning plans, Kolb's (1984) development of awareness of the benefits of active learning – these and other mainstays of contemporary educational discourse and practice are no longer considered radical or off the wall, but derive from the pioneering and sometimes ridiculed work of those outlined above.

SOME OTHER RADICAL INSIGHTS

Often regarded as one of the most significant educational thinkers of the last century, John Dewey (1859–1952) also influenced many of the ideas we might now regard as mainstream. He argued that education had to provide, engage with and develop pupils' experiences, that time to reflect rather than to go from one piece of knowledge to another was an essential component in learning, that the physical and social contexts of learning were part of the experience of learning, and that democracy depended upon involving people in their own learning. He proposed that education could improve society by encouraging individuals to develop their full potential as human beings and was particularly critical of rote learning of facts. (See Dewey, 1966.) Again we can see an influence on current practice of ideas from a time when the English education system was based on teacher authority, pupil conformity, and a move towards selection and the continued emphasis on role allocation. The current entitlement of pupils to be non-voting associate members of school governing bodies[1] might be the beginning of the democratisation of schools, but still falls far short of the practice at Summerhill School and the ideals of Dewey.

Paolo Freire (1921–1997) was highly critical of what he referred to as the 'banking' concept of education, in which the student was viewed as an empty account to be filled by the teacher – an analysis similar to Bowles and Gintis' (1976) 'Jug and Mug' theory. Freire (1972) argued instead for a model of classroom practice where the teacher also learns and the learners also teach, where education is a process to be shared and experienced rather than a commodity to be consumed. Mutual respect between all involved in processes of learning, lacking from most formal and much informal education in Freire's view, is central to this process, as is action which is informed by and linked to personal and social values. As with Pestalozzi and others mentioned in the previous section, Freire considered education to be a tool for making a difference, for developing social capital and making a contribution to communities. By situating learning in the experiences of all participants, it was argued, learners bring a new interpretation to theory and to each other, thus enhancing their own development and the development of those with whom they are learning. Freire was aware that such an approach was not in the self-serving interests of educators and, although notions of respect and understanding might appear within the new National Curriculum, particularly within Citizenship Education, there is little evidence of a sea-change in teacher attitude or behaviour in this regard.

There are similarities between much of Freire's analysis and that of Ivan Illich (1921–2002), who developed a critique of the power of central social institutions such as health and education which, he asserted, ended up more concerned with self-promotion and self-perpetuation than with meeting and serving their original objectives. Just as Michels (1949) demonstrated how all organisations become oligarchies no matter how well-intentioned or careful its members might be, Illich argued this was inevitable in complex technological societies and was true of all attempts to organise and provide for universal social welfare. He argued that such systems aspire to deliver services that are fair and reliable, which requires codes, protocols and procedures. These in turn become complex and rule-bound, rendering them dehumanised. The dominant professions – in our context, teachers and education administrators – not only provide services for people, they also define what people need and what the nature of provision should be. In this way, the professionals become part of the problem they are in place to solve. Indeed, far from encouraging people to learn, formal school trains many people to reject learning. School creates the impression that learning is something we do only in special places, at special times in our lives, with the help of qualified teachers. Education is seen as detached from the day-to-day world. By extension, the world cannot be about learning. Education is not seen as a personal project of self-development, but rather a process of gaining qualifications which show that you have learned what the system expects.

Illich (1973) offered guidance for how a more enabling education system could work. This included access to resources at any time for anyone wishing to learn, not only in schools but also in the workplace, museums and libraries – akin to what is now termed 'life long learning'. He also advocated the opportunities to exchange skills and knowledge now seen in virtual social networks such as Second Life (although these obviously have myriad other applications) and the University of the Third Age. His desire for professionals to work together to nurture and support all aspects of children's existence could be seen as embodied in the multiagency approach of the *Every Child Matters* agenda in England, *Getting it Right for Every Child* in Scotland, and some variants of the *No Child Left Behind* program in the USA, if not for the fact that such initiatives remain government-directed and professional-led. As such there is a likelihood that they will go the way of *Operation Head Start* in the USA in the 1960s, which attempted to engage children living in poverty with opportunities for success in education without addressing the needs or desires of those children or their communities but instead imposing a structure which addressed professionals' perceptions and goals.

The 1960s and 1970s produced a significant amount of radical insight into education without a great deal of measurable impact on mainstream provision. Rosenthal and Jacobson (1968) clearly demonstrated a tendency for teachers to label pupils and to teach to those labels, fitting what Merton (1968) described as a self-fulfilling prophecy, while Jackson and Marsden (1970) demonstrated the negative effects of selection on pupil progress, based as it was on culturally determined, poorly operationalised and inaccurately measured notions of IQ.[2] While the introduction of comprehensive schools was claimed to be aimed at ending such practices so that all pupils would have an equal opportunity to fulfil their potential, there is little evidence of success. Over 40 years later selection remains in many parts of England, by test or by post-code, and schools continue to set, stream or band pupils according to test scores and/or teacher assessment.

Jackson and Marsden (1968) also showed the effects of social class on the possibility of educational success, concluding that working class pupils who held working class social attitudes were doomed to educational failure. To succeed in education, they argued, pupils had to become middle class. This was further demonstrated by Willis (1977) in his account of working class boys' complicity in their educational failure which, in their terms, was not failure at all. Their values were not the values of the school, the characteristics they admired were those which teachers abhorred. It remains the case today that social class is the most reliable determinant of educational engagement and level of success, showing a continued lack of understanding of the needs, aspirations, interests and desires of a significant proportion of the population. With minority ethnic community pupils also tending towards the lower reaches of success criteria tables, this lack of understanding or inclusion of pupils and the communities to which they have allegiance continues to compound social problems. Educational capital continues to reside largely in middle class values.

Even the concept of meritocracy as bandied about by advocates of comprehensivisation shows a lack of understanding of this term, coined by Young (1958). Young despaired of the misuse and appropriation of this term when he wrote in the *Guardian* newspaper in June 2001 that '[t]he book was a satire meant to be a warning (which needless to say has not been heeded) against what might happen to Britain'. Far from being a society based on equality of opportunity for all where everyone works for the common good, Young showed that a meritocracy was characterised by a self-serving elite claiming legitimacy through the illusion of equality while ensuring its own interests were secure and perpetuated. It would perhaps be overly cynical to conclude that advocates of the term, including former prime ministers Thatcher, Major and Blair, were aware of the true meaning of the term; but, if they did not, it shows that they had not read Young's work or not understood it.

Other radical writers of this period made their allegiances clear in the titles of their publications as well as the content of their analyses. Postman and Weingartner (1976) pulled no punches in advocating that teaching should be subversive, that it was essential for pupils to question and critique if they were to develop and if society was to progress. Their observation that teachers were routinely asking questions to which they already knew the answers, and criticising those pupils who questioned the questions or sought 'new' knowledge or information, was redolent of the comments made by Pestalozzi roughly two centuries earlier.

Keddie (1978) offered a collection which questioned a prevailing notion of victim blaming – that working class pupils were culturally deprived and could therefore succeed if their culture changed. It is their own fault, the argument goes; opportunities are there to be taken or ignored as the individual chooses. One example of the fatuous nature of this argument can be found in the contribution from Labov (1969), where he clearly demonstrates that it is the limitations of teachers' culture – their inability to understand pupils' language, in this case – which inhibits working class, black pupils' achievement. Pupils understand the teacher's language but the teacher is not familiar with that of the pupils. As the teacher is in a position of power and the pupil relatively powerless, it is the teacher's definition of 'right' and 'wrong', of 'lucid' or 'incoherent' which holds sway. In Labov's analysis, it was teachers' ethnocentricity and middle class world view, underpinned by their professional status, which created an environment in which black working class pupils in particular were likely to 'fail'. As Labov wrote then, and which continues to be true today, 'the myth of verbal deprivation is particularly dangerous, because it diverts attention from real defects of our education system to imaginary defects of the child' (Labov, 1969: 22).

Attention was also drawn, primarily by feminist writers, theorists and educators, to the nature of the formal school curriculum, particularly focusing on the stereotyping – often the seeming invisibility – of women in subjects and text books (Dixon, 1979; Kelly, 1981). The language of teaching and learning, and the power relationships within schools and other educational settings, were demonstrated by Spender (1980) and others to perpetuate a masculine hegemony, thereby excluding or belittling women and their experiences. Many of these analyses emphasised the interconnectedness of family, school and work, and argued that women were allocated a specific and subservient role in each context. As the problem was structural so must the long-term solution be structural.

It is clear that much has changed in respect of women's place in education. From early reading schemes to advanced textbooks, there is a wealth of material which address to differing extents the previous omission or denigration of women. Girls are outperforming boys in virtually every public examination subject. Projects such as Women Into Science and Engineering (WISE) have broken – or at least seriously cracked – the glass barriers protecting some traditional male employment and education enclaves from female encroachment. However, improved female academic performance has given rise to concerns about boys being 'left behind' despite both sexes continuing to raise their achievement and aspirations – measuring success in relation to gendered competition rather than individual needs and talents. The 'family, school, work' nexus continues to wield a significant influence.

RADICAL EDUCATION AND 'THE RIGHT'

Most of the ideas and actions discussed so far could be placed within the broad spectrum of 'The Left', or at least identified as emanating from progressive perspectives and movements. To some extent this is inevitable as to be conservative, in the words of Oakeshott, himself a conservative philosopher, is

> to prefer the familiar to the unknown, to prefer the tried to the untried, fact to mystery, the actual to the possible, the limited to the unbounded, the near to the distant, the sufficient to the superabundant, the convenient to the perfect, present laughter to utopian bliss.
>
> (Oakeshott, 1962: 169)

Nisbett summarises this position by quoting Falkland – whom he describes as a hero of the English Civil War – 'when it is not *necessary* to change, it is necessary *not* to change' (Nisbett, 1986: 26).

At the same time, conservatism proclaims opposition to all but the minimum of state intervention, management and control, in the belief that it is not necessary to manage that which it is not necessary to change. Where change does come about it should be evolutionary rather than radical. It might appear from this that there can be no such thing as conservative radicalism, but those who might be positioned within 'The New Right' would challenge such a perception. Gray argued that the National Curriculum for England 'embodies an indefensible degree of centralisation' (Gray 1993: 31) – notwithstanding that this National Curriculum was introduced by a Conservative Government – and advocated a degree of autonomy for state as well as independent schools, with less reliance on local authority and state provision and intervention. Such relative freedom from interference might now be identified in the development of city technology colleges, specialist schools and colleges and, more recently, the establishment of academies.

Just as those with progressive radical ideas and agendas have perceived themselves as outside the establishment and seeking to develop social justice in and through education, the New Right tries to place itself in a similar position. The tone of Lawlor's (1995) introduction to a series of pamphlets produced by the Centre for Policy Studies – a conservative 'think tank' – is one of outsiders valiantly trying to reclaim education from an unwieldy and uncaring establishment. That these 'outsiders' include a member of the House of Lords, a knight of the realm, professors, senior Anglican clergy and a Conservative Party director of research who subsequently became a Conservative MP, appears to be an oxymoron which Lawlor does not address.

This group of self-perceived disadvantaged outsiders advocates a return to the teaching of knowledge, 'the training and cultivation of the mind' (Lawlor, 1995: 10), and a move away from experiential or exploratory learning and the development of skills. Teacher training, the reader learns, should return to the halcyon days of subject specialists being trained to teach their subjects. Education vouchers should be introduced so that children are valued. The only language structure which schools should accept is Standard English and received pronunciation. Such moves might be more easily considered radical if it were not for conservatism's own dictum, originating in the mid-seventeenth century and cited above, that change should arise only from necessity – assuming that such moves would necessarily be changes.

The central issues here are those of power and of perceptions of civil society. Where Oakeshott writes of the conservative preference for the familiar, the tried and tested, facts, sufficiency, convenience, the present, etc., we must ask to whose benefit did or would such a system operate. Indeed, it is pertinent to ask whose laughter is heard if the vast majority of learners are downtrodden, have their cultures ignored or derided, their skills devalued, their needs suppressed. In the middle of the nineteenth century, Marx argued that, if you 'assume a particular civil society . . . you will get particular political conditions' (Marx and Engels, 1973: 660), and it is clear that the New Right has a vision of and for society based on a return not only to old values but to old inequalities.

SUMMARY

We have seen that education certainly has had a radical past but that it would be highly inaccurate to describe all past education as radical. If we were to compare state educational provision in England 130 years ago with what is in place today, we would certainly see remarkable differences, but these changes have come about slowly rather than radically; they have been evolutionary rather than revolutionary.

This chapter has offered only a flavour of some of the radical arguments and ideas regarding education. They should be placed in a wider theoretical context in order to understand their full significance. Few have argued for changes only in education; the arguments have rather been for changes too in social structure and organisation. In the same way as Beveridge claimed it was necessary to attack the five evils, radical theorists have tended to take the apparently paradoxical view that changes in educational provision alone will not result in changes to education. Better physical learning environments, more engaging and active lessons, experiential learning in place of didacticism, involving pupils in their own learning and its structure – none of these things will matter to people who are hungry, impoverished, unwell, poorly housed, who feel disenfranchised, isolated, frightened and rejected.

There have been many changes in the content and structure of education in England and in the other members of the UK – some radical, some influenced by radical thought, some pragmatic, some reactionary, some significant and some ineffectual.

Analyses based on inequalities of educational access and provision based on class, gender and ethnicity continue to be put forward. As our understanding develops regarding the complexities of these social constructs and lived social experiences, and of their interrelationships, so will the range of potential responses and radical solutions become better informed. More is being understood about the range and diversity of learning needs of young people, particularly those whose skills and attributes might appear to render them less immediately and obviously either academic or employable, but who are beginning to be recognised as entitled to an education which develops and supports them. There are moves to recognise what young people can do rather than what they cannot.

Developments such as the movement to give pupils a voice in their education and the running of their schools could yet produce radical changes in the conduct, structure and content of education, depending on the extent to which those voices are given freedom of expression and the extent to which attention is paid to what they say. The growing awareness of cosmopolitanism rather than multiculturalism might yet have a significant impact, where education demonstrates and promotes recognition and respect for the complexities of ethnicity and encourages young people to place themselves in a series of global contexts rather than being limited to parochial, simplistic national boundaries – physical and intellectual. Until the impact and reality of the range of cultural influences and allegiances which pupils and teachers bring to the process of education, the situation will remain where

> student non-school lives and associations are "checked in at the door", as schools focus fervently on academic learning and attainment of . . . political values as if these were independent of ethnic, linguistic, or social identity. Thus, pupils and teachers experience . . . a "culturalectomy".
>
> (Florio-Ruane, 2001: 23)

Student voice, active learning, the overt development of political literacy and an awareness of cosmopolitanism, all have come to the fore with the advent of Citizenship Education as part of the National Curriculum in England. The Report which paved the way for the introduction of Citizenship had the avowed intention to bring about 'no less than a change in the political culture of this country' (QCA, 1998: 7). The Report concluded with a lengthy quotation from the then Lord Chancellor, Lord Irvine of Laing, advocating a particular form of Citizenship Education which fosters respect for law, justice and democracy, relates rights to obligations, and encourages voluntary work. To some extent this is the advocacy of 'being good and doing good' but, when considered in the light of a perception that young people are politically apathetic, and which ignores alternative forms of political engagement and reasons why formal political structures do not excite the young, there is a danger that it is simply a late twentieth-century rendition of Lowe's comment from the late nineteenth century quoted earlier in this chapter.[3] As Gillborn (2006) points out, there is a danger that a potentially radical departure from conventional education will prove to be no more than a placebo, that much will be expected and little achieved other than an illusion of the consideration and resolution of social and educational ills.

Most radical educationists would argue that education cannot of itself solve society's problems, but it can reflect them. While society has divisions, unequal opportunities, abuses of power and people of unfulfilled potential, radical educators will seek to offer remedies within a framework of other remedies for other social ills. This has been the past of radical education, and there is every likelihood that it will be the future.

KEY QUESTIONS

1. What is radical education?
2. Have the radical educators of the past influenced today's education system?
3. Are there any radical forms of education in existence today? Explain your answer.

FURTHER READING

Freire, P. (1972) *Pedagogy of the Oppressed*, Harmondsworth: Penguin.
Illich, I. (1973) *Deschooling Society*, Harmondsworth: Penguin.

Keddie, N. (ed) (1978) *Tinker, Tailor . . .: The myth of cultural deprivation*, London: Penguin.
Postman, N. and Weingartner, C. (1976) *Teaching as a Subversive Activity*, London: Penguin.

NOTES

1 As discussed by Hallgarten, Breslin and Hannam, 2004.
2 For a detailed discussion of the limitations of IQ testing, and the consequential social damage thus caused, see the work of Stephen J Gould, e.g. Gould 1981.
3 'We must educate our masters' (Jarman, 1966: 264).

This chapter links with readings 16 and 20 of *The Routledge Education Studies Reader.*

CHAPTER 16

E-LEARNING
The future?

Caroline Daly and Norbert Pachler

The rationale for this chapter is:

- to argue why e-learning is a vital matter for *all* teachers in all phases of education;
- to examine the impact of technologies on the education environment and why change is not only desirable but unavoidable;
- to explore the key challenges which e-learning brings to traditional concepts of teacher–learner relationships, the curriculum and assessment.

INTRODUCTION

The growth in technologies which is now a part of everyday life for people in Western societies and beyond, has brought fundamental changes in learning opportunities across every phase of the education sector and in wider society. The concept of 'ubiquitous' technology is already a reality in the world outside of formal education: individuals now rely on technologies to conduct their everyday lives in a multitude of social and work-related ways, including using the internet to access information on-demand, carry out work roles, conduct social arrangements, book holidays, access entertainment, buy goods and services and conduct banking, to mention but a few examples in a countless range of interactions with technology which are the norm for an increasing majority of people. In fact, for young people who are fully acclimatised to this technological environment, it seems paradoxical to think of 'e-learning' as 'the future', when other core social practices involving technologies are 'the present'. In the wider world, engaging with technology is increasingly not an 'extra' or a 'special' way of conducting social processes. It is embedded within what it is to communicate, conduct friendships, find out information, solve problems and fully inhabit society.

This chapter considers the key implications for education of this fundamental shift in the ways individuals access and share information and communicate using technologies. It examines: key theorisation of the role of technology in learning; young people as learners in contemporary contexts; the potentials for enhancing educational opportunities in schools, and the challenges such a shift creates for traditional concepts of knowledge and the practices by which it is made and shared.

WHAT IS E-LEARNING?

E-learning has been described by Garrison and Anderson (2003) thus:

> Broadly defined, e-learning is networked, on-line learning that takes place in a formal context and uses a range of multimedia technologies. . . . The essential feature of e-learning extends beyond its access to information and builds on its communicative and interactive features.
>
> (pp. 2–3)

The term 'e-learning' is not stable, however, and this is a broad definition as part of a wider claim that the 'dominant feature' of e-learning is 'to support asynchronous, collaborative learning' (ibid.). Like most educational concepts, this should be seen in relation to other related perspectives, such as 'mobile learning' or 'cyberlearning' which emphasise the role of technologies for learning in contexts where the boundaries between formal and informal learning become permeable and where learning at school is seen on a continuum with learning across a life-span. These concepts are important to consider in terms of the broader context in which technologies are so embedded within individuals' lives that they become 'invisible'. The following examples of prevalent concepts of cyberlearning (a term popular in the United States) and, more recently, mobile learning, offer alternative ways of conceptualising e-learning, and have different emphases in viewing an individual's learning in terms of their wider integration with society:

> [Cyberlearning is] the use of networked computing and communications technologies to support learning. Cyberlearning has the potential to transform education throughout a lifetime, enabling customized interaction with diverse learning materials on any topic – from anthropology to biochemistry to civil engineering to zoology . . . cyberlearning supports continuous education at any age.
>
> (Borgman *et al.*, 2008, p. 5)

Mobile learning emphasises much more than 'anywhere, anytime' engagement with learning. In addition to the point that mobile handheld devices such as telephones and Personal Digital Assistants (PDAs) allow learning to take place away from fixed locations, Kress and Pachler (2007) emphasise that mobile learning is a 'habitus' – a way of being in the world – and that

> mobility resides in respect to who produces knowledge and how . . . those who 'have' it are accustomed to immediate access to the world . . . the habitus has made and then left the individual constantly mobile . . . a constant expectancy, a state of *contingency*, of *incompletion*, of moving toward completion . . . .
>
> (p. 26)

These concepts emphasise important aspects of e-learning as embedded within a 'whole life' view of the individual and their relationship to wider society. What is crucial is that in each perspective, learning is conceived of as a social practice – being 'networked' is a core element here, both technologically *and* socially. For the purposes of this chapter, we propose a working definition of e-learning as a set of practices which enhance the potential of people to learn with others via technology-aided interaction, in contexts which can be 'free' of barriers of time and place. It involves the utilisation of a range of digital resources – visual, auditory and text-based – which enable learners to access, create and publish material which serves educational purposes. Essentially, this material can be shared electronically with fellow learners and teachers both within and beyond the bounds of formal education contexts.

E-LEARNING: REVOLUTION OR EVOLUTION?

Whilst there is general agreement that new technologies have brought fundamental changes in communicating to learn within a context of local and global societal change, such changes have been conceptualised from different theoretical perspectives, which can be broadly characterised as 'revolutionary' or 'evolutionary'. These are located in differing historical perspectives on the degree and types of change which are brought about by learning with technologies. Harasim (2000) has argued that a 'paradigm shift' has been brought about by a 'knowledge revolution'; Andriessen *et al.*'s (2003) evolutionary perspective claims that a new 'knowledge age' has replaced the first 'information age' in the contemporary history of learning and technologies; Lanham's (1993) early technocentric claim was that knowledge is being reconstituted in terms of ownership and power relations brought about by the electronic word, while Kress (2003) has focused on the potential learning revolution contained within the transformed semiotics of multimodal communication. Some have argued (Harasim, 2000; Lapadat, 2002; Laurillard, 2002; Garrison and Anderson, 2003) that the results offer the potential for *improvements* in learning, which Harasim (2000) claims to be the twin potentials of 'the improved quality of learning' and 'the improved opportunities to participate'. Garrison and Anderson have argued that the key potential of e-learning lies in text-based computer-mediated communication (CMC), which has the 'capacity to support reflective text-based interaction, independent of the pressures of time and the constraints of distance' (2003, p. 6).

Kress (2003) and Snyder (2002) assert that the term 'revolution' is apt to indicate the far-reaching future significance of economic, technological and social changes: Snyder insists that the impact of new technologies on learning and pedagogy is 'more of a revolution than an evolution' (2002, p. 18) and argues that it has brought about a fundamental shift in the way knowledge is organised and accessed. To date though, the theoretical claims for 'revolution' are not well supported by research into how e-learning brings about conceptual change in participants. It is clear that technology has 'revolutionised' learning contexts in terms of tools, and the conditions of time and place which affect relationships between learners and teachers. But talk of 'revolution' in the field of learning with technologies is contested. Much theorisation of e-learning is based on social constructivist ideas about knowledge-building which takes place through forms of interaction between learners in shared communicative contexts. Oliver (2003) argues that, therefore, we have experienced a 'dynamic evolution' in learning with technologies, rather than a 'revolution'. 'Evolution' suggests changes in the practices of things with which we are already familiar, the incorporation of the new within existing frameworks, social and literate, of cultural reference and a shift in ways of understanding that are different from what has gone before but are inextricably linked to it. Certainly, in terms of schools as sites for learning, there is evidence that considerable investment in technologies does not necessarily bring about 'revolution' in the learning experiences of students or the pedagogies of teachers, and it is not clear that 'revolution' is a desirable goal of e-learning, despite the fact that undoubtedly technologies provide radically new ways for learners to interact with information and with each other.

YOUNG PEOPLE AS E-LEARNERS

Recent studies in the United Kingdom and United States have reported on the extent to which technology is embedded in the everyday lives of young people. In the UK, the Media Literacy Audit (Ofcom, 2008) showed that children are familiar with the use of key media such as television, games consoles and the internet, by the age of five. Although differences exist in access to technologies according to socio-economic group, almost all children 'access the internet in some way'. There is a considerable range of evidence which points out the extent of the divide between the young people's experiences of learning inside and outside of school. The MacArthur Report (Ito *et al*., 2008) has shown the extent of immersion in digital cultures of young people in the USA, examining these as new sites of learning. The report is based on a study which explored the impact of digital cultures on the ways learning is conceptualised, examining 'the dynamics of youth–adult negotiations over literacy, learning, and authoritative knowledge' (p. 1):

> By its immediacy and breadth of information, the digital world lowers barriers to self-directed learning. . . . New media allow for a degree of freedom and autonomy for youth that is less apparent in a classroom setting. Youth respect one another's authority online, and they are often more motivated to learn from peers than from adults. Their efforts are also largely self-directed, and the outcome emerges through exploration, in contrast to classroom learning that is oriented toward set, predefined goals. . . . New media forms have altered how youth socialize and learn, and this raises a new set of issues that educators, parents, and policymakers should consider.
>
> (p. 2)

This report, together with others based in the USA (*The Horizon Report*, The New Media Consortium and Educause, 2008) and the UK (ESRC Series, 2008; Ofcom, 2008) provides emphatic evidence of the altered social and cultural conditions brought about by technology, in which young people negotiate their lives. The message is that educational policy-making struggles to keep up with the realities of learners' lives, and 'the future' is an elusive world which young people are already experiencing, and are doing so very differently from the ways that educators are planning for their projected formal educational experiences. This divide is reported by a recent study for the UK Economic and Social Research Council which funds research and training in social and economic issues: 'While educationalists are rethinking formal learning environments, young people themselves are using new technologies for informal learning in a far wider array of social settings, public and private, shared and individual' (2008, p. 4). The annual *Horizon Report* offers further indications of the far-reaching impact of technological innovations on teaching and learning in organisations beyond school. In 2008, it identified the innovations which are likely to affect education within the following one to five years as web-based tools: *grassroots video* and *collaboration webs* (already widely in use); use of *mobile broadband* and *data mashups* (evident in more advanced technology-focused organisations); *collective intelligence* and *social operating systems* (currently rarer, but longer-term expectations of adoption). The anticipated (or already current) ubiquity of these technologies however is not matched by the teaching of information, visual, and technological literacy in many instances. To match the expectations and experiences of learners in the second decade of the twenty-first century, higher education is facing growing expectations to revise the ways in which learning is conceptualised and organised. This includes: making learning resources available 'on-demand' via a range of mobile devices; considering the validity of visual and multimedia representations of knowledge; and revising approaches to assessment within a shift to increasing collaborative learning via social software.

From the perspective of life-long e-learning, the challenge for all phases of education is to understand how it can effectively harness young people's engagement with digital cultures. Policy-making in the UK has seen a considerable mobilisation of funding and resources to support the development of 'e-confident' learners and teachers in schools (Becta, 2008a; DfES, 2005), who benefit from fully integrated technological infrastructures for learning. One problem, historically, with the development of e-learning in UK schools has been the emphasis on techno-centric development which is not well-matched by appropriate pedagogical development or education for teachers. There is a strong need to develop teachers' knowledge, understanding and skills regarding *learning* with technologies, and hitherto teachers' professional learning in this area has been largely under-theorised and problematic in terms of effective policy and strategy (Preston, 2004). Changing pedagogical practice involves several inter-related focuses for change: a reassessment of the teacher's role in considering appropriate pedagogies, as well as learner roles; a review of what constitutes an appropriate curriculum and forms of knowledge which have currency in contemporary society; and a revision of the assessment practices by which forms of knowledge are validated. The key need is to re-conceptualise how the world of school relates to the world beyond.

Despite the claims made for the potentially revolutionary impact of technologies, it is increasingly acknowledged that there is a need for greater understanding of the ways in which new technologies affect learning and learner experiences (JISC, 2005; Seale, 2003). Without this understanding, and without a commitment to the broader goals of education beyond preparing workers, it has been argued (Cuban, 2001) that technologies are 'oversold and underused' in education institutions.

CHALLENGES FOR EDUCATIONAL INSTITUTIONS

For the vast majority of young people, the 'future' is already here. On transition to university, there is an expectation that e-learning will be embedded in the learning experience, despite widely varying previous educational experiences (JISC, 2007, p. 32). Learners expect to use technologies in personalised ways, to enable them to control aspects of their learning environment. By the time students leave school, e-learning involves the appropriation of technologies such as laptops, mobile phones and social software into their lifestyles 'to make their learning experiences more congenial, manageable and appropriate to their needs' (ibid.).

In a recent study, Conole, de Laat, Dillon and Darby (2008) report this clear shift in the ways higher education students approach their studies. The changing contexts in approaches to learning this research suggests the need to be factored into the way teachers, and the institutions in which they work, approach the 'business' of teaching and learning. In a modified way, we would argue, these trends also apply to how younger learners approach their educational tasks. On the basis of the analysis of the data they gathered, Conole *et al.* (2008, pp. 521–522) suggest eight factors influencing changing student practice:

- pervasive (technologies are used to support all aspects of study);
- personalised (technologies are appropriated to suit personal needs);
- niche/adaptive (particular tools are used for specific purposes);
- organised (technologies are used in a sophisticated manner to find and manage information);
- transferable (skills gained through non-education use of technologies are applied to learning contexts);
- time/space boundaries (changes to where and how students are working);
- working patterns (new working practices attendant to new tools); and
- integrated (suiting individual need).

Technology, they argue, is not simply seen as an 'add on',

> it is central to how (the students) organise and orientate their learning. The technologies provide them with a rich variety of alternatives for interaction and communication in relation to learning and a flexibility of use which enables them to take control of their learning.
>
> (Conole *et al.*, 2008, p. 522)

Educational institutions, their social, cultural and technological structures and inherent practices need to reflect the socio-cultural practices of the everyday lives of students in order not to be perceived as irrelevant by them.

One key affordance of new technologies, for example, is that they allow users not just to generate their own content but also contexts for their learning in and across formal and informal settings (for a detailed discussion see e.g. Pachler *et al.*, 2009). Matt Locke, in a blog posting in August 2007 (http://test.org.uk/2007/08/10/six-spaces-of-social-media/), for example, distinguishes six spaces of social media, which we list here not as a definite map but as a useful attempt of charting the changing landscape in which learning increasingly takes place:

- secret spaces (SMS, MMS, IM);
- group spaces (Facebook, MySpace, Bebo);
- publishing spaces (Blogger, Flickr, YouTube);
- performing spaces (Second Life, World of Warcraft);
- participation spaces (Meetup, Twitter); and
- watching spaces (mobile tv).

Locke does note some of the limitations of this conceptualisation, in particular the overlap between some of the categories as well as their existence offline as well as online. However, the particular strength of this representation, we think, lies in its user- rather than technology-centredness. In other words, we see the socio-cultural practices underpinning the use of technology as the driving force, not specific technologies themselves.

Electronic mobile devices, especially mobile phones with a wide range of functions, are more and more central features of our everyday lives. Yet, they remain mostly excluded from schools and key aspects of school-based learning. Whilst media use in everyday life and school belong to separate socio-cultural practice domains, the devices and services prevalent in everyday life do lend themselves as learning resources. This we consider to be one of the main challenges in coming years for educational institutions in general, and schools in particular. This is not in terms of an educational modernisation agenda or in terms of instrumentalising the school as a vehicle for technological advancement of society. It is rather for the benefit of learners in their attempt to come to terms with the divergent social and cultural realities around them in line with one of the traditional aims of schooling, namely to prepare young people for adult life in relation to their level of preparedness to participate adequately in dominant cultural and societal practices in an increasingly fragmented society characterised by individualised risk (see Bachmair *et al.*, forthcoming, for a detailed discussion).

The MacArthur Report (Ito *et al.*, 2008) claims that 'notions of expertise and authority have been turned on their heads' (p. 2) and schools need to capitalise far more on the informal, collaborative, peer-learning networks which their students inhabit. This would constitute a considerable shift in the ways that school-based learning has been organised to date, and it is in the challenge of implementation that the term 'revolution' becomes relevant to e-learning. There is extensive research into the challenges of embedding e-learning within pedagogical practices in schools. Valentine (2008), whilst broadly welcoming the integration of informal e-learning practices in schools, has warned against simplistic beliefs that school and home-based learning practices can easily be integrated, and indeed argues that elements of separation are important for learner well-being:

> The danger is that the more formal implementation and monitoring of home–school links might rob children's home-based ICT activities of their association with 'fun' and 'experimentation' with the result that children re-define these activities as school-related activities

> and consequently as 'boring' or 'uncool' things to spend their time doing (as well as blurring the association of home with leisure time and 'private' space and the school with work time and public space). There is therefore a need to understand how a strengthening of the relationship between the spaces of home and school through ICT links may affect young people's perceptions of what learning is, their willingness to use ICT at home and their learning styles in this space.
>
> (p. 17)

The Rose Report (2008), which proposes a major revision of policy and curriculum development in English primary schools to begin in 2011, emphasises that ICT should be embedded within the curriculum as one of the 'skills for learning and life' (p. 37) and should also be taught discretely:

> A sound grasp of ICT is fundamental to engagement in society, and the foundations for this engagement must be laid in primary schools. Along with literacy and numeracy, the use of technology to develop skills for learning and life should be at the core of the primary curriculum.
>
> (p. 15)

This reflects something of the broader conceptualisation of e-learning discussed earlier in the chapter, and its relevance to schools. The Rose Report also however adds further to concerns that experience with technologies in both primary and secondary phases does not effectively support the learners' stages of development. Successive reports have indicated that, despite a huge investment in providing technology resources in English schools, the learning gains have not been as great as anticipated. The *Harnessing Technology Review* (Becta, 2008b), a report from the government agency which is responsible for the development of technology-related learning in English schools, suggests that the learner experience of technologies is inconsistent, with a continuing deficit in teachers' pedagogical awareness of ways of working with technologies in ways which bring learning benefits. The review found that a key area where change is slow is in the use of technologies for collaborative peer-learning. This is a major conceptual component of 'e-learning', and reveals the gap between learning-focused developments in education and the ways in which technologies have been adopted by many schools.

The need to focus on the development of relevant pedagogies by which technologies are embedded in meaningful learning activities is a key outcome of such recent reports. In summary, although there has been a marked increase in availability of technologies in schools and in teachers' use of them, there is a lack of impact on practice relative to the considerable mobilisation of policy-making and resources which it has attracted. Questions of e-learning therefore address fundamental issues about the social organisation of knowledge and relationship between private/public spaces for learning. These types of issues lie beneath queries such as the following:

> How can [mobile] devices be folded into the learning processes of school, how can they be adapted to serve the function of the school? And that's a lively debate about, let's say the potential of MP3 podcast-type devices or texting as a way in which teachers and pupils can be in communication with each other.
>
> (Prout, 2008, p. 12)

E-learning involves more than the incorporation of the digital into school. It is about recognising the permeable boundaries between school and the rest of the world, between formal and informal learning, between 'school work' and 'homework' in e-learning contexts and about the impact of learning platforms in schools which make 'school-learning' into 'anywhere learning'.

THE IMPACT OF DIGITAL TECHNOLOGIES ON TEACHING, LEARNING AND ASSESSMENT

Our discussion of challenges of 'e-learning' for educational institutions above has already highlighted one important impact of digital technologies, namely the questions it requires policy makers and teachers to ask themselves about the nature of the curriculum, be it in terms of content and attendant skills, knowledge and understanding or be it in terms of appropriate tools for teaching and learning. In relation to tools, digital technologies, just like analogue ones, are characterised by a perpetual obsolescence. This poses a considerable challenge to any education system, both in terms of the cost involved in keeping hardware and software up to date and in terms of the professional development needs for the entire children's workforce as these technologies are not only increasingly permeating pedagogical practices but, of course, also the administrative ones supporting them.

According to a teacher voice omnibus survey conducted in 2007 by the National Foundation for Educational Research (NFER, 2008), around a third of respondents feel unprepared to maximise the use of the technology at their disposal. The lack of preparedness includes a demand for basic skills training in relation to comparatively established technologies such as computers, mobile devices and interactive whiteboards. Kitchen *et al.* (2007, p. 11) report that most teachers feel the need for professional development in using technology, with primary school teachers mentioning development needs in the area of digital video material creation and with secondary teachers foregrounding the need for support in learners' use of digital video. This despite a concerted effort by initial teacher education providers to develop technological pedagogical content knowledge (TPCK) in student teachers (see Mishra and Koehler, 2006) as well as some major government schemes in recent years such as the New Opportunities Funding (NOF) scheme to upskill the workforce (see e.g. Preston, 2004). In policy circles, the term 'e-maturity' has become popular of late, which refers to the 'integration of technology-based applications and processes into all key aspects of . . . practice and operation' (Becta, 2007, p. 19), to capture the degree of preparedness by all stakeholders at all levels.

Research into the use of mobile devices by teachers (McFarlane *et al.*, 2008, p. 7) suggests that teachers' confidence, their attitude to risk-taking together with their relationship with their classes are the factors with the greatest effect on the pace of implementation of digital technologies.

Fisher, Higgins and Loveless (2006, p. 2) argue that there is very little research on how teachers might learn with digital technologies and they identify the activities in Figure 16.1 as purposeful for teacher learning.

Ostensibly, this list is not very different from one that might be drawn up for student learning, which suggests, as do the findings by McFarlane referred to above, that 'learning partnerships' between teachers and students might well be a way forward in ensuring greater embedding of 'e-learning' in the work of schools as well as the interface between learning inside and outside of school. Indeed, a recent piece by Bachmair, Pachler and Cook (forthcoming) strongly suggests that the 'expert patterns' young people display in relation to media use outside of school can be made very fruitful for curriculum-orientated learning.

One possible model of how such learning partnerships might be operationalised is Diana Laurillard's (2002; 2007) Conversational Framework, which is based on the notion of the learning process as a 'conversation' between the teacher and the student. According to Laurillard the conversations are iterative and operate at a discursive and interactive level linked by reflection and adaptation. The conversations take place with the external world and its artefacts, the learner is seen

Knowledge building	• adapting and developing ideas • modelling • representing understanding in multimodal and dynamic ways
Distributed cognition	• accessing resources • finding things out • writing, composing and presenting with mediating artefacts and tools
Community and communication	• exchanging and sharing communication • extending the context of activity • extending the participating community at local and global levels
Engagement	• exploring and playing • acknowledging risk and uncertainty • working with different dimensions of interactivity • responding to immediacy

Figure 16.1 Purposeful activities for teacher learning

Source: Fisher, Higgins and Loveless, 2006, p. 2

as conversing with herself, with other learners and, of course, the teacher. Laurillard sees it as important for the learner to be in control of activities and able to test ideas by various means.

In the context of e-learning it is important to stress here that technology can feature variously in this model: for example, computer-based mediation (CMC) could be used as a vehicle for/medium of the learning conversations; concepts could be represented with the help of visual technologies such as mind-mapping software; outputs could be in the form of digital, multimodal artefacts; activities could be based around technology-supported simulations; the teacher-constructed environment could be virtual or mixed-mode; indeed, comments and questions by the teacher could be automated.

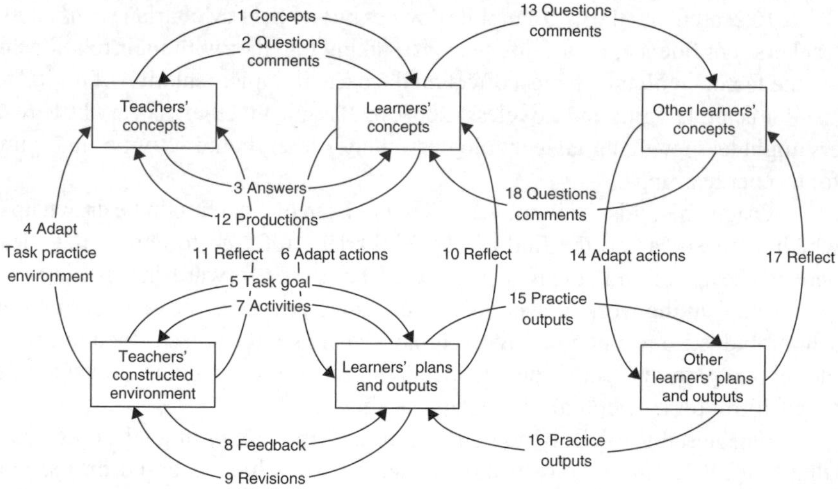

Figure 16.2 The Conversational Framework for supporting the formal learning process

Source: Laurillard, 2007, p. 160

In addition to teaching and learning, assessment is another dimension in which there is considerable potential for innovation. The tools most readily associated with e-assessment are e-portfolios, which are best understood as electronic tools that offer the user the opportunity to store and present digital material of personal relevance to her. In the context of e-assessment, such portfolios tend to contain artefacts produced/authored by the user rather than those derived from third parties. However, assessment of e-learning is increasingly faced with the social and distributed nature of artefact creation, i.e. the fact that such material tends not to be produced by one individual learner on her own, but as part of a collaborative effort in which existing digital material is readily appropriated, for example through cut and paste, and augmented in personally meaningful ways. This paradigm shift in socio-cultural practices associated with the production of new knowledge, which also includes an increasing prominence of sound and images as means of representation and meaning-making, creates significant challenges for the education system not only in terms of what it considers to be dominant literacy practices but also how to assess learning. The recent rise of plagiarism to the top of the agenda of many learning and teaching committees in higher education institutions, as well as a concern in schools, bears witness to this challenge. E-portfolios can have a range of functions in addition to that of a repository. In relation to its use as an assessment tool, processes of selection of artefacts for inclusion predicated on acts of reflection on the part of learners as well as the making of connections between individual items, seem to be of particular importance and relevance here.

KEY QUESTIONS FOR CONSIDERATION

This chapter has argued that, for the educational potentials of technologies to become embedded within education, significant changes are needed in approaches to pedagogy, curriculum and assessment. Currently, there is still a considerable way to go before most UK schools can effectively harness technologies for learning, despite being in a relatively advantageous position regarding pupil access to computers and internet connection, and teachers' skill levels (Becta, 2008b; Empirica, 2006). It is important to ask: What obstacles are presented for the successful development of e-learning in schools by the current ways in which knowledge is organised within the curriculum? What new forms of assessment are needed to reflect the types of knowledge, understanding and skills which young people develop through engagement with e-learning? Fundamentally, there needs to be a review of the models of teacher education which are needed to meet the needs of contemporary learners. What forms of initial teacher education and continuing professional development are needed, beyond skills acquisition? What should these models look like in Further Education, Higher Education and Adult Learning contexts?

The focus on teacher education is critical, but this needs to be teacher education which is critically informed by research into the learning benefits of types of pedagogical approaches. It is not *inevitable* that technologies will bring worthwhile enhancement to life-long learner experiences:

> Considering the ubiquity of e-learning, and the enormous opportunities and risks it presents for higher education, we need more than a fragmented approach to studying and understanding this phenomenon. . . . Is e-learning to be used simply to enhance inherently deficient existing practices (e.g., lecturing)? Or does this technology have the potential to transform the educational transaction . . .?
>
> (Garrison and Anderson, 2003, p. xi)

Finally, the MacArthur Report (Ito *et al.*, 2008) raises further questions about the relationship between formal and informal learning, and places considerations about e-learning within a much broader view of the social responsibilities of the education system:

> Youths' participation in this networked world suggests new ways of thinking about the role of education. What would it mean to really exploit the potential of the learning opportunities available through online resources and networks? Rather than assuming that education is primarily about preparing for jobs and careers, what would it mean to think of it as a process guiding youths' participation in public life more generally? Finally, what would it mean to enlist help in this endeavor from engaged and diverse publics that are broader than what we traditionally think of as educational and civic institutions?
>
> (Ito *et al.*, 2008, p. 3)

SUMMARY

This chapter has explored the key issues for e-learning within contemporary education contexts. It has asserted the importance of a clear definitional basis for e-learning, particularly in the context of new academic fields such as 'mobile learning' emerging. We have tried to show that the effective and appropriate use of digital technologies are not questions for future approaches to teaching and learning, but are of pressing importance for the here and now. We have noted that a new 'habitus' of being in, and acting (semiotically) upon the social and cultural world is implicit in technology-enhanced socio-cultural practices and we have urged for a re-evaluation of the lifeworlds of learners vis-à-vis their formal educational practices. We conclude that it is incumbent upon socially conscious education professionals to engage meaningfully with digital technologies if nothing else in order to ensure that young people learn how to contribute actively to the world in which they live and into which they grow up. And, whilst, at least in the foreseeable future, technologies are unlikely to replace teachers, teachers competent in the use of digital technologies are likely to replace those that are not.

KEY QUESTIONS

1. Is e-learning merely a fad or does it introduce new forms of learning?
2. What forms of assessment are needed to reflect the types of knowledge, understanding and skills which young people develop through engagement with e-learning?
3. What potential does e-learning have concerning young people's participation in public life?

FURTHER READING

Conole, G., de Laat, M., Dillon, T. and Darby, J. (2008) '"Disruptive technologies", "pedagogical innovation": what's new? Findings from an in-depth study of students' use and perception of technology', *Computers & Education 50*, pp. 511–524.

Ito, M., Horst, H., Bittanti, M., Boyd, D., Herr-Stephenson, B., Lange, P., Pascoe, C. and Robinson, L. (2008) *Living and Learning with New Media: Summary of findings from the digital youth project*, The John D. and Catherine T. MacArthur Foundation Reports on Digital Media and Learning, Chicago: The MacArthur Foundation.

Pachler, N. (2007) *Mobile learning: Towards a research agenda*, London: WLE Centre, Institute of Education.

This chapter links with reading 17 of *The Routledge Education Studies Reader*.

DEBATE 5

DO TRADITIONAL AND PROGRESSIVE TEACHING METHODS EXIST OR ARE THERE ONLY EFFECTIVE AND INEFFECTIVE METHODS?

Chris Kyriacou and Anne Cockburn

Chris Kyriacou and Anne Cockburn have written extensively on various aspects of effective teaching in schools, and have conducted numerous research studies on classroom practice since the 1980s. Over this period government policy has swung back and forth between favouring traditional teaching methods and favouring progressive teaching methods. Here they give their thoughts on how best to make sense of this ongoing debate that shows no signs of coming to an end. Chris Kyriacou begins by noting that defining the features of a particular teaching method is more problematic than might be assumed and argues that what really matters is not what you do but how you do it. Anne Cockburn develops this idea by asking you to reflect on your own experiences of learning. As the debate develops, it leads to a reframing of the initial question in terms of what characteristics of a teaching method need to be in place for effective learning to occur.

CHRIS KYRIACOU

One of the great schisms in educational ideology is that between two approaches to teaching – a *traditional approach* characterised by viewing the teacher as someone who transmits their knowledge and understanding to pupils through lecturing, explaining, asking leading questions, and giving emphatic evaluative feedback to pupils regarding whether their answers are right or wrong, on the one hand, and a *progressive approach* characterised by viewing the teacher as someone who allows pupils to find things out for themselves through the use of investigational activities, pupil–pupil and teacher–pupil discussion, the use of a range of resources and sources of information, and giving feedback to pupils which is supportive and collaborative rather than judgemental. These two extremes rarely exist in a pure form in the classroom – teachers will often use a mix of both approaches. However, this schism can be traced through writings on teaching over many centuries and clearly exists in contemporary discussion about what type of teaching methods are the most effective.

In my years as a teacher educator, researcher and writer, I have pondered hard on various aspects of effective teaching, and come to the conclusion that it's not what you do but the way that you do it that matters. By this, I mean that what has most struck me when observing teachers and looking at research findings, is that any particular teaching method can be used effectively and ineffectively. This first became evident to me when the notion of *active learning* (the use of activities in which pupils are given a markedly greater degree of autonomy and control over their learning) was being widely advocated in the 1980s (Kyriacou, 1992). When I observed lessons involving active learning, it was clear that some lessons involved a high level of pupil enthusiasm and involvement in their work and that high-quality learning was taking place, whilst in other lessons involving active learning, pupil enthusiasm, involvement and the quality of learning was at a low level. In considering whether the use of active learning was an effective method of teaching, I was forced to conclude that it depends on how the learning activities are managed.

At the same time I began to wonder what was meant by 'being active'. Was it simply evidence of physical activity (pupils were moving around the room, sharing ideas, discussing, using different resources, constructing posters) or was being active more a state of mind (the pupils were fully engaged mentally in the work they were doing)? If the latter, it occurred to me that listening to an excellent lecture, or reading an excellent chapter in a book, would be more effective in engaging pupils mentally than being in a poorly managed lesson involving lots of physical activities.

Of course, making a comparison between teaching methods often implies that there needs to be a level playing field – that is, comparing a good example of method A with a poor example of method B is not a fair comparison. But, then, what does it mean to ask, other things being equal, 'is a good use of traditional teaching methods more or less effective than an equally good use of progressive teaching methods?'

At the same time, advocates of active learning often referred to a wide range of learning outcomes and other benefits it offered compared with traditional methods. For example, it was claimed that by engaging in active learning, pupils developed a greater sense of independence, developed better communication and planning skills, and became more interested in doing school work. This raised the issue of to what extent when comparing traditional methods and progressive methods, we need to be clear about the learning outcomes and other benefits we have in mind. For example, let us suppose the main objective for a lesson is for pupils to be able to recall the chemical formulae for some common acids.

A traditional method might be to use a mix of explaining how and why the molecular structures of common acids take the form that they do. The teacher might then explain that it is important to be able to recall these formulae easily. As such, pupils will be given ten minutes to look at the formulae for some common acids, test themselves, and then the teacher would formally test the pupils and record their performance.

A teacher adopting progressive methods with the same learning outcomes in mind might divide the class into groups of four pupils, and provide them with some information resources from which they need to identify why the molecular structure of common acids take the form that they do. The teacher might circulate around the room to give help and assistance whilst the group work was in progress. Each group might then be asked to design a poster in which the molecular structure was drawn. The teacher would not formally test their recall, but might devise a competition or game in which recalling the formulae correctly was required; such an activity would be expected by the teacher to consolidate their ability to recall these formulae.

Which teaching method, in this example, is more effective? Well, it all depends on what the teacher is trying to achieve, and to what extent pupils respond positively to these two types of lessons. In addition, the way a teacher teaches conveys all sorts of messages to pupils about their role and identity as learners, and about the nature of knowledge, understanding and how it is acquired. Simply because pupils tended to score more highly in a test of recall after one type of lesson compared with another may not be sufficient grounds for saying one type of method is more effective. Moreover, we might also need to take account of the lesson's impact over the longer term, the impact it had on the classroom climate, and the impact it had on pupils' self-perceptions.

Another issue that forcefully struck me when looking at active learning in the classroom was that active learning was not a single method, but rather a family of methods. A teacher using small group work and a teacher who sets a pupil an independent project to carry out could both be said to be using active learning, but to what extent are they really using the same method? Indeed, the more I thought about any method or activity, the more I could see ways in which any method could be subdivided. For example, two teachers may both make very frequent use of asking questions in their lessons. However, the type of questions, how and when, and to what purpose they used questions, could be quite different. In thinking about traditional teaching methods and progressive teaching methods, we are faced with the same problem, but on a larger scale – both these approaches cover a vast array of activities, and how each particular activity is used will also vary immensely from teacher to teacher.

Does this mean that we cannot say whether traditional teaching methods are more/less effective than progressive teaching methods? My view is that trying to say a particular style of teaching method is more/less effective than another style is fraught with problems. The complex interaction between how these styles are manifest, the context of the classroom, the subject matter, the learning outcomes intended, and the differing needs of pupils, all conspire against reaching any simple conclusions.

Perhaps this is why recent policy guidelines on pedagogy in schools emphasise the need for teachers to make use of a mix of teaching methods, and shy away from advocating which particular methods, or set of methods, might constitute a teaching approach/style which is more effective than another. For example, in the recent review of mathematics teaching in primary schools (DCSF, 2008), the review group took the view that it was not possible to identify a single 'most effective' approach, but it could sensibly attempt to identify key features of teaching activities that, when taken together, constitute best practice.

Neither 'traditional teaching methods' nor 'progressive teaching methods' are sufficiently homogeneous concepts to be able to say with confidence that one set of teachers is exclusively using the former in a similar way and that another set of teachers is exclusively using the latter in a similar way. Moreover all teaching methods can be used either effectively or ineffectively. There are no teaching methods that are always effective, and no teaching methods that are always ineffective. For me, the key issues are thus: what are the merits and shortcomings of particular teaching methods?; are some teaching methods generally more effective in some circumstances than others?; and what factors can help ensure that any particular teaching method used by a teacher is used as effectively as possible? The answers to these questions will be complex, but that is why effective teaching presents such a challenge.

ANNE COCKBURN

Take a few minutes to think about the best teacher you ever had. Jot down what they did and why you thought they were so good. Now think about a teacher you did not rate and note down what you didn't like and why, in your view, he/she was not a very good teacher. Compare what you have written for both teachers and check to see whether there is any mention of learning!

Certainly some readers will have included learning in their lists but I am confident many will not. If you don't believe me try it on some friends: people may write what they *did* but not necessarily what they *learnt*. So the first point I want to make is that we are being asked the wrong question in this debate or, put another way, the question is incomplete in terms of a worthwhile educational discussion. It would have been more appropriate to phrase it as, for example, 'There is no such thing as traditional or progressive methods of education. There are only effective and ineffective methods.'

My second point is that, without making these amendments to the statement we are asked to consider, the debate would be very short for, from a pedant's point of view, there are, indeed, 'traditional' and 'progressive' teaching methods. There might be slight variations in how they might be defined but five of the key features of each – as agreed by Bennett (1987) and Pollard (1997) – are summarised in the table below.

Table D5.1 Progressive vs traditional

Progressive	Traditional
Much learning through discovery techniques	Rote learning involving practice and memory
Children's social and emotional development as important as academic attainment	Highest priority to academic attainment
Continuous informal forms of monitoring	Regular formal testing
Active pupil role	Passive pupil role
Intrinsic motivation (e.g. interest and fulfilment emphasised)	Extrinsic motivation (e.g. rewards and penalties used)

Seen in black and white such descriptions may seem fairly straightforward but my third point is that, if you stop to think about it, almost certainly some of the things you have learnt will fall into one category and others will fall into another. The balance between the two may, in part, be a factor of your age and, in part, a factor of the type of teachers you had. So, for example, if you are over a certain age or had a teacher brought up in the Haylock tradition (Haylock and Cockburn, 2003), it is likely that you were taught your times tables. It is also likely that you were required to memorise them using practice and rote which is classified as 'traditional' above. Looking back on it – although, for some, the process might have seemed tedious and painful – I suspect that, as an adult, you are quite glad you made the effort when it comes to decorating, cooking, budgeting and so on.

Not everyone benefited from the above approach, however: some because they were not exposed to it and others because it proved unsuccessful as a teaching method. Haylock (2006) describes various individuals who suffered great trauma during maths lessons at school including one person who explained, 'I had nightmares about maths . . . Numbers and figures would go flashing through my head. Times tables, for example' (p. 4). In the light of this and various other accounts of learning, for example, mathematics (see, Ashcraft and Krause, 2007; Buxton, 1981; Ma, 1999), my fourth point is that perhaps there is something to be said for the progressive rather than traditional approach: apart from the fact that the learning might be less effective if someone is anxious, I have grave doubts about the moral dimension of traumatising a child in the name of education.

If you left school within the last few years it is highly likely that you are only too familiar with the experience of frequent formal testing and assessment as opposed to a more progressive approach. Concern with academic standards resulted in many passionate debates in the 1970s and

1980s (see, for example, Chitty, 1992; Lawton, 1994; Simon, 1988) leading to the formation of the Task Group on Assessment and Testing (TGAT). The TGAT report (DES, 1988) introduced the idea of formally testing children in Enhools – particularly in the late spring – will find many teachers and children in years 6 and 9 poring over past test papers and desperately trying to cover as much ground as possible so that they and their schools will perform well in the national league tables.

You might, from the previous paragraph, have got a sense as to how I feel about the current approach to testing! Testing, in and of itself, is not, in my view, necessarily a bad thing as an effective test properly administered can provide valuable information as to someone's knowledge and – to a lesser extent – their understanding. There are several flaws with the present system and, at some point, you might consider what they are but, for the sake of this debate, just take a few minutes to ponder on whether frequent and rigorous testing enhances or hinders children's educational progress.

Interestingly early on in the TGAT report (see above) it states that, 'Promoting children's learning is a principal aim of schools. Assessment lies at the heart of this process' (1988, para 3). It goes on, 'The assessment process itself should not determine what is taught and learned. It should be the servant, not the master, of the curriculum' (para 4). So my fifth point is that, although the regular monitoring of children's progress – which does not necessarily need to be in the form of testing – is an important component of teaching and learning, we need to be vigilant that it is not managed in an overly traditional manner such that it distorts the educational process.

Having contemplated some of the potential horrors of testing, hopefully you can now think of something you learnt and understood at school. Take a few minutes to think about how you acquired such knowledge and understanding. Perhaps it was something you discovered as you were investigating something in science or maths. Perhaps it was when you were sitting quietly at your desk listening to your teacher describing events of long ago or far away or maybe it was on a fieldtrip as you contemplated the exploits of various minibeasts within their natural habitats. Possibly you have experienced successful learning in most or, indeed, all of these situations. Before unpacking the implications for this debate stop to think about how you learnt to ride a bicycle, use a computer or construct a flat pack. Compare and contrast this to sitting back in a comfortable armchair and watching, for example, one of David Attenborough's many programmes exploring the natural world.

My guess is that most of you will conclude that you have learnt effectively in a range of situations – some of them while you were being active and others when you were more passive. I would also guess that the extent of your learning would depend partly on the subject matter but also on your interest and your teacher's capability and enthusiasm. All of these are interrelated: David Attenborough being an excellent example of someone else's fascination and passion for a subject igniting interest among even the most reluctant learners. So my sixth point is that sometimes our learning tends towards the more progressive and other times the more traditional.

Before drawing a conclusion, what subjects do you really enjoy? What do you want to learn more about? Think back to when your curiosity and enthusiasm for this subject were ignited. Without a doubt it was not when you were being rewarded or punished but rather when you were intrinsically interested in the subject matter. My seventh point, in other words, was that you were fascinated in the work for its own sake rather than merely because it was something you were expected to do.

So what is real education? How is it best achieved? You and your friends might come up with slightly different answers. If you travel around the world you will find further variations in response and, indeed, you will find some very traditional teachers and some very progressive ones but, even considering this short discussion, it is clear that neither one approach nor the other encompasses the most effective ways to educate a child. Over 20 years ago Bennett (1987, p. 12) concluded, '. . . whether teachers teach in a so-called progressive or traditional mode is largely irrelevant. Teachers need a repertoire of teaching styles.'

So, yes, I believe it is more a case of effective and ineffective teaching methods of education rather than a strict divide between progressive and traditional practices but, on a personal note, I find that I much prefer involving you – the reader – in my writing than preparing more detached and formal papers which may make me more of a progressive at heart . . . .

CHRIS KYRIACOU

Response to Anne Cockburn

Anne makes five key points in her piece. First, she argues that the debate concerning traditional and progressive teaching methods is really about 'education' rather than teaching methods. This point reminds us that we are essentially dealing with ideological positions when we think about teaching methods, as the use of a particular teaching method is bound up with our view of the nature of education as a whole. Anne's second point is that strictly speaking, traditional and progressive teaching methods can be defined and seen in classroom practice. I agree, but when observing teachers in action, the distinction is harder to sustain than one might imagine, and that all pupils will have learnt some things from both methods (which is Anne's third point). Her fourth point concerns her moral anxiety about the use of traditional methods, if the way it is used can traumatise pupils. My response to this point is that any teaching method, in particular circumstances, can generate high levels of anxiety in pupils – I can recall how some pupils reported that they found lessons involving active learning quite threatening. Anne's fifth point about the current emphasis on testing in schools, highlights that the ideology underpinning the use of traditional teaching methods is often focused on the importance of test performance and cognitive learning outcomes. This raises a very important issue facing all teachers: if the government continues to place an emphasis on the use of regular tests of cognitive learning outcomes, will that pressure some teachers to adopt traditional teaching methods if they believe such methods will enhance test performance? We certainly need to guard against the danger that the regular monitoring of pupils' progress using testing in this way, in Anne's words, 'distorts the educational process'.

Anne's piece highlights how difficult and complex it is to make sense of current practice in schools using broad labels such as traditional methods versus progressive teaching methods. For example, the increasing use of information and communications technology (ICT) in schools, particularly the use of interactive whiteboards, has in many ways transformed how classroom practice appears. However, studies of ICT-based teaching methods can sometimes be interpreted as exemplifying a traditional teaching method (e.g. the teacher may be using an interactive whiteboard as a teaching aid to support an expository mode of teaching) but a few minutes later when a pupil might take centre-stage the use of the interactive whiteboard can appear to exemplify a progressive teaching method. I began my piece by saying I thought it is not what you do but the way that you do it that matters. I still think that, but reading Anne's piece has reminded me that the teacher's intention for a teaching method and their broader view of education as a whole, need to be taken into account before we can properly interpret and label what we think is going on in the lesson.

ANNE COCKBURN

Response to Chris Kyriacou

There is much I agree with in Chris' discussion and, in particular, that there is a wide range of teaching methods, many of which are effective much of the time but none of which is effective all of the time.

The other day a candidate for a place on a teacher training course suggested a very appealing definition of an effective teacher: 'An effective teacher is someone who knows their subject well enough to have fun with it'. In my experience both as a teacher and an observer of teachers, this is certainly true. Indeed, I would go so far as to say that it is an important part of being an effective teacher as enthusiasm is generally an excellent motivator: if learners want to learn they are often well on the way to success. Think about your most enthusiastic teachers: did you learn from them? If so, how and what? If not, why not?

Reflecting on my own experiences, some teachers can be a little over-enthusiastic or, probably more accurately, insufficiently aware of their audience; the result being that, if they lose me in the first few minutes they may well have lost me altogether. A more sensitive – albeit possibly less enthusiastic teacher – is more likely to pick up on my lack of comprehension and adjust their teaching accordingly if, of course, they have the knowledge and understanding to do so.

What knowledge and understanding might such a teacher require? Familiarity with the subject certainly. Second, they need to be able to 'unpack' (Ball, Bass and Hill, 2004, p. 10) the information to be conveyed into bite-size chunks suitable for learner consumption. A third requirement is the ability to teach. And of crucial importance, teachers need to understand how children in classrooms operate. Doyle's (1979) phrase that learners 'exchange performance for grades' springs to mind: what you praise is what you get. I once observed a wonderfully inspiring introduction to a *creative* writing session complete with a model (and highly active!) volcano. The class of seven-year-olds then began their writing and their teacher praised them for writing the date, producing neat work and so on: there was no mention of imaginative writing and creativity and, as a result, there was none in the children's writing.

The thing about classrooms, of course, is that they are highly unpredictable places. One minute a teacher might be having high-level discussions about the meaning of life and the next minute adding one and one. An effective teacher is constantly on the go, thinking ahead, responding to children's intellectual and emotional needs, managing this, that and the next thing. Modifying a phrase Chris used, I would say that an effective teaching method is an *active teaching* method: one where a teacher is able to employ all of the qualities described above but in ways that are most appropriate to the situations in which they find themselves. As these are ever changing so too is the description of the effective teacher. Thus, for example, a teacher's enthusiasm will be predominant one minute, sensitivity the next, and subject knowledge the next . . . .

CONCLUSION FROM CHRIS KYRIACOU AND ANNE COCKBURN

Looking at our two initial statements and our subsequent responses it is interesting to see how we have moved from a focus on comparing two types of teaching methods (traditional versus progressive) to a focus on the nature of effective teaching. In a way this is not surprising. An analysis of an educational issue often starts with what appears to be a clear and straightforward question, but after some probing, it becomes apparent that the issue, as presented, begs a number of questions, assumptions and value positions. How these are dealt with has a major impact on how the initial question posed can be addressed. Thus, in this case, the assumption that there are two clearly identifiable types of teaching methods that can be compared in terms of effectiveness, raises underlying issues concerning the extent to which teachers can be said to adopt one of these teaching methods, what criteria can be used to judge effectiveness, and what value positions concerning the nature and purposes of education are implicit in this.

It is also evident that although the distinction between 'traditional' and 'progressive' appears to endure, how these approaches manifest themselves in classroom practice needs to be identified anew. For example, an email sent by a teacher to a pupil as part of an internet discussion board can be expositional in tone or take the form of raising and sharing questions. Does this make the former a 'traditional' use and the latter a 'progressive' use of this ICT? Indeed, reading our two outline pieces above, one can say they both take the same format (you are reading a text in a book), but you, as the reader, may find differences in the style of presentation engage you differently.

As such, like many conceptual dichotomies that are used in education, the distinction between traditional and progressive teaching methods provides us with a critical cutting edge to explore classroom practice, and thereby enriches our understanding of key issues involved, but it cannot provide a simple answer to a complex question.

KEY QUESTIONS

1. Are 'traditional' and 'progressive' meaningful labels in discussions about teaching methods?
2. Does 'high-status knowledge' mean the same thing as 'traditional knowledge'? If so, does this have any implications for what teachers should teach?
3. To what extent should students be allowed to decide what they learn?

FURTHER READING

The following three sources address important aspects of classroom practice which are relevant to the debate on traditional versus progressive teaching methods.

Galton, M. (2008) *Learning and Teaching in the Primary Classroom*. London: Sage.
Petty, G. (2006) *Evidence Based Teaching: A Practical Approach* (2nd edn). Cheltenham: Nelson Thornes.
Rudduck, J. and McIntyre, D. (2007) *Improving Learning through Consulting Pupils.* Abingdon: Routledge.

This debate links with reading 13 of *The Routledge Education Studies Reader.*

SECTION 3

DOING EDUCATION STUDIES

CHAPTER 17

ACCESSING AND UNDERSTANDING RESEARCH IN EDUCATION

Stephen Gorard

The rationale for this chapter is:

- to outline the fantastic range and sources of available evidence relevant to education;
- to suggest craft tips on seeking and using existing research evidence;
- to propose a few areas for improvement and further work.

INTRODUCTION

This chapter describes the range of evidence that exists relevant to educational studies, and discusses how to locate, read, and use such evidence. The evidence exists in publicly available datasets as well as in the writings of others. The chapter introduces some generic methods of assessing the quality and usefulness of evidence, including a key quality control principle. The chapter ends by outlining some ideas for future research.

THE SCALE OF RESEARCH EVIDENCE IN EDUCATION

In all developed countries including the UK, and most other countries, education is a huge industry. It is increasingly lifelong, from cradle to grave (or more formally from pre-school to adult learning in the third-age). It is society-wide, taking place in families, schools, colleges, prisons, the workplace, libraries, on-line, and in numerous informal settings. Education is also the only major area of public policy which is compulsory for all citizens – hospitals are for the unwell, prisons are for offenders, benefits are intended for a disadvantaged minority, and so on. But everyone is required by law to attend school, or to make equivalent arrangements at home. And education is held responsible by policy-makers for a bewildering range of phenomena including the economy (a trained workforce), social mobility, social cohesion, and social justice. So, although education research is only a small part of all this education it is still a large undertaking itself. There are more education researchers in the UK than in any other field or discipline (Gorard *et al.*, 2004).

Education research in the UK is funded by central and local government, by near-government bodies like the Qualifications and Curriculum Development Agency, the Training and Development

Agency, or the Learning and Skills Council, by research councils such as the Economic and Social Research Council, by learned bodies such as the Royal Society or the British Academy, by think tanks such as the Social Market Foundation or the Institute for Public Policy Research, by practitioner bodies such as the NUT or ATL, by large charities like the Nuffield Foundation, Gatsby, or Joseph Rowntree, by individual benefactors such as the Sutton Trust or Bowland Trust, and by many of the same kinds of bodies in Europe, the USA and worldwide including the OECD, the EC Directorate for Education and Culture, and the Spencer Foundation. The research is conducted by these bodies themselves as well as by academics, practitioners, and increasingly by private consultants.

This means that there is a vast amount of data collected on education, and a vast amount written about education research. For any topic, as broadly conceived, the first problem you will face is how you will manage the scale of that evidence.

LOOKING FOR RESEARCH EVIDENCE

A hierarchy of evidence

Primary evidence is based on first-hand data that you collect yourself. This has the advantages of being new, fresh, directly relevant to your own area of investigation, and more easily comprehensible to you. Primary evidence has the disadvantages that it is likely to be small-scale due to lack of time and resources, it could be biased by your selection of the cases to be involved, and will often anyway be a replication of evidence already collected by others.

Secondary evidence is based on existing data collected by others. Where you can gain direct access to the evidence collected by others this often allows you much larger-scale data, but still with many of the advantages of primary data. For example, if you wish to find out whether the number of applicants to study undergraduate mathematics at universities in the UK has been going up or down in the last ten years it is difficult to imagine that you could collect better data on this than the Higher Education Statistics Agency (HESA). HESA makes these data available to all would-be analysts (see below). A fantastic range of existing evidence is available on almost all education studies topics. Such secondary evidence has the disadvantages, for you, that it was usually collected for another purpose and so may not be ideal, that you have no real idea of the conditions under which the data were collected, and you may therefore be misled about its completeness and accuracy. Nevertheless, when considering an educational issue, secondary evidence is usually at least as useful as primary evidence, and much cheaper to get hold of (Gorard, 2001).

Where primary evidence is not possible, and secondary evidence is not available, it is also worth considering the conclusions of others, drawn from their own analysis of primary or secondary data ('tertiary' data if you like). But remember, whatever the flaws and limitations of any direct evidence (primary or secondary), these are made worse by being summarised at third hand. One has only to read two different newspaper accounts of the same governmental policy announcement to see the truth of this. The accounts may be contradictory and such contradictions may only be resolved by reading the announcement for yourself. This principle is widely misunderstood in education studies, where new authors rush to repeat the *opinions* of others, when it is just as easy to read that author's evidence at first-hand and come to your own opinion. Any author summarising their own evidence faces exactly the same flaws and relative disadvantages as you would when reading the evidence itself, but they put you at the added disadvantage of only 'seeing' the evidence through their eyes. This does not mean that we should not read the accounts of others. My purpose here is to illustrate the dangers of relayed and packaged information for those seeking a greater understanding of education, and to recommend the use of direct evidence wherever possible.

One advantage of reading about evidence at second-hand is that it might allow you to use a larger number of studies and datasets in any given time period. This advantage occurs especially when you have access to a synthesis of evidence from more than one source, such as might appear in a meta-analysis or systematic review.

Reports of single studies are therefore towards the bottom of the hierarchy of useful evidence. They are valuable but require considerable time to use effectively, and lead to an increased danger of being misled by a poor-quality and un-replicated study. For some reason, reports of primary research often give very little detail about the evidence uncovered. It should be a simple matter to provide the relevant research instruments, full transcripts of interviews, spreadsheets of responses, and so on, either as appendices or as linked websites. This kind of good practice is still only attempted by a minority. Many research reports make quite bold claims illustrated by selective interview quotations or tables, in such a way that readers are unable to judge for themselves whether the claims are warranted by the evidence. Just because the author claims that something is so does not make it so. Your task as a reader of evidence is to make critical and informed judgements about the relative quality of different sources of evidence, and about the conclusions others have drawn from this evidence. In order to complete that task you must have reasonably good access to the evidence, and providing that access is part of the task of the author. Where an author does not create that access through the clarity of their writing they are failing in that basic task. It is then quite rational for you to cast doubt on both their evidence and their conclusions.

Beware also of articles that look like summaries of evidence, but which are mere opinion. Reviews of literature in a number of fields report encountering a large number of papers published in peer-reviewed research journals that contain no direct accounts of evidence at all (Gorard *et al.*, 2007). Perhaps one-third of all education 'research' publications are thought pieces, and of course some of these are valuable. There are discussions and debates about innovative research methods, and the occasional piece with a new idea that has the power to completely change the way we look at a topic. However, far too many are largely pointless theorising or posturing. Do not mistake the opinion of others for evidence, however important the source and however forcefully expressed.

To recap, there are at least five different ways of uncovering apparent evidence on a topic. Direct access to primary and secondary evidence are the best and most secure routes. Failing these a rigorous synthesis of available evidence, performed by someone else, is a time-saving and useful alternative, as long as the quality of the synthesis is made clear and the route (or audit trail) to the primary data is available for interested readers. Failing this you can produce your own rigorous synthesis of the evidence published in single studies. You may also find useful techniques and approaches in published articles with no evidence in them, but do not mistake these for evidence of any kind.

Searching for secondary evidence

Once you have opened your eyes to the possibility of using existing data, rather than just reports about existing data, the difficulty is not so much whether what you want exists but where you can find it. I suggest some likely sources here for illustration, but the details of internet resources are likely to date rapidly, and to vary between countries.

An obvious place to start your search for existing data is the national UK Data Archive (http://www.data-archive.ac.uk/). This is, or should be, a repository of all datasets generated through research paid for by the taxpayer-funded Research Councils (such as the Economic and Social Research Council), and from a number of other sources. It includes historical archives, policy and other documents, and transcripts of interviews undertaken as part of previous research projects. Some of it is relevant to education studies. You can register for access to these resources, and then reanalyse the evidence for your own purposes. The National Digital Archive of Datasets (http://www.ndad.nationalarchives.gov.uk/) similarly contains a fantastic array of data – perhaps most obviously a database of the annual schools census for all schools, undertaken in January each year, collecting data at school level on pupil intake characteristics (poverty, special needs, ethnicity, sex, first language) and on the teaching and support staff. Linking such school characteristic data to the corresponding records of school examination entry and attainment is a very powerful approach. The Department for Children, Schools and Families has a website full of data on all aspects of school and childhood, including an archive of examination and key stage results for each school up to the current year (http://www.dcsf.gov.uk/performancetables/).

If you want comparative data, or to place your evidence in an international context then the OECD website has a wonderful collection of educational evidence, including the annual Education at a Glance, and the results of successive rounds of the international PISA study. The most recent PISA study at the time of writing was in 2006 (http://pisa2006.acer.edu.au/), and the database includes the views of teachers and students, student test results in a range of subjects, and school-level data. It can be downloaded from the website, giving records for individuals within schools, in around 80 countries. For more on where to find data and how to analyse it, see Gorard (2001).

One of the many websites with downloadable data about post-school education is the Higher Education Statistics Agency (http://www.hesa.ac.uk/). Here you can find an archive of applications and admissions to higher education, and discover changes over time or regional variations in what kinds of students study what kinds of subjects at university, for example.

The (Office for) National Statistics is a one-stop shop for evidence on almost anything. It includes evidence at small area level on all ten-yearly national censuses of the population, most recently from 2001; the next will be run in 2011 (http://www.statistics.gov.uk/census2001/topics.asp). Here you can find such things as the highest educational qualification of everyone in the population aged 16–74, broken down by sex, age, area of residence, type of accommodation, health, religion, occupation, marital status, and so on. You can also request bespoke tables and specific analyses. It is a public service.

These few examples really only touch the surface of the local, national and international datasets made available specifically so that you and I can use them for our own purposes. Whatever you want to know about education it is very likely that someone or some department of government has already collected the evidence you need on a far grander scale than you would be capable of. Perhaps the most original new use of these existing datasets lies in combining evidence from two or more in a way that has not been done before. I have already pointed out how useful it is to use the schools census data on pupil intakes to help explain and understand the DCSF figures on school attainment. This is a well-known link. What about others that you could be combining for the first time? Can you imagine linking the schools data with the HESA data – who is missing out on university? Or the population data with the schools intake data – do schools represent their local residents? Or whether pupil views on citizenship (from PISA, 2006) are related to the type of school they attend (schools census)? One of the many interesting projects I have conducted involved comparing present-day stories of adult learning with those in the taped oral archive of families living in the South Wales coalfields in the 1890s (Gorard and Rees, 2002). The possibilities are endless, but largely ignored by UK scholars who just do not seem to realise this potential, and continue with their small-scale and often pointless recreation of these same bases of evidence.

Searching for tertiary evidence

What about searching for research literature? I propose two main methods. Whatever else you do, do not start your review of the research literature by using a book or books. Books recounting research evidence are, by definition, out of date. They take some time to write and a long time to get published. A book dated 2010 probably only refers to other literature up until 2009, and will be based on primary evidence collected in or before 2007. They will only give a partial picture. To get a much more recent and more complete list of research reports relevant to your topic you need to visit one or more of the databases maintained for precisely that purpose. As with databases of existing evidence it is shocking how few scholars use these resources. For example, the British Education Index holds a vast database of complete reports available to download and read (http://www.leeds.ac.uk/bei/). Many of the reports are what is termed 'grey literature', meaning that they are like pre-publications. They are less prestigious than journal articles in some people's eyes, but they compensate for this by being more up to date. It takes almost as long to get a journal article published as it does a book (longer for some journals), but the Education Index can receive an electronic paper and put it up the same day.

An even wider literature on education is available to search at the Education Resources Information Center (http://www.eric.ed.gov/), and at PsycINFO (http://www.apa.org/psycinfo/). These do not always lead to a complete text, but usually to an abstract, keywords, and full bibliographic reference list. You can then use the references to find the full text in your library or on the internet, if the abstract sounds as though the piece is really relevant to your own work. A key advantage of the electronic search engines for these databases and others like them is that as well as searching by titles and authors you can search for terms or phrases appearing in the documents, and you can combine all of these with Boolean logical operators like AND, OR and NOT. The precise instructions for doing this vary with each database, but imagine you were interested in bullying at school. You might search for 'bullying' and get thousands of hits (documents containing the word bullying). You then refine your search to look for 'bullying' AND 'secondary school' AND 'Scotland', and this reduces the hits only to those documents that mention all three search terms. It takes a few goes to get enough hits but not too many. It is very similar to using Google. Talking of which, Google has a specialist search engine called Google Scholar used for looking at academic writing in particular, which can be very useful (http://scholar.google.co.uk/). A final example from the many databases of research publications relevant to education is the Campbell Collaboration (http://www.campbellcollaboration.org/). This contains systematic reviews of evidence on almost every imaginable topic in formal education, and reports of randomised controlled trials of educational interventions.

In addition to these resources it is always useful to conduct a smaller search of your own. You might start with the electronic library in your own institution which has access to a number of research journals. However, these are usually organised for the benefit of someone who knows what they are looking for (such as you, once armed with a list of useful references from the ERIC database). I find a better way of finding material at the very start of a new search is to visit the library in person (it also makes a nice change from using the computer). Your library probably has hard copies of the most up-to-date issues of each journal lying face out on the shelves. You can walk along the education shelves, picking up each journal that might be relevant and reading the list of contents – usually on the back cover. Some of the most useful journals at this stage are the generic ones covering a whole range of issues, such as the *British Educational Research Journal*, *Oxford Review of Education*, *Cambridge Journal of Education*, and so on. Scan the list of contents and turn to the page for any paper that looks relevant. Read the abstract and decide to note the reference or discard it. Remember that any article does not have to be specifically about your topic. Nor do you have to use all of any article. An article might give you an idea, a description of a method, or a way of writing or presenting evidence, as well as or instead of substantive information about your topic. Perhaps the most valuable resource will be the references cited in each article. This is why you start with the most recent journals. Any paper can only cite prior papers, so if you start with last year you are going to miss the most recent evidence. You use the first set of articles to daisy-chain back to further articles, books and reports. Coupled with a search of electronic databases this should give you a fairly accurate picture of the state of evidence in your field.

Also consider looking at student theses if these are available in your library. Masters and doctoral dissertations are usually on the shelves. And remember that if a crucial paper or book is not in your library they will probably order it for you (most libraries are desperate for suggestions) or they can get it via inter-library loan. Remember also how the library catalogue system works. If you go to the shelf with the classification mark for the book or report you want and it is not there, all of the other nearby volumes will, by definition, be on similar themes. They might be even better than the one you were looking for.

Once you have located a useful publication or piece of information, ensure that you note down the full bibliographic or website details at the same time – including the date of access for websites, and the page numbers for any direct use of evidence or quotations. You do not want to waste time looking for the citation details again later when you come to write an assignment or dissertation. Incidentally, your course or institution will have an agreed set of standards for how you cite and list references in your work (such as Harvard, Chicago or Oxford). It is a really simple matter to master these rules early on, and it is a surprise to me that so much time is wasted in incorrect or incomplete references. Save your anarchic protest for something more substantial.

CONSUMING RESEARCH EVIDENCE

Clearly, having located some useful evidence in whatever form, you must now read and understand it. Mere possession of a photocopied article or a library-loaned book is of no use. So this is not the time to relax. On the other hand you do not need to read all and everything you locate. In the same way as you will exclude some material at first glance as being irrelevant or too dated, so you will come to realise that some of the material you have retained is not as useful as you first thought. Skimming the abstract, conclusions and references of a published article can help you decide whether to read further. Using the list of contents and figures and preface in a book can help you decide which, if any, chapter to read. Academic work is not like a detective novel designed to be read in order, in full, and once. You can start at the end and work backwards. Sometimes you need very little from a reference – perhaps all you glean from it is that there is a debate about some topic. It is perfectly proper to cite the reference as simply showing the existence of the debate. In this case, you are truthfully pointing out that the debate appears in the paper. As soon as you go further than this and venture an opinion or even implicit support for one side in that debate then you need to have read the paper much more carefully.

It is important for you to realise that the publication of education research has no real quality control. Weblogs and wikis are written by individuals with differing approaches to the truth, and cannot always be relied upon to give factual information. In the same way, electronic papers and pieces linked to websites, even those of well-known academics, cannot always be relied on. It is what they report that matters, not where they appear or who wrote them. The major attempt at quality control in education research comes from peer-review. In top journals, papers submitted for publications are sent without identifying information to two or more other academics for their comments and advice on whether to publish. Several problems arise. Innovative and controversial papers may be rejected, while anodyne ones that do not threaten the status quo are accepted. There is sometimes clique review, where a group of academics working in the same area review and approve each other's work to advance their own careers. There is sometimes competitor review, where a group of academics combine to inhibit the publication of work that is critical of their own approach. The journals are businesses that need a supply of papers to be published and so their 'standards' vary with time, popularity and the number of papers they receive for review. There are other attempted quality controls in education research but they are also defective. This is clear from reading almost any journal carefully. The papers in it will be mostly a combination of the anodyne and unexciting, poorly written and crafted, illustrating weak research and drawing unjustified or illogical conclusions.

This last passage should give you a few clues as to how to do your own form of quality control. For example, the author of any education research paper is writing to tell the story of their research to you and I – and people exactly like us. If, after careful reading, you do not understand what the author is saying, what the evidence means or how their conclusions follow from the evidence then the author is generally the one at fault. It is not only bad manners to treat their readership like that. It is also suggestive of flaws in their own logic or research that they are attempting to cover up by obfuscation. I find that, in addition to the one-third of papers I read that contain no evidence or new ideas (see above), around another third do not make sense at all. But rather than ignoring these problems, why not join me in pointing this out when you write your summaries of evidence or literature reviews? Explain which or how many papers were vacuous and which were impossible to read.

For the minority of pieces you come across, which contain substantive reports of evidence *and* are explained clearly for their intended audience, try applying the following quality control principle. If the conclusion(s) of each report were not actually true how else could we explain the evidence they found? This simple-sounding question is actually a very powerful discriminator between good and bad research (Gorard, 2002). Imagine a study providing evidence that school pupils today report high levels of stress, concluding that school life today is more stressful than in previous decades. The author then begins to suggest explanations for this change – such as increased pressure of exams or shorter break times. Apply the principle. If it were not actually true that school life today is more stressful than in previous decades then how could we explain the evidence that pupils today report high levels of stress? There are many explanations that would fit. Most obviously, perhaps pupils might always have reported high levels of stress. The author is making a comparative claim without the necessary comparator (the levels of stress from previous decades). Yet this is a real example written by a professor of education in a UK university. It was written in all seriousness, peer-reviewed (for quality control) and then published. Unfortunately, I do not think this is some kind of freak outlier, but the normal weak standard of education research.

Try another real example. A study is based on education lecturers at a university interviewing their trainee teacher students about what they think of the course. The evidence is that most students are complimentary about the course, and the researchers conclude that their course is good, and so begin to characterise what they do well on the course so that other institutions can copy them. Again, apply the principle. If the course were not actually that good, how else could we explain why the students reported that they were happy with it? Again, there are numerous explanations. One obvious one is that the lecturers were not just the researchers; they were also the people who decided on the students' results, and this inhibited critique. Yet this study was also peer-reviewed and published without consideration of this apparently key point by the authors, peer-reviewers or journal editors. There is no decent quality control in education research. You have to be the judge of quality for each piece.

I would say that the majority of education research in the UK is incomprehensible or fatally flawed. It is important for us as users of research evidence to be able to admit this so that we can discriminate and use more easily the minority of good research that does not have these flaws. Such research *does* exist and we should seek it out and treasure it. Of course, all research faces problems and requires the researcher to compromise. We are not looking, mistakenly, for perfection. We are looking, ethically, for scrupulousness. The problem with the two examples above and others like them is not so much with the evidence but about how the results are explained. The first author could have said that although they did not have evidence from previous decades, the levels of stress among pupils today were so high that they believed this to be a new phenomenon, though this would be a weaker conclusion. In the second, the authors could have said that they realised that their students may have felt constrained about being critical in front of them, but they did not have the resources to employ outsiders to conduct the interviews, and anyway the students did not have to be so complimentary. Thus, they might still conclude more tentatively that most students seemed genuinely happy with the course. Being critical and cautious in the use of evidence is, ironically, more persuasive than being gung ho.

You will come across different kinds of evidence in databases, and different kinds of studies in the literature. Evidence may differ in scale, completeness, quality, age, methods of data collection and analysis. There is insufficient space here to discuss how to read, critique and summarise every type. Two general points will have to suffice. First, anyone genuinely concerned about evidence in education research cannot exclude any data or reports solely on the basis of their type or the methods used (Gorard with Taylor, 2004). A synthesis of evidence must use all relevant available material. This might sound obvious but you will soon discover ridiculous and supposedly incommensurable schisms, often based on the q words 'quantitative' and 'qualitative', that encourage research users to focus on only a subset of available evidence. Don't fall into this trap. Second, at a general level all types and methods of evidence can be handled in the same way, using the principle above (for example), or using the same kind of common sense judgement you use in everyday life. If the writers do not make themselves clear, that is their fault. Education research does not, or at least should not, generally use any complex techniques beyond the comprehension of education studies students (Gorard 2010). If the author puts tables in their writing which are in fact the undigested output from analytical software and you do not understand the table, it is not your fault. If the author uses long and unfamiliar words, in lengthy sentences of low readability, again this is not your fault.

USING TERTIARY EVIDENCE

In general, your main use of existing evidence will be to synthesise it. Your task will be to report the overall picture of what we know about a specific topic. This means that you will have to convert what you have – often a list of references with notes attached – into a coherent story. This usually entails changing the subject and object of the discussion. In note form, the subject heading may quite naturally be the author of the research report, while the topic takes a back seat. You need to avoid carrying this incorrect emphasis into your writing. One clue to this problem in any report is a sequence of paragraphs and sentences starting something like:

> Gorard (2002) claims that . . .
> Gorard (2004) found that . . .

Ensure that you avoid this error. Instead, make the topic of discussion the subject and use the references to substantiate your claims. For example:

> Is UK education research of the quality that the taxpaying public have a right to expect? It has many deficiencies according to Gorard (2002, 2004). These include . . .

In this way as well as making the more important issue the topic of discussion, you can avoid repetition. If two (or more) authors or studies say similar things you can run their accounts together. Note that you should also avoid the opposite flaw of 'sandbagging', where each point or sentence is accompanied by a bracketed list of dozens of references. Sometimes, of course, you will make a deliberate choice to focus on one study for detailed discussion, not because that is how your notes were taken but because it is interesting enough to be a topic in its own right. It may be a key finding, or a particularly innovative piece of research that appears to contradict the rest of the field. It is also often a very poor piece of research that you want to focus on, because it is not enough simply to disagree with something or to write it off as poor. If there is a study in your area that would be important if its findings were true but with which you disagree then you owe it to the author of that study and to your readers to explain why, in more detail. This means, of course, that when you are searching for and reading literature you do not throw away or ignore poor research. You use it to illustrate why your own conclusion is not going to take it into account.

Thus, summarising evidence is not simply a question of vote-counting. Intellectual argument does not rely, at least initially, on any kind of democracy. Ten studies may conclude one thing, and only two the opposite but the two studies may have the right answer. Perhaps the ten studies had not used the quality control principle and so had no comparator, or something similarly essential for making the claims they do. Maybe their support is circular, citing each other, and making it difficult to locate the primary evidence on which any original claim was based. And, of course, when summarising evidence and conclusions from evidence, the mere opinion of academic writers is irrelevant. It is for this reason, among others, that you should refrain from using extended quotations from the writing of others to 'support' your argument. What the writer says is not really any kind of *evidence*. You can summarise what they say if it is important (and incidentally therefore also avoid any appearance of plagiarism). There are a few occasions when you might want to quote another author directly. If you are going to dispute what they say then it is important to be accurate and so only fair to put their position in their own words (to avoid the 'straw person' error). And just occasionally a good writer has expressed what you want to say so perfectly, succinctly, or wittily that you quote them in admiration.

You should present your evidence as part of an argument. Evidence only becomes informative, rather than being dull facts, when placed in the relevant context of an argument. This argument might consist of a claim or conclusion that you want to draw, grounds for the claim, which is where your existing evidence comes in, the warrant linking the grounds logically to the claim, and any qualifiers and reservations (Toulmin *et al.*, 1979).

WHAT KIND OF EVIDENCE IS MISSING?

I have been critical of the quality and usefulness of much education research, too much of which seems to have been conducted for the sake of it with no genuine curiosity or concern for scrupulousness. It follows then that what I would like to see is far less of this 'fake' research and far more genuine attempts to answer explicit and relevant questions (Gorard, 2004, 2005). I know that people find this plea unsatisfying since it is so generic, specifying neither topics nor methods to be used. But that is the situation we face. There is no magic bullet of methods or topic. Increasing the proportion of 'quantitative' research, having more randomised controlled trials, or more work on pre-school is not, in itself, likely to improve anything. Put another way, persuading a researcher who currently does sloppy work involving interviews with primary school teachers to undertake a sloppy questionnaire with secondary school parents, for example, will lead to no overall improvement in the quality of research. Education really needs new people (you perhaps) who care much more about the quality of their research results. The sceptical quality principle – if the conclusion I want to draw were not true how else could I explain the evidence? – is of greatest help if we can persuade researchers to use it from the outset. At the beginning of a new study it would help researchers to consider the kind of evidence they would need in order to be able to draw the kinds of conclusions they want to (Gorard and Cook, 2007).

Imagine that a researcher wanted to help decide whether some new kind of school (perhaps Academies in England) 'performed' better than the kind of school it replaced (perhaps the 'bog standard comprehensive'). The sceptical principle immediately reminds the researcher that they need a comparator. So they imagine comparing Academies with their predecessor schools. But even if the exam scores in Academies are higher than in predecessor schools it would be easy to find alternatives to the explanation that Academies therefore performed better. Many other things may have changed over time as well, including the prevalence of exam scores. Every year qualifications tend to rise across all schools (more students get more high grades at GCSE or equivalent, for example). So the question is not whether scores in Academies rise but whether they rise faster than in other schools or faster than they would have been predicted to rise in the predecessor schools. So now the researcher realises they need at least two comparators – the predecessor schools and the non-Academy existing schools. Another thing that might change over time is the student intake to the Academies. As a consequence of new building or extra funding perhaps the Academies are attracting a different kind of student. If these students have higher prior attainment at primary school than the previous student intake of the predecessor school then we would expect higher scores from the Academies anyway, even if they did not perform any better as schools. So we need to look not at the raw scores of students but at the scores of equivalent students in the three groups (Academies, predecessor schools, and existing non-Academies). And so on. All of this and much more becomes quite clear before the study takes place, simply by imagining how it would be possible to warrant a claim that Academies were or were not more effective than the kinds of schools they replaced.

Thus, we could avoid the kind of weak 'research' that fills most UK education research journals. Using such an approach both as authors and as reviewers of the work of others, it simply should not be possible for researchers to make comparative claims without a comparator, and other distressingly common errors. What I am talking about here is an emphasis on design. Design is not about the topic, approach, research questions or methods used. What we need more of is research in which these elements hang together logically in a coherent design (http://www.tlrp.org/rcbn/capacity/Links.html).

I will end by suggesting just four areas in which I feel future research could be crucial, but this can only be a partial picture.

1 Rigorous teaching experiments (or design experiments) examining different techniques and pedagogies are essential to discover how to help students of all ages to learn best. At present research tends to be dismissed in favour of professional judgement (perhaps rightly so), but in the cumulation of small-scale practitioner work with professional judgement we can hope for the best of both kinds of knowledge to work together and not in stand off.
2 Decades of work in the sociology of education tradition have shown that student background, including socio-economic status and prior attainment, makes a difference to school outcomes and beyond. But no one has satisfactorily addressed why this is so. Raking through data from the past can only advance the field so far. We need more genuinely evaluated interventions, to try to find out.
3 We all know that teachers make a difference, in comparison to not having a teacher. But it is also assumed that different teachers are differentially effective. If this is actually true it ought to be easy to establish via randomised controlled trials, and so provide pointers for the improvement of others.

4 Above all, we need to educate the potential users of evidence from education research about what evidence they can rely on and what they ought to ignore. Currently, academic writers on the impact of research seem to assume that all research is good and should simply be taken more account of. But practitioners and policy-makers, while paying lip-service to evidence-based approaches, actually ignore research because they know much of it is flawed. This stand-off requires several changes, the most important of which are that academics start rejecting poor research and that users start recognising good research (Gorard, 2008).

SUMMARY

This chapter looked at the range of evidence relating to educational studies that can be explored, including studies done by the government, charities and international bodies, as well as individual academic research, and discussed ways of finding and using this evidence, whether primary data, collected by yourself, secondary data, collected by others, or tertiary evidence, the interpretations others have drawn from this data. It is equally important to be able to assess the quality and usefulness of evidence once found, and thus it is vital to ask the quality-control question: 'If the conclusion(s) of each report were not actually true how else could we explain the evidence they found?'. Finally, possible areas for future research were suggested.

KEY QUESTIONS

1. What are the advantages and costs of using different kinds of evidence?
2. How can I find a wider range of evidence in my own area of interest?
3. What one thing would I do to improve the use of research evidence in education?

FURTHER READING

Booth, W., Colomb, G. and Williams, J. (1995) *The craft of research*, Chicago: University of Chicago Press

Gorard, S. (2002) Fostering scepticism: the importance of warranting claims, *Evaluation and Research in Education*, 16, 3, 136–149

Toulmin, S., Rieke, R. and Janik, A. (1979) *An introduction to reasoning*, New York: Macmillan

This chapter links with readings 21, 22 and 23 of *The Routledge Education Studies Reader.*

CHAPTER 18

DOING EDUCATIONAL RESEARCH

Alan Sears

The rationale for this chapter is:

- to present educational research as a public enterprise designed to inform policy discussions about practice in the field;
- to provide an overview of key approaches to educational research including attention to the philosophical assumptions underlying each; the kinds of questions asked; and the research methods employed;
- to describe how research develops from general topics through focused research questions to the design of specific studies.

INTRODUCTION

Education is a contentious area of public policy that is almost always embroiled in some kind of crisis or overlapping crises. Headlines and media reports send out a constant stream of worries such as: children cannot read or calculate at appropriate levels; bullying makes school intolerable for many students; international test scores indicate students in one country are significantly behind those in others in important areas of skills and knowledge; obesity is growing to epidemic proportions despite school programmes in health and physical education; and young people are disengaging from civic responsibilities while schools are doing too little to foster good citizenship. These are just some of the many issues that have animated discussions and debates about educational policy and practice in the recent, and not so recent, past.

Unfortunately, these deliberations more often take the form of 'debates in ignorance' (Sears, 1989, p. 158) than informed consideration. That is, public policy discussions about education are often not informed by evidence accumulated from research and practice but driven by participants' common sense notions of what might work or not work. The trouble is, however, more than a century of research in the field demonstrates that common sense ideas about teaching and learning 'are often common nonsense' (Gardner, 2006, p. 3).

There are two reasons for this propensity for uninformed debate in the field. First, as Richardson (2006) points out, 'We have a unique situation in education. Nearly everyone has been a student, and on the basis of that experience, many claim knowledge of the field, perhaps even consider themselves to be experts.' Unfortunately, as Richardson goes on to contend, 'Their beliefs are deep, strong and often incorrect, or at least misguided and unworkable' (p. 258). Second, educational scholarship has often been dominated by advocacy rather than research literature. In other words, much has been written about what we should do with relatively little systematic investigation of whether or how any of that works.

The good news is that in many areas the latter situation is changing. As will be discussed below, important bodies of research are being developed in education and these have the potential to enrich the conversations that scholars, practitioners and the public have about how best to conduct the enterprise. The purpose of this chapter is to introduce research in the field through an examination of the multiple forms research in education takes; how research develops to produce substantial bodies of knowledge; and the ways in which educational research is used (and sometimes abused). By introducing educational research in this way, I want to begin the process of including you in an informed conversation about educational practice; just the type of conversation good research should stimulate.

THE MULTIPLE VARIETIES AND FORMS OF EDUCATIONAL RESEARCH

Before describing the range of forms research takes in education, I will focus on the word itself. Research is a common term used often in many situations. Depending on the situation, it can mean very different things. High school or university undergraduate students, for example, talk about doing research in order to write a paper for a course and what they normally mean is reading articles and books written by others in order to pull together relevant information for their work. Someone planning a trip will talk about doing research in order to chart the best route or find out what kind of attractions and activities are available at their destination. Another person planning to buy a new car might do research on which vehicles have the best fuel efficiency or safety ratings. All of these are quite legitimate uses of the word research and they all have an important element in common: the activities are focused on accumulating information that is already available. Research from this perspective is simply a matter of finding existing knowledge. This, however, is not what I mean by educational research.

While educational research is rooted in and flows from an understanding of the knowledge and information already available, its primary purpose is the creation of new knowledge. Educational researchers do read books and articles already written on their field of study, but they do so not only to find what is already known but also where there are gaps in knowledge. They want to find out what remains unknown. Their research is then designed to create new knowledge to fill in some of those spaces.

I will take an example from my own work as an illustration. Research on cognition over the past century has demonstrated that people come to learning situations with well-developed cognitive frameworks that Howard Gardner (2006) calls 'mental representations' (p. 76). Learners use these frameworks to interpret, shape, and classify new learning. Good teaching, therefore, requires taking students' pre-existing cognitive frames into account. As Gardner writes, 'If one wants to educate for genuine understanding, then it is important to identify these early representations, appreciate their power, and confront them directly and repeatedly' (p. 77).

A problem in social education generally, and citizenship education in particular, is that not much is known about students' conceptions of key ideas related to the social world (Hughes & Sears, 1996). My colleagues and I decided to begin a research programme to address the lack of knowledge in this area. Over the past ten years we have been conducting research into how children and young people understand ideas like ethnic diversity, dissent and democratic participation (Chareka & Sears 2005; 2006; Peck & Sears, 2005; Peck, Sears & Donaldson, 2008). This programme of work has helped develop a more complete picture of children's understandings of the social world.

While educational research includes myriad forms and approaches, a common purpose of it all is to contribute new knowledge or insights to the field. A number of other characteristics are common to all research but two of particular importance are:

1 'Research is disciplined inquiry characterized by accepted principles' (McMillan, 2004, p. 4). Discipline and rigour are characteristics of all good research in education. All approaches to educational research include well worked-out and generally agreed-upon standards of practice for things such as setting questions, collecting and analysing data, reporting results, and drawing out the implications of those results. These standards are set by the community of scholars working in particular traditions and maintained by peer review and other collegial procedures. Standards do evolve, but in the context of discussion within the intersecting communities of research and practice, not based on the whims of individual researchers.

2 Research is a public endeavour. Richardson (2006) argues a major purpose of scholarship in education is 'to help understand and improve the enterprise' (p. 252). If the knowledge generated by research is going to improve education it has to be shared, argued about, refined, and reexamined. Fundamental to the research process is the publication and discussion of results in conference presentations, journal articles, books, websites, professional workshops, and other public venues. At its core research is about informing discussions and decisions regarding what constitutes good practice in education and to do that it must be a public enterprise from start to finish.

With these commonalities in mind, I will now move on to consider the range of approaches to educational research. There are a number of possible ways to categorise research approaches or paradigms around issues such as the philosophical premises underlying particular approaches; the kinds of methods used for collecting and analysing data; relationships between researchers and others involved in the work; and beliefs about how findings, and implications that flow from them, might be applied. For the purposes of the discussion here, I will use four categories: analytic, quantitative, qualitative, and critical. Keep in mind that any such categorisation is somewhat arbitrary and fails to do justice to the complex and overlapping nature of the categories. Models like this do, however, help illustrate important differences among approaches to research. Space does not allow for a full exploration of each so what follows is a very general summary.

Analytical research: Issues of language and logic

Analytical research in education is generally rooted in the disciplines of philosophy, history, and sociology. It focuses on close examination of language and policies, trying to determine the range of meanings of key concepts and how logically and consistently these are worked out in policy and practice over time. Conceptual philosophy is one of the major fields in this approach and research in this tradition focuses on the often contested meanings of concepts. Participants in educational discussions and debates often use the same terms but with different meanings. Coherent and effective policy depends partly on shared understandings of key ideas and their implications. Current debates about standards provide a good example. Virtually everyone agrees that there should be standards in education but that can mean very different things. For some, standards are general goals toward which to work; for others, standards are precise measures of achievement that can and should be regularly assessed and reported on. Standards are sometimes developed collaboratively by teachers and policy makers paying close attention to the relevant conceptual frameworks of students, but more often are imposed on education systems from above with little or no reference to the characteristics of students or particular teaching and learning contexts (Peck, Sears & Donaldson, 2008). The meanings adopted for policy concepts like standards make a big difference in what actually happens in educational systems, schools, and classrooms. Good conceptual analysis makes clear the range of possible meanings for these ideas and the implications of adopting particular ones.

Analytical work on citizenship and character education provides another example of research in this field. Like many other countries across the democratic world, England has recently introduced major initiatives in these areas. Both fields are infused with the language of good citizenship and some people think they are synonymous. Davies and his colleagues (Davies, Gorard & McGuinn, 2005) examined programmes in each, however, and found that while they make common claims, they are quite different in terms of: 'academic traditions; curricular organization; preferred view of the relationship between individuals and the state; curricular content; attitude toward "right" answers; attitude toward stages of learning' (p. 347). They go on to argue that, 'Character and citizenship exponents view the purpose of teaching very differently. Generally, character educators insist on the acceptance of "right" answers by learners' while 'in citizenship education it is common for teachers to use a dynamic exploration of dilemmas within a specific framework of values and that this is very different from the insistence on right answers from at least some of the character educators' (p. 350). This kind of detailed analysis can help policy makers and practitioners decide which type of programme would work best for their purposes and avoid having areas of the curriculum operating at crosspurposes to one another.

Analytical research in education, then, closely examines premises and practices that are often taken for granted. This kind of scrutiny often reveals important new insights and possible directions.

Quantitative research: Issues of predictability and prescription

For most of its time as a distinct field educational research has been dominated by work in the quantitative paradigm. Work of this nature emerged from experimental and correlational research in psychology and sociology. It is generally focused on discovering predictable patterns in human behaviour and institutions and using those discoveries to make policy prescriptions. Central to the quality of this work is the creation of valid and reliable instruments (usually tests and surveys) to measure relevant variables. Common 'outcome variables' include student achievement, beliefs, and attitudes, while typical 'predictor variables' are socio-economic status (SES), demographic characteristics (age, gender, urban/rural) and particular school programmes or initiatives (Kahane & Sporte, 2008, p. 746).

Research in this tradition is often conducted on a very large scale. Kahane and Sporte (2008), for example, studied the impact of civic education programmes on students' levels of commitment to participation and included data from 4,057 students from 52 high schools across the city of Chicago. They were interested in the relationship between a range of predictor variables and students' commitment to civic engagement. They found that

> experiences that focus directly on civic and political issues and ways to act (e.g. undertaking service learning projects, following current events, discussing problems in the community and ways to respond, providing students with a classroom in which open dialogue about controversial issues is common and where students study topics that matter to them, and exposure to civic role models) are highly efficacious means of fostering commitments to civic participation.
>
> (p. 754)

They go on to argue these findings have clear implications for policy and programme development.

Not all quantitative work is carried out on such a large scale. Curtis (1980) conducted a quasi-experimental study to find out if an approach to teaching social studies that included discussion of current public issues would enhance the critical thinking abilities of slow learners. The study included 225 students in eight classrooms. The students were given a pre-test and then for four months experimental classes were taught using the treatment programme while control classes

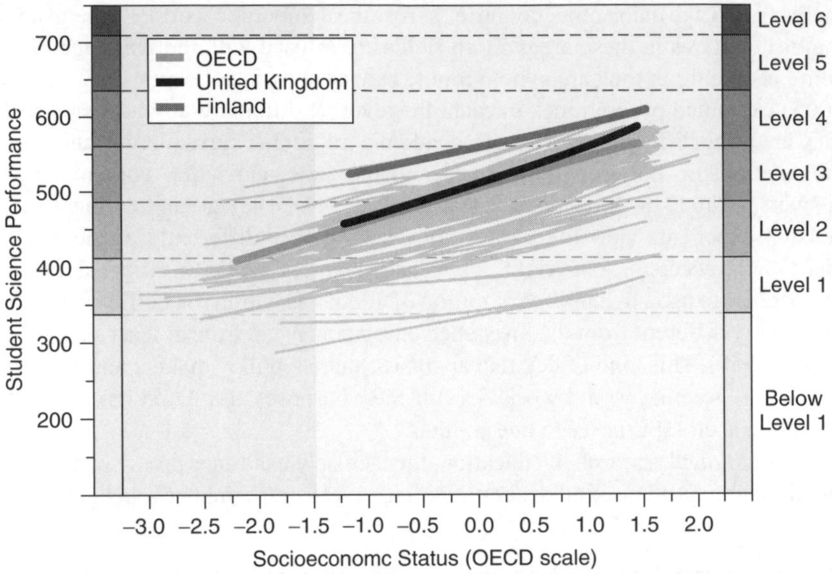

Figure 18.1 Socio-economic gradients for England and Finland

continued with the normal programme. Following the treatment period a post-test was given and the scores compared. Curtis concluded, 'that the treatment program had a significant effect upon critical thinking skills' (p. 81).

An interesting programme of quantitative research in education is on studies of predictor and outcome variables associated with international achievement tests including the Programme for International Student Assessment (PISA) and the Progress in International Reading Study (PIRLS). Part of this research examines the correlations between SES and student achievement, which are often reported as socio-economic gradients like the two shown in Figure 18.1 (Willms, 2006). The relatively steep gradient for England emphasises the gap in achievement between students with lower SES and those with higher SES. The higher and flatter gradient for Finland shows achievement is both higher on average and much more even in that country. In exploring other predictor variables it is clear that a key factor in the difference between countries is the degree of streaming or tracking in the educational systems. Jurisdictions that separate students into streams or tracks in school based on academic ability tend to have results more like England while those that do not stream students produce results more like Finland. This finding has generated calls to eliminate streaming in many countries.

Quantitative research in education focuses on discovering variables that are well-founded predictors of school improvement and student progress and using those findings to prescribe interventions to improve education.

Qualitative research: Issues of interpretation and understanding

Over the past 30 years research in the qualitative paradigm has come to the fore in education. This orientation to research largely emerged from work in anthropology, sociology and feminist theory drawing on specific approaches such as ethnography, phenomenology, grounded theory, and action research. Scholars working in this tradition were concerned about the dominance of quantitative research and would join Barr (2008) in arguing, 'The world does not consist . . . of mere repetition, but of individual, contingent, unique, and unrepeatable events' (p. 30). Their concern is not to identify large-scale trends that can be used to make predictions about what will and will not work in educational policy and practice but, rather, to interpret the unique and multileveled meanings of particular educational contexts and experiences as well as to understand how those meanings shape institutions, relationships, and practices.

Qualitative work is almost always small in scale in terms of the number of participants but makes up for limited numbers by developing 'thick description'; that is, description that explains particular situations at a number of levels and from a range of perspectives. This kind of research often takes much longer to carry out as it can involve extensive fieldwork.

Eyre (1991), for example, spent a year following a class of year 8 students in the home economics/technical studies component of their programme. She had been a home economics teacher involved in advocating an end to segregation by sex in home economics and technical studies classes. She wanted to find out how that policy reform actually played out on the ground with a particular class in a large city in Western Canada. Typical of this kind of research, Eyre collected several types of data including detailed field notes of her observations in class; interviews with teachers and students; and a personal diary of her 'subjective experience in the research enterprise' (p. 197). She sought to confirm her interpretations of these data by showing the transcripts of her notes to the teachers involved and talking with them about her emerging analysis. This kind of member-check is used quite frequently in qualitative research and emphasises the commitment to a collaborative relationship with participants central to the paradigm.

Eyre's study provides a deep and layered look at the relationships in this class and how they constructed and reinforced particular conceptions of femininity and masculinity. Among her more disturbing findings was that 'misogyny and homophobia is a serious problem. Classroom observations day after day showed that a group of boys not only dominated student–teacher interaction, but they also corrected, interrupted and ridiculed girls and quieter boys and woman teachers' (p. 215). For Eyre it is clear that more has to be done than developing progressive policy statements or simply allowing boys and girls access to the same programmes. She writes, 'Gender equity involves more than questions of access, sex stereotyping, and gender bias in student–teacher interactions'. Among other things 'it means understanding the inequities that result when traditional power relations enter into our daily lives in classrooms' (p. 217).

Like virtually all qualitative researchers, Eyre does not claim her findings are widely generalisable or that they can be used to predict outcomes or prescribe reforms for other contexts. She writes, 'Although I gave careful attention to the accuracy of findings, the information presented here does not claim to represent reality' (p. 198). This does not mean the findings are completely idiosyncratic and cannot be used by others, but that others must make their own sense of the implications of the findings for them and the contexts in which they work. Eyre again, 'Readers must take it from here and mediate it through their own experiences' (p. 198).

As Eisner (1998) points out, qualitative researchers do not rely on representative samples or statistically valid and reliable instruments for assessing the quality, trustworthiness, and implications of their research but on three general criteria:

- coherence – the degree to which the account makes sense and is well supported;
- consensus – the degree to which the findings resonate with other work in the area and readers' own experiences; and
- instrumental utility – the degree to which the account helps in bringing some insight and clarity to other contexts and situations.

Qualitative research in education focuses on interpreting and understanding particular educational experiences and contexts. It seeks to lay bare the meanings of those experiences and situations for the various people involved and explore those meanings in light of relevant social theory. Its findings are presented not as prescriptive truths to be implemented, but as contingent perspectives to be explored and assessed by others in light of their own circumstances.

CRITICAL RESEARCH: ISSUES OF IDEOLOGY AND HEGEMONY

Critical research in education emerges from continental philosophy and, in particular, postmodernism and critical theory. It is overtly political, seeking to expose the underlying ideologies inherent in educational structures, relationships and arguments and, most importantly, to show where those have become hegemonic – or taken for granted as natural and right. Critical researchers are interested in issues of power: who has it; who does not have it; how it is used to privilege some groups and marginalise others; and how situations of unequal power relations can be exposed, resisted, and changed. Researchers in this tradition pay close attention to discourse, institutional structures, and relationships between and among participants in educational enterprises.

Nason and her colleagues, for example, are particularly interested in the relationships between parents, schools, and educational professionals and how those relationships are expressed in institutional arrangements and practices (Gorham & Nason, 1997; Nason, 1997). Despite considerable policy rhetoric about the importance of parental involvement in their children's education, these researchers argue that parents, particularly poor ones, are often seen by educational professionals as at best secondary assistants in the educational enterprise or, at worst, as hindrances. Traditionally, they claim, educators see parents as people who can assist in processes and procedures that are determined by the professionals and not as collaborators who might make valuable contributions in their own right to the education of their children.

In one study Nason (1997) 'examines the practices and products of school culture: jokes, hallway conversations, home–school correspondences and interpersonal interactions between parents and teachers' (p. 117). Quite contrary to the ideal of partnerships, she argues, these practices constitute parents 'in the subordinate position, required to read only so they can follow the direction the school has set and comply with its regulations. The school orders and parents obey' (p. 119). Consistent with the concept of hegemony, Nason contends that this

> regulation of parents to a subordinate position is not a conscious deliberate or individual decision. Rather, it is a social construction, an idea which has been collectively produced. It arises from a dominant ideology which presumes the relationship between teachers and parents to be hierarchical.
>
> (p. 120)

The power of this research – its usefulness – lies in the exposing or opening up of this kind of taken for granted assumptions. Nason argues that when parents, teachers, and school administrators begin to reflect on 'how the texts of schooling relegate parents to a subordinate position' (p. 123), possibilities for resistance and reform emerge.

Critical research in education probes deeply beneath the surface of policy and practice seeking to expose the ways in which power is established, maintained, and extended through the normalising of particular ideologies. It casts itself as an explicitly democratic enterprise, dedicated to finding ways for otherwise excluded groups and individuals to resist domination and participate as equal partners in educational discourse and practice.

As Noddings (2007) points out, there are often vigorous disputes between and among practitioners of these different approaches to educational research. Quantitative research is often described as dehumanising, limiting, and out of date, while qualitative and critical approaches are criticised for not being rigorous and scientific. I agree with Noddings that there is room both for multiple kinds of research and specific studies that employ mixed methods. Most educational issues are so complex any single way of examining them is sure to leave much unknown.

Recent reform initiatives in education provide an example of this complexity. Hargreaves (2003) writes about the impact of economic globalisation and particularly what he calls 'market fundamentalism' (p. 73) on schools around the world. He documents a range of similar reforms in Britain, the USA and Canada focused on standardising practice across the field. There is no doubt the reforms

Table 18.1 Varieties of research approaches to studying the same phenomenon

Research Type	Possible Research Questions	Research Methods and Data
Analytical		
Conceptual	What is meant by the key concepts or ideas driving the reform (accountability, standards, etc.) and what implications do those meanings have for practise?	Analysis of different ways of understanding and operationalising key ideas or concepts.
Quantitative		
Correlational	Is there a relationship between components of the reform and student achievement?	Survey measures of various components of reform, data about student achievement and statistical correlation of those.
Quasi-Experimental	Does reform (or any component of it) improve student scores?	Pre-test, post-test scores of students from an experimental group (in a school which has implemented reform) and a control group (no reform) and statistical comparison of those.
Qualitative		
Case Study	How does reform impact my classroom/school?	Analysis of multiple data sets — student products (projects, test scores), interactions between students and teachers, the treatment of various subjects in the curriculum, etc.
Phenomenological	What has been the lived experience of reform for students and teachers?	Analysis of interviews with participants and/or their reflective writing about the experience.
Ethnographic	How has reform impacted the community and culture in particular schools or classrooms?	Analysis of long-term observation of schools and classrooms.
Critical	What or whose interests have been served by reform? Who has been marginalised or left out?	Analysis of the underlying assumptions of the language and practices of reform and the setting of those in the context of broader social theories and analysis.

took place including an increasingly narrow focus on literacy and numeracy; increased scrutiny of schools and teachers; and the widespread use and reporting of standardised tests. What is in doubt is the effects they have had on education. Gaining the fullest possible understanding of those effects would require examining the reforms from a number of perspectives. Table 18.1 provides an illustration of the ways in which various approaches to educational research might study this phenomenon.

HOW EDUCATIONAL RESEARCH DEVELOPS AND GROWS

Contradictory advice from researchers can be quite frustrating. It seems, for example, that almost every week health researchers discover something that contradicts what they told us only a little before. Experienced educators are able to tell similar tales of research evidence being used to justify particular reforms at one point and to attack those same reforms sometime later. If research produces such contradictory results how can we ever rely on it as a basis for acting?

Part of the problem is that recommendations are sometimes being made based on the results of one or two studies and that is almost never a solid basis for action. That is not to say the studies relied on were ill-conceived or poorly carried out, but that individual investigations are usually very narrowly focused. Substantive knowledge is normally produced by combining findings from a range of studies to build a solid platform on which to base recommendations for change. As Noddings (2007) writes, 'we do not learn a lot about the working of science simply by studying individual investigations. We must analyze *programs* of research' (p. 136, emphasis in the original). I will return to this idea later but first I want to explore the process of constructing individual studies.

Researchers come to a particular line of work for a number of reasons but a key motivation is always interest in a topic or area of study. For example, as a social studies teacher I have always been interested in citizenship education. That is a very general area, however, so when I decided that I wanted to make a contribution to research in the field I had to find an issue or question within citizenship education that had not already been fully explored. Wide reading in the field told me there were a number of big issues, one being the perceived disengagement of young people from civic life and particularly processes like voting, joining political parties and running for office. That issue was still too broad for focused research, so I had to narrow that to a researchable question. Drawing on the literature on cognition I decided to contribute to the field by helping to map young people's conceptions of democratic participation. Even then, my focus was too broad for there is no way I could study all young people or even all young people of a particular age. For each study I needed a much more focused research question such as, How do the students in a particular school or area understand democratic participation? Figure 18.2 demonstrates visually this narrowing of focus. Once an investigator arrives at the focused research questions there are still other decisions to make, such as which methods and/or procedures will best help address the question in a substantive way.

All researchers go through a similar process of moving from a general topic; through issues related to that topic; to general research questions that address gaps in knowledge related to an issue; and, finally, to the question or questions that drive their particular studies. Individual enquiries, while important, normally address very narrow areas and it normally takes a compilation of studies to build sufficient knowledge to support recommendations for policy and practice.

The narrow focus of much educational research means that individuals can often make important contributions to bodies of work with small-scale studies that do not require significant funding or large research teams. Over the past 20 years I have worked with a number of graduate students who were all educational professionals and conducted important research in or about their own work contexts – classrooms, schools or school districts. That work has ranged over all the approaches to educational research discussed above. Table 18.2 provides examples of some of that work.

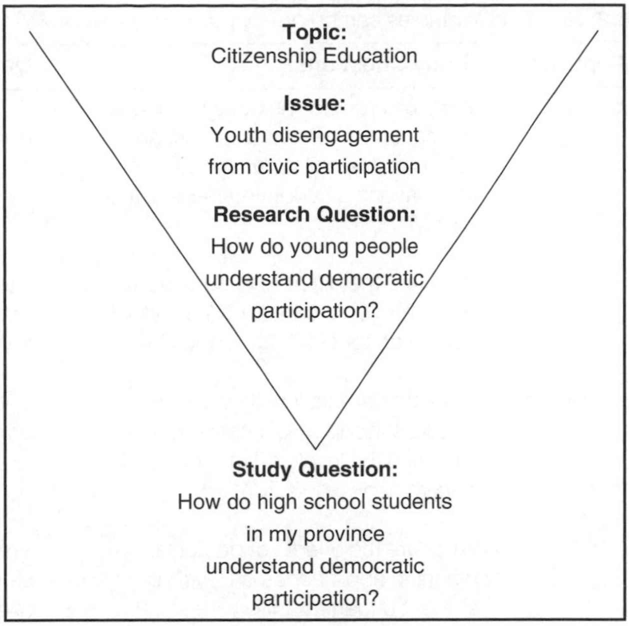

Figure 18.2 Moving from topics to study questions in educational research

All of these studies helped the researchers better understand their own work and also made a contribution to broader knowledge in the relevant areas. Graduate theses are one of the public forms research takes and are often the source of the latest work in a particular field.

Programmes of work grow in several ways. First, there is the simple cumulation of discrete studies carried out by researchers in their own settings. In this way the international history education community has developed a significant pool of complementary and overlapping small-scale research that provides a strong knowledge base for how students understand historical ideas and processes (Lévesque, 2008; Sandwell, 2006; Stearns, Seixas & Wineburg, 2000).

Second, individual research teams embark on long-term programmes of research in a single area. Brophy and his colleagues in the USA have conducted a range of studies on children's understandings of cultural universals. These have included hundreds of children across a number of cities in the US and are both a significant body of work in their own right and make a substantial contribution to broader work on the prior conceptions of students (Brophy & Alleman, 2002; Brophy, Alleman & O'Mahony, 2003; Brophy & Alleman, 2006).

Third, large-scale longitudinal studies often constitute a programme of work in and of themselves. The Citizenship Education Longitudinal Study (CELS) being carried out by the National Foundation for Educational Research (NFER) in England is a good example. Described as 'the biggest and longest-running study about the impact of citizenship education anywhere in the world' (NFER, 2008), it runs from 2001–2010 and incorporates a combination of case study visits to schools and regular large-scale surveys of students and teachers. It has already produced dozens of research reports, conference papers, journal articles and book chapters and provides a range of information on the website dedicated to the study.

Table 18.2 Small-scale studies carried out by practising educators

Research Approach	Study Questions	Data Sets
Analytical Research	What different forms does Holocaust education take in North American school systems? What are the implications of adopting particular forms?	Curriculum and policy documents related to Holocaust education.
	What are the differences between social and civic capital? What would education for civic capital look like?	Literature on social capital and civic engagement, curriculum and policy documents.
Quantitative Research	How are parents involved in local middle schools? How satisfied are they with the level and range of their involvement?	Survey data and statistical correlations.
	What are the effects of particular teaching approaches on levels of student engagement?	Pre-test, post-test measures of student and teacher perceptions of engagement.
Qualitative Research	What are year 7 students' conceptions of ethnic diversity?	Transcripts of interviews with 20 students.
	Can teaching the use of graphic organisers improve students' writing?	Transcripts of interviews with 20 students, samples of students' writing pre and post working with graphic organisers.
Critical Research	How has neo-liberalism shaped policy and practice in citizenship education?	Popular media, policy and curricular documents.
	How does the discourse of disability shape the way students are constructed by teachers and their peers?	Cultural products discussing ability/disability, experience in schools.

SUMMARY

Research can be an important tool to help improve practice in education but it is often not very well used. There are a number of reasons for this including the fact that education is a political enterprise and politicians responsible for it recognise that 'beliefs drive political action and voting intentions much more than do facts' (Levin, 2005, p. 20). Therefore their policy prescriptions are often more designed to respond to those beliefs than to act on evidence. Some reasons, however, lie within the realm of the research context itself. Research is often not offered as a tool for practitioners to use in improving their schools and classrooms but rather as a hammer with which to beat them. Educators are told they are not doing a good job or that they should uncritically implement the pronouncement of researchers. As Hargreaves (2003) points out, 'Research in best classroom practice is imposed on [teachers] rather than offered as a source of professional reflection and adaptation to their own classroom circumstances' (p. 80).

Some years ago Robert Bellah and his colleagues (Bellah *et al.*, 1985) argued that as research in social sciences became an activity almost exclusively located in universities it grew increasingly detached from policy and practice. Researchers began to write and speak in a language only they could decipher and were far more likely to pronounce than engage in discussions about the meaning and implications of their work. Bellah's team called for researchers to rethink their role and conceive of their work as 'public philosophy' (p. 302). They argued research should be 'public not just in the sense that its findings are publically available or useful to some group or institution outside the scholarly world. It is public in the sense that it seeks to engage the public in dialogue' (p. 303).

That commitment to research as a tool to foster informed dialogue about education is the central theme of this chapter. For that to happen a number of conditions need to exist including:

1. Researchers who present their results in language and forms that are accessible to practicing educators and the public;
2. Researchers who are willing to engage with educators and the public in dialogue about the implications of their work for particular contexts;
3. Educators and the public who are knowledgeable about the research process and able to ask and answer questions such as, 'Do researchers' claims correspond to what we regularly observe in schools? Do their premises, methods, and conclusions hang together in a convincing way, or are there contradictions in their accounts?' (Noddings, 2007, p. 124);
4. Educational practitioners who are researchers themselves engaging in studies of their own work and educational contexts and thereby contribute to the building of new knowledge as well as improving practice in education.

Debates about the forms education takes are often very intense because they go right to the heart of deeply held social values. As Barton and Levstik (2004) point out, research cannot tell us what to do about contested aspects of educational policy and practice, it can, however, 'force us to think about the unquestioned assumptions that impede [those] discussions' and thereby enrich them significantly. For that to happen the research process has to be open to public scrutiny and engagement at all levels.

KEY QUESTIONS

1. What is the difference between common sense and research-based knowledge?
2. Is research necessary for the improvement of education?
3. Is it possible that researchers who have conducted their work effectively can come up with contradictory findings?

FURTHER READING

Creswell, J. W. (2008). *Research Design: Qualitative, Quantitative, and Mixed Methods Approaches* (3rd ed.). London: Sage.

Eisner, E. (1998). *The Enlightened Eye: Qualitative Inquiry and the Enhancement of Educational Practice*. Upper Saddle River, New Jersey: Prentice-Hall.

Gall, M. D., Gall, J. P., & Borg, W. P. (2007). *Educational Research: An Introduction* (8th ed.). Upper Saddle River, NJ: Merrill.

This chapter links with readings 21, 22 and 23 of *The Routledge Education Studies Reader*.

DEBATE 6

EDUCATIONAL RESEARCH

A foundation for teacher professionalism?

Andrew Pollard and Mark Newman

In this chapter Andrew Pollard (Director of the UK's largest-ever programme on teaching and learning, TLRP, www.tlrp.org) and Mark Newman (Associate Director of the UK's leading centre on research synthesis, EPPI-Centre, www.eppi.ioe.ac.uk) reflect on recent debates in education about the role of research as a basis for classroom decision-making and on its implications for teacher professionalism.

ANDREW POLLARD

Teaching, professionalism and pedagogy

The expertise of teachers in making subtle and complex judgements about teaching and learning and in managing large groups of children is not very well understood in our societies. And maybe we are not too good at explaining it either? One consequence is that teachers may not get the credit and respect they deserve. Another is that governments can sometimes introduce new policies and practices with inadequate consultation.

Indeed, both media and politicians are susceptible to reaching for simple 'solutions' which fail to recognise the nature and range of the educational issues which teachers routinely consider. In this, they are sometimes encouraged by researchers offering to pinpoint 'what works' so that these methods can be disseminated to teachers for classroom application.

These are impoverished positions for two major reasons. First, the reality is that, however much we may know about effective teaching and learning, implementation is always mediated by teacher judgement. There are no magic bullets. Second, education has moral purposes and consequences, so that teaching is never simply a technical activity. As a consequence, judgements about appropriateness must always be made.

The essence of teacher professionalism might therefore be viewed as: 'the exercise of skills, knowledge and judgement about teaching, learning and education for the public good'.

But how can such a position be developed, promoted and defended so that the profession can be better understood? My view is that we need to start by reasserting the role of pedagogy and teacher expertise. Indeed, a challenging chain of argument starts from a definition of what we mean by 'pedagogy':

1 Pedagogy is the practice of teaching as informed by a structured body of knowledge and combined with moral purpose.
2 By progressively acquiring such knowledge and mastering pedagogical expertise – through initial formation, continuing development and reflective experience – teachers are entitled to be treated as professionals.
3 Teachers should scrutinise and evaluate their practice to make rationally defensible professional judgements beyond pragmatic constraints and/or ideological concerns.

Put another way, this line of reasoning suggests the various forms of reflective practice, classroom-based research and other forms of professional enquiry are essential to the improvement of teachers' own understanding and, in turn, to public perception and respect for the activity of teaching. We have to establish ourselves as an 'evidence-informed profession'.

The resources contained in my handbook on *Reflective Teaching* (Pollard *et al.*, 2008) are all about activities of this sort and will support enquiry on a very wide range of topics from classroom behaviour to curriculum planning and from pupil consultation to home–school relationships. Of course, such detailed work cannot happen all the time but the use of occasional, but explicit, classroom enquiries has been found to be extremely effective in providing reflective learning experiences. When planning a classroom study, whether a teacher or researcher, we are faced by three decisions:

1 Which facet of classroom life should be investigated and why?
2 What evidence should be collected and how?
3 How should the findings be analysed, interpreted and applied?

But teachers do not need to tackle these challenges in isolation for it has been found to be much more effective, if possible, to work as a group of colleagues working on a shared topic (e.g. MacGilchrist *et al.*, 2004).

Additionally, outputs from organisations such as the Teaching and Learning Research Programme (TLRP) have been explicitly designed to support teachers in developing the quality of evidence-informed judgements. For example, evidence from 22 TLRP school projects led to the production of a set of 'principles for effective teaching and learning'. This was sent out in poster form to all UK schools (and can be downloaded from http://www.tlrp.org/findings).

Building on experience as well as evidence, these principles seem to apply across the board and provide a yardstick for reflection and analysis.

The suggestion then is that successful policy implementation and sustainable improvement are best achieved through the expert judgement of skilled and knowledgeable professionals – and TLRP's contention is that such judgements are best informed by educational principles, rather than by decontextualised prescription. Teachers are key mediators and must use judgements about circumstances, contexts, pupils, objectives and teaching approaches, bearing in mind appropriate values, goals and educational principles.

If we can focus on this, and on processes for the continuous improvement of understanding and judgement, then the status and respect of the profession will grow. Nor should we ever forget that teaching continues to present wonderful opportunities for making a difference to the life of every child who comes through the classroom door. Today we have the evidence and the tools at our disposal to help children become skilled and enthusiastic lifelong learners, and to grow and learn themselves throughout their own lives and careers. As they develop, so should we.

MARK NEWMAN

Knowledge and professional teaching

The practice of effective teaching requires the development, use and continual updating of many different kinds of knowledge. One approach to professional reasoning (Higgs & Titchen 2000) suggests that professional reasoning comprises of three distinct types of knowledge. *Professional craft knowledge* is sometimes referred to as wisdom or intuition and concerns the procedural or practical knowledge that guides the everyday activities of practice. *Personal knowledge* can be defined as the unique frame of reference and knowledge of the self through which propositional and professional craft knowledge are translated into decisions for practice. *Propositional knowledge* is the public objective knowledge of the field that includes formal statements concerning interactional and causal relationships between events. These different types of knowledge play different roles in helping the teacher act to create learning in whichever context they are working. Each is essential to effective teaching and it is important therefore to consider how these different types of knowledge might be generated and used by the teacher.

Experience and observation lie at the heart of the development of all knowledge of social phenomena like education. What varies is the scale (number and/or depth) of the experiences and observations, the degree to which the experience/observation was undertaken systematically and the teacher's distance from the actors in the event. Table D6.1 illustrates for a sample of the main types of knowledge development experiences how they vary on these three dimensions. For each category of knowledge development experience the typical position in each category is shown. An individual teacher is obviously close to their own teaching experience but knowledge developed on the basis of personal experience will usually be less systematic because the focus of practice is on doing the job of teaching rather than collecting evidence about doing the job. Furthermore an individual's teaching experience is small compared to the total pool of teaching experiences in the world. The 'typical' position can be varied. For example developing knowledge from one's own teaching experience can be done more systematically through the use of structured approaches such as reflection and the closely related mechanism of teacher research.

Table D6.1 Characteristics of knowledge development experiences

Type of knowledge development experience	Teachers distance from actors	How systematic	Amount of experiences
Own teaching	Close	Low	Small
Training	Close	Medium	Medium
Textbook	Far	Medium	Medium
Teacher researcher	Close	High	Small
Academic research	Far	High	Large

Do these differences on each dimension matter? When answering this question there are four things we need to consider. First, we are all biased. Selective perception and memory recall appears to be an inextricable part of being human. What this means is that we tend to remember and/or favour events, actions, outcomes, in a way that fits with our pre-existing conceptions of how things are or ought to be and forget/reject those that don't fit with our pre-existing conceptions. So systematic approaches that minimise this problem may be important for certain types of knowledge. Second, if learning from others is valuable, presumably the more others we learn from the better? Third, how important these differences are will vary depending on the type of knowledge that is being generated and the use to which that knowledge is put. Finally there also appear to be some 'trade-off' type of difficulties. For example academic research may be more systematic and include a large depth or amount of experiences but it will be at a greater distance from the teacher's own experience, thus increasing the difficulty for the teacher of using the knowledge in their own practice.

The ability of teachers to recognise the type of knowledge required to address a particular practice issue, to find such knowledge, to appraise its quality and relevance, and to interpret it for their own practice environment are therefore key features of professional teaching practice. This process and the set of skills/knowledge required to apply it are what is referred to as evidence-informed practice. Evidence-based medicine was initially taken up by doctors, but in the guise of evidence-informed practice, it has been taken up also by nurses, and the professions allied to medicine, in social work and in education. It is both a model for practice decision making (see Figure D6.1) and a five-stage process for systematically considering research evidence in decision making (see Figure D6.2). As the model indicates, research is treated as one of a number of groups of factors that influence teachers' decision making. It should be obvious that this process bears the hallmarks of the process of reflection to which Andrew refers but it adds to this the explicit, systematic consideration of 'academic' research.

For propositional knowledge it would seem to be important that it is generated using an approach which is more systematic, thus reducing the effects of our individual and collective biases, and is based on as much experience as possible. For example if we want to know whether on average

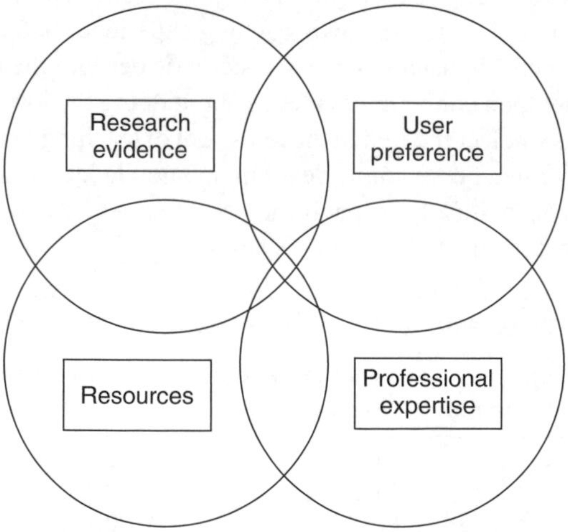

Figure D6.1 Evidence-based practice: a model for professional decision making

Source: Adapted from DiCenso, A., Cullum, N. & Ciliska, D. (1998) Implementing evidence-based nursing: some misconceptions. In *Evidence-Based Nursing* 1(2), p. 38. Reproduced with permission from BMJ Publishing Group Ltd.

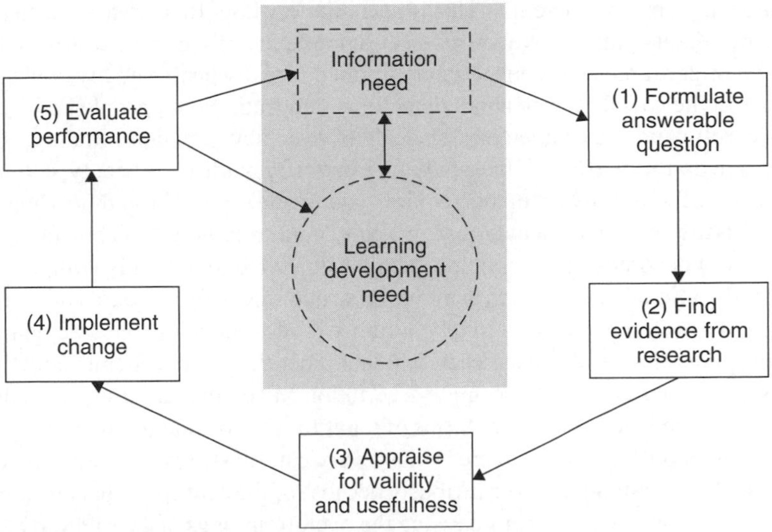

Figure D6.2 The stages of evidence-informed practice

Source: Newman, M., Thompson, C. & Roberts, A. (2006) Helping practitioners understand the contribution of qualitative research to evidence-based practice. In *Evidence-Based Nursing* 9(1), p. 6. Reproduced with permission from BMJ Publishing Group Ltd.

using phonics or the 'whole book' method is more effective for helping children to learn to read then we would have more confidence in the results of evidence collected systematically on a large scale. This is where the 'what works' type of approach is of value. What this approach is actually trying to do is identify which teaching and learning approach demonstrates better outcomes for which children in which circumstances. Where there is systematic high-quality evidence on a sufficient scale we might be persuaded that an answer that indicates that on average one approach produces better outcomes than another for a particular group of children should, unless we have good reason to think otherwise, be implemented.

However because this knowledge is generated at a distance from the teacher it presents the potentially difficult but not insurmountable problem of putting the knowledge generated to use in practice. We could, as Andrew suggests, think of such 'what works' type of presentation as 'a prescription'. But the caveat's 'on average' and 'unless we have good reason to think otherwise' are important. The individual teacher will need to use her expert professional craft knowledge to work out whether and how the results of the academic research, i.e. the propositional knowledge, apply to the children whom they are teaching. Just as in medicine 'the prescription' is given not by the researcher but by the practitioner who interprets the evidence and decides on the basis of their expert knowledge of their craft and of their students to whom and how the indicated approach should be used.

ANDREW POLLARD: RESPONSE TO MARK NEWMAN

The role of teacher judgement: a response

Mark makes a lot of important points, but what are the foundations of his argument? The first element is the concept of 'propositional knowledge'. He expertly defines this as 'public, objective knowledge of the field that includes formal statements concerning interactional and causal relationships between events'. This is an extremely important idea because it sets a standard of scientific understanding. However, given the complexity of social processes such as teaching and learning, I wonder if the confident certainty implied is really possible? My doubt reflects a long-running debate in the social science about objectivity and truth. Some people believe it is possible, through very careful and systematic research designs, to achieve categoric findings. Others, and I am one of them, are doubtful. It's a bit like studying a butterfly, with all its beauty, colour and movement, if the precision of your measurements requires you to stick a pin through it! I'm exaggerating of course, but the issues have technical terms – 'validity' and 'reliability'. So one fundamental question in this discussion becomes: Is it possible to achieve knowledge of highly complex teaching, learning and other educational issues which achieve the strong scientific standards of propositional knowledge?

My preference here is to take a rather modest position. This demands the same rigour and open-mindedness of the researcher, whether practitioner or academic, and the same search for patterns in the data to generate accurate description and evidence-informed analysis. But such findings are then placed alongside other forms of input for the consideration of the classroom practitioner or government policy-maker. There is thus a very careful struggle to understand and an expectation to have such understanding taken seriously because of the care taken, but no claim to privileged insight. This is the reason why, in summarising the overall findings of TLRP, Mary James and I (James and Pollard, 2006) used the concept of '*principles*' of effective teaching and learning. We feel that there is lots of evidence that the principles we identified contain some important insights – but the relative openness of the concept calls for significant professional input in application.

There is a second foundation of Mark's argument which I think we need to notice. This concerns the consequence of being 'close to' or 'far from' the action. Being close, in reflecting on one's own practice, seems to be a problem because of being less systematic and having a small range of experiences – and human selectivity distorts our perception. On the other hand, the inherent human capacity to make sense of situations means that teachers do develop the capability to interpret events in their context. Mark treats this as risking 'bias', which of course is perfectly correct in terms of pure research design. However, it is exactly this capacity to interpret the meaning of patterns of evidence in context which makes professional judgement so valuable. Indeed, in a sense, it is the essence of professional expertise as deployed by lawyers, doctors, social workers, teachers, etc.

It is worth noticing too that, in his initial response to my text, Mark has not mentioned the 'moral purposes' of teaching or the observations which I made about this issue. I don't actually think that he takes the view that teaching is simply a technical matter, though an emphasis on 'what works' can, in some hands, sometimes give this impression. My view that the effectiveness and moral purpose are inextricably linked in pedagogic practice is another reason why I think we have to place considerable reliance on the quality of professional judgement. This has big implications for initial and continuing teacher education of course which is reflected strongly in the requirements of at least three countries of the UK.

Of course, Mark and I are not at all far apart when it comes to his suggestion that it is necessary for teachers to be able to recognise the 'type of knowledge' required, to judge its quality and relevance, and interpret it for application. Indeed, I can readily identify with Mark's models of overlapping types of knowledge and of the stages of evidence-informed practice (see the similar concepts in Pollard *et al.*, 2008: Chapter 1).

Now why should all this matter? Well, there is a big difference between a profession which waits to be told 'what works' and one which plays an active part in the generation of its own professional expertise. In recent decades the extent of central control has grown enormously – first over the curriculum, then assessment, then pedagogy and accountability. Standards arguably did rise for a time. However, these have levelled off to a considerable extent and many countries round the world are re-evaluating the merit of large-scale, centralised policy prescription. Has the time now come to trust teachers more? Will new policies based on this propensity, in the end, be more beneficial for learners?

The answer to this question will, in large part, depend on the way in which teachers tackle the dilemma which Mark and I have posed in this discussion. To really connect to the learners in one's classroom, contextual validity is vital. But constant awareness of the nature of the available evidence is also extremely important. There are some good technical terms for this too. What is the 'warrant' of the finding being claimed or the judgement being made? Is the evidence dependable?

If teachers can rise to this challenge, can find ways of drawing on both academic research and contextual insight, then we might just get somewhere in raising the expertise and status of the profession.

MARK NEWMAN: RESPONSE TO ANDREW POLLARD

Understanding the warrant of knowledge claims: a response

Andrew raises many issues in his original argument and his response to my initial argument. As he points out I have not explored all of the points he makes as I feel there are too many of great complexity to do justice in this short space available here. On the issue of the purposes of 'teaching' I am happy enough with the goal of 'facilitating learning' the complexity of which, as I have already indicated, requires the development and application of different types of knowledge of which knowledge of the self (which may correspond to Andrew's 'moral purpose') is one.

In his response Andrew argues that the basis of my initial argument is the claim that there can exist something that I referred to as 'propositional knowledge' and wonders whether this and the 'certainty implied' can ever be the case in such a complex field as education. However *he* also refers in his original argument to the 'structured body of knowledge' that underpins teaching and learning and in his response he also refers to the 'principles for effective teaching and learning' developed by the TLRP. I find this confusing as 'structured body of knowledge' sounds to me very much like the 'propositional knowledge', i.e. knowledge of 'interactions' and 'causal relationships between events' that I referred to in my initial argument. And furthermore the Oxford English dictionary defines 'principle' as 'a fundamental truth or a general law or doctrine that is used as the basis of reasoning or action' and/or specific laws of physics, nature, etc. Again this sounds to me rather like the propositional knowledge I was referring to. Furthermore the TLRP principles can certainly be read as 'prescriptions'. For example 'Effective pedagogy promotes the active engagement of the learner' seems to me much like saying that to be effective your teaching should promote active learning.

There are different types of propositional knowledge that may be generated in different ways. Some of these will use particular research designs and concomitant measures to estimate effects. However to cast this as a claim of or for 'certainty' is I feel a misinterpretation (albeit one in which researchers themselves can sometimes overenthusiastically promote). Rather, such studies provide an estimate of effect and seek to estimate the range of *uncertainty* of that effect should these results apply in a wider population/context. It is therefore important that the context in which such studies are carried out is reported in great detail and in this sense such research is not any more decontextualised than for example the TLRP's principles. However as with all propositional knowledge it is decontextualised from its intended place of use. This caveat is of course important and as I indicated in my earlier argument the further the research is carried out from the intended place of application the more difficult such judgements become.

The variations I referred to in Table D6.1 raise for the individual teacher the issue of 'which' knowledge to choose to act upon in what way. Let's take an example. Imagine you are a secondary school mathematics teacher who wants to do something to improve the mathematics capabilities of your students. Your Head of Mathematics, who has 20-plus years of teaching experience and whose students appear to understand maths well (and get good grades), tells you that setting lots of individual tests and tasks according to individual student ability is the way to improve grades. You also come across a systematic review of evidence about interventions for middle and high school mathematics. This states that that there is strong evidence of effectiveness for something called 'power teaching' – a cooperative learning programme in which students work in four-member heterogeneous groups to help each other master academic content, and teachers follow a schedule of teaching, team work, and individual assessment (Slavin, Lake & Groff, 2008). What do you do? Both recommendations are 'prescriptive' in tone and both combine propositional, personal and professional knowledge. Both, insofar as the limited framing of the teacher's question permits, would appear to correspond with the TLRP's evidence-informed pedagogic principles and both sources present evidence claims that say that their particular approach will lead to improved learning in your students. But they would appear to be opposing pedagogic strategies. Surely they cannot both be correct?

Actually both could be correct, both could be wrong or one correct and the other not. Let's assume that they are indeed different strategies (the ascertainment of which would require more information than provided here). How could they both be correct? To take just one possible explanation the Head of Mathematics may teach the 'top' group of students, i.e. those who through some mechanism have been identified as already having a greater understanding of mathematics. For this group of students setting individual tasks and exercises may be an effective pedagogic strategy. The systematic review however was concerned with 'average' students, i.e. students whose mathematics abilities run across the ability spectrum. If you were teaching a group of high-ability mathematics students, all other things being equal, you might want to try the Head of Mathematics strategy and see how it worked, but presumably you would want to check and see if there were any other evidence to support this approach. If however, you are teaching mathematics to a mixed-ability group then you might want to try the 'power teaching' approach. As Andrew points out, the important issue is that an individual teacher needs to be able to understand the strengths and weaknesses (i.e. the warrants) of any particular 'knowledge claim' in order to make a professional judgement about the potential consequences of applying any recommended pedagogical approach in her own setting. As the discussion above illustrates, both sources of evidence are potentially valuable.

I would agree with Andrew that the importance of this aspect has been underplayed in many recent debates about the use of evidence to improve teaching and learning in that the efforts to help teachers develop the skills and knowledge to use research to inform their decisions have been comparatively limited. Perhaps even more importantly there appears to have been little discussion about how the cultural and organisational contexts in which teachers work affects their capacity for the necessary structured reflection. Further with few notable exceptions (such as the various TLRP projects that have explored 'pupil voice') I would also argue that there appears to have been even less attention paid to involving parents and pupils in these decision-making processes.

This is not only an issue for 'policymakers' (whoever they may be) but also for the teaching profession itself. In discussion on this issue with colleagues who are involved in teacher education, I have often heard the response that this is something for 'Masters' level courses and/or to be developed through engagement in 'teacher research'. But teachers start their teaching as soon as they are qualified and should surely have the capability and capacity to critically appraise, interpret and apply all propositional knowledge (including research) at this point also.

CONCLUSION FROM ANDREW POLLARD AND MARK NEWMAN

There are many shared perspectives between Mark and Andrew. For example, both highlight the importance of reflection and teachers' professional judgement in the process of making decisions about pedagogy. There are however also some key differences which may have significant potential consequences for policy, practice and the role of teachers' professional judgement. Mark argues that 'what works' type research is just one type of propositional knowledge no different to any other. Andrew raises a concern with the claims to certainty implied by those who believe that 'what works' can be scientifically identified. He points to an important tension in Mark's reasoning in that the personal knowledge of the teacher which may make them susceptible to bias is also the knowledge which makes them uniquely capable of making professional judgements about practice in their own setting.

Andrew advocates a more cautious approach to science suggesting that evidence-informed 'principles' about teaching and learning are a sufficient guide to teacher decision making. This has the advantage of not prescribing decisions and makes clear the role of expert judgement – thus providing a rationale for teacher professionalism and, consequentially, for public trust and esteem. However, Mark suggests that such principles are still based on a form of propositional knowledge and look not at all dissimilar to prescriptions. He argues that all forms and sources of knowledge including 'what works' are potentially useful.

Both Andrew and Mark suggest that the exercise of professional judgement and development of teachers' ability to understanding the warrants for particular knowledge claims should be given more priority in teacher initial training and in continuing professional development.

KEY QUESTIONS

1. What is meant by 'evidence-based practice' in relation to education?
2. To what extent can we develop an overarching sense of what works in education?
3. Which individuals or groups should be responsible for deciding what counts as good practice and how should they reach that decision?

FURTHER READING

Cohen, L., Manion, L. & Morrison, K. (2007) *Research Methods in Education* (6th ed) (pages 289–296, on evidence-based educational research and meta-analysis). London: Routledge.

Pollard, A., Anderson, J., Maddock, M., Swaffield, S., Warin, J. & Warwick, P. (2008) *Reflective Teaching: Evidence-informed Professional Practice* (3rd ed) (pages 3–30 on reflective teaching and 47–87 on developing an evidence-informed classroom). London: Continuum.

This debate links with readings 15, 21, 22 and 23 of *The Routledge Education Studies Reader.*

REFERENCES

CHAPTER 1

Apple, M. (1979) *Ideology and Curriculum*, Boston, MA: Routledge and Kegan Paul

Apple, M. (1982) *Education and Power*, New York: Routledge

Apple, M. (2000) *Official Knowledge: Democratic Education in a Conservative Age*, New York: Routledge

Carr, D. (1978) 'Practical pursuits and the curriculum', *Journal of Philosophy of Education*, 12, 69–80

Carr, D. (1996) 'The dichotomy of liberal versus vocational education: some basic conceptual geography', in Nieman, A. (ed.), *Philosophy of Education 1995*, Urbana, IL: Philosophy of Education Society

Carr, W. (1997) 'Professing education in a post-modern age', *Journal of Philosophy of Education*, 54, 31, 309–327

Carr, W. (2006) 'Education without theory', *British Journal of Educational Studies*, 54, 2, 136–159

Frege, G. (1978) *The Foundations of Arithmetic: A Logico-Mathematical Enquiry into the Concept of Number*, Oxford: Blackwell

Freire, P. (1972) *Pedagogy of the Oppressed*, Harmondsworth: Penguin

Gallie, W.B. (1955–1956) 'Essentially contested concepts', *Proceedings of the Aristotelian Society*, 56, 167–198

Giroux, H. (1981) *Ideology, Culture and the Process of Schooling*, London: Falmer

Giroux, H. (1992) *Border Crossings: Cultural Workers and the Politics of Education*, London: Routledge

Goodman, P. (1971) *Compulsory Miseducation*, Harmondsworth: Penguin

Gribble, J. (ed) (1967) *Matthew Arnold*, London: Collier Macmillan, Educational Thinkers Series

Hirst, P.H. (1974) 'Liberal education and the nature of knowledge', in *Knowledge and the Curriculum*, London: Routledge and Kegan Paul

Illich, I. (1973) *Deschooling Society*, Harmondsworth: Penguin

MacIntyre, A.C. (1973–1974) 'The essential contestability of some social concepts', *Ethics*, 84, 1–9

MacIntyre, A.C. (1987a) *Whose Justice, Which Rationality?*, Notre Dame, IN: Notre Dame Press

MacIntyre, A.C. (1987b)'The idea of an educated public', in Haydon, G. (ed.), *Education and Values: The Richard Peters Lectures*, London: Institute of Education, University of London

MacIntyre, A.C. (1999) 'How to appear virtuous without actually being so', in Halstead, J.M. and McLaughlin, T.H. (eds), *Education in Morality*, London: Routledge

Marx, K. and Engels, F. (1968) *Selected Writings*, London: Lawrence and Wishart

Neill, A.S. (1968) *Summerhill*, Harmondsworth: Penguin

Peters, R.S. (1964) 'Mental health as an aim of education', in Hollins, T.H.B. (ed.), *Aims of Education: The Philosophical Approach*, Manchester: Manchester University Press

Peters, R.S. (1966) *Ethics and Education*, London: George Allen and Unwin

Peters, R.S. (1973) 'Aims of education', in Peters, R.S. (ed.), *The Philosophy of Education*, Oxford: Oxford University Press

Plato (1961) *Theaetetus*, in Hamilton, E. and Cairns, H. (eds), *Plato: The Collected Dialogues*, Princeton, NJ: Princeton University Press

Pring, R. (1995) *Closing the Gap: Liberal Education and Vocational Education*, London: Hodder and Stoughton
Pring, R. (2005) *Philosophy of Education: Aims, Theory, Common Sense and Research*, London and New York: Continuum
Reimer, E. (1971) *School is Dead*, Harmondsworth: Penguin
Scheffler, I. (1960) *The Language of Education*, Springfield, IL: Thomas Press
Warnock, M. (1973) 'Towards a definition of quality in education', in Peters, R.S. (ed), *The Philosophy of Education*, Oxford: Oxford University Press
Warnock, M. (1977) *Schools of Thought*, London: Faber and Faber
Winch, C. (2000) *Education, Work and Social Capital*, London: Routledge
Winch, C. (2002) 'The economic aims of education', *Journal of Philosophy of Education*, 36, 1, 101–117
Wittgenstein, L (1953) *Philosophical Investigations*, Oxford: Blackwell
Young, M.F.D. (ed.) (1971) *Knowledge and Control*, London, Collier-Macmillan

CHAPTER 2

Arnot, M. (2004). Male Working-Class Identities and Social Justice: A Reconsideration of Paul Willis' *Learning to Labor* in Light of Contemporary Research. In N. Dolby & G. Dimitriadis (Eds.), *Learning to Labor in New Times* (pp. 17–41). New York, London: RoutledgeFalmer
Birkan, T. (2002). Solun Son Sözü Kültürel Çalışmalar mı? [Cultural Studies: The Last Words of the Left?]. *Toplum ve Bilim*, 94: 6–16
Boas, F. (1920). Methods of Ethnology. *American Anthropologist*, 22: 311–322
Bowles, S. & Gintis, H. (1976). *Schooling in Capitalist America: Educational Reform and the Contradictions of Economic Life*. New York: Basic Books
Clifford, J. & Marcus, G.E. (Eds.) (1986). *Writing Culture: The Poetics and Politics of Ethnography*. Berkeley, CA: University of California Press
Culler, J. (1976). *Saussure*. Glasgow: Fontana/Collins
Dworkin, D. (1997). *Cultural Marxism in Postwar Britain*. London: Duke University Press
Hall, S. (1980). Cultural Studies: Two Paradigms. *Media, Culture and Society*, 2: 57–72
Hall, S. (1988). *The Hard Road to Renewal*. London: Verso
Hall, S. (1996). Cultural Studies and Its Theoretical Legacies. In D. Morley & K.-H. Chen (Eds.), *Stuart Hall: Critical Dialogues in Cultural Studies* (pp. 262–276). London: Routledge
Hegel, G.W.F. (1977). *Phenomenology of Spirit*, trans A.V. Miller, with analysis of the text and foreword by J.N. Finlay. Oxford: Oxford University Press
Jakobson, R. (1973). *Main Trends in the Science of Language*. London: Allen & Unwin
Johnson, R. (1986–1987). What is Cultural Studies Anyway? *Social Text*, 16: 38–80
Katz, A. (1997). Postmodern Cultural Studies, *Cultural Logic*, 1, 1. Available at: http://eserver.org/clogic/1-1/katz.html (accessed 17 July 2009)
Kaye, H. (1984). *The British Marxist Historians: An Introductory Analysis*. Cambridge: Polity Press
Lee, R. (2003). *Life and Times of Cultural Studies*. Durham, NC: Duke University Press
Logue, J. & McCarthy, C. (2008). Rereading Class, Rereading Cultural Studies. In L. Weis (Ed.), *The Way Class Works* (pp. 363–379). New York: Routledge
McLaren, P. & Annibale, V. (2004). Paul Willis, Class Consciousness, and Critical Pedagogy. In N. Dolby & G. Dimitriadis (Eds.), *Learning to Labor in New Times* (pp. 41–61). New York, London: RoutledgeFalmer
McRobbie, A. (1980). Settling Accounts with Sub-culture. *Screen Education*, 34: 37–50
Mills, D. & Gibb, R. (2004). "Centre" and Periphery – An Interview with Paul Willis. In N. Dolby & G. Dimitriadis (Eds.), *Learning to Labor in New Times* (pp. 197–227). New York: Routledge
Nolan, K. & Anyon, J. (2004). Learning to Do Time: Willis' Model of Cultural Reproduction in an Era of Postindustrialism, Globalisation, and Mass Incarceration. In N. Dolby & G. Dimitriadis (Eds.), *Learning to Labor in New Times* (pp. 133–151). New York, London: RoutledgeFalmer

Sökefeld, M. (1999). The Concept of Culture between Politics and Social Anthropology: From Difference to Continuity, available at: http://www.uni-muenster.de?EthnologieHeute/eh3/culture.htm (accessed 3 January 2007)

Sparks, C. (1996). Stuart Hall, Cultural Studies and Marxism. In D. Morley & K.-H. Chen (Eds.), *Stuart Hall: Critical Dialogues in Cultural Studies* (pp. 71–102). London, New York: Routledge

Steele, T. (1997). *The Emergence of Cultural Studies: Cultural Politics, Adult Education and the 'English' Question*. London: Lawrence and Wishart

Turner, G. (2003). *British Cultural Studies: An Introdction* (third ed.). London: Routledge

Tylor, E.B. (1903). *Primitive Culture*. London: John Murray [1871]

Walker, J. (1985). Rebels With Our Applause? A Critique of Resistance Theory in Paul Willis' Ethnography of Schooling. *Journal of Education*, 167 (2): 63–83

Willis, P. (1981). *Learning to Labor: How Working Class Kids Get Working Class Jobs*. New York: Columbia University Press

Willis, P. (1983). Cultural Production and Theories of Reproduction. In L. Barton & S. Walker (Eds.), *Race, Class and Education* (pp. 107–139). London: Croom Helm

Willis, P. (1990). *Common Culture*. Bristol: Open University Press

Willis, P. (2000). *The Ethnographic Imagination*. Cambridge: Polity Press

Willis, P. (2003). Foot Soldiers of Modernity: The Dialectics of Cultural Consumption and the 21st-Century School. *Harvard Educational Review*, 73 (3): 390–415

CHAPTER 3

Anderson, R.D. (1995) *Education and the Scottish People, 1750–1918*. Oxford: Oxford University Press

Curtis, S.J. and M.E.A. Boultwood (1966) *An Introductory History of English Education Since 1800* (fourth edition). London: University Tutorial Press

Gardner, R. (2005) 'Faith Schools Now: an overview'. In Gardner, R., Lawton, D. and Cairns, J. (eds) *Faith Schools: consensus or conflict?* London: Routledge

Green, A. (1990) *Education and State Formation: the rise of education systems in England, France and the USA*. London: Macmillan

Jones, K. (2003) *Education in Britain: 1944 to the present*. Cambridge: Polity Press

Organisation for Economic Co-operation and Development (2006) *Starting Strong II: early childhood education and care*. Paris: OECD Publishing

Stevens, R. (2004) *University to Uni: the politics of higher education in England since 1944*. London: Politico's

West, E.G. (1994) *Education and the State: a study in political economy*. Indianapolis, IN: Liberty Fund

CHAPTER 4

Arnot, M., & Miles, P., 2005. A reconstruction of the gender agenda: the contradictory gender dimensions in New Labour's educational and economic policy. *Oxford Review of Education*, 31 (1), pp. 173–179

Becker, J., 1995. Women's ways of knowing in mathematics. In P. Rogers, & G. Kaiser, eds. *Equity in mathematics education: influences of feminism and culture*. London: Falmer Press, pp. 163–174

Carrington, B., Tymms, P., & Merrell, C., 2008. Role models, school improvement and the 'gender gap': do men bring out the best in boys and women the best in girls? *British Educational Research Journal*, 34 (3), pp. 315–327

Clarricoates, K., 1978. Dinosaurs in the classroom: a re-examination of some aspects of the 'hidden' curriculum in primary schools. *Women's Studies International Forum*, 1, pp. 353–364

Connell, R.W., 1989. Cool guys, swots and wimps: the interplay of masculinity and education. *Oxford Review of Education*, 15 (3), pp. 291–303

Connolly, P., 1998. *Racism, Gender Identities and Young Children*. London: Routledge

Connolly, P., 2006. The effects of social class and ethnicity on gender differences in GCSE attainment: a secondary analysis of the Youth Cohort Study of England and Wales 1997–2001. *British Educational Research Journal*, 32 (1), pp. 3–21

Davison, K.G., & Frank, B.W., 2006. Masculinities and femininities and secondary schooling. In C. Skelton, B. Francis, & L. Smulyan, eds. *The SAGE Handbook of Gender and Education.* London: SAGE Publications, pp. 152–165

Delphy, C., 1993. Rethinking sex and gender. *Women's Studies International Forum*, 16 (1), pp. 1–9

Demack, S., Drew, D., & Grimsley, M., 2000. Minding the gap: ethnic, gender and social class differences in attainment 1988–1995. *Race, Ethnicity and Education*, 3 (2), pp. 117–143

Eden, C., 2007. Gender and educational achievement. In S. Ward, ed. *Education Studies: A Student's Guide*, second edition. London: Routledge, pp. 28–37

Epstein, D., Elwood, J., Hey, V., & Maw, J., eds. 1998. *Failing Boys? Issues in Gender and Achievement.* Buckingham: Open University Press

Francis, B., 1998. *Power Plays: Primary School Children's Constructions of Gender, Power and Adult Work.* Stoke-on-Trent: Trentham Books

Francis, B., 1999. Lads, lasses and (New) Labour: 14–16-year-old students' responses to the 'laddish behaviour and boys' under achievement' debate. *British Journal of Sociology of Education*, 20 (30), pp. 355–371

Francis, B., & Skelton, C., 2005. *Reassessing Gender and Achievement: Questioning Contemporary Key Debates.* London: Routledge

Gillborn, D., & Gipps, C., 1996. *Recent Research on the Achievement of Ethnic Minority Pupils.* London: Office for Standards in Education

Gillborn, D., & Mizra, H.S., 2000. *Educational Inequality: Mapping Race, Class and Gender, a Synthesis of Research Evidence.* London: Office for Standards in Education

Gilligan, C., 1982. *In a Different Voice: Psychological Theory and Women's Development.* Cambridge, MA: Harvard University Press

Gorard, S., & Smith, E., 2004. What is 'underachievement' at school? *School Leadership and Management*, 24 (2), pp. 205–225

Gorard, S., Rees, G., & Salisbury, J., 1999. Reappraising the apparent underachievement of boys. *Gender and Education*, 11 (4), pp. 441–454

Gordon, T., Holland, J., & Lahelma, E., 2000. *Making Spaces: Citizenship and Difference in Schools*. New York and London: St. Martin's Press and Macmillan Press

Jackson, S., 2005. Sexuality, heterosexuality and gender hierarchy: getting our priorities straight. In C. Ingraham, ed. *Thinking Straight: New Work in Critical Heterosexuality Studies.* London: Routledge, pp. 15–38

Jackson, S., & Scott, S., 2001. *Gender: A Sociological Reader*. London: Routledge

Jones, S., & Myhill, D., 2004. Seeing things differently: teachers' constructions of underachievement. *Gender and Education*, 16 (4), pp. 531–546

Martin, J., 2004. Gender in Education. In D. Matheson, ed. *An Introduction to the Study of Education*, second edition. London: David Fulton, pp. 126–141

Mills, M., Martino, B., & Lingard, B., 2004. Attracting, recruiting and retaining male teachers: policy issues in the male teacher debate. *British Journal of Sociology of Education*, 25 (3), pp. 355–369

Myhill, D., & Jones, S., 2006. 'She doesn't shout at no girls': pupils' perceptions of gender equity in the classroom. *Cambridge Journal of Education*, 36 (1), pp. 99–113

Norris, S., 2005. Habitus, social identity, the perception of male domination – and agency? In S. Norris, & R.H. Jones, eds. *Discourse in Action: Introducing Mediated Discourse Analysis.* London: Routledge

O'Hara, R., 2005. Gender in math, science and engineering: Stanford researchers discuss new and important evidence. http://www.stanford.edu/group/IRWG/NewsAndEvents/Forum.html

Pollack, W., 1998. *Real Boys.* New York: Owl Books

Raphael Reed, L., 1999. Troubling boys and disturbing discourses on masculinity and schooling: a feminist exploration of current debates and interventions concerning boys in school. In M. Arnot, & M. Mac an Ghaill, eds. *The RoutledgeFalmer Reader in Gender and Education.* London: RoutledgeFalmer, pp. 33–48

Reay, D., 2001. ‘Spice girls’, ‘nice girls’, ‘girlies’, and ‘tomboys’: gender discourses, girls’ cultures and femininities in the primary classroom. In M. Arnot, & M. Mac an Ghaill, eds. *The RoutledgeFalmer Reader in Gender and Education.* London: RoutledgeFalmer, pp. 117–130

Renold, E., 2006. Gendered classroom experiences. In C. Skelton, B. Francis, & L. Smulyan, eds. *The SAGE Handbook of Gender and Education.* London: SAGE Publications, pp. 439–453

Salisbury, J., & Jackson, D., 1996. *Challenging Macho Values: Practical Ways of Working with Adolescent Boys*. London: Falmer Press

Skelton, C., 2001. *Schooling the Boys: Masculinities and Primary Education.* Buckingham: Open University Press

Skelton, C., 2006. Boys and girls in the elementary school. In C. Skelton, B. Francis, & L. Smulyan, eds. *The SAGE Handbook of Gender and Education.* London: SAGE Publications, pp. 139–151

Smith, E., 2005. *Analysing Underachievement.* London: Continuum

UNICEF, 2007. *A Human-rights-based Approach to Education for All.* New York: United Nations Children’s Fund

Willis, P., 1977. *Learning to Labour: How Working Class Kids get Working Class Jobs.* Farnborough: Saxon House

Younger, M., & Warrington, M., 1996. Differential achievement of girls and boys at GCSE: some observations from the perspective of one school. *British Journal of Sociology of Education*, 17 (3), pp. 299–313

CHAPTER 5

Abraham, J. (1993) *Divide and School: Gender and Class Dynamics in Comprehensive Education*. London: Falmer Press

Arnold, M. (1869) *Culture and Anarchy*. London: Penguin (1969 edn.)

Baldick, C. (1983) *The Social Mission of English Criticism*. Oxford: Oxford University Press

Ball, S. (1981) *Beachside Comprehensive: A Case Study of Secondary Schooling*. London: Cambridge University Press

Ball, S., Kenny, A. and Gardiner, D. (1990) ‘Literacy, Politics and the Teaching of English’ in Goodson, I. and Medway, P. (eds) *Bringing English to Order*, London: Falmer Press

Bernstein, B. (1971) *Class, Codes and Control, vol 1*, London: Paladin

Blanden, J. and Machin, S. (2007) Recent Changes in Intergenerational Mobility in the UK. *Sutton Trust Report*, available at: http://www.suttontrust.com/annualreports.asp (accessed 17 July 2009)

Boocock, S. (1980) *Sociology of Education: An Introduction*, 2nd edition. Boston: Houghton Mifflin

Board of Education (1910) *Circular 753*. London: HMSO

Board of Education (1921) *The Teaching of English in England* (Newbolt Report). London: HMSO

Board of Education (1938) *Report on Secondary Education* (Spens Report). London: HMSO

Bourdieu, P. (1973) ‘Cultural Reproduction and Social Reproduction’ in Brown, R. (1973)

Bourdieu, P. (2007) *Distinction: A Social Critique of the Judgment of Taste* [trans Nice, R.]. Harvard: Harvard University Press

Bowles, S. and Gintis, H. (1976) *Schooling in Capitalist America: Education and the Contradictions of Economic Life*. London: Routledge and Kegan Paul

Brown, R. (ed.) (1973) *Knowledge, Education and Cultural Change*. London: Tavistock

Davison, J. and Dowson, J. (2009) *Learning to Teach English in the Secondary School: A Companion to School Experience*, 3rd edition. London: Routledge

DeMarrais, K.B. and LeCompte, M.D. (1990) *The Way Schools Work: A Sociological Analysis of Education.* White Plains, NY: Longman

DES (1975) *A Language for Life* (The Bullock Report). London: HMSO

DES (1987) *The Report of the Task Group on Assessment and Testing*. London: HMSO

DES (1993) *English in the National Curriculum*. London: HMSO

Dittmar, N. (1976). *A Critical Survey of Sociolinguistics: Theory and Application* [trans. Sand, P., Seuren, P.A.M. and Whiteley, K.). New York: St. Martin’s Press

Douglas, J. (1964) *The Home and the School*. London: MacGibbon and Kee
Eagleton, T. (1983) *Literary Theory: An Introduction*. Oxford: Blackwell
Eisner, E. (1984) *Cognition and Curriculum*. London: Longman
Fairclough, N. (1992) *Critical Language Awareness*. London: Longman
Floud, J., Halsey, A.H. and Martin, F.M. (1966) *Social Class and Educational Opportunity*. Bath: Chivers
Galindo-Rueda, F., Marcenaro-Gutierrez, O. and Vignoles, A. (2004) 'The Widening Socio-Economic Gap in UK Higher Education'. *National Institute Economic Review*, 190 (1): 75–88
Gaskell, J. (1985) 'Course Enrollment in High School: The Perspective of Working Class Females'. *Sociology of Education*, 58: 48–59
Gavron, K. (2009) 'Introduction' in Runnymede Trust (2009)
Gee, J.P. (1991) 'What is Literacy?' in Mitchell, C. and Weiler, K. (eds) (1991)
Graff, H.J. (1987) *The Labyrinths of Literacy: Reflections on Literacy Past and Present*. New York: Falmer
Gossman, L. (1981) 'Literature and Education'. *New Literary History*, 13: 341–371
Gould, S.J. (1981) *The Mismeasure of Man*. New York: W.W. Norton & Co
Halsey, A.H. (1998) 'Leagues Apart'. *Times Higher Education Supplement*, 6 February: 17
Hargreaves, D. (1967) *Social Relations in the Secondary School*. London: Routledge and Kegan Paul HMI (1984) *English from 5 to 16*. London: HMSO
Lacey, C. (1970) *Hightown Grammar*. Manchester: Manchester University Press
Lankshear, C. (1987) *Literacy, Schooling and Revolution*. London: Falmer Press
Lankshear, C. (1997) *Changing Literacies*. Buckingham: Open University Press
Lupton, R. (2004) *Do Poor Neighbourhoods Mean Poor Schools?* London: Centre for Analysis of Social Exclusion/ESRC
MacSwan, J. and McLaren, P. (1997) 'Basil Bernstein's Sociology of Language'. *Bilingual Research Journal*, 21 (4): 334–340
Mitchell, C. and Weiler, K. (eds) (1991) *Rewriting Literacy: Culture and the Discourse of the Other*. New York: Bergin and Garvey
Palmer, D. (1965) *The Rise of English Studies*. Oxford: Oxford University Press
Patten, J. (1992) Speech to Conservative Party Annual Conference, 7 October
Runnymede Trust (2009) *Who Cares about the White Working Class?* London: Runnymede Trust
Sampson, G. (1921) *English for the English*, Cambridge: Cambridge University Press
Smithers, A. (2000) 'Woodhead Sparks Row over Value of Degrees'. *The Independent*, 3 March
Sunday Times (1978) 'Crucial Data Faked by Eminent Psychologist', 29 November *Times Educational Supplement* (1915) Report on Lancashire Headteachers' Report. London: Times Newspapers
Trudgill, P. (1974) *Sociolinguistics: An Introduction to Language and Society*. London: Penguin Books
Willis, P. (1977) *Learning to Labour: How Working Class Kids Get Working Class Jobs*. Sheffield: Saxon Press
Willis, P. (1981) 'Cultural Production is Different from Cultural Reproduction'. *Interchange* 12 (2–3): 48–67
Woodhead, C. (2000) 'Teenage Culture Harming Pupils, says Woodhead'. *The Guardian*, 12 February
Woodhead, C. (2008) 'A GCSE in Jade'. *Daily Mail*, 19 April UNESCO (2003) *Education for All: United Kingdom Perspectives*. Paris: UNESCO

CHAPTER 6

Abbas, T. (2002). 'The Home and the School in the Educational Achievements of South Asians', *Race Ethnicity and Education*, 5 (3): 291–316
Ajegbo, K., Kiwan, D. and Sharma, S. (2007) *Curriculum Review: Diversity and Citizenship*. London: DfES
Aspinall, P.J. (2002) 'Collective Terminology to Describe the Minority Ethnic Population', *Sociology*, 36 (4): 803–816
Blair, M. (2001) *Why Pick on Me? School Exclusion and Black Youth*. Stoke-on-Trent: Trentham Books
Carrington, B. and Short, G. (1997) 'Holocaust Education, Anti-racism and Citizenship', *Educational Review*, 49 (3): 271–281

Codjoe, H.M. (2006) 'The Role of an Affirmed Black Cultural Identity and Heritage in the Academic Achievement of African-Canadian Students', *Intercultural Education*, 17 (1): 33–54

Cordeiro, A. *et al*. (1994) *Multiculturalism and TQE: Addressing Cultural Diversity in Schools*. London, New Delhi and Thousand Oaks, CA: Sage Publications

Gay, G. (2004) 'Educational Equality for Students of Colour'," in J. Banks & C.M. Banks (Eds.) *Multicultural Education: Issues and Perspectives*, 5th ed. (pp. 211–241), Hoboken, NJ: Wiley & Sons

Johnson, S.M. and Lollar, X.L. (2002) 'Diversity Policy in Higher Education: The Impact of College Students' Exposure to Diversity on Cultural Awareness and Political Participation', *Journal of Education Policy*, 17 (3): 303–320

Kiwan, D. (2008) *Education for Inclusive Citizenship*. Abingdon, Oxon: Routledge

Lawson, H. (2001) 'Active Citizenship in Schools and the Community', *The Curriculum Journal*, 12 (2): 163–178

Leighton, R. (2004) 'The Nature of Citizenship Education: An Initial Study', *The Curriculum Journal*, 15 (2): 167–181

Lukes, S. (1974) *Power: A Radical View*. London: Macmillan

Macpherson, Sir W. (1999) *The Stephen Lawrence Enquiry*, Cm 4262. London: The Stationery Office

Moll, L.C. (1988) 'Some Key Issues in Teaching Latino Students', *Language Arts*, 65: 465–472

Olssen, M. (2004) 'From the Crick Report to the Parekh Report: Multiculturalism, Cultural Difference, and Democracy – the Re-visioning of Citizenship Education', *British Journal of Sociology of Education*, 25 (2): 179–192

Potter, J. (1999) *Education for Life, Work and Citizenship*. London: CSV

Tomlinson, S. (1998) 'New Inequalities? Educational Markets and Ethnic Minorities', *Race, Ethnicity and Education*, 1 (2): 207–224

Tomlinson, S. (2005) 'Race, Ethnicity and Education under New Labour', *Oxford Review of Education*, 31 (1): 153–171

Warren, S. and Gillborn, D. (2004) *Race, Equality and Education in Birmingham* (Report commissioned by Birmingham City Council and Birmingham Race Action Partnership)

DEBATE 2

Banks, J. (2004a) Multicultural education: historical development, dimensions and practice, in Banks, J. and McGee Banks, C.A. (Eds) *Handbook of research on multicultural education*, San Francisco, CA: Jossey-Bass

Banks, J. (2004b) Introduction: citizenship education in multicultural societies, in Banks, J. (Ed) *Diversity and Citizenship Education: global perspectives*, San Francisco, CA: Jossey-Bass

Banks, J. (Ed) (2004c) *Diversity and Citizenship Education: global perspectives*, San Francisco, CA: Jossey-Bass

Barry, B. (2001) *Culture and equality*, Cambridge: Polity Press

Berube, M.R. (1994) *American school reform: progressive, equity and excellence movements, 1883–1993*, Westport, CT: Praeger

Brierly, P. (Ed) (2004) *UK Christian handbook: religious trends no 4*, London: Christian Research

Brighouse, H. (2006) *On education: thinking in action*, London: Routledge

British Humanist Association (2009) Religious schools: the case against, extract from a report from the Humanist Philosopher's Group at http://www.learning-together.org.uk/docs/called5.htm (accessed 20 July 2009)

Bruce, S. (2002) *God is dead: secularisation in the West*, Oxford: Blackwell

Bryk, A.S., Lee, V.E. and Holland, P.B. (1993) *Catholic schools and the common good*, Cambridge, MA: Harvard University Press

Buruma, I. (2007) *Murder in Amsterdam: The death of Theo Van Gogh and the limits of tolerance*, London: Atlantic Books

Cairns, J., Gardner, R. and Lawton, D. (Eds) (2005) *Faith schools: consensus or conflict*, London: Routledge

Coleman, J.S., Hoffer, T. and Kilgore, S. (1982) *High school achievement: public, Catholic and private schools compared*, New York: Basic

Conroy, J. (2004) *Betwixt and between: The liminal imagination, education and democracy*, New York: Peter Lang

Conroy, J. (2008) Prejudice and schooling, in Bryce, T. and Humes, W. (Eds) *Education*, Edinburgh: Edinburgh University Press

Cormack, R., Gallagher, A. and Osborne, R. (1991) Religious affiliation and educational attainment in Northern Ireland: the financing of schools in Northern Ireland, in *The sixteenth annual report of the Standing Advisory Commission on Human Rights* (pp. 117–212), London: HMSO, House of Commons Paper 488

European Values Study (2008) Available at http://www.europeanvaluesstudy.eu/evs/surveys/values-surveys-1981-2004.html (accessed 20 July 2009)

Fitzmaurice, J. (1996) *The politics of Belgium: a unique federalism*, London: Hurst

Gallagher, T. (2007) Desegregation and resegregation: the legacy of Brown *versus* Board of Education, 1954, in Bekerman, Z. and McGlynn, C. (Eds) *Addressing ethnic conflict through peace education*, New York: Palgrave/Macmillan

Galston, W. (2003) Church, state and education, in Curren, R. (Ed.) *A companion to the philosophy of education* (pp. 412–429), London: Blackwell

Goodlad, J.I. (1997) *In praise of education*, New York: Teachers College Record

Goodlad, J.I., Soder, R. and McDaniel, B. (Eds) (2008) *Education and the making of a democratic people*, Boulder, CO: Paradigm Publishers

Greeley, A. (2002) *Catholic high schools and minority students*, New Brunswick, NJ and London: Transaction Publishers

Gutmann, A. (2004) Unity and diversity in democratic multicultural education: creative and destructive tensions, in Banks, J. (Ed) *Diversity and Citizenship Education: global perspectives*, San Francisco, CA: Jossey-Bass

Haydon, G. and Halstead, M. (Eds) (2007) *Journal of Philosophy of Education special issue: the common school and the comprehensive ideal. A defence by Richard Pring with complementary essays*, 42 (4)

Judge, H. (2002) *Faith-based schools and the state*, Oxford: Symposium Books

Kelly, P. (Ed) (2002) *Multiculturalism reconsidered*, Cambridge: Polity Press

Lijphart, A. (1975) *The politics of accommodation: pluralism and democracy in the Netherlands*, Berkeley, CA: University of California Press

NicCraith, M. (2003) Politicised linguistic consciousness: the case of Ulster-Scots, *Nations and Nationalism*, 7 (1), 21–37

Obama, B. (2008) *The audacity of hope*, Edinburgh: Canongate Books

O'Keefe, J., Connors, M., Goldschmidt, E., Green, J., Henderson, S. and Schervish, K. (2004) *Sustaining the legacy: urban Catholic Schools in the United States*, Washington, DC: NCEA

Parekh, B. (2000) *Rethinking multiculturalism: cultural diversity and political theory*, Basingstoke, UK: Palgrave

Postman, N. (1996) *The end of education*, New York: Knopf

Scruton, R. (2009) Forgiveness and irony, *City Journal*, 19 (1), available at http://city-journal.org/2009/19_1_the-west.html (accessed 20 July 2009)

Sniderman, P.M. and Hagendoorn, L. (Eds) (2009) *When ways of life collide: multiculturalism and its discontents in the Netherlands*, Princeton, NJ: Princeton University Press

Sturm, J., Groenendijk, L., Kruithof, B. and Rens, J. (1999) Educational pluralism: a historical study of so-called 'pillarization' in the Netherlands, including a comparison with developments in South African education, *Comparative Education*, 34 (3), 281–297

Swann Report (1985) *Education for all: report of the Committee of Enquiry into the Education of Children from Ethnic Minority Groups*, House of Commons Cmnd. 9453, London: HMSO, available at http://www.dg.dial.pipex.com/documents/docs3/swann.shtml (accessed 20 July 2009)

United States Government (2004) The Elementary and Secondary Education Act (The No Child Left Behind Act of 2004), available at http://www.ed.gov/policy/elsec/leg/esea02/index.html (accessed 20 July 2009)

Voas, D. (2006) Religious decline in Scotland: new evidence on timing and spatial patterns, *Journal for the Scientific Study of Religion*, 45 (1), 107–118

Walford, G. (1995) Faith-based grant-maintained schools: selective international policy borrowing from the Netherlands, *Journal of Education Policy*, 10 (3), 245–257

Walford, G. and Miller, H. (1991) *City Technology College*, Milton Keynes, UK: Open University Press

Wells, A.S. (2009) *Both sides now: the story of school desegregation's graduates* (The George Gund Foundation Imprint in African American Studies), Berkeley, CA: University of California Press

CHAPTER 7

Baltes, P.B. & Kunzmann, U. (2003). Wisdom. *The Psychologist*, 16, 131–132

Belmont, L. & Marolla, F.A. (1973). Birth order, family size, and intelligence. *Science*, 182, 1096–1101

Bernstein, B. (1971). *Class, codes and control, vol. 1.* London: Paladin

Bouchard, T.J. & Segal, N.L. (1985). Environment and IQ. In B.B. Wolman (Ed.), *Handbook of intelligence: Theories, measurements, and applications* (pp. 391–464). New York: Wiley

Caldwell, B.M. & Bradley, R.H. (1978). Home observation for measurement of the environment. Little Rock: University of Arkansas

Carroll, J.B. (1993). *Human cognitive abilities: A survey of factor analytic studies*. Cambridge: Cambridge University Press

Catell, R.B. (1971). *Abilities: Their structure, growth, and action*. Boston: Houghton Mifflin

Ceci, S.J. (1990). *On intelligence . . . more or less: A bio-ecological treatise on intellectual development.* Englewood Cliffs, NJ: Prentice Hall

Das, J.P. (1994). Eastern views of intelligence. In R.J. Sternberg (Ed.), *Encyclopedia of intelligence* (pp. 91–97). New York: Macmillan

Demetriou, A. & Papadopoulos, T.C. (2004). Human intelligence: From local models to universal theory. In R.J. Sternberg (Ed.), *International handbook of intelligence* (pp. 445–474). Cambridge: Cambridge University Press

Dweck, C.S. (2002). Beliefs that make smart people dumb. In R.J. Sternberg (Ed.), *Why smart people can be so stupid* (pp. 24–41). New Haven, CN: Yale University Press

Dweck, C.S. (2006). *Mindset*. New York: Random House

Flynn, J.R. (1984). The mean IQ of Americans: Massive gains 1932 to 1978. *Psychological Bulletin*, 95, 29–51

Flynn. J.R. (1987). Massive IQ gains in 14 nations: What IQ tests really measure. *Psychological Bulletin*, 101, 171–191

Galton, F. (1869). *Hereditary genius.* London: Macmillan and Co

Gardner, H. (1983). *Frames of mind: Theory of multiple intelligences: The theory of multiple intelligences.* New York: Basic Books

Gardner, H. (1999a). *Intelligence reframed: Multiple intelligences for the 21st century*. New York: Basic Books

Gardner, H. (1999b). *The disciplined mind: Beyond facts and standardized tests, The K-12 education that every child deserves*. New York: Simon and Schuster

Gardner, H. & Hatch, T. (1989). Multiple intelligences go to school: Educational implications of the theory of multiple intelligences. *Educational Researcher*, 18 (8), 4–9

Gonzales, P., Williams, T.J., Jocelyn, L., Roey, S., Kastberg, D. & Brenwald, S. (2008). *Highlights from TIMSS 2007: Mathematics and science achievement of U.S. fourth- and eighth-grade students in an international context.* Washington, DC: National Center for Educational Statistics

Gordon, H.W. & Lee, P. (1986). A relationship between gonadotropins and visuospatial functions. *Neuropsychologia*, 24, 563–576

Gottfredson, L.S. (1994). Mainstream science on intelligence. *Wall Street Journal*, December 13, p. A18

Gottfredson, L.S. (1997). Why g matters: The complexitiy of everyday life. *Intelligence*, 24, 79–132

Gottfried, A.W. (Ed.). (1984). *Home environment and early cognitive development: Longitudinal research.* New York: Academic Press

Halpern, D.F., Benbow, C.P., Geary, D.C., Gur, R.C., Hyde, J.S. & Gernsbacher, M.A. (2007). The science of sex differences in science and mathematics. *Psychological Science in the Public Interest*, 8 (1), 1–51

Harkness, S. & Super, C.M. (2008). Why African children are so hard to test. In R.A. LeVine & R.S. New (Eds.), *Anthropology and child development: A cross-cultural reader* (pp. 182–186). Malden, MA: Blackwell Publishing

Hart, B. & Risley, T.R. (1992). American parenting of language-learning children: Persisting differences in family–child interaction observed in natural home environments. *Developmental Psychology*, 28, 1096–1105

Horn, J.L. (1985). Remodeling old models of intelligence. In B.B. Wolman (Ed.), *Handbook of intelligence: Theories, measurements, and applications* (pp. 267–300). New York: Wiley

Jensen, A.R. (1980). *Bias in mental testing*. New York: Free Press

Luria, A.R. (1976). *Cognitive development and its cultural and social foundations*. Cambridge, MA: Harvard University Press

Lynn, R. (1994). Sex differences in intelligence and brain size: A paradox resolved. *Personality and Individual Differences*, 17 (2), 257–271

Lynn, R. & Longley, D. (2006). On the high intelligence and cognitive achievements of Jews in Britain. *Intelligence*, 34 (6), 541–547

Mackintosh, N.J. (1998). *IQ and human intelligence.* Oxford: Oxford University Press

Neisser, U.N., Boodoo, G., Bouchard, T.J., Boykin, A.W., Brody, N., Ceci, S.J., Halpern, D.F., Loehlin, J.C., Perloff, R., Sternberg, R.J. & Urbina, S. (1996). Intelligence: Knowns and unknowns. *American Psychologist*, 51 (2), 77–101

Räty, H. & Snellman, L. (1997). Children's images of an intelligent person. *Journal of Social Behavior and Personality*, 12, 773–784

Scarr, S. (1997). Behavior-genetic and socialization theories of intelligence: Truce and reconciliation. In R.J. Sternberg & E. Grigorenko (Eds.), *Intelligence: Heredity and environment* (pp. 3–41). New York: Cambridge University Press

Schaler, J.A. (Ed.). (2006). *Howard Gardner under fire: The rebel psychologist faces his critics.* Chicago: Open Court

Seligman, M.E.P. (1975). *Helplessness: On depression, development and death.* San Francisco, CA: W.H. Freeman

Sinha, D. (1983). Human assessment in the Indian context. In S.H. Irvine & J.W. Berry (Eds.), *Human assessment and cultural factors* (pp. 27–34). New York: Plenum

Spearman, C. (1904). General intelligence: Objectively determined and measured. *American Journal of Psychology*, 15, 201–293

Sternberg, R.J. (1985). *Beyond IQ: A triarchic theory of intelligence.* Cambridge: Cambridge University Press.

Sternberg, R.J. (1996). *Successful intelligence.* New York: Simon and Schuster

Sternberg, R.J. (2007). Intelligence and culture. In S. Kitayama & D. Cohen (Eds.), *Handbook of cultural psychology* (pp. 547–568). New York: The Guilford Press

Sternberg, R.J. & Detterman, D.K. (Eds.). (1986). *What is intelligence: Contemporary viewpoints on its nature and definition.* Norwood, MA: Ablex

Sternberg, R.J. & Kaufman, J.C. (1998). Human abilities. *Annual Review of Psychology*, 49, 479–502

Sternberg, R.J. & Wagner, R. (1986). *Practical intelligence: Nature and origins of competence in the everyday world.* Cambridge: Cambridge University Press

Sternberg, R.J., Conway, B.E., Ketron, J.L. & Bernstein, M. (1981). People's conception of intelligence. *Journal of Personality and Social Psychology*, 41, 37–55

Stevenson, H.W., Lee, S.Y. & Stigler, J.W. (1986). Mathematics achievement of Chinese, Japanese, and American children. *Science*, 231, 693–699

Thorndike, R.L., Hagen, E.P. & Sattler, J.M. (1986). *Stanford-Binet intelligence scale: Technical manual.* 4th edition. Chicago, IL: Riverside

Thurstone, L.L. (1938). *Primary mental abilities*. Chicago, IL: University of Chicago Press

Thurstone, L.L. (1957). *Primary mental abilities*. Chicago, IL: University of Chicago Press

Triandis, H.C. (1989). Cross-cultural studies of individualism and collectivism. *Nebraska Symposium on Motivation*, 37, 41–134. Lincoln: University of Nebraska Press

Turkheimer, E., Haley, A., Waldron, M., D'Onofrio, B. & Gottesman, I. (2003). Socioeconomic status modifies heritability of IQ in young children. *Psychological Scienece*, 14 (6), 623–628

White, K.R. (1982). The relation between socioeconomic status and academic achievement. *Psychological Bulletin*, 91, 461–481

Zajonc, R.B. (1983). Validating the confluence model. *Psychological Bulletin*, 93, 457–480

Zigler, E. & Muenchow, S. (1992). *Head Start: The inside story of America's most successful educational experiment.* New York: Basic Books

CHAPTER 8

Alexander, R.J. (2008): *Towards dialogic teaching: rethinking classroom talk*, fourth edition. York: Dialogos

Banich, M.T. (1997): *Neuropsychology: the neural bases of mental functions*. New York: Houghton Mifflin

Boardman, J., Griffin, J. & Murray, O. (1986): *The Oxford history of the classical world*. Oxford: OUP

Bruner, J.S. (1983): *Child's talk: learning to use language*. London: Norton

Burns, C. & Myhill, D. (2004): Interactive or inactive? A consideration of the nature of interaction in whole class teaching. *Cambridge Journal of Education*, 34 (1), 35–49

Canter, L. & Canter, M. (1976): *Assertive discipline: A take-charge approach for today's educator*. Los Angeles, CA: Canter and Associates. Summarized on the following website: http://maxweber.hunter.cuny.edu/pub/eres/EDSPC715_MCINTYRE/AssertiveDiscipline.html (accessed 20 July 2009)

Caspi, A., McClay, J., Moffitt, T.E., Mill, J., Martin, J., Craig, I.W., Taylor, A. & Poulton, R. (2002): Role of genotype in the cycle of violence in maltreated children. *Science*, 297, 851–854

Claxton, G. (1990): *Teaching to learn*. London: Cassell

Dann, R. (2002): *Promoting assessment as learning: improving the learning process*. London & New York: Routledge Falmer

Donaldson, M. (1978): *Children's minds*. London: Fontana

Eraut, M. (2000): Non-formal learning and tacit knowledge in professional work. *British Journal of Educational Psychology*, 70, 113–136

Eysenck, M. & Keane, M. (2005): *Cognitive psychology*. Hove, UK: Psychology Press

Fisher, R. (1990): *Teaching children to think*. New York: Simon & Schuster

Froebel, F. (1906): *The autobiography of Friedrich Froebel*. London: Swan Sonnenschein

Goswami, U. (2004): Neuroscience, education and special education. *British Journal of Special Education*, 31 (4), 175–183

The Haddow Report (1931): *The primary school*. London: HM Stationery Office

Hargreaves, A. (2003): *Teaching in the knowledge society: education in the age of insecurity*. London: McGraw-Hill

Hewitt, D. (2008): *Understanding effective learning*. London: OUP

Hibbert, C. (1986): *The English: a social history 1066–1945*. London: Guild Publishing

Newman, D. (1982): Perspective-taking versus content in understanding lies. *Quarterly Newsletter of the Laboratory of Comparative Human Cognition*, 4, 26–9 (Cited in Rogoff, B. (1991): The joint socialisation of development by young children and adults. In P. Light, S. Sheldon and M. Woodhead (Eds.), *Learning to think* (pp. 67–96). London: Routledge)

Pintrich, P.R. & Schunk, D.H. (1996): *Motivation in education: theory, research and applications*. Englewood Cliffs, NJ: Prentice-Hall

Pollard, A. (1985): *The social world of the primary school*. London: Holt, Rinehart and Winston

Pollard, A. (1988): *Sociology and teaching*. London: Crown Helm

Pollard, A. (3rd. Ed.) (1997): *Reflective teaching in the primary school*. London: Cassell

QCA (1999): *The national curriculum*. London: HMSO

Rutter, M. (1975): *Helping troubled children*. Baltimore, MD: Penguin Books

Seifert, J., Scheuerpflug, P., Zillessen, K.E., Fallgater, A. & Warnke, A. (2003): Electrophysiological investigation of the effectiveness of methylphenidate in children with and without ADHD. *Journal of Neural Transmission*, 110 (7), 821–829

Smith, P.K., Cowie, H. and Blades, M. (2003): *Understanding children's development*, fourth edition. Oxford: Blackwell

Sutton-Smith, B. (1986): *Toys as culture*. New York: Gardner Press

Sylva, K., Roy, C. & Painter, M. (1980): *Child watching at playgroup and nursery school.* Bath: Pitman Press

Vygotsky, L.S. (1962): *Thought and language*. New York: Wiley

Vygotsky, L.S. (1978): *Mind in society: the development of higher psychological processes*. Cambridge, MA: Harvard University Press.

Weinstein, C.E., Husman, J. & Dieking, D.R. (2000): Self-regulation interventions with a focus on learning strategies. In M. Bokaerts (Ed.), *Handbook of self-regulation*. New York: Academic Press

Wood, D. (1988): *How children think and learn*. Oxford: Blackwell

Wood, D. (2nd Ed) (1998): *How children think and learn*. London: Blackwell

CHAPTER 9

Arnot, M., David, M. and Weiner, G. (1999), *Closing the Gender Gap: Postwar education and social change*, Cambridge: Polity Press

Bracey, G.W. (1996), International comparisons and the condition of American education, *Educational Researcher*, 25 (1), 5–11

Cohen, M. (1998), 'A habit of healthy idleness': boys' underachievement in historical perspective, in *Failing Boys? Issues in gender and achievement*, Epstein, D., Elwood, J., Hey, V. and Maw J. (eds), Buckingham: Open University Press

Cox, C.B. and Dyson, R.E. (eds) (1969), *Black Paper 1: Fight for Education*, London: The Critical Quarterly Society

Delamont, S. (1999), Gender and the discourse of derision, *Research Papers in Education*, 14 (1), 3–21

Francis, B. and Skelton C. (2005), *Reassessing Gender and Achievement: Questioning contemporary key debates*, Abingdon, Oxon: Routledge

Gorard, S. (2000), *Education and Social Justice*, Cardiff: University of Wales Press

Millard, E. (1997), Differently literate: gender identity and the construction of the developing reader, *Gender and Education*, 9 (1), 31–48

NCES (2005), NAEP 2004: Trends in academic progress, three decades of student performance in reading and mathematics, National Center for Education Statistics, available at http://nces.ed.gov/pubsearch/pubsinfo.asp?pubid=2005464 (accessed 20 July 2009)

OECD (2001), *Knowledge and Skills for Life: First results from PISA 2000*, Paris: OECD

Prais, S. (2003), Cautions on OECD's recent educational survey (PISA), *Oxford Review of Education*, 29 (2), 139–163

Rees, G. and Delamont, S. (1999), Education in Wales, in *Wales Today*, Dunkerley, D. and Thompson, A. (eds), Cardiff: University of Wales Press

Slavin, R.E. (2002), Evidence-based education policies: Transforming educational practice and research, *Educational Researcher*, 31 (7), 15–21

Smith, E. (2005), *Analysing Underachievement in Schools*, London: Continuum

Younger, M. and Warrington, M., with McLellan, R. (2005), *Raising Boys' Achievement in Secondary Schools: Issues, dilemmas and opportunities*, Buckingham: Open University Press

CHAPTER 10

Ball, S. (1987) *The Micro-Politics of the School: Towards a Theory of School Organization*, London: Methuen.

Ball, S. (1994) *Education Reform: A Critical and Post-Structural Approach*, Buckingham: Open University Press

Cochran-Smith, M., & Lytle, S. (1993) *Inside/Outside: Teacher Research and Knowledge*, New York: Teachers College Press

Dana, N., Gimbert, B., & Silva, D. (2001) Teacher inquiry as professional development for the 21st century in the United States, *Change: Transformations in Education*, 4 (2): 51–59

Darling-Hammond, L. (2000) How teacher education matters, *Journal of Teacher Education*, 51 (3): 166–173

Dewey, J. (1933) *How We Think*, Chicago, IL: Henry Regnery

Dewey, J. (1958) How we think, in Kolesnick, W. (ed.) *Mental Discipline in Modern Education*, Madison, WI: University of Wisconsin Press (Original work published in 1933)

Farrell, T. (2004) *Reflective Practice in Action*, Thousand Oaks, CA: Corwin Press

Fullan, M. (1999) *Change Forces: The Sequel*, London: RoutledgeFalmer

Fullan, M. (2001) *The New Meaning of Educational Change*, 3rd Edition, New York: Teachers College Press

Fullan, M. (2003) *Change Forces with a Vengeance*, London: RoutledgeFalmer

Gewirtz, S., Ball, S., & Bowe, R. (1995) *Markets, Choice and Equity in Education*, Buckingham: Open University Press

Goodman, J. (1984) Reflection and teacher education: a case study and theoretical analysis, *Interchange*, 15: 19–27

Hargreaves, A., & Fink, D. (2003) Sustaining leadership, *Phi Delta Kappan*, May: 693–700

Hargreaves, A., & Goodson, I. (2006) Educational change over time? The sustainability and nonsustainability of three decades of secondary school change and continuity, *Educational Administration Quarterly*, 42 (1): 3–41

Hubbard, R., & Power, B. (1993) *The Art of Classroom Inquiry*, Portsmouth, NH: Heinemann

Kelly, P. (1992) *The End of Certainty*, St. Leonards, NSW, Allen and Unwin

Kress, G. (2000) A curriculum for the future, *Cambridge Journal of Education*, 30 (1): 133–145

Osterman, K., & Kottkamp, R (1993) *Reflective Practice for Educators*, Newbury Park, CA: Corwin Press

Reid, A. (2004) Towards a culture of inquiry in DECS, *Occasional Paper Series*, 1: 1–19, Adelaide, SA: South Australian Department of Education and Children's Services

Reid, A., & O'Donoghue, M. (2004) Revisiting enquiry-based teacher education in neo-liberal times, *The International Journal of Teaching and Teacher Education*, 20 (6): 559–570

Schon, D. (1983) *The Reflective Practitioner*, New York: Basic Books

Schon, D. (1990) *Educating the Reflective Practitioner: Towards a New Design for Teaching and Learning*, San Francisco, CA: Jossey-Bass

Smyth, J., Dow, A., Reid, A., Shacklock, G., & Hattam, R. (2000) *Teachers' Work in a Globalising Economy*, London: Falmer Press

Wells, G. (1994) *Changing Schools from Within: Creating Communities of Inquiry*, Toronto: OISE Press

Zeichner, K., & Liston, D. (1996) *Reflective Teaching: An Introduction*, Mahwah, NJ: Lawrence Erlbaum

CHAPTER 11

Barber, M. (1997) *The Curriculum, the Minister, His Boss and Her Hairdresser: The rise and fall of Kenneth Bakers plan*, London, British Curriculum Foundation

Berieter, C. and Scardamalia, M. (1993) *Surpassing Ourselves: An inquiry into the nature and implications of expertise*, Chicago, Open Court

Bruner, J.S. (1960) *The Process of Education*, Cambridge MA, Harvard University Press

Bruner, J.S. (1996) *The Culture of Education*, Cambridge MA, Harvard University Press

Central Advisory Council for Education (1967) *Children and their Primary Schools* [The Plowden Report], London, HMSO

Chevellard, Y. (1991) *La Transposition Pedagogique: Du savoir savant au savoir enseigné*, Paris, La Pensee Sauvage

Dewey, J. (1901) 'The situation as regards the course of study', *Journal of the Proceedings and Addresses of the Fortieth Annual Meeting of the National Education Association*

Freire, P. (1998) *Teachers as Cultural Workers: Letters to those who dare teach*, translated by Donald Macedo, Dale Koike and Alexandre Oliveira, Boulder CO, Westview Press

Gardner, H. (1995) *The Unschooled Mind*, New York, Basic Books

Larson, E.J. (1997) *Summer for the Gods: The Scope Trial and America's continuing debate over science and religion*, Cambridge MA, Harvard University Press

Leach, J. and Moon, B. (1999) *Learners and Pedagogy*, London, Paul Chapman

Leach, J. and Moon, B. (2008) *The Power of Pedagogy*, London, Sage

Moon, B. (2002) 'Beyond the bell curve: new policies for the National Curriculum' in Demaine, J. (ed.) *Education Policy and Contemporary Politics*, New York, Palgrave

The Schools Inquiry Commission (1868) The Taunton Commission, London

Shulman, L.S. (1986) 'Those who understand: knowledge growth in teaching', *Educational Researcher*, 15 (5), pp. 4–14

Shulman, L.S. (1987) 'Knowledge and teaching: foundations of the new reforms', *Harvard Educational Review*, 57 (1), pp. 4–14

Shulman, L.S. (2006) *The Wisdom of Practice*, New York, John Wiley

Spruce, G. (1999) 'Music, music education and the bourgeois aesthetic: developing a music curriculum for the new millennium' in McCormick, R. and Paechter, C. (eds) *Learning and Knowledge*, London, Paul Chapman

Taylor, T. (1995) '"Movers and shakers": high politics and the origins of the national curriculum', *The Curriculum Journal*, 6 (2), pp. 161–184

CHAPTER 12

Ausubel, D.P. (1968) *Educational Psychology: A Cognitive View.* New York: Holt, Rinehart and Winston

Department for Education and Skills (2003) *Key Stage 3 National Strategy Key Messages: Pedagogy and Practice.* London: DfES

Department for Education and Skills (2007) *Primary and Secondary National Strategies: Pedagogy and Personalisation.* London: DfES

Department for Children, Schools and Families (2008a) *Policy Statements on Pedagogy.* London: DCSF

Department for Children, Schools and Families (2008b) *Personalised Learning: A Practical Guide.* London: DCSF

Evertson, C.M. and Weinstein, C.S. (eds) (2006) *Handbook of Classroom Management: Research, Practice, and Contemporary Issues.* Mahwah, New Jersey: Lawrence Erlbaum

Galton, M. (2007) *Learning and Teaching in the Primary Classroom.* London: Sage

Goswami, U. (2008) *Cognitive Development: The Learning Brain.* Hove: Psychology Press

Hayes, D. (2006) *Inspiring Primary Teaching: Insights into Excellent Primary Practice.* Exeter: Learning Matters

Kounin, J.S. (1970) *Discipline and Group Management in Classrooms*. New York: Holt, Rinehart and Winston.

Kyriacou, C. (2007) *Essential Teaching Skills*, 3rd edn. Cheltenham: Nelson Thornes

Kyriacou, C. (2009) *Effective Teaching in Schools*, 3rd edn. Cheltenham: Nelson Thornes

Kyriacou, C. and Goulding, M. (2006) A systematic review of strategies to raise pupils' motivational effort in Key Stage 4 Mathematics. In: *Research Evidence in Education Library.* London: EPPI-Centre, Social Science Research Unit, Institute of Education. [available online at the EPPI-Centre website: http://eppi.ioe.ac.uk]

Mercer, N. and Littleton, K. (2007) *Dialogue and the Development of Children's Thinking: A Sociocultural Approach.* London: Routledge

Muijs, D. and Reynolds, D. (2005) *Effective Teaching: Evidence and Practice*, 2nd edn. London: Paul Chapman

Ofsted (2007) *The Annual Report of Her Majesty's Chief Inspector of Education, Children's Services and Skills 2006/07.* London: The Stationery Office. [available online at the Ofsted website: www.ofsted.gov.uk]

Opdenakker, M.-C. and Van Damme, J. (2006) Teacher characteristics and teaching styles as effectiveness enhancing factors of classroom practice. *Teaching and Teacher Education*, 22 (1), 1–21

Rogers, B. (2006) *Classroom Behaviour: A Practical Guide to Effective Teaching, Behaviour Management and Colleague Support*, 2nd edn. London: Paul Chapman

Schunk, D.H. (2008) *Learning Theories: An Educational Perspective*, 5th edn. Upper Saddle River, New Jersey: Pearson

Smith, F., Hardman, F., Wall, K. and Mroz, M. (2004) Interactive whole class teaching in the National Literacy and Numeracy strategies. *British Educational Research Journal*, 30 (3), 395–411

Smith, P.K., Cowie, H. and Blades, M. (2003) *Understanding Children's Development*, 4th edn. Oxford: Blackwell

Wilen, W., Hutchinson, J. and Ishler, M. (2008) *Dynamics of Effective Secondary Teaching*, 6th edn. London: Pearson

CHAPTER 13

Assessment Reform Group (ARG) (2002a) *Testing, Motivation and Learning*, Cambridge: University of Cambridge Faculty of Education

Assessment Reform Group (ARG) (2002b) *Assessment for Learning: 10 Principles*, available online at: www.assessment-reform-group.org (accessed 23 July 2009)

Assessment Systems for the Future (on-line undated) *Purposes, Properties and Methods in Summative Assessment*, ASK Working Paper No. 3, available online at: http://www.assessment-reform-group.org/images/Working_paper_03_Final.pdf (accessed 23 July 2009)

Black, P. (2001) *Testing: Friend or Foe? The theory and practice of assessment and testing*, London: RoutledgeFalmer

Black, P. & Wiliam, D. (1998) *Inside the Black Box: Raising standards through classroom assessment*, London: King's College School of Education

Black, P. & Wiliam, D. (2006) 'The Reliability of Assessments' in J. Gardner (Ed.) *Assessment and Learning*, London: Sage (119–132)

Black, P., Harrison, C., Lee, C., Marshall, B. & Wiliam, D. (2002) *Working Inside the Black Box: Assessment for learning in the classroom*, London: King's College Department of Education and Professional Studies

Black, P., Harrison, C., Lee, C., Marshall, B. & Wiliam, D. (2003) *Assessment for Learning: Putting it into practice*, Maidenhead: Open University Press

Broadfoot, P. (2007) *An Introduction to Assessment*, London: Continuum

Children, Schools and Families Committee (House of Commons) (2008) 'Testing and Assessment', Third Report of Session 2007–08, Vol. 1, HC169-I, London: The Stationery Office

Davies, A. (1999) *Educational Assessment: A critique of current policy*, Impact No. 1, Philosophy of Education Society of Great Britain

Ecclestone, K. & Pryor, J. (2001) '"Learning Careers" or "Assessment Careers": The impact of assessment systems on learning', paper presented at the *British Educational Research Association Conference*, University of Leeds, 13–15 September

Elwood, J. (2006) 'Formative Assessment: Possibilities, boundaries and limitations', *Assessment in Education*, 13 (2), 215–232

Gillborn, D. (2008) *Racism and Education: Coincidence or conspiracy?* Abingdon: Routledge

Gillborn, D. & Mirza, H.S. (2000) *Educational Inequality: Mapping race, class and gender – a synthesis of research evidence*, Report HMI 232, London: Office for Standards in Education

Gillborn, D. & Youdell, D. (2000) *Rationing Education: Policy, practice, reform and equity*, Buckingham: Open University Press

Gipps, C. & Murphy, P. (1994) *A Fair Test? Assessment, achievement and equity*, Buckingham: Open University Press

Lambert, D. & Lines, D. (2000) *Understanding Assessment: Purposes, perceptions, practice*, London: RoutledgeFalmer

Miliband, D. (2004) 'Using Data to Raise Achievement', speech by Minister of State for School Standards at a conference of The Education Network, London, 11 February
Sadler, R. (2007) 'Perils in the Meticulous Specification of Goals and Assessment Criteria', *Assessment in Education*, 14 (3), 387–392
Smith, E. & Gorard, S. (2005) '"They Don't Give Us Our Marks": The role of formative feedback in student progress', *Assessment in Education*, 12 (1), 21–38
Stobart, G. (2006) 'The Validity of Formative Assessment', in J. Gardner (Ed.) *Assessment and Learning*, London: Sage (133–146)
Stobart, G. (2008) *Testing Times: The uses and abuses of assessment*, Abingdon: Routledge
Torrance, H. (2007) 'Assessment *As* Learning? How the use of explicit learning objectives, assessment criteria and feedback in post-secondary education and training can come to dominate learning', *Assessment in Education*, 14 (3), 281–294

DEBATE 4

Brook, P. (1972). *The Empty Space*. Harmondsworth: Pelican
Callender, C. (1997). *Education for Empowerment: Practice and Philosophies of Black Teachers*. London: Trentham
DCSF (2008). *Learning to be Safe: A Toolkit to Help Schools Contribute to the Prevention of Violent Extremism*. London: DCSF
Freud, S. (2001). Civilization and its Discontents (1930), in *The Standard Edition of the Complete Psychological Works of Sigmund Freud*, Volume XXI, trans. James Strachey, pp. 57–145. London: Vintage
Gillborn, D. (2008). *Racism and Education: Coincidence or Conspiracy*. London: Routledge
Green, A., Preston, J. and Janmaat, G. (2006). *Education, Equality and Social Cohesion*. London: Palgrave
Lockwood, D. (1964). Social Integration and System Integration, in G. Zollschan and W. Hirsch (eds.), *Explorations in Social Change*. Boston: Houghton Mifflin
McLaren, P. (2005). Revolutionary Pedagogy in Postrevolutionary Times: Rethinking the Political Economy of Critical Education, in P. McLaren (ed.), *Capitalists and Conquerors: A Critical Pedagogy against Empire*. Lanham, MD: Rowman and Littlefield
OECD (2006). *Society at a Glance* [social cohesion indicators]. Paris: OECD
Owen, H. (2008). *Open Space Technology: A User's Guide*. San Francisco: Berrett-Koehler
Preston, J. (2008). Protect and Survive: 'Whiteness' and the Middle Class Family in Civil Defence Pedagogies. *Journal of Education Policy*, 23, 5, 469–482
Putnam, R. (2000). *Bowling Alone: The Collapse and Revival of American Community*. New York: Simon and Schuster
Putnam, R. (2007). E Pluribus Unum: Diversity and Community in the Twenty-first Century – The 2006 Johan Skytte Prize Lecture. *Scandinavian Political Studies*, 30, 2, 137–174
Rai, M. (2006). *7/7: The London Bombings, Islam and the Iraq War*. London: Pluto Press
Rich, A. (1981). *Compulsory Heterosexuality and Lesbian Existence*. London: Onlywomen Press
Rousseau, J. (1991). *Emile: Or On Education*. London: Penguin
Royle, N. (2003). Literature, Teaching and Psychoanalysis, in *The Uncanny*. Manchester: Manchester University Press
Schuller, T., Preston, J., Hammond, C., Brassett-Grundy, A. and Bynner, J. (2004). *The Benefits of Learning: The Impact of Education on Health, Family Life and Social Capital*. London: RoutledgeFalmer
Siddique, H. (2008). Racism Would Block British Barack Obama, says Trevor Phillips, *The Guardian*, 8 November

CHAPTER 14

Aldrich, R. (1990) 'History of Education in Initial Teacher Education in England and Wales'. *History of Education Society Bulletin*, 45 (1), 47–53

REFERENCES

Aldrich, R. (2006) *Lessons from History of Education: The Selected Works of Richard Aldrich.* London and New York: Routledge

Brooks, V. (2006) 'A "Quiet Revolution"?: The Impact of Training Schools on Initial Teacher Training Partnerships'. *Journal of Education for Training*, 32 (4), 379–393

Coppock, D.A. (1997) 'Respectability as a Prerequisite of Moral Character: The Social and Occupational Mobility of Pupil Teachers in the Nineteenth Century'. *History of Education*, 26 (2), 165–186

Dewey, J. (1916) *Democracy and Education*, online http://www.ilt.columbia.edu/Publications/dewey.html, accessed 3 August 2009

Dombkowski, K. (2002) 'Kindergarten Teacher Training in England and Wales and the United States'. *History of Education*, 31 (5), 475–489

Dyhouse, C. (1997) 'Signing the Pledge?: Women's Investment in University Education and Teacher Training before 1939'. *History of Education*, 26 (2), 207–223

Edwards, A. and Mutton, T. (2007) 'Looking Forward: Rethinking Professional Learning through Partnership Arrangements'. *Oxford Review of Education*, 34 (4), 503–519

Ellis, A.C.O. (1979) 'The Training and Supply of Teachers in the Victorian Period'. *History of Education Society Bulletin*, 24 (1), 22–38

Furlong, J. (2005) 'New Labour and Teacher Education: The End of an Era'. *Oxford Review of Education*, 31 (1), 119–134

Furlong, J. (2008) 'Does the Teaching Profession Still Need Universities?', in Johnson and McClean (2008), 85–97

Furlong, J., McNamara, O., Campbell, A., Howson, J. and Lewis, S. (2008) 'Partnership, Policy and Practice: Initial Teacher Education Under New Labour'. *Teachers and Teaching: Theory and Practice*, 14 (4), 307–318

Goodson, I. (2005) *Learning, Curriculum and Life Politics. The Selected Works of Professor I.F. Goodson.* London: RoutledgeFalmer

Goodson, I. and Hargreaves, A. (1996) *Teachers' Professional Lives*. London: Routledge

Harris, S. (2005) 'Professionals, Partnerships and Learning in Changing Times'. *International Studies in Sociology of Education*, 15 (1), 71–86

Heafford, M. (1979) 'Women Entrants to a Teacher Training College, 1852–1860'. *History of Education Society Bulletin*, 23 (1), 14–20

Heward, C. (1993) 'Men and Women and the Rise of Professional Society: The Intriguing History of Teacher Educators'. *History of Education*, 22 (1), 11–32

Hill, D. (2007) 'Critical Teacher Education, New Labour and the Global Project of Neo-liberal Capital'. *Policy Futures in Education*, 5 (2), 204–225

Hobson, A.J., Malderez, A. Tracey, L., Giannakaki, M.S., Pell, R.G., Kerr, K., Chambers, G.N., Tomlinson, P.D. and Roper, T. (2006) *Becoming a Teacher: Student Teachers' Experiences of Initial Teacher Training in England. Research Report RR744*. London: DfES

Hobson, A.J., Malderez, A., Tracey, L., Marina, G., Pell, G. and Tomlinson, P.D. (2008) 'Student Teachers' Experiences of Initial Teacher Preparation in England: Core Themes and Variation'. *Research Papers in Education*, 23 (4), 407–433

Hughes, J., Jewson, N. and Unwin, L. (eds) (2007) *Communities of Practice: Critical Perspectives*. London and New York: Routledge

Hurd, S. (2008) 'Does School-based Initial Teacher Training Affect Secondary School Performance? *British Educational Research Journal*, 34 (1), 19–36

Hurd, S., Jones, M., McNamara, O. and Craig, B. (2007) 'Initial Teacher Education as a Driver for Professional Learning and School Improvement in the Primary Phase'. *Curriculum Journal*, 18 (3), 307–326

Johnson, R. and McClean, D. (eds) (2008) *Teaching: Professionalization, Development and Leadership Festschrift for Professor Eric Hoyle*. London: Springer

Marx, K. and Engels, F. (1848) *Manifesto of the Communist Party*, online http://www.marxists.org/archive/marx/works/1848/communist-manifesto/index.htm, accessed 24 July 2009

McNally, J. (2008) 'Teaching the Teachers', ESRC Briefing on the 'Enhanced Competence-Based Learning in Early Professional Development' project, online http://www.esrcsocietytoday.ac.uk/, accessed 3 August 2009

Menter, I., Brisard, E. and Smith, I. (2006) 'Making Teachers in Britain: Professional Knowledge for Initial Teacher Education in England and Scotland'. *Educational Philosophy and Theory*, 38 (3), 269–286

Meyer, J.W. and Rowan, B. (2007) 'The Structure of Educational Organizations', in Ballantine, J.H. and Spade, J.Z. (eds.) *Schools and Society: A Sociological Approach to Education*, 3rd edition. Thousand Oaks, CA: Pine Forge Press, 217–221

Mill, J.S. (2008) [1859] *On Liberty, with related documents*, edited by A. Kahan. Boston: Bedford/St. Martins.

Murray, J. (2005) 'Re-addressing the Priorities: New Teacher Educators and Induction into Higher Education'. *European Journal of Teacher Education*, 28 (1), 67–85

Murray, J. and Male, T. (2005) 'Becoming a Teacher Educator: Evidence from the Field'. *Teaching and Teacher Education*, 21 (2), 125–142

Mutton, T. (2008) 'We Will Take Them Anywhere: Schools Working within Multiple Initial Teacher Training'. *Journal of Education for Teaching*, 34 (1), 45–62

Mutton, T. and Butcher, J. (2007) 'More than Managing?: The Role of the Initial Teacher Training Coordinator in Schools in England'. *Teacher Development*, 11 (3), 245–261

Oancea, A. (2005) 'Criticisms of Educational Research: Key Topics and Levels of Analysis'. *British Educational Research Journal*, 31 (2), 157–184

Pring, R. (2004) *Philosophy of Education Research*, 2nd ed., London and New York: Continuum

Raffo, C. and Hall, D. (2006) 'Transitions to Becoming a Teacher on an Initial Teacher Education and Training Programme'. *British Journal of Sociology of Education*, 27 (1), 53–66

Schon, D. (1995) *The Reflective Practitioner: How Professionals Think in Action*. Aldershot: Ashgate

Smith, A. (2008) [1776] *An Inquiry into the Nature and Causes of the Wealth of Nations*, edited by K. Sutherland. Oxford: Oxford World's Classics

Smith, E. and Gorard, S. (2007) 'Who Succeeds in Teacher Training?' *Research Papers in Education*, 22 (4), 465–482

Vroede, M. de (1981) 'The History of Teacher Education: Opening Address of the International Standing Conference on the History of Education, 24–27 September 1979'. *History of Education*, 10 (1), 1–8

Wenger, E. (1998) *Communities of Practice: Learning, Meaning and Identity*. Cambridge: Cambridge University Press

West, E.G. (1979) 'Literacy and the Industrial Revolution'. *Economic History Review* 31 (3), online: http://www.ncl.ac.uk/egwest/test/egwet/pdf/education and the state/Literacy and the Industrial Rev.pdf, accessed 24 July 2009

West, E.G. (1991) 'The Rise of the State in Education'. *Policy: A Journal of Policy and Ideas*, online: http://www.ncl.ac.uk/egwest/test/egwest/pdf/education and the state/Independent1.pdf, accessed 24 July 2009

West, E.G. (1994) 'Education Without the State'. *Economic Affairs*, 14 (5), 12–15

Willis, P. (1997) 'The Role of the College of Preceptors in Providing Teacher Examinations in Educational Theory and Practice 1846–1907'. *History of Education Society Bulletin*, 60 (1), 14–23

Williams, A.R. (1971) 'Teacher Training: A Victorian Ideal'. *History of Education Society Bulletin*, 7 (1), 19–23

CHAPTER 15

Bowles, S. and Gintis, H. (1976) *Schooling in Capitalist America*, London: Routledge & Kegan Paul

Dewey, J. (1966) *Democracy and Education: An introduction to the philosophy of education*, New York: Free Press

Dixon, B. (1979) *Catching Them Young*, London: Pluto Press

Freire, P. (1972) *Pedagogy of the Oppressed*, Harmondsworth: Penguin

Florio-Ruane, S. (2001) *Teacher Education and the Cultural Imagination*, London: Lawrence Erlbaum
Gardner, H (1983) *Frames of Mind: The theory of multiple intelligences*, New York: Basic Books
Gillborn, D. (2006) 'Citizenship Education As Placebo: 'Standards', institutional racism and education', *Education, Citizenship and Social Justice*, 1: 83–104
Gould, S.J. (1981) 'The Mismeasurement of Man', *New Scientist*, 6 May: 349–352
Gray, J. (1993) *Beyond The New Right*, London: Routledge
Hallgarten, J., Breslin, T. and Hannam, D. (2004) *I was a Teenage Governor – Project report phase 1:Pupil Governorship: initial thoughts and possibilities*. Available at: http://www.citizenshipfoundation.org.uk/lib_res_pdf/0158.pdf (accessed 24 July 2009)
Illich, I. (1973) *Deschooling Society*, Harmondsworth: Penguin
Jackson, B. and Marsden, D. (1970) *Education and the Working Class*, London: Penguin
Jarman, T.L. (1966) *Landmarks in the History of Education*, London: John Murray
Keddie, N. (ed.) (1978) *Tinker, Tailor . . .: The myth of cultural deprivation*, London: Penguin
Kelly, A. (ed.) (1981) *The Missing Half: Girls and science education*, Manchester: Manchester University Press
Kolb, D. (1984) *Experiential Learning*, New Jersey: Prentice Hall
Labov, W. (1969) 'The Logic of Non-Standard English', in N. Keddie (ed.) (1978) *Tinker, Tailor . . .: The myth of cultural deprivation*, London: Penguin
Lawlor, S. (1995) *An Education Choice: Pamphlets from the Centre 1987–1994*, London: Centre for Policy Studies
Lukes, S. (1974) *Power: A radical view*, London: McMillan
Marx, K. and Engels, F. (1973) *Selected Works*, London: Lawrence & Wishart
Merton, R.K. (1968) *Social Theory and Social Structure*, New York: Free Press
Michels, R. (1949) *Political Parties*, Glencoe, IL: The Free Press
Neill, A.S. (1960) *Summerhill: A Radical Approach to Child Rearing*, New York: Hart
Nisbett, R. (1986) *Conservatism*, Milton Keynes: Open University Press, Harmondsworth: Penguin
Oakeshott, M. (1962) *Rationalism in Politics and Other Essays*, London: Methuen
Postman, N. and Weingartner, C. (1976) *Teaching as a Subversive Activity*, London: Penguin
Qualifications and Curriculum Authority (1998) *Education for Citizenship and the Teaching of Democracy in Schools: Final Report of the Advisory Group on Citizenship*, London: QCA
Rosenthal, R. and Jacobson, L. (1968) *Pygmalion in the Classroom*, New York: Holt, Rinehart & Winston
Spender, D. (1980). *Man Made Language*, London: Routledge & Kegan Paul
Willis, P. (1977) *Learning to Labour*, Farnborough: Saxon Press
Young, M.D. (1958) *The Rise of the Meritocracy, 1870–2033: An essay on education and equality*, London: Thames and Hudson
Young, M.D. (2001) 'Down with Meritocracy', *The Guardian*, 29 June. Available at http://www.guardian.co.uk/politics/2001/jun/29/comment (accessed 24 July 2009)

CHAPTER 16

Andriessen, J., Baker, M. and Suthers, D. (2003) 'Argumentation, computer support, and the educational contexts of confronting cognitions', in J. Andriessen, M. Baker and D. Suthers (eds) *Arguing to Learn: Confronting Cognitions in Computer-supported Collaborative Learning Environments*, Dordrecht: Kluwer Academic Publishers
Bachmair, B., Pachler, N. and Cook, J. (forthcoming) 'Mobile phones as cultural resources for learning: an analysis of educational structures, mobile expertise and emerging cultural practices'. Submitted to *MedienPädagogik*, available at http://www.medienpaed.com/zs/
Becta (2007) *Harnessing Technology Review 2007: progress and impact of technology in education*, Coventry: Becta. Available at: http://partners.becta.org.uk/upload-dir/downloads/page_documents/research/harnessing_technology_review07.pdf (accessed 24 July 2009)

Becta (2008a) *Harnessing Technology: Next Generation Learning 2008–14*, Coventry: Becta.

Becta (2008b) *Harnessing Technology Review 2008*, Coventry: Becta

Borgman, C., Abelson, H., Dirks, L., Johnson, R., Koednger, K., Linn, M., Lynch, C., Oblinger, D., Pea, R., Salen, K., Smith, M. and Szlaly, A. (2008) 'Fostering learning in the networked world: the cyberlearning opportunity and challenge', Report of the National Science Foundation Task Force on Cyberlearning. Available at: http://www.nsf.gov/pubs/2008/nsf08204/nsf08204.pdf (accessed 24 July 2009)

Conole, G., de Laat, M., Dillon, T. and Darby, J. (2008) '"Disruptive technologies", "pedagogical innovation": what's new? Findings from an in-depth study of students' use and perception of technology', *Computers & Education* 50, 511–524

Cuban, L. (2001) *Oversold and Underused: Computers in the classroom*, Cambridge, MA: Harvard University Press

Department for Education and Skills (2005) *Harnessing Technology: Transforming learning and children's services*, Nottingham: DfES

Economic and Social Research Council (2008) *Changing Spaces: Young people, technology and learning*, No 2 in the series *The educational and social impact of new technologies on young people in Britain*, London: ESRC

Empirica (2006) *Benchmarking Access and Use of ICT in European Schools 2006*, Bonn: Empirica

Fisher, T., Higgins, C. and Loveless, A. (2006) *Teachers Learning with Digital Technologies: A review of research and projects*. Available at: http://www.futurelab.org.uk/resources/documents/lit_reviews/Teachers_Review.pdf (accessed 24 July 2009)

Garrison, D. and Anderson, T. (2003) *E-Learning in the 21st Century: A framework for research and practice*, London: RoutledgeFalmer

Harasim, L. (2000) 'Shift happens: Online education as a new paradigm in learning', *The Internet and Higher Education* 3, 41–61

Ito, M., Horst, H., Bittanti, M., Boyd, D., Herr-Stephenson, B., Lange, P., Pascoe, C. and Robinson, L. (2008) *Living and Learning with New Media: Summary of findings from the digital youth project*, The John D. and Catherine T. MacArthur Foundation Reports on Digital Media and Learning, Chicago: The MacArthur Foundation

Joint Information Systems Committee (2005) *Understanding My Learning: Background and rationale*. Available at: http://www.jisc.ac.uk/media/documents/funding/2005/04/understanding_mylearning.pdf/ (accessed 25 July 2009)

Joint Information Systems Committee (2007) *In Their Own Words: Exploring the learner's perspective on e-learning*. Available at: http://www.jisc.ac.uk/media/documents/programmes/elearningpedagogy/iowfinal.pdf (accessed 25 July 2009)

Kitchen, S., Finch, S. and Sinclair, R. (2007) *Harnessing Technology Schools Survey 2007*, Becta: Coventry. Available at: http://partners.becta.org.uk/upload-dir/downloads/page_documents/research/harnessing_technology_schools_survey07.pdf (accessed 25 July 2009)

Kress, G. (2003) *Literacy in the New Media Age*, London: Routledge

Kress, G. and Pachler, N. (2007) 'Thinking about the 'm' in m-learning', in N. Pachler (ed.) *Mobile Learning: Towards a research agenda*, London: WLE Centre, pp. 7–32

Lanham, A. (1993) *The Electronic Word: Democracy, technology and the arts*, Chicago: University of Chicago Press

Lapadat, J. (2002) 'Written interaction: A key component in online learning', *Journal of Computer-Mediated Communication* 7 (4), article 5. Available at: http://www.jcmc.indiana.edu/vol7/issue4/lapadat.html (accessed 25 July 2009)

Laurillard, D. (2002) *Rethinking University Teaching: A conversational framework for the effective use of learning technologies*, London: RoutledgeFalmer

Laurillard, D. (2007) 'Pedagogical forms of mobile learning: Framing research questions', in N. Pachler (ed) *Mobile Learning: Towards a research agenda*, London: WLE Centre, Institute of Education, pp. 153–176. Available at: http://www.wlecentre.ac.uk/cms/files/occasionalpapers/mobilelearning_pachler_2007.pdf (accessed 25 July 2009)

McFarlane, A., Triggs, P. and Yee, W. (2008) *Researching Mobile Learning: Interim report to Becta, April–December*, Coventry: Becta. Available at: http://partners.becta.org.uk/upload-dir/downloads/page_documents/research/mobile_learning.pdf (accessed 25 July 2009)

Mishra, P. and Koehler, M. (2006) 'Technological pedagogical content knowledge: A new framework for teacher knowledge', *Teachers College Record* 108 (6), 1017–1054

NFER (2008) *Teacher Voice Omnibus Survey: November 2007*. Available at: http://www.nfer.ac.uk/what-we-offer/teacher-voice/ExampleReport.pdf (accessed 25 July 2009)

Ofcom (2008) *Media Literacy Audit: Report on UK children's media literacy*, London: Ofcom

Oliver, M. (2003) 'Looking backwards, looking forwards: An overview, some conclusions and an agenda', in J. Seale (ed.) *Learning Technology in Transition*, Lisse: Swets & Zeitlinger

Pachler, N., Bachmair, B., Cook, J. and Kress, G. (2009) *Mobile Phones: Structures, agency, practices*, New York: Springer

Preston, C. (2004) *Learning to Use ICT in Classrooms: Teachers' and trainees' perspectives. An evaluation of the English NOF ICT teacher training programme 1999–2003*, London: Mirandanet and the Teacher Training Agency

Prout, A. (2008) 'Changing childhood in a globalizing world', in *Changing Spaces: Young people, technology and learning*, No 2 in the series *The educational and social impact of new technologies on young people in Britain*, London: ESRC

Rose, J. (2008) *The Independent Review of the Primary Curriculum: Interim report* [The Rose Report]. Available at: http://publications.teachernet.gov.uk (accessed 25 July 2009)

Seale, J. (2003) *Learning Technology in Transition*, Lisse: Swets & Zeitlinger

Snyder, I. (2002) *Silicon Literacies: Communication, innovation and education in the electronic age*, London: Routledge

The New Media Consortium and Educause (2008) *The Horizon Report*. Available at: http://www.nmc.org/publications/2008-horizon-report (accessed 25 July 2009)

Valentine, G. (2008) 'Home-school links: The implications of information and communication technologies for sites of learning and spaces of childhood', in *Changing Spaces: Young people, technology and learning*, No 2 in the series *The educational and social impact of new technologies on young people in Britain*, London: ESRC

DEBATE 5

Ashcraft, M.H. and Krause, J.A. (2007) Working memory, math performance, and math anxiety. *Psychonomic Bulletin and Review*, 14 (2), 243–248

Ball, D.L., Bass, H. and Hill, H.C. (2004) Knowing and using mathematical knowledge in teaching: learning what matters. Invited paper presented at the Southern African Association for Research in Mathematics, Science and Technology, Cape Town, April

Bennett, N. (1987) The search for the effective teacher. In S. Delamont (Ed.) *The Primary School Teacher* (pp. 45–61). Lewes: Falmer Press

Buxton, L. (1981) *Do you Panic about Maths?* London: Heinemann

Chitty, C. (1992) *The Education System Transformed.* Manchester: Baseline Books

Department for Children, Schools and Families (2008) *Review of Mathematics Teaching in Early Years Settings and Primary Schools: Final Report*. London: DCSF

Department of Education and Science (1988) *National Curriculum Task Group on Assessment and Testing: A Report*. London: HMSO

Doyle, W. (1979) Making managerial decisions in classrooms. In D.L. Duke (Ed.) *Classroom Management* (pp. 42–74). Chicago: University of Chicago Press

Haylock, D. (2006) *Mathematics Explained for Primary Teachers*. London: Sage

Haylock, D. and Cockburn, A.D. (2003) *Understanding Mathematics in the Lower Primary Years* (2nd edn). London: Sage

Kyriacou, C. (1992) Active learning in secondary school mathematics. *British Educational Research Journal*, 18 (3), 309–318

Lawton, D. (1994) *The Tory Mind on Education*. London: Falmer Press

Ma, X. (1999) A meta-analysis of the relationship between anxiety toward mathematics and achievement in mathematics. *Journal for Research in Mathematics Education*, 30 (5), 520–540

Pollard, A. (1997) *Reflective Teaching in the Primary School* (3rd edn). London: Cassell

Simon, B. (1988) *Bending the Rules*. London: Lawrence and Wishart

CHAPTER 17

Gorard, S. (2001) *Quantitative methods in educational research: The role of numbers made easy*, London: Continuum

Gorard, S. (2002) Fostering scepticism: the importance of warranting claims, *Evaluation and Research in Education*, 16, (3), 136–149

Gorard, S. (2004) The British Educational Research Association and the future of educational research, *Educational Studies*, 30, (1), 65–76

Gorard, S. (2005) Current contexts for research in educational leadership and management, *Educational Management Administration and Leadership*, 33, (2), 155–164

Gorard, S. (2008) Research impact is not always a good thing: a re-consideration of rates of 'social mobility' in Britain, *British Journal of Sociology of Education*, 29, (3), 317–324

Gorard, S. (2010) All evidence is equal: the flaw in statistical reasoning, *Oxford Review of Education* (forthcoming)

Gorard, S., with Adnett, N., May, H., Slack, K., Smith, E. and Thomas, L. (2007) *Overcoming barriers to HE*, Stoke-on-Trent: Trentham Books

Gorard, S. and Cook, T. (2007) Where does good evidence come from?, *International Journal of Research and Method in Education*, 30, (3), 307–323

Gorard, S. and Rees, G. (2002) *Creating a learning society?*, Bristol: Policy Press

Gorard, S., Rushforth, K. and Taylor, C. (2004) Is there a shortage of quantitative work in education research?, *Oxford Review of Education*, 30, (3), 371–395

Gorard, S., with Taylor, C. (2004) *Combining methods in educational and social research*, London: Open University Press

Toulmin, S., Rieke, R. and Janik, A. (1979) *An introduction to reasoning*, New York: Macmillan

CHAPTER 18

Barr, S.M. (2008). Theology after Newton. *First Things*, 187, 29–33

Barton, K.C., & Levstik, L.S. (2004). *Teaching History for the Common Good*. Mahwah, New Jersey: Lawrence Erlbaum Associates

Bellah, R.N., Masden, R., Sullivan, W.M., Swidler, A., & Tipton, S.M. (1986). *Habits of the Heart: Individualism and Commitment in American Life*. New York: Harper and Row

Brophy, J., & Alleman, J. (2002). Primary-grade students' knowledge and thinking about the economics of meeting families' shelter needs. *American Educational Research Journal*, 39 (2), 423–468

Brophy, J., & Alleman, J. (2006). *Children's Thinking About Cultural Universals*. Mahwah, New Jersey: Lawrence Erlbaum Associates

Brophy, J., Alleman, J., & O'Mahony, C. (2003). Primary-grade students' knowledge and thinking about food production and the origins of common foods. *Theory and Research in Social Education*, 31 (1), 10–49

Chareka, O., & Sears, A. (2005). Discounting the political: Understanding civic participation as private practice. *Canadian and International Education*, 34 (1), 50–58

REFERENCES

Chareka, O., & Sears, A. (2006). Civic duty: Young people's conceptions of voting as a means of political participation. *Canadian Journal of Education*, 29 (2), 521–540

Curtis, C.K. (1980). Developing critical thinking skills in nonacademic social studies classes. *The Alberta Journal of Educational Research*, XXVI (2), 75–84

Davies, I., Gorard, S., & McGuinn, N. (2005). Citizenship education and character education: Similarities and differences. *British Journal of Educational Studies*, 53 (3), 341–358

Eisner, E. (1998). *The Enlightened Eye: Qualitative Inquiry and the Enhancement of Educational Practice*. Upper Saddle River, New Jersey: Prentice-Hall

Eyre, L. (1991). Gender relations in the classroom: A fresh look at coeducation. In J.S. Gaskell & A.T. McLaren (Eds.), *Women and Education* (pp. 193–219). Calgary: Detselig

Gardner, H. (2006). *The Development and Education of the Mind: The Selected Works of Howard Gardner*. London and New York: Routledge

Gorham, P.J., & Nason, P.N. (1997). Why make teachers' work more visible to parents? *Young Children*, 52 (5), 22–26

Hargreaves, A. (2003). *Teaching in the Knowledge Society: Education in the Age of Insecurity*. New York: Teachers College Press

Hughes, A.S., & Sears, A. (1996). Macro and micro level aspects of a programme of citizenship education research. *Canadian and International Education*, 25 (2), 17–30

Kahne, J.E., & Sporte, S.E. (2008). Developing citizens: The impact of civic learning opportunities on student's commitment to civic participation. *American Educational Research Journal*, 45 (3), 738–766

Lévesque, S. (2008). *Thinking Historically: Educating Students for the Twenty-First Century*. Toronto: University of Toronto Press

Levin, B. (2005). *Governing Education*. Toronto: University of Toronto Press

McMillan, J. (2004). *Educational Research: Fundamentals for the Consumer* (4th ed.). Boston: Pearson

Nason, P. (1997). Telling tales out of school: The construction of parental literacy in school culture. *School Leadership & Management*, 17 (1), 117–124

National Foundation for Educational Research. (2008). *CELS: The Citizenship Education Longitudinal Study*. Retrieved November 18, 2008, from http://www.nfer.ac.uk/research-areas/cels/cels_home.cfm

Noddings, N. (2007). *Philosophy of Education* (2nd ed.). Boulder, CO: Westview Press

Peck, C., & Sears, A. (2005). Uncharted territory: Mapping students' conceptions of ethnic diversity. *Canadian Ethnic Studies*, 37 (1), 101–120

Peck, C., Sears, A., & Donaldson, S. (2008). Unreached and unreachable? Curriculum standards and children's understanding of ethnic diversity in Canada. *Curriculum Inquiry*, 38 (1), 63–92

Richardson, V. (2006). Stewards of a field, stewards of an enterprise: The Doctorate in Education. In C.M. Golde, G.E. Walker & Associates (Eds.), *Envisioning the Future of Doctoral Education: Preparing Stewards of the Discipline, Carnegie Essays on the Doctorate* (pp. 251–267). San Francisco: Jossey-Bass

Sandwell, R.W. (2006). *To the Past: History Education, Public Memory, and Citizenship in Canada*. Toronto: University of Toronto Press

Sears, A. (1989). Ben Johnson and social studies teaching: Classroom use of current social issues. *The History and Social Science Teacher*, 24 (3), 158–161

Stearns, P., Seixas, P., & Wineburg, S.S. (Eds.). (2000). *Knowing, Teaching, and Learning History: National and International Perspectives*. New York & London: New York University Press

Willms, J.D. (2006). *Learning Divides: Ten Policy Questions About the Performance and Equity of Schools and Schooling Systems* (No. UIS/WP/06-02). Montreal: UNESCO Institute for Statistics

DEBATE 6

Higgs, J.& Titchen, A. (2000) Knowledge and reasoning. In Higgs, J. & Jones, M. (Eds) *Clinical reasoning in the health professions*, pp. 22–33.Oxford: Butterworth Heinemann

James, M. & Pollard, A. (Eds) (2006) *Improving teaching and learning in schools – TLRP commentary.* London: TLRP

MacGilchrist, B., Myers, K. & Reed, J. (2004) *The Intelligent School.* London: Sage

Pollard, A., Anderson, J., Maddock, M., Swaffield, S., Warin, J. & Warwick, P. (2008) *Reflective Teaching: Evidence-informed Professional Practice.* London: Continuum

Slavin, R., Lake, C. & Groff, C. (2008) *Effective Programs in Middle and High School Mathematics: A Best-Evidence Synthesis.* Available at: http://www.bestevidence.org/math/mhs/top.htm (accessed 25 July 2009)

INDEX